*Display
PostScript®
Programming*

Display PostScript® Programming

David A. Holzgang

Addison-Wesley Publishing Company, Inc.
Reading, Massachusetts   Menlo Park, California   New York
Don Mills, Ontario   Wokingham, England   Amsterdam   Bonn
Sydney   Singapore   Tokyo   Madrid   San Juan

Many of the designations used by manufacturers and sellers to distinguish their products are claimed as trademarks. Where those designations appear in this book, and Addison-Wesley was aware of trademark claim, the designations have been printed in initial caps or all caps.

The name *PostScript*® is a registered trademark of Adobe Systems Incorporated. All instances of the name *PostScript* in the text are references to the *PostScript language* as defined by Adobe Systems Incorporated unless otherwise stated. The name *PostScript* also is used as a product trademark for Adobe Systems' implementation on the PostScript language interpreter.

Any references to "PostScript printer," "PostScript file," or "PostScript driver" refer to printers, files, and driver programs (respectively) that are written in or support the PostScript language. The sentences in this book that use "PostScript language" as an adjective phrase are so constructed to reinforce that the name refers to the standard language definition as set forth by Adobe.

Library of Congress Cataloging in Publication Data

Holzgang, David A.
    Display PostScript programming / David A. Holzgang.
        p.   cm.
    ISBN 0-201-51814-7
      1. PostScript (Computer program language) I. Title.
QA76.73.P67H63   1990
005.26'2--dc20   90-35725
                                                                               CIP

Copyright © 1990 by David A. Holzgang. Portions of this book have been reprinted from *Understanding PostScript Programming*, *Second Edition*, copyright 1988, Sybex Publishing, Alameda, CA.

All rights reserved. No part of this publication may be reproduced, stored in a retrieval system, or transmitted, in any form or by any means, electronic, mechanical, photocopying, recording, or otherwise, without prior written permission of Addison-Wesley. Printed in the United States of America.

Sponsoring Editor: Carole McClendon
Cover design by Doliber Skeffington
Text design by Michael Swider
Set in 11.5-point Times

ABCDEFG-MW-943210
First Printing, July 1990

CONTENTS

Acknowledgments   ix

Introduction   1
> What is PostScript?   2
> Purpose of this Book   4
> How to Use this Book   8

Chapter 1: Getting Started   13
> The PostScript Language   14
> Concepts   25
> Setting Up the First Examples   33
> Programming the First Example   37
> Programming the Second Example   39
> Language Operations   41

        Text and Commentary Exercise   51
        Conclusion   61

Chapter 2: Dictionaries and Procedures   63
        Dictionaries   64
        Text and Commentary Exercise Revisited   69
        Program Structure and Style   76
        Referencing Objects   82
        Object Types   88
        Procedure Definitions   93
        Integrating C and Display PostScript   104
        Business Report Exercise   107
        Managing Display PostScript Resources   123
        Conclusion   131

Chapter 3: Text and Graphics   133
        Display PostScript Imaging Model   134
        Display PostScript Basic Graphics Operators   135
        Fonts   162
        Additional Display PostScript Graphics   169
        Creating a Logo Graphic   199
        Conclusion   204

Chapter 4: Window Operations   207
        Setting Up the Exercise   209
        Creating a Blank Form   221
        Entering Text   241
        Integrating the Exercise into an Application   245
        Using Form Sets   251
        Conclusion   252

Chapter 5: Font Creation and Modification 255

    Font Mechanics   256
    Font Modifications   285
    Additional Font Techniques   307
    Conclusion   309

Chapter 6: Advanced Screen Handling 311

    Handling the Screen   312
    Displaying Sampled Images   337
    Placing EPS Graphics   351
    Error Handling   357
    Conclusion   367

Appendices 369

    A: Operator Review   369
    B: Specific Implementations   387

Index 397

ACKNOWLEDGMENTS

All books require the patient and willing help of a variety of persons besides the author whose name appears on the cover. This book, in particular, would not have been possible without the support and active participation of many people, both those mentioned here and others, who have helped turn an idea into a finished product.

From beginning to end I have been very lucky in and very appreciative of the fine, consistent support that I have received from Addison-Wesley. Carole McClendon has been both enthusiastic and patient, in equal measures—which says a lot for her enthusiasm, since her patience has surely been stretched to biblical lengths in the series of delays and problems that she has dealt with, always and unfailingly cheerfully. All good editors, by the nature of the task, must be both detail-oriented and visionary to transform a manuscript into a book. Joanne Clapp Fullagar, my editor, has raised these virtues to the level of art by her careful and thoughtful contributions to the form and structure of this book. It is commonplace for authors to say that the good features of a work are based in the constructive help of someone or another, while any failings are strictly personal; in this case, the commonplace is also the simple truth. Finally, Rachel Guichard provided constant support for all my administrative and logistical problems with good humor and competent efficiency.

These professionals, functioning as a team, have provided an environment that challenges an author to produce a book worthy of this support.

Of course, a book such as this is very dependent also on technical support from a variety of sources. At Adobe Systems, I was provided with several important boosts that have helped the book. To start with, Cynthia Johnston provided the original Display PostScript reference materials so that I could get started. Ellen Nold and Deborah Mackay provided valuable direction and guidance at the outset. Jim King, unfailingly courteous, provided access to technical and hardware support at a point when I thought that no one would ever return my telephone calls. Without Jim's support, this book might have died.

Access to hardware was a constant problem, which was helped by the generous access provided by two companies. Randy Adams of Emerald City Software graciously allowed me to use one of their NeXT systems to test and review the initial Display PostScript work. Mike Diamond also was more than generous in both answering questions and, more importantly, adjusting his schedule to allow me access to the NeXT machine. Chuck Price of DEC ISV support provided the system and set up the software that allowed me to finish the work and make a final test of the exercises and examples here.

On the personal side, Shirley kept a flood of disasters from interfering with the work, while listening with unflagging interest and concern to my minor tragedies.

INTRODUCTION

This book is a guide and tutorial in the use of the Display PostScript system. Display PostScript was designed and developed by Adobe Systems as an extension of their PostScript page description language, which has been enriched to provide special capabilities for creating and managing displays, especially interactive displays. Display PostScript therefore has and uses all of the functionality of PostScript itself. The PostScript language is a general-purpose programming language that also contains many graphics operations that are defined within it. Display PostScript additionally provides special features that allow you, as a programmer, to embed PostScript code into a C application and thus access the graphic power and flexibility of PostScript from your own application code. The entire concept of programming in Display PostScript is to combine basic PostScript operations with specialized procedures that you can define yourself so that you can create, display, and print complex pages of text and graphics.

WHAT IS POSTSCRIPT?

Because the power and utility of Display PostScript grow directly out of the PostScript environment, you first must understand certain aspects of PostScript itself to appreciate and use Display PostScript effectively.

PostScript is a *page-description* language. It has been designed specifically to communicate a description of a unit of output—generally thought of as a page, but might be a window or even a single graphic element—from a computer-based composition system to a raster-output device. The raster-output device may be a computer display, a laser printer, a high-resolution typesetter, or one of many specialized graphics output devices. This is a *high-level* description because it describes pages as a series of abstract graphic objects rather than as a series of detailed, device-dependent commands.

PostScript is embedded in an interpreter program that may run in an independent device such as a laser printer, or may share the processing power of the computer host. The interpreter program (or just the *interpreter*) translates PostScript operations and data into device-specific codes and controls the output device to generate the graphics being described on the page. The interpreter completely processes each element—a name, string, array, number, or whatever—that is presented to it before it proceeds to the next element. You will learn all about these *syntactic objects* in the following chapters as we discuss PostScript programming and its requirements.

The Display PostScript System

Remember that the Display PostScript system is an extension of the PostScript language. Everything about PostScript in this book applies equally to Display PostScript. Thus this text most often discusses PostScript as a single display or output environment, making no distinction between PostScript and Display PostScript. You will be alerted to the rare instances of divergent approaches. Any variation will, generally, be in the direction of expanding the facilities and the environment that is provided by PostScript itself.

Because the Display PostScript system is an extension of the basic PostScript language, some of its language extensions may not be supported on current PostScript printers. When this is the case, the application or system printer driver must interpret these extensions so that these devices can correctly render the output desired. You should note that, in such cases, using the newer extensions within the Display PostScript system, which are more efficient in the display environment, may produce slower and less efficient output when this conversion takes place. This should not discourage you from sticking to the Display PostScript programming methods; in the long run, all PostScript devices will implement as much of these extensions as is appropriate for the given device. You simply should understand that pages produced in this manner may require additional processing and additional output time on existing PostScript devices.

If you are familiar with or fluent in PostScript but do not know Display PostScript, it is entirely possible for you to learn Display PostScript by building on your PostScript knowledge. Basically, however, that is not the approach taken here. Instead, PostScript and Display PostScript are presented as an integrated whole. Although the imaging model in Display PostScript is identical to that in PostScript, and the operators and the concepts involved in programming remain the same, the conceptual approach to programming taken in Display PostScript is definitely different from that taken in standard PostScript. Display PostScript is integrated into a C language (or other higher level language) in a natural way, which makes the nature of the program code generated for Display PostScript somewhat different from that for basic PostScript. More importantly, Display PostScript operates in a dynamic, event-driven display environment that is quite distinct from the more static, batch-oriented environment prevalent in standard PostScript. So, although the language and concepts are virtually identical, the planning and execution are quite new and individual.

The Display PostScript system extensions provide new or improved facilities that support the display environment. These facilities include the ability to integrate PostScript code into a C application in a relatively natural way, by translating ordinary PostScript code into a format that can be accessed and used within an application, along with a library of PostScript functions that are available to your C program. Although Display PostScript itself does not create or manage windows, it does provide extended PostScript functions that support windowing displays in a variety of ways. Finally, Display PostScript provides new operations that expand or support color output and text display. These operations will, no doubt, become standard in all PostScript environments at some point in the future; and, as such, may simply be regarded as part of the natural evolution of the PostScript language.

An Integration of Output Methods (WYSIWYG)

The PostScript language represents a new and exciting way of creating complex units of output that include both graphics and text. In many ways, using the PostScript language requires both artistry and craftsmanship, an interaction among a hand and a mind and the physical output. PostScript has much more in common with lettering and calligraphy than with spreadsheets and word processing.

By design, PostScript treats letters as graphic objects, as shapes to be painted onto the output page. Moreover, PostScript provides features and operations that allow you to control the precise rendering of text and graphics in many ways that would be difficult with existing display and printing technologies. You can stretch, bend, shade, and clip letters, using their shapes as graphic elements to create interesting (sometimes even bizarre) effects. Display PostScript provides the perfect communication mechanism for moving such beautiful and complex displays to the printed output.

One of the driving forces behind the use of Display PostScript is the need to be able to represent the potential range of output on raster devices in some high-level, device-independent way. Graphics artists and applications programmers alike have come to realize that a new, effective tool is available to them, one that can also perform the old tasks, such as text display or charts and graphs, very well. It minimizes the repetitive portion of such tasks, allowing both users and programmers to concentrate on creative, rather than housekeeping, aspects. It also provides scope for innovative approaches that were not feasible before, for example, using text in special graphic effects or providing seamless translation of color output. This freedom has been enhanced by the development and acceptance of electronic page-composition systems that use PostScript as their link to the individual devices, thus greatly expanding the potential for high-quality output.

PURPOSE OF THIS BOOK

The purpose of this book is to teach you to understand and use the Display PostScript system. PostScript is an extremely powerful language, and Display PostScript provides an additional layer of functionality. Unfortunately the power of a computer language is often directly related to its complexity, and Display PostScript is no exception. PostScript itself is not inherently difficult to use; it is only unfamiliar and complex. Moreover, as you learn PostScript operations, you will quickly understand how they mesh with the Display PostScript environment. This book is structured to minimize complexity by introducing you to both PostScript and Display PostScript operations step by step, and to help you become familiar and comfortable with both basic PostScript and Display PostScript through doing and discussing many examples.

Objectives

We have already broadly stated this book's goal: to help you understand and use the Display PostScript system. This goal can be refined into three more precise objectives, which we will discuss in order of priority.

The first objective is to teach you to read basic PostScript code. This means more than just looking up the operators in a manual. Sometimes that kind of reading is necessary, but it is not the kind of fluency that you need to develop. This objective means that you should be able to understand PostScript concepts and operations with depth and accuracy. You will learn the basic PostScript vocabulary and structure so that you can follow most PostScript code without resorting to a reference guide (including this book). Having completed this book, you should be able to follow most PostScript programs and comprehend at a general level what the program does and how it does it. In other words, you should be able to read PostScript pretty much the same way you can read English—sometimes referring to a dictionary or grammar, but mostly able to follow ordinary constructions without difficulty.

The second objective is to teach you to write PostScript programs. This involves several steps that are probably not obvious to you now. You will learn to analyze and set up output in units. You will use these setups to generate the necessary procedure definitions, and you will then program those procedures to generate the output that you have analyzed. This process of structuring output, designing solutions to create the desired display, and then implementing them in PostScript is at least as important a component of learning to write the language as is the use of the various operators.

The third objective is to teach you how to integrate your PostScript code into your application by using Display PostScript. It may surprise you that this is the third objective, and not the first, but there is reason behind it. To use Display PostScript effectively is very similar to being able to integrate assembly language code into your applications. It requires more than just a little familiarity; it requires a level of comfort and control that must be earned. If you achieve the first two objectives, with some aid from this book, integrating the resulting PostScript code into your application will be quite easy.

Obviously these objectives are intertwined so closely that each supports and involves both of the others. The book does not distinguish each objective but, like any good text, tries to teach all of them with each exercise or lesson. In this way, you will learn the PostScript operators individually as well as the process of combining those operators into Display PostScript procedures in a unified way.

Who This Book Is For

Besides setting objectives for a book, we must have some vision of the type of reader who is going to use the book. This vision of a typical reader forms the basis for the discussion of requirements. Note that there is nothing restrictive here; there are no prerequisites for making effective use of the book. This simply tells you what material in the book does not include long explanations, because you are expected to either already know the material or to be able to work out what needs to be done.

To begin with, this book is designed for both current PostScript programmers and for programmers who are new to PostScript. Current PostScript programmers will be introduced to the new extensions and way of working that Display PostScript provides. Beginning programmers will be shown both PostScript and Display PostScript in a unified way that will allow them to use Display PostScript from the beginning.

The only thing I ask is that you be willing to work through the examples. PostScript really is like any other language in that ease and proficiency come from practice. So you should do the exercises and examples, perhaps even more than once. I would encourage you to try alternative approaches and to print out your variations to see how you are progressing. One of the most interesting things about PostScript, in my experience, has been how much pure fun it is to play with. You can generate an amazing variety of graphics just by trying options and operators. Enjoy this experience; it will make the whole process more satisfying.

General computer concepts and operations are not covered here. Although I try to precisely define all terms that are intrinsic or even related to PostScript, a number of concepts that apply to computer operations and computer languages generally are not defined. I take more or less for granted that you understand what a window is and what a computer language does.

This book also assumes that you are reasonably familiar with your operating environment and with the C language. It does not try to teach you C programming. Also, because Display PostScript provides direct access from a C application, C code appears in the text and examples. The code is quite straightforward; even a beginning C programmer should have no trouble following it. However, it is presented without any discussion of standard C practices and procedures. If you have any problems, a good C tutorial would be advised.

The most obvious thing that is not covered here is the specific operating system and windowing environment that you might be using. Display PostScript does not directly support window creation or manipulation. It leaves these tasks to the operating system because each workstation platform has different requirements and features that are integrated into the window or display environment. In the book, we adopt the same approach, showing standard Display PostScript code and associated C functions without any direct window connections.

The net result then is that you should know your workstation and its operating system. You should know the C programming language at least well enough to create, compile, link, and execute a program. You should be able to open an output window using the C language and perform all the basic tasks needed to manage that window. The appendices give some information about how this can be done in the NeXT and DECWindows environments, but the text's fundamental assumption is that you have all this in hand. The general tendency has been to avoid device- or operating-system–dependent text and examples and to allow you to work out how to talk to the PostScript device on your own. This presumes, of course, that you are familiar with the computer and operating system that you're using. If you have trouble, look first at the operations documentation that came with the computer, then try the more general operating system references (particularly if you are using UNIX or a variant), and finally try the appendices in this book or the Display PostScript environment-specific references that should be available with your system.

Additional Resources

Let's look at what resources, besides this book, you might want to have handy. Note that you don't absolutely need any of the references mentioned here to use this book; all the required definitions and materials are provided here. Even if you have these other references, you don't want to be flipping back and forth among several books to try to learn the material.

But as you grow beyond what you have learned here, you will need precise and complete definitions for every possible PostScript operator.

To begin with, it would be ideal if you could have a workstation system that supports the Display PostScript system. You certainly can follow the examples in the book without actually doing them yourself, but the learning experience will be measurably improved and much easier if you can input and execute these examples for yourself. The book expects you to do so, and in fact meeting our second objective can only be accomplished through a hands-on approach.

If you are going to do much PostScript work, you will also want to own the *PostScript Language Reference Manual* and the associated *Display PostScript System Reference* manuals. These are written by Adobe Systems, the creators of PostScript, and they are the definitive source for all PostScript operators and operations. The *PostScript Language Reference Manual,* published by Addison-Wesley, is available in most technical bookstores. The associated Display PostScript references should come with your workstation, or they may be available elsewhere. In several places throughout the book you are referred to the *Language Reference Manual* or various components of the *Display PostScript System Reference* for further detail or explanations of various operations.

At the time this is written, the definitions of all these concepts and operators are spread out in several sources. These sources break down into two or three places: the *Language Reference Manual,* the *Display PostScript System Reference,* and—depending on whether or not you have a PostScript printer—a PostScript supplement for your specific output device. This last documentation is not provided on the NeXT computer system if you are using the NeXT printer as your output device because the PostScript interpreter that creates the printed image is the same one that creates the screen. All of these materials are easily available, but you may have to assemble them piece by piece.

HOW TO USE THIS BOOK

The book follows a regular pattern that grows out of the established objectives. It is organized in a sort of spiral, in that certain topics recur regularly but with increasing depth and complexity. For example, you first encounter simple text output in Chapter 1, using the most basic operations and relying, in so far as possible, on default parameters in the language. Then you explore PostScript procedures and dictionaries in Chapter 2, using somewhat more advanced text operations, and followed by basic graphics. Then you return to text processing in Chapter 5, this time using the procedures and graphics techniques already developed to help you build more complex text output. This continues through advanced fonts and dictionaries, more text, and finally very advanced graphic concepts.

Built into this book are three proven techniques that can help expand your understanding of Display PostScript. First, the book follows a course of study, a plan that is designed to present the various operations in PostScript in a natural way. The book also proceeds in a cumulative manner, with each topic and exercise building on the previous ones. Finally, the book provides ample exercises and examples to help you practice the concepts presented in a concrete setting and allow you sufficient drill to make these concepts and operations really familiar.

How the Text Is Organized

The basic orientation of the book is to act first and talk later. The idea is that you will have a much better appreciation of the discussion of what the program means after you have executed it, instead of analyzing it to death before running it. This is an excellent basic approach to language instruction generally, whether for natural languages or computer ones—just ask Berlitz.

However, this approach cannot be followed entirely. Page composition is inherently a process that depends on some analysis and planning in order for it to work properly. Moreover, you must make some choices before you start programming; otherwise, the program and the associated procedures will look entirely arbitrary and capricious. To this extent, the exercises include preliminary setup and analysis. Beyond what is required for that reason, no preliminary programming is undertaken. Instead, the exercises and examples all have extensive discussions after the program is presented and run. The intent is to provide you with the concepts necessary for the program before you write it, use the actual program as an example, and then discuss the specific use and results of these concepts as embodied in the program after the exercise is completed.

As you will learn, the nature of Display PostScript divides this process into two pieces: wraps and procedures. Therefore, the general structure of the major exercises and examples is to analyze the output, create the wraps, discuss the wraps, and then create and document the procedures. I believe this to be a very understandable process that you will find perfectly clear and rewarding.

Using the Coding Examples

The coding examples presented in this book are to some extent cumulative. Because of the structure of programming languages, it is both appropriate and useful to create procedures that do certain tasks and then repeatedly reuse these procedures, occasionally reworking them to fit the current need. That is not to say that you must work the examples in order; most of them are complete programs in themselves and can be entered and executed on their own without error. However, the explanations that accompanied them initially are not repeated in the text when the procedure is reused. Therefore, if you are skipping around and you need to look up a specific procedure to understand some point, you may have to look back at the first instance of its use in the book to find a complete discussion. When code is reused, the text mentions the origin of the example in case you need to consult it.

The concepts used in the book are also cumulative. As you might have guessed from the discussion of the spiral nature of the material, much use is made of previous concepts and techniques as you proceed further on into the book. Indeed, some of the material in the later chapters will be almost incomprehensible if you are not fully familiar with certain PostScript operations and ideas that have been explained, discussed, and illustrated in earlier portions of the book. This is, to some extent, a process of developing vocabulary to enable further discussions to proceed quickly and precisely.

If you do want to skip around in the book, I would recommend that you use the Conclusions sections at the end of the chapters as a quick guide to the material covered in the chapter. I would also suggest that you at least read through the code examples before you skip the chapter; if the code is clear, you can proceed with the assurance that you understand the work done so far in the book; if the code is not clear, however, you should read the explanations and discussions before proceeding. Finally, you might wish to look at Appendix A, which lists all the operators that are discussed in the text by chapter and so forms a rough index of the concepts contained in the chapters themselves.

Using the Operator Review

Appendix A provides a quick and convenient review of the operators that are presented in each chapter. You will also see definitions for some new operators when they seem to fit in naturally and when the use of the operator does not require additional explanation over and above what can be presented there. The same format is used here as throughout the book, and indeed in all the PostScript and Display PostScript reference materials. Lists like this will help you recall the operators presented in each chapter, and it also provides an informal index for the topics presented in the chapter.

Every possible operator does not appear in these chapter reviews; only the operators used in the chapters, or operators closely associated with them, are covered. As I suggested earlier, the best way to learn a language is to learn the primary functions well and then to broaden your scope to include the more specialized functions. That is the rule followed here: only the most common or most useful—generally one and the same—operators are presented and explained. Related operators may only be noted; some operators are omitted entirely.

If you want a full list of the operators that are available on your system, you should review the list of operators provided by your system manufacturer in the complete reference manuals listed earlier. Remember, also, that we have deliberately excluded environment-specific operators. For all these reasons, you should become very well acquainted with your environment's individual set of operators. This is certainly not an attempt to discourage you from using the full set of operators; in fact, to make truly effective displays for your machine, you will almost have to use some device-specific techniques. In this book, however, the purpose is to keep to basic, common output functions. You should be able to understand the language better and achieve your objective of writing Display PostScript more quickly by sticking, at least at first, to a subset of the language that contains the operators most often used.

Using Device-specific Implementations

All of the work in this book, both text and examples, relies on generic PostScript and Display PostScript features and is not tied to any specific implementation of Display PostScript in any specific device. Any exercise or example should execute correctly on any Display PostScript–equipped device. Moreover, the PostScript concepts and techniques that you will learn are as applicable to a laser printer or typesetter as they are to a computer screen. Of course, changes must be made to run them on a page-oriented (which essentially means "batch-oriented") device instead of a workstation. Nevertheless, once you have mastered this material, you will be able to read and modify standard PostScript without much trouble.

The work in the book is based solely on PostScript and Display PostScript. With the single exception of the C programming language, there is no use of any language or program other than PostScript with the Display PostScript extensions in this book. That means that you can complete all of the examples using only a Display PostScript–equipped device. The requirement for C comes from the integration of Display PostScript with that language and should not cause you any problems.

A serious attempt has been made to keep the C code as well as the PostScript code as general and universal as possible. For this reason, I have followed the ANSI standard format and conventions in all the C code presented here. Of course, this may not match the compiler available in your environment. If this is a problem, you should review the excellent material in Kernighan and Ritchie, *The C Programming Language, Second Edition* (Prentice-Hall), which discusses the variation between the new ANSI standard C and previous versions. Alternatively you may be able to get information on this from the compiler manufacturer.

Obviously each reader will have some specific configuration of hardware and software. The book is structured for use by everyone; but what do you do if you have a specific problem? Unfortunately I am not able to provide detailed information on every possible configuration. However, Appendix B contains specific information for two common configurations: one for a NeXT system and the other for a DEC. Even if your specific setup is not included, you may want to read whichever of these is most similar to your configuration if you have a problem. It may give you some ideas or helpful information.

CHAPTER 1

Getting Started

This chapter presents the basic concepts that you need to grasp in order to understand and write PostScript code. You will learn how the Display PostScript extensions to the PostScript language are integrated into your application to give you access to a complete graphic language. Specifically you examine how PostScript describes a unit of output, you review housekeeping issues such as how to set up a window, and you see how to position text within a window. With these concepts, you will write a short PostScript program to generate some text.

Once you have written some code, you will undoubtedly have some questions. To answer these questions, the chapter presents PostScript stack operations, a standard notation for PostScript examples, and a short discussion of how PostScript handles strings and comments.

The next section introduces the specifics of Display PostScript coding and the concept of "wrapped PostScript," which will form the basis of most of your Display PostScript code. A second exercise then uses wrapped PostScript procedures to set several paragraphs of text and commentary in a two-column format. This exercise shows you some of the ways you can easily use Display PostScript to accomplish things that may look quite difficult.

THE POSTSCRIPT LANGUAGE

PostScript is both a graphics language and a complete programming language; you can use it to create any kind of function or algorithm that is required to generate the output you want. PostScript was designed with certain points in mind that give it useful and powerful features. These distinctive characteristics, which are important from the viewpoint of both the programmer and the user, are as follows:

- Interpreted
- Dynamic
- Encoded
- Device-independent
- Graphically oriented

These characteristics are important for you to understand before you begin programming in PostScript.

Interpreted

PostScript is an interpreted language, like APL or BASIC, and is not compiled, as C and Pascal usually are. This means that PostScript operators and functions are understood and acted on by another program, the interpreter, which actually executes these commands as it receives them. The interpreter may reside in the output device controller, as it does in most laser printers or typesetters, or it may reside within your computer, as it does in the NeXT computer. In either case, using an interpreter offers both advantages and disadvantages to the programmer. On the plus side, it allows definition of many program requirements as the commands are being executed, which provides both flexibility and sensitivity to the current state of the output and the device being used. It also allows for immediate feedback, error handling, and command execution, which improves error diagnosis and debugging. Finally, it allows you to easily prototype visual effects without having to compile (and recompile) many times.

However, there is a negative aspect to interpreted languages, particularly in a shared execution environment, which is where Display PostScript typically executes. For example, because the interpreter is itself a program, it adds another layer of software that must be executed before the image is created. This can slow things down, and such hesitation is particularly noticeable and potentially annoying on a screen display. Speed of display is, therefore, always a concern for a programmer, particularly one creating commercial applications. For the examples presented in this book, however, speed is not an issue since these examples are all quite short. We will discuss in later chapters how to use the Display PostScript extensions to extract the maximum speed out of your graphics.

Interpreted languages do have the advantage of being naturally recursive, meaning that PostScript functions may call themselves, either directly or indirectly. This is of some benefit. Also, interpreted languages are not very demanding as to program format or layout. In all this, PostScript is much like C, which also has a minimum of required or language-enforced formatting and which supports recursive functions. However, PostScript does not have any kind of function prototyping or data casting or formatting. All of these issues, as you will see, are either handled automatically or left to the programmer for control and analysis. This can be a negative point if programmers do not restrict themselves to a clear structure and do not follow the desired format and rules quite strictly. Generally such rules and structure—and the self-discipline to follow them—come only with experience in the language. In the case of Display PostScript, you have the additional challenge of integrating PostScript routines and C functions into a seamless and yet manageable whole. These issues are discussed and examined throughout the following chapters precisely because self-discipline and structure are essential in an interpreted environment.

Dynamic

PostScript is dynamic in two ways. First, it is dynamic in that it can provide feedback both to its own routines and to its associated C programs as to the current state of the execution environment. For example, it can determine whether a given font is currently loaded and available and, if it is not, PostScript can either remedy the situation or return a status message to the calling program. This, of course, is essential in a display environment, but PostScript is also able to do this in the more traditionally static environment of an output device. Such self-analysis and correction capabilities are generally quite beyond the normal escape mechanism used in simpler output devices.

Second, PostScript is dynamic in that the screen output, or page output, can be modified as it is created. This is done by creating new functions that can interact intelligently with your C code, using the basic set of graphic and procedural operators as building blocks. In this case, the interpreter acts as a sort of operating system, creating, cataloging, retrieving, and executing the procedures you have defined.

Because of the nature of a display environment, Display PostScript provides additional functionality to manage resources, such as memory, that were not treated dynamically in the basic PostScript model. Although such changes are critical to the successful implementation of a display, these extensions, from a programmer's viewpoint, do not require much direct attention beyond a reasonable care in using and controlling certain types of objects because they are mostly concerned with routine housekeeping tasks that can be left on "automatic" once the basic concerns are taken care of.

Encoded

PostScript and Display PostScript are converted, or *encoded*, into units before processing, which allows a certain flexibility. This encoding provides several options that improve certain factors in handling the PostScript commands that flow to the interpreter. In ordinary PostScript, all commands and other objects are created and transmitted in simple ASCII codes, using the printable subset of the standard ASCII encoding.

This form of encoding provides several great advantages. First, the codes can be interpreted and understood by machines (the interpreter) as well as by humans. You can easily read an ordinary PostScript program. Second, the programs and procedures can be created and manipulated by any standard editing software, without any special handling requirements. Finally, the resulting programs can be transmitted over any network without loss of information and without any concern about transparency.

However, this method of storing and executing programs has its drawbacks. Primarily it requires a long string of characters to deliver any command, and it takes a correspondingly long time to transmit and interpret these commands. Particularly in an environment such as Display PostScript, which requires quick and accurate communications between the PostScript interpreter and the application that is creating and sending the PostScript commands, alternative methods of encoding are desirable. Display PostScript, therefore, offers two additional methods of encoding commands. In the first form, called *binary token encoding*, all the commands and other PostScript objects are transformed into a binary code format that provides compact storage and reasonable execution of the code.

In addition, the Display PostScript system provides a very fast and efficient, but somewhat less compact, encoding called *binary object sequence encoding*. This process is handled by the Display PostScript Client Library, which is a library of procedures that handle communications with the interpreter. The Client Library is supported by the *pswrap* translator, which generates a C source file from standard PostScript commands and operations that contains calls to the Client Library functions. We will discuss *pswrap* and its requirements later in the chapter.

Really, this is all just for formality and completeness. There are just two points to keep in mind as you go about creating your code. First, all these different encoding schemes do not add any functionality to the language. All versions of PostScript are identical in what they can do; they only differ in how they store commands. Second, in actual use, you simply write your PostScript code in the ordinary way or call C functions that are predefined in the Display PostScript Client Library from your program to get the output that you want. The *pswrap* translator, which changes your PostScript code into functions that can be accessed from your C application; the Client Library, which contains all the predefined PostScript functions; and the interpreter do all the rest. As the rest of this chapter demonstrates, the real action is in getting your thoughts and creations into PostScript; the encoding is secondary.

Device-independent

As mentioned earlier, one of PostScript's great strengths is that it is independent of any specific output device. The basic set of PostScript operators is designed to be appropriate to the general class of raster-output devices, and the specific needs of screen output are covered by the Display PostScript extensions. In this way, the complete PostScript language can control and command a wide variety of devices, leaving the programmer free to concentrate on the graphics issues. However, where there is a special need, specific device-dependent operations are available to construct images or to control the device.

This freedom from the constraints of a specific device provides two major benefits to the PostScript programmer. First, you can write your software without being especially concerned about the nature of the platform on which you are running, the class of the display, or the quality of the output device. In all these cases, the PostScript interpreter transforms your Display PostScript into the best output that is available on the given device. Second, you can create the output on a low-resolution screen, transfer it to a high-resolution workstation for editing or revision, proof it on a relatively low-cost output device such as a laser printer, and finally output it on a high-quality and high-resolution device such as an imagesetter for final processing.

Graphically Oriented

PostScript is especially designed to create and manipulate graphic objects on a raster-output device. This graphics orientation is such a major component of the language that probably the best way to think about PostScript is as a method of electronic drawing—an electronic pen-and-ink, if you like. More than 30 percent of the primitive PostScript operators deal directly with graphics, and many of these operators are intuitively similar to the action of an artist handling a pen: raising it, positioning it on the drawing surface, inking it, and then stroking each line onto the surface. Using these techniques, PostScript can easily draw both graphics and text onto the output surface. In addition, PostScript provides a number of powerful primitive operators, for example, **scale** and **rotate**, which can be combined in many ways and used to produce dramatic and surprising results.

PostScript's flexibility makes it the language of choice for serious graphics work, particularly work that integrates text and graphics. In addition, the same techniques can be used on both the screen and the printed output, further simplifying the programming process. Where other languages or mechanisms may impede the combining of quality text and graphics, PostScript makes it easy and natural. This facility for combining what have often been, up to this point, two separate modes of output derives in large measure from PostScript's approach to text. Within PostScript, the individual characters that make up text are themselves graphic objects that can be positioned, scaled, rotated, and used in a variety of functions, just as any other graphic could be.

The PostScript language consists of more than 250 basic operators that provide a complete set of graphics and text handling operations as well as all the traditional functions of a programming language. Display PostScript, which adds approximately another 80 operators to the basic PostScript set, provides extensions that handle various screen functions and also adds some new operations that are part of the basic graphics and text management.

Before you can begin reading or writing PostScript code, whether Display PostScript for screen handling or basic PostScript for page layout, you need to acquaint yourself with a basic subset of these operators and to become familiar with the format and structure of the PostScript language itself. Although by no means unique, PostScript is quite individual, and indeed distinctive, in its presentation.

As you can readily see from the relative numbers of operators, Display PostScript is simply an extension of the basic PostScript language with some additional operations to make screen handling faster, easier, and more effective. Therefore the concepts and functions discussed in this section are fundamental to both systems. Indeed, it is the very power of these concepts and the elegance of the concepts that have made PostScript the de facto industry standard page-description language.

The basic imaging model in Display PostScript is still that of the underlying PostScript language. PostScript was intended from its creation as a complete programming language with powerful graphic operators built into it at the fundamental level. It has many features in common with other computer languages such as C because it addresses the same or similar tasks and must overcome the same limitations and problems as they do. But PostScript goes far beyond traditional computer languages by providing the ability to handle and output graphic images of all types. In many ways, all the other features of PostScript are centered on and support this unique capacity to describe graphic objects.

Graphic Objects

When you say "graphics," you naturally think of pictures, and picture elements, which make up a substantial portion of our visual means of communication. Human beings have a strongly visual orientation. Our language is full of visual metaphors, and we typically say "I see" to mean that we understand something. The saying "a picture is worth a thousand words" has become a cliché because the graphic presentation of information is so obviously and inherently useful. It is this utility that drives our need to render images of things seen or understood into the permanent and concrete form of pictures and other graphics.

The methods for creating images generally fall into two basic techniques that are used alone or in combination to create the final result. Surely the more ancient is the application of paint or some other opaque or partially opaque medium to a prepared surface. This method and its variations gives us paintings and drawings of all types: oils; watercolors; sketches in pencil, crayon, chalk, or charcoal; and so on. By extension of this process we also have collage and similar assembly techniques. On the other hand is the process perhaps best exemplified by photography where light is used to change millions of molecular-sized particles into dots to create or capture an image.

Printing, in these terms, is generally most like painting, using ink as the opaque medium to mark out shapes on the page. In text or line art, the desired image is placed onto the page as a continuous line of ink, just as the artist makes a line with paint on the canvas. When it comes to reproducing images that do not consist simply of lines, however, modern high-speed presses use a technique much more like photography than like painting. In these cases, the image is broken down into a series of dots of varying sizes that create the illusion of shades and patterns to the human eye. The dots are then grouped by size and area to create the desired image on the page. This process of making dots of ink to re-create an image is called *screening*, and it plays an important part in PostScript image processing. A simple example of this process is shown in Figure 1-1.

Figure 1-1. Simple screened image.

Raster-output Devices The graphics operators provided by the PostScript language are designed to create images out of dots essentially because the language was designed to work with a general class of devices, known collectively as *raster-output devices*, that use this technique to create all their output. Perhaps surprisingly, the original raster-output device is the television; and, in fact, that is where the term "raster" originated. Raster devices are characterized by having a number of dots that are activated in some manner to make up an image. On a television screen, these dots are made out of a phosphorescent material and are activated—that is, made to shine—by the action of a beam of electrons. Essentially the image is created by using dots in a manner very similar to the printing process mentioned earlier. Unlike printing, however, there are no continuous lines of any sort on a raster-output device, so text and lines must also be composed by a series of dots.

Each dot on a raster-output device represents one picture element, or *pixel*. Although these elements are conveniently and conventionally referred to as "dots," this is a generic reference and does not necessarily represent the actual shape of a pixel. Actual pixels may be round, square, oval, or rectangular—whatever suits the nature of the device and the requirements of the manufacturer. The simplest form of pixels are simply off or on, zero or one, like binary numbers. You can readily see how naturally this fits into a digital processing framework.

However, many devices have pixels that are not simply on-and-off, but that can vary by color or brightness. Television, for example, has dots that vary in brightness by the strength of the electronic beam that activates them, providing darker and lighter shades of images. Some computer systems have similar features; for example, the NeXT computer display has four levels of brightness on its screen. In such cases, more than a simple binary number must be associated with each dot. However, even in devices with only on-and-off pixels, various levels of shading can be created by using the screening process mentioned earlier.

This process of composing in dots has advantages and disadvantages. The advantage is that this method produces text as well as graphics, line art, and shaded images, without any change in technique or approach. Each character or image is simply a set of pixels to be set appropriately. The disadvantage is that neither characters nor lines have continuous boundaries; at the finest and smallest level, every object looks ragged and uneven.

With the possible exception of certain exaggerated "pop art" images, the intention is to produce text and graphics that appear continuous and shaded to the eye, even though they are actually a simple collection of dots. This illusion is created by having a large number of relatively small dots, or pixels, in a given area. The number of pixels per unit area is called the *device resolution*.

Because resolution is measured by area, it has both horizontal and vertical components. Many devices have identical numbers of pixels in both dimensions; such devices generally provide resolution measurements as *dots per inch*, or dpi. Where the resolution differs in the horizontal and vertical directions, both figures are usually given, as 240 by 300 dpi. Obviously the greater the resolution, the better the output from the device will fool the eye into thinking that its lines are continuous instead of a string of dots. At the highest level, where resolutions typically are 2500 dpi or more, it becomes impossible for the unaided eye to distinguish the individual dots, and lines and text become continuous shapes for all practical purposes.

Even on high-resolution devices, there is still a problem of determining the precise boundary of an image. Somehow the device must be told where to start and stop turning pixels on. This process is particularly critical for text characters because long training and association make the distinctive shapes of the characters quite familiar to the eye, and any distortions, at even the finest levels, will often adversely affect speed and ease of reading. This issue of adjustment of pixels at an image boundary is called *tuning*, and it is both important and extremely device dependent. Using an intermediary language like PostScript to create and display images on various devices not only allows you flexibility and control, but also saves you from worrying about specific device characteristics.

Device Classification Some familiar forms of output devices are not raster-output devices. For example, typewriters and similar letter-quality devices work by imprinting preformed characters or shapes onto the page. Such devices have no mechanism for producing general images since they can only represent those forms that were predefined for their output.

Dot-matrix printers, even though they use impact printing techniques borrowed from typewriters, are raster-output devices because they form characters and images by a series of dots. Resolutions on such devices are quite low, typically between 100 and 200 dpi. Most page printers—laser printers, ink-jet printers, and so on—are medium-resolution devices, with resolutions ranging from 300 to 600 dpi. Typesetting machines—or as they are more commonly called now, imagesetting machines—use photographic techniques to create their pixels, and achieve resolutions between 1000 and 2800 dpi. Some special-purpose, high-resolution devices go even higher.

Obviously, high resolution imposes some constraints and problems for device output. Each time the resolution increases, the number of pixels per unit area increases by the square of that new value, and so more information must be generated to control the device and create the desired image. The increase in information imposes significantly greater demands on system resources such as computational power and data transmission facilities. All of this is reflected in higher costs—both in dollars and in required skills—for using such devices.

Since Display PostScript is primarily intended for drawing onto a screen, we should also examine the characteristics of screen-output devices. Displays on computer systems are also raster-output devices, as you might expect, because they are directly derived from television technology. These displays generally have the lowest resolution of all the raster-output devices, ranging from 60 to 100 dpi. To some extent, however, they can compensate for this by using pixels that have varying intensity to create shading and texture. At such low resolutions, tuning becomes critical, and poor tuning is most noticeable. For this reason, text characters and graphic figures may appear ragged on the screen, but they print smoothly on a higher resolution output device such as a laser printer.

Screen and Printer Management

One of the challenges of creating images that are both displayed on a screen and printed onto paper arises from the screening considerations for raster-output devices discussed earlier and the differences between high- and low-resolution devices. As we mentioned, screens are generally low-resolution devices, but their dots may vary in intensity. Printing output devices, on the other hand, have only black dots—where the ink or toner is left on the image—but often have much higher resolution images. In such cases, it is common to mimic the visual effect of gray or color tints by grouping dots into grids and filling the grid according to some pattern. If the *tiles* that make up the grid are small enough and the dots are small relative to the tile size, a set of tiles with part of the dots inked in will look like a shade of gray to the eye.

A simple, theoretical example should help illustrate this issue. Suppose that you are running on the NeXT computer, where the MegaPixel display provides four varying intensities of pixels and therefore four shades of gray: black, dark gray, light gray, and white. Suppose that you draw a simple 2-inch square on the screen and color it light gray, which is about one-third of the way between black and white. If you were writing directly to the screen, you would have sent some hardware command to set the intensity of the pixels that you calculated were within the area of the square to the correct value.

Now you want to print this square on the laser printer that is attached to the NeXT machine. However, the printer only has black and white pixels.

Moreover, the screen has 94 dpi, so that the square extends about 188 pixels in each direction; and, as a final problem, the screen is not shaped like a page at all. Where do you start and end the square?

All of this can, of course, be calculated. The relationship between the screen coordinates and the page is always the same. Thus the 2-inch square becomes 800 pixels in each direction instead of 188 since the resolution of the printer is 400 dpi. The conversion of a white sheet to a light gray involves a simple screening process. In this case, the screening process divides the square into smaller regions, called tiles, and allocates a certain number of pixels to each tile. Then individual pixels within each tile will be turned black in a distinct pattern to create the illusion that the tile is light gray. If the tiles match seamlessly and fill the square, the entire square will appear light gray to the eye. An example of this is shown in Figure 1-2.

Figure 1-2. Tiling and gray values.

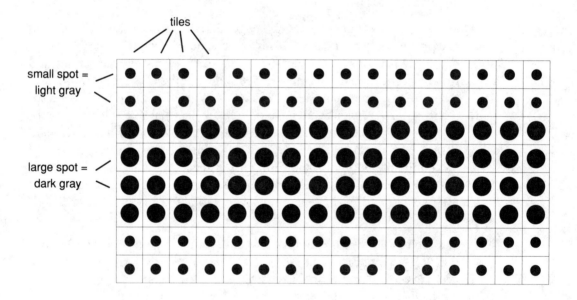

As you see, this is a lot of computation, and a lot of programming to get it right the first time. Once you have it, of course, it can easily be done again and again; it's only the first time that's the problem. Furthermore, you would have to redo these calculations for each different display, and each different output device, and for all possible combinations of display and output resolution. Naturally no one actually does all this, even in as simple a display environment as MS-DOS; you always have some help. But "some" is really not enough to get you away from the hair-pulling, teeth-grinding problems that still have to be addressed.

The PostScript language handles all of these complex and difficult issues automatically for you, while still leaving you with the operators you need to directly control the device if you wanted. This is, in a nutshell, the power and promise of PostScript. Plainly and simply, if you learn PostScript and its Display PostScript extensions, you can minimize device interface considerations and concentrate on the more valuable and interesting issues of user interface and output that will make your software stand out from the crowd. Like C itself, PostScript allows you to work at as high or low a level as you need to feel comfortable and to create the output effects that you want. If you need direct access to the device, you can get it; but if you don't need it, you can just code along and trust the interface to create the desired results.

CONCEPTS

Before proceeding, you will need to know a few basic PostScript concepts. You will, of course, hear more about them later, but the intent here is to give you a simple overview that will accomplish two purposes. First, it allows you to see these basic ideas clearly and free of other, perhaps confusing, details. A sort of "forest view" before we get into the trees. Second, it gives you enough basic information to allow us to work through several simple exercises, so that you can begin to get some feel for hands-on Display PostScript.

The PostScript interpreter processes a series of entities known as *objects*, or *tokens*. These are simply a convenient way to refer to those things that the PostScript interpreter can work with and understand. For now, you can think of these objects as falling into one of three intuitive categories: literals, names, and procedures. Literals are, as you might expect, all objects of a fixed nature: numbers, strings, arrays, and so on. Names are labels that allow you to reference other objects—either literal or procedure objects. Names are created and tied to their reference object by means of dictionaries. Procedures are groups of objects, meant to be executed in sequence, that are stored and referenced as a single object. Like most programming jargon, all of this sounds much more complex than it really is when you use it.

The first key concept is that PostScript works through a *stack* mechanism. This is a place where PostScript operators look for data and return results. You may already be familiar with stacks from other work in computers; if not, for now just think of this as a temporary storage area within the interpreter.

As you already know, PostScript is a language of operators and each operator performs a single function, although that function may be quite complex as it is, for example, when executing certain graphics operators. Most operators require some form of information to work from; the required data are called *operands*. These operands are made available to the operator by placing them on the stack. This leads to the second key concept: that PostScript, unlike most other computer languages (such as C) requires that all the operands come before the operator. This makes life easy for the interpreter but hard for the user and programmer. It means, for example, that you must enter the coordinates where you want to go before you can tell PostScript to move there.

Each PostScript operator has been provided with a matching C library function, stored in the *Client Library*, which is simply the operator name preceded by the letters "PS". The operands that the operator needs are provided by the function arguments, with real numbers being float values, strings being * char values, and so on. Note, however, that many operators that require operands are designed to obtain them from the operand stack rather than from the function call. All these functions, including a definition of the required arguments, are presented in your Display PostScript documentation and are also available in the *psops.h* header in the Client Library.

In Display PostScript, if you used only the Client Library facilities, this would not be an issue because the library calls work just like ordinary C procedures. In that case, the coordinates for a move are passed to the procedure as parameters in parentheses, as float values, after the function call. However, when you write your own PostScript procedures, you will have to be aware of this difference.

Output Structure

A unique and powerful characteristic of PostScript is that it is independent of special device characteristics, making it quite general and portable. It accomplishes this, in part, by removing the programmer and the application from any specific device output structures. Instead, PostScript provides a simple and common output unit that the interpreter manages, and then the interpreter maps this output unit into the device output. For both historical and practical reasons, this output unit is called a page. Note, however, that this does not represent any specific size, shape, or medium of output. The "page" may be long or short; it may be a piece of paper, a strip of film, or a display screen. This is simply a convenient way to refer to a standard output unit.

PostScript maintains a simple conceptual model of a "page" as a two-dimensional space. Images are "built" on the page by placing "paint" in selected areas. The paint may be put on the page in the form of letters, lines, filled shapes, or halftone representations of images. The paint may be in color, black, white, or any intermediate shade. The paint is generally opaque so that the last mark on the page completely overlays any previous marks. In some devices, however, you can control the transparency of the paint so that previous marks will be more or less visible. Any element of the page may be cropped, as it is painted onto the page, to fit within any desired region or shape.

In all this, the PostScript language follows the natural model of moving a pen or brush across a page of paper. Even though the "page" may be a metal drum or phosphorescent screen and the "paint" may be electrons or light waves, the concept remains the same. The major conceptual change follows from PostScript's ability to generate and fill a path—in the same way that an artist lightly pencils in a letter or figure, fills in the outline with ink or paint, and then removes the original line to leave the final image. Even though PostScript's "pencil lines" are invisible, the way that Post-Script behaves in this model is natural and intuitive, especially from a graphic artist's standpoint.

Current Page The PostScript artist—the programmer—begins work on an "ideal page," which is independent of any specific output device. PostScript calls this the *current page*, and this is the two-dimensional space where PostScript operators leave their marks.

When PostScript begins, the current page is blank. Painting operators, which form a subset of the complete set of graphics operators, place marks on this page. The principal painting operators are as follows:

Operator	Function
fill	Fills in an area on the page.
stroke	Marks lines on the page.

show	Paints character shapes onto the page.
image	Paints an image such as might come from a scanner or other device onto the page.

Display PostScript has extended these basic painting operators by adding the following painting operators that take advantage of the special Display PostScript graphics concepts:

Operator	*Function*
ufill	Fills in an area that is defined in a special format, known as a user path.
ustroke	Marks lines that are defined in the special user path format.
xyshow	Paints character shapes onto the page at specified locations.

Each of these operators, along with the other graphics operators, has various operands, which may be both implicit and explicit. (All of these issues are discussed more fully in Chapters 3 and 4.)

Current Path Most of the painting operators, namely, **fill**, **stroke**, and **show**, have one common and important implicit operand, which is called the *current path*. This is the invisible "pencil line" we mentioned earlier. It describes for the PostScript interpreter where to apply paint onto the current page. The current path is an arbitrary sequence of points, which may be both connected (as in a line or curve) and disconnected (as a separate point). Taken together, this sequence of points describes not only the shapes on the page, but also the position and orientation of the shapes with respect to the overall page. The last point placed on the existing current path is called the *current point*.

Figure 1-3 is an example of a current path (shown here as a dashed line because the real path would be invisible) consisting of two disconnected *subpaths* with the current point at the end of the current subpath. The starting point has no name and no direct bearing on the path; it is shown here for reference, so you can follow how the path was constructed. In the same way, the arrows show the direction in which the path was built—they are not actually part of the path.

Figure 1-3. Current path and current point.

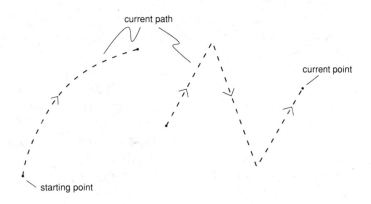

You can construct more than one path on a page. There is no requirement that a page be output before you start a new path. Display PostScript does provide methods for switching from one current path to another on the same page without losing the first. Even in this case, however, only one path on a page may be current at any given time.

Path Construction Operators The current path is built as your application program executes the PostScript path construction operators. Each of these operators alters the current path in some way, generally by adding a new segment to the existing path. Typical path construction operators are shown in the following list:

Operator	Function
newpath	Starts a new path.
moveto	Moves to a defined point and makes that the current point.
lineto	Creates a line from the current point to a defined point.
curveto	Creates a curved line from the current point to a defined point; the shape of the curve is controlled by two additional points, called control points.
rlineto	Creates a line from the current point to a new point that is defined by its position relative to the current point.

Remember that these operators only move the current path; they do not mark the page. All marking is done by means of the painting operators.

User Paths Display PostScript has extended the idea of the current path by providing a new facility for creating and using paths: the *user path*. The user path is a description of a path, consisting of path construction operators and their associated coordinate operands, contained in one unit. In other words, it is a self-contained description of a complete path in user space. This new facility provides several advantages for the display environment. First, since it contains both the path construction operators and the coordinates that describe the path, it can be executed much more efficiently by the interpreter than an arbitrary sequence of operations that may construct an identical path. Second, because of its construction, the path can be stored in a cached form, eliminating redundant interpretation of the same operators within the program and significantly speeding up the display operation.

The user path is a PostScript procedure that must follow a well-defined form to be used correctly. In particular, the path must be provided with a bounding box that determines the limits of the visible path, and can only consist of specific path construction operators and their numeric operands that describe the path itself. As described earlier, the Display PostScript system has included additional painting operators to work with these user paths. You will learn how to create and use user paths in Chapter 4.

Measurement and Coordinates

As you might expect, paths and points on the current page are specified in terms of coordinates. Since a PostScript page is two-dimensional, two rectilinear coordinates are required; these are conventionally designated as x and y. With this method, every point on a PostScript page can be uniquely described by a pair of independent numbers (x, y) that precisely define its location on the ideal page. Remember that, at this point, these coordinates have no relationship to the actual output medium. These are ideal coordinates only, and they always maintain a fixed relationship to the current page no matter what the underlying medium may be or what its physical characteristics are. This coordinate system is called the *user space*.

Default User Space To understand precisely where a specific pair of x, y coordinates places us on a standard PostScript page, we must define three things:

1. Location of the origin. The point (0, 0), or the *origin*, is at the *bottom-left corner* of the page.
2. Direction of the x-axis and y-axis. The *positive* direction on the x-

axis extends *horizontally to the right*. The *positive* direction on the y-axis extends *vertically upward*.

3. The scale, or unit of measure, on the *x*-axis and the *y*-axis. The length of one unit along either axis is *1/72 inch*.

If you are not familiar with printing, the choice of 1/72 inch may seem to be somewhat strange or arbitrary. In fact, it is almost precisely a printer's *point* (which is fractionally larger than 1/72 inch). In this way, the default *x* and *y* values become the equivalent of point values as you move around the page, which is quite convenient when you are setting up and moving around the page. Note also that, by this choice of origin and orientation, every point on the page is described by a positive value of *x* and *y*.

This entire set of conventions now precisely defines every point on an ideal page in terms that are convenient, natural, and practical. This set of conventions defines what is called the *default user space*. The entire set of conventions is shown in Figure 1-4.

Figure 1-4. Default user space.

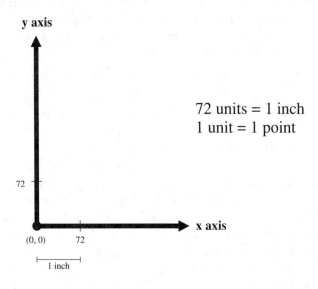

These are, however, just conventions that either you, as the programmer, or the operating system may alter. This may be done for a variety of reasons and, if it is done by the system, may replace the conventions so that a different default space is presented to a program. For example, on the

NeXT system, the scale on the display is 1/94 inch instead of 1/72. This allows a page that is 612 by 792 units to be displayed. Such a page translates into a standard 8 1/2 by 11 inch output page when the standard 1/72-inch coordinates are used. In this way, the application can display an area on the screen that maps exactly into a physical page of paper, with obvious benefits.

There are two points here for you to remember. First, the default user space, although not necessarily ideal for all applications, gives you a clear and well-defined place to begin your work. Second, you can easily change the coordinate system that defines the default user space in order to create your own set of conventions.

Window Operations

Before you can actually create any display operations, you need to create a place on the screen for the display. In modern computer operations, display ordinarily takes place in a *window*. The window is a defined area of the display screen, usually a rectangle, that is allocated to the executing program by the operating system. Windows have proven themselves to be a natural and intelligible way for users to understand and communicate with a program. For maximum efficiency, graphics applications often draw the desired information or output into an area in memory, such as a screen buffer, and then transfer the completed image directly into the display window, but the concept is the same.

Even though windows are such wonderfully useful tools, they are so tied to specific display hardware and to an operating environment that they are not implemented directly in Display PostScript. We could argue the theoretical benefits and drawbacks of this approach, but the simple fact is that each operating system has its own set of windowing controls and conventions, and any attempt to bring yet another set to a wide range of platforms would probably have been a failure. Instead, Display PostScript operates within whatever windowing structure exists on the workstation that you are using and is generally subordinate to it. This allows the workstation manufacturer to customize and control the windowing environment and often, by extension, the total interface for all applications. Display PostScript then operates within a defined window to create the output that you want. Since the output page generally maps directly into a window, when you are marking on the page, you are marking on the window.

However the window is created and managed, certain features of a window are common to all systems, and we should review them here before you create your first application. The window is generally allocated at some position on the overall screen and is given some dimensions. Within the window there is also some coordinate system that defines a position inside the window. Coordinates within the program may be relative to the window origin or relative to the screen origin, but generally you use the window coordinates because this makes your display independent of the actual window position. For this reason, the default coordinates in your PostScript program generally map into window coordinates and not into screen coordinates.

A lot of overhead is associated with window management. The operating system provides for much of it, but the application must handle a certain amount. Generally an application that is displaying in a window works on some event-driven mechanism, where the operating system signals the application when the user takes some action such as moving or resizing a window, and the application must then respond to that action. Because these actions involve changing the display within the window as well as changing the window size and location, Display PostScript does provide many operators that support typical responses to window events. For example, it can clip a display to a given area, save graphic objects in a cache for faster display, and synchronize display execution to external or application events.

In addition to the standard Display PostScript operators, every implementation has some operators that are specific to the windowing system in use. Such operators can be quite important under certain circumstances, but we avoid them here so as to remain as independent of specific windowing systems as possible.

SETTING UP THE FIRST EXAMPLES

With these window preliminaries out of the way, we can now begin work to actually create some displays. We begin with the simplest type of text output. Since we know that Display PostScript is intended to work within a C programming framework, we can expect that the application code that is creating and managing the window and plans to display output in that window is written in C. As a small tribute to the famous first exercise in the text by Kernighan and Ritchie, our first output is a display of text that includes the phrase "hello, world" from their first C example.

We are not going to show any code that creates, synchronizes, or manages the display. All of this is within the windowing environment that you are using and is thus outside of Display PostScript. Instead, we concentrate on coding the Display PostScript segments of the program and merely describe what additional functions you need to perform outside this environment, leaving it up to you to create and test such code. In fact, you still must perform several tasks in order to actually create and view the examples that are presented in the rest of this book.

Window Setup

We presume here that you have created a C program that opens a window in some way or other. In the code that creates the window, you have placed a call to the runPSInline function, which is intended to create the output that will show in the window. We assume that all window management, including setting up access to the window and so on, has been handled outside of the current function.

For the next two chapters, all this code is placed into one function, which we will call runPSInline. This is a standard C function, which, as set up for this example, neither receives nor returns any arguments. The function prototype would therefore be

```
void  runPSInline(void)
```

In actual programming, of course, the function will probably need some parameters. Certainly it will almost always require one that would tie it to the correct window. Most often this is a value, called a Display PostScript *context*, which associates a specific window with a specific Display PostScript output environment. We will discuss contexts and their properties later in this chapter. The operating system will usually also provide a separate connection to the window itself, often referred to as a *window handle*. For this exercise, you are assumed to have associated the window that you have created with a specific Display PostScript output environment, or context. In fact, such a short piece of display code would usually be placed in the function that created the window itself. Here, of course, we have isolated it for clarity and commonality. ("Commonality" here means the capability to be run on both the NeXT and DEC systems, which have very different window-handling and creation mechanisms. By isolating the procedure, we can use it in both environments without changes.)

You may create a window of any size larger than 4 inches wide by 4 inches high. Initialize the window in the normal way for the operating system.

Then connect the window to the Display PostScript environment, and make it the active window and the current context.

Because Display PostScript doesn't "do windows," all the exercises and examples in this book assume that a window has been created and is being controlled outside the Display PostScript system. The necessary calls to the operating system to allocate and display a window are assumed to have already been done. Appendix B is designed to help you with this process; it gives some specific directions on how this can be accomplished in two different Display PostScript environments. However, it's really going to be up to you, as the programmer, to determine how to create and access the window itself; if you have any trouble, consult the technical documentation for the system that you are using or Appendix B for the hardware with which you are working.

Text Setup

Let's look at how you will display your text. This first exercise produces a single line of text output in your window on the screen. Since almost every type of output contains text somewhere, this seems like a good place to start.

PostScript displays text on the output page by means of the **show** operator. This is one of the PostScript painting operators that place marks on the current page. In this case, the marks are in the form of letters, as described by the currently selected font. Each font contains a precise description of letters and symbols that defines for **show** how to mark them on the page.

Text is presented and handled in PostScript as *strings*. A string in PostScript is a line of characters enclosed in parentheses, like this:

> (This is the first string to display)

In C, of course, strings (usually called *string constants*) are coded slightly differently, being enclosed in double quotes, like this:

> "This is the first string to display"

The result of this difference is that, when you call a PostScript function from C, you send the string in double quotes (as you would to *printf*, for example), but if you create and use strings inside your own PostScript code, you must enclose them in parentheses. Like C, however, PostScript strings may contain a variety of characters.

PostScript contains built-in descriptions of a variety of common fonts; the exact set of fonts available depends on the implementation of Display PostScript that is currently running on your device. However, four basic fonts are present in almost every PostScript device: Helvetica, Times Roman, Courier, and Symbol. The Helvetica and Times Roman are classic fonts; Courier is a simple typewriter font; and Symbol provides mathematical and other special characters. Many other fonts are available for PostScript, any or all of which may be available on your device. The examples here use only the most basic fonts to ensure that they can be run on all varieties of output device. You can easily substitute other fonts if you have them available; it won't change the basic effect of the exercises at all—although it will change the output to the new font.

Before you can display a line of text, you must do some work to set up a font for output. First, you have to tell PostScript the name of the font you want to use. Second, you must specify the size you want the printed letters to be. This is done by providing a size number, in user units, which corresponds (in the default PostScript coordinates) to points—a convenient text measurement. With these two tasks taken care of, you are ready to make the given font the currently active font. In basic PostScript, this process requires three steps, using the **findfont**, **scalefont**, and **setfont** operators. In Display PostScript, this process has been streamlined into one operation, using the new **selectfont** operator.

Next, you must set the current point, which defines where on the output display window to paint the desired string of text. Anytime you start a new page, the current point is undefined; there are no defaults in PostScript displays. The **show** operator paints a string of text beginning at the current point and leaves the current point set to the end of the string when it's done. In this way, successive **show**s place output strings one after another, as you would expect and want. However, the operators do not sense when you have left the visible portion of the display; if you write a string that goes past the edge of the window, you do not get an error; the excess text simply does not display, and the current point ends up off the visible output region. Of course, some windowing systems keep this information and allow the user to move the window (by scrolling or other means) to display the additional text. It is up to the programmer to determine where the application output is in the window and what to do about long text lines.

Going back to our initial problem of setting the current point, for this example let's display the string about in the middle of the window, assuming that the window is about 4 x 4 inches. In that case, the point

(70, 200) should display the line of text about in the center of the window. Since the default coordinate units are 72 per inch, a point (70, 200) will be slightly less than an inch from the left edge of the window and just less than 3 inches from the bottom of the window. We use the PostScript **moveto** operator to set this point. This operator takes a pair of numbers—the *x*, *y* coordinates—and sets the current point to the position specified by these coordinates.

PROGRAMMING THE FIRST EXAMPLE

Here is the first cut at the runPSInline procedure.

#include <psops.h>

```
void    runPSInline(void)
{
PSselectfont("Helvetica", 12.0);
PSmoveto(70.0, 200.0);
PSshow("This is the first string to display");
}
```

Enter this code into the system in the same way that you would enter any other C procedure. Then save it, and compile the result. You may have another header file that serves the Display PostScript library; use that instead of *psops.h* if your system requires it.

In your calling code, you may need to add an event test to pause the display long enough for you to see it. This would usually be to wait for a mouse button or to wait for the window to be closed manually. Just be sure that you do not display the message in the window and then close it right away, before you can read your handiwork. You should see something like Figure 1-5 (with suitable modifications for the specific hardware that you have, of course).

Figure 1-5. First display output.

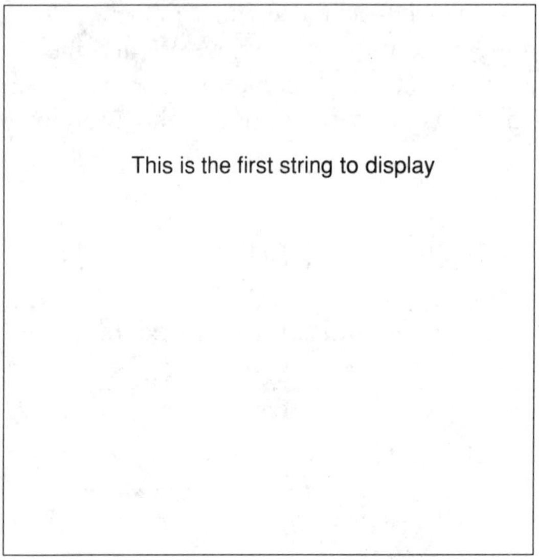

This is the first string to display

Let's look at this code in detail. This is obviously a short and simple program that creates a single line of output in the window. It does, however, show you the beginnings of writing Display PostScript.

To begin with, you include the Display PostScript Client Library header that contains the procedures you will be calling. When using Display PostScript, you must always include the necessary header file or files for the Client Library procedures you are calling. Because these are standard and generally unchanging within a given system environment, we only show them as part of the code this one time. From here on, we assume that you have included the necessary reference for these in all the procedures.

The function body consists of three calls to Display PostScript library functions. These calls actually invoke specific PostScript operators and pass the arguments in the function calls to the operators as operands. Here we have used just three PostScript operators to print a string of information on the screen. First, we selected a font, in this case, Helvetica, which we scaled to a 12-point size and then made into the current font. This makes it the font that all text display operations will use. Next, we moved to a specific position on the output window. The position is (70, 200), which gives a reasonable margin around the display. The coordinates are those of the window itself. Finally, we displayed the string 'This is the first string to display' at the point (70, 200) using the 12-point Helvetica font.

Let's consider the sequence here for a moment. Obviously, from the preceding discussion of **show,** you can see that the first two function calls had to be made before the call to PSshow. However, there is the issue of which function to call first. You may think the sequence chosen here was arbitrary; and, from the viewpoint of the PostScript interpreter, it was. All that the interpreter requires is that both items be set before it attempts to place the letters onto the page. But to you as a programmer, the order is important. Setting fonts requires some time and resources, and the font will probably persist for some fairly large part of the document. For efficient applications, therefore, you generally want to minimize how often you change fonts. Movement around the page, on the other hand, is quite common; it is one of the most frequent commands that you will issue. If you were going to print multiple lines of text, you would probably have to move for each line, whereas you would only set the font once. Therefore, it makes sense to set the font first, followed by the **moveto** to the desired position, rather than the other way around.

PROGRAMMING THE SECOND EXAMPLE

Let's add some more code to this function and redisplay the output. Here again, the output is to be some simple lines of text. Modify the runPSInline function as follows:

```
void  runPSInline(void)
{
PSselectfont("Helvetica", 12.0);
PSmoveto(30.0, 200.0);
PSshow("This is the first string to display");
PSshow(": hello, world!");
PSmoveto(30.0, 180.0);
PSshow("And this is the second string.");
}
```

If you substitute this new version for the first one and rerun your program, you should see an output in the window something like Figure 1-6.

Figure 1-6. Second example output.

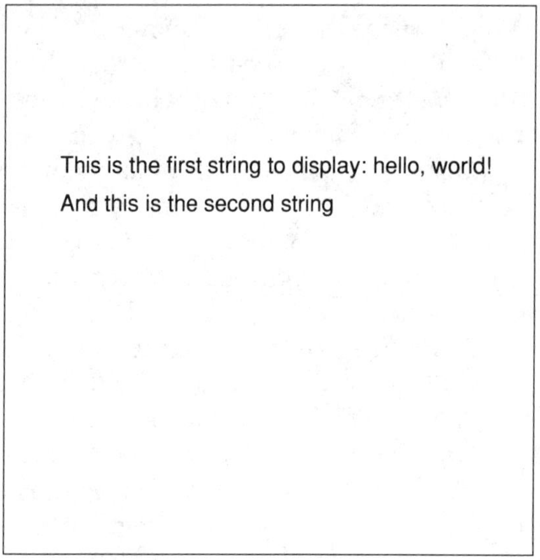

```
┌─────────────────────────────────┐
│                                 │
│                                 │
│   This is the first string to display: hello, world!
│   And this is the second string │
│                                 │
│                                 │
│                                 │
│                                 │
│                                 │
│                                 │
│                                 │
└─────────────────────────────────┘
```

Let's discuss this second version of the function in some detail. The first part is identical to the first function that you used earlier, except that you have moved the display to the left to accommodate a second string. This is followed by a second **show** command, which displays another string, ": hello, world!". Recall that there are certain requirements for a **show** command: a current font must be set and the current point must be defined. The first **show**, as you would expect, left the current font unchanged, and it set the current point to the end of the first string. This is illustrated in the output by the placement of the colon (:) exactly after the first string. This is just what you want because normal operations place one string of text after another without any intervening space.

The next line is another **moveto**, which sets the current point to (30, 180), slightly below the first line. The x coordinate is set to 30, where it was for the first string. This lines the beginning of the second string up with the first. The y coordinate is set to 180, which is 20 less than the first line. This is a large enough distance to allow the lines of text to be printed without running into one another. Note here that we have subtracted an amount to move down the window. Remember that the default positive direction on the x-axis is to the right, and the default positive direction on the y-axis is upward. If you had added the 20 units instead of subtracting them, you would have moved up the window instead of down.

LANGUAGE OPERATIONS

Now that you have done some simple output, you probably want to know some more about how PostScript and Display PostScript work. Before we can continue with another exercise, we need to develop some of the ideas that have just been introduced. We need to establish some points about PostScript stacks and develop a standard notation for our examples and for discussing and defining PostScript operators. This is the same format as is used in the standard PostScript references, so, if you are already familiar with that, this will be quite familiar. We also define some points about PostScript strings and comments. Then, after a short introduction to integrating PostScript and C, you are ready for the next exercise.

Stack Operations

One of the important characteristics of PostScript is that it works through a series of stacks. Physically a stack is an area of memory that holds items to be referenced by the PostScript interpreter. Unlike the stacks that you may have used in microcomputer programming, however, all the stack management is done internally by the interpreter so that the use of these stacks is, to a great extent, transparent to the programmer. PostScript uses four distinct stacks:

- Execution stack
- Dictionary stack
- Graphics state stack
- Operand stack

All of these stacks are independent of one another; what happens to one does not directly affect the others, although it may have indirect consequences. Each stack has its own method of access, but all of them are similar in concept and operation. If you understand how one works, you will be well on your way to understanding how they all function.

The first of these, the *execution stack*, is directly under the control of the PostScript interpreter in all respects, and only the interpreter can enter or remove items from it. An application can interrogate but not modify it. For our purposes, we can treat it as a black box. The second and third stacks, the *dictionary stack* and the *graphics state stack*, are special stacks accessed by certain specific PostScript operators. We will examine the most useful of these operators later. They have a particular importance in program structure and display control.

The last stack, the *operand stack*, is the most important stack from a programmer's viewpoint and the one that you will work with most often. This stack contains the operands for PostScript operators and receives the results as the operators are executed. All PostScript operands and results pass through the operand stack, and the majority of PostScript operators get their data to operate on from this stack, or they return data to this stack, or both. This is the stack we mean when we refer to "the stack." Remember that all the other PostScript stacks operate in essentially the same way.

Like all the PostScript stacks, the operand stack is a push-down, pop-up stack. It can also be described as a last-in, first-out (LIFO) stack, but the push-pop nomenclature is preferred because it seems easier to visualize. Each new object is placed on the top of the stack, and all previous entries are moved down one place; similarly, any access to the stack removes the top item, makes the item below it accessible, and moves all the lower items up one place.

It may help to visualize how the stack might be represented in operation. Suppose that we present the token representing the integer number 25 to the interpreter—for the moment, let's not consider where the number originated nor how it is presented to the interpreter. The interpreter takes the number (the first "object") and puts it—we usually say "pushes it"— onto the stack, which might then look like this:

    25

Imagine that this is a side view of the stack area, from top to bottom. Next we present the interpreter with the number 60, which once again gets pushed onto the stack. Now the stack looks like this:

    60

    25

Finally suppose that we present the interpreter with the number 12. Now the final state of the stack looks like this:

    12

    60

    25

However you keep track of the stack contents, you will find that you must keep in mind the following three basic points:

    1. The next item available is always the one on the top of the stack; nothing beneath it can be reached without removing the top item.

2. The next item down automatically becomes the top item when the previous top item is used or otherwise removed.
3. As you begin to construct reasonably complex procedures, you must remember to think ahead about the required sequence of operator operands and results on the stack.

This chapter's examples of various PostScript and Display PostScript concepts are shown as fragments of programs. These examples are presented in addition to practical, working exercises such as the one you just finished. To facilitate this process, we should establish a few points about these examples. First, they are written as PostScript code and are not embedded into any window or display context. That's really a nice way of saying that these are not executable from a C program as they stand, although they are correct and executable in a standard PostScript environment.

Second, the examples require the use of the following mathematical operators:

Operator	Function
add	Adds two operands together.
sub	Subtracts two operands.
mul	Multiplies two operands.
div	Divides two operands.

Each of these operators requires certain items of information to execute; you may recall that we named these *operands*.

Let's consider the following sequence of actions as examples of stack operations. These examples display the operand stack on one side and the results, after the execution of the indicated operator, on the other.

Operand Stack	Operator	Result
15 60	**add**	75
15		

The exact steps are as follows. First, the integer 15 is presented to the interpreter. This is pushed onto the stack. Next we present the integer 60 to the interpreter, as shown in the next column, where the 60 is on top of the stack and the 15 is now underneath. Then we execute the **add** operator, shown alone in the third column, which takes the two items from the operand stack and adds them, pushing the result, 75, back onto the stack, as shown in the fourth column.

To see how this works, let's look at two more examples. The next one shows the same sequence as the previous example, but uses the **mul** operator instead of the **add**.

Operand Stack	Operator	Result
15 60	**mul**	900
15		

Here we present two integers, 15 and 60, to the interpreter and execute the **mul** operator, which takes the two items from the operand stack and multiplies them, and pushes the result, 900, back onto the operand stack.

The third example shows the same structure, but illustrates an important point about stack control.

Operand Stack	Operator	Result
15 60	**sub**	−45
15		

Here the number 60, which is the last number presented to the interpreter and therefore on the top of the stack, is subtracted from the number beneath it, in this case, 15, giving a negative result. This shows how important the order of presentation is.

This issue of sequence is not only important, but it is also very different from that of the C language that you are accustomed to. PostScript, unlike C and most other programming languages, has no controls on sequence of execution and no order of precedence for various operations. In most languages, the various operators are executed in some fixed order, and any alternative sequences of operation are usually specified by the use of parentheses. None of this is available in PostScript. For example, consider the C sequence

$$25 - 3 * 4$$

Because of the precedence of C operators, this is exactly equivalent to the mathematical expression

$$25 - (3 * 4)$$

which yields a result of 13. If you wanted an alternative, you could use parentheses to force the computation

(25 – 3) * 4

which gives the quite different result of 88.

In PostScript, you have no such alternatives. You control the sequence of operations by controlling the sequence of operands onto the stack. For example, to create the first result, you would enter

Operand Stack			Operator	Result
25	3	4	**mul**	12
	25	3		25
		25		
	12		**sub**	13
	25			

To generate the second result, you would use the following sequence:

Operand Stack		Operator	Result
25	3	**sub**	22
	25		
22	4	**mul**	88
	22		

Note that, in each case, the correct result was only obtained by presenting the operands and the operators in a specific sequence. In fact, the seemingly obvious sequence, shown here, yields an entirely incorrect result.

Operand Stack		Operator	Result
3	4	**mul**	12
	3		
12	25	**sub**	−13
	12		

Postfix Notation Because of the interpreted nature of PostScript and its stacked operation mechanism, it requires an unusual syntax for execution. As you saw in the preceding examples, the interpreter executes an operator when it receives it, taking the required number of operands off the operand stack. Therefore, operands must precede their operators for proper and successful operation. This is known as *post-fix notation.* Although eminently rational, and both convenient and practical for the interpreter, this is not how humans usually operate. We would normally write "1 plus 2" or "add 1 to 2" or even, in some computer languages, "add 1, 2."

In C, which uses operator symbols instead of names, you would write "1 + 2." But PostScript requires the sequence

    1 2   **add**

So you need to begin thinking "backwards" as you read PostScript code. This becomes especially necessary when you start to read procedures (described in the next section), which may contain several nested levels of operation. This way of thinking was also reflected in the issues of sequence of operations in which some operands had to be presented in "reverse" order to get the correct sequence of operations, and hence of results. PostScript does have operators that you can use to help with this process, as we will see.

Example Notation The preceding examples were presented graphically to help you visualize the state of the stack during a PostScript operation. For obvious reasons of space, however, we cannot continue this type of presentation. Instead, we will use the notational conventions established in the PostScript and Display PostScript operator and reference manuals. This will establish a standard method of presentation that will allow you to follow our examples.

Let us assume, as a convention, that the PostScript interpreter reads and processes objects from left to right, as we do. That means that the sequence of operations presented in our first stack example could be written, using this notation, as follows:

    25   60   12

and the second set of stack operations would be written

    15   60   **add**

    15   60   **sub**

    15   60   **mul**

From now on, our examples will follow the notation illustrated here; you must envision the operands going onto the stack, with items on the left being below items to the right on the stack. The correct visualization of the current state of the stack is essential to successful PostScript programming.

We also need a notation to show the results that the operators place onto the stack as shown by the stack diagrams on the right above. Where an explicit result is returned to the top of the stack, we will illustrate that as follows:

    15   60 **add** ->   75

    15   60 **sub** ->   −45

    15   60 **mul** ->   900

Where multiple results are returned to the stack, they will also be presented in the order of left to right, so that the first item pushed onto the stack appears on the left and the last item (which would be the item on the top of the stack at the end of the operation) appears on the right. An example of this would be as follows:

    15   60 **add** 15   60 **sub** ->   75   −45

The same presentation would, of course, be used if you were showing multiple results from a single operator.

Operator Notation Now that we have agreed how we will present PostScript operators and operands in a program context, we must also establish how to write the operators for general reference purposes because the conventions that we have established are specific to a program context. In other words,

    10   20 **add** ->   30

adds two specific numbers, 10 and 20, and returns a specific result, 30. Now we need to establish how to write this in a generic fashion, so that you will know as you read them how the operators work, what operands they require, and what results are returned.

Let us establish the following general notation for writing operators. On the left of the operator we will show the operands required, in the same order as just described, namely, with the operand that must be on the bottom of the stack on the left and the operand that must be on the top of the stack on the right. Where no operands are required, we will use the symbol —. Further, we will use names for operands that are descriptive of the nature of the operand, for example, *num* for numbers, *int* for numbers that must be integers, *string* for strings, and so on. Where there are several operands or results, we will try to use names that are suggestive of the nature of each;

for example, *width* and *height* might be used to represent numeric results from certain operators. Finally, the PostScript operators will be presented in boldface type, to clearly show you what the name of the operator is. In this way, we would present the **add** operator as

    num1   num2   **add**   sum

On the right of the operator we will show the results in the same order as the operands; again, with the rightmost result on the top of the stack. This is similar to the notation we established for writing explicit results except that it omits the -> symbol before the results. Where the operator does not return a result, we will show —. Then the full set of notation for operators will look like this:

    num1 num2   **sub**   diff

subtracts *num2* from *num1* and pushes the difference, *diff*, onto the operand stack.

    num1 num2   **mul**   result

multiplies *num1* by *num2* and pushes *result* onto the operand stack.

Now you should also review the three operators that you have already seen in the preceding exercise. Using the notation that we have just established, these three operators are defined as follows:

    fontname scale   **selectfont**   —

gets the font whose name is given by *fontname* and scales it to the point size specified by *scale* and then makes that the current font.

    x y   **moveto**   —

moves to the point (*x*, *y*) and makes that the current point.

    string   **show**   —

displays *string* in the current font beginning at the current point.

Strings and Comments

You were introduced earlier to the use of strings in PostScript code. Now you need to learn some more about strings and find out how to add comments to your PostScript code in preparation for the next exercise. This is still not a complete or exhaustive discussion of these important objects; that comes in Chapter 2 when you will read about all the types of PostScript objects.

Strings You saw strings used in the first exercise as the arguments for the call to the **show** operator. This is one of the most typical uses of strings in

PostScript because strings are the natural method for representing and handling text material. However, as you will see, there are some differences between C string constants and PostScript strings. For this reason, you should know something about PostScript strings.

A string in PostScript usually consists of a collection of characters bounded by left and right parentheses. The first character of the string is the first character after the initial left parenthesis, and the string ends with the last character before the final, matching right parenthesis. In this you can immediately see one major difference between PostScript and C: there is no special string terminator in PostScript like the '\0' in C. Like C, PostScript provides some special escape sequences for placing unusual characters within a string; however, PostScript strings can contain any characters within the delimiters. Even the delimiter characters themselves, (and), can be placed within a string as long as each is part of a matched set. You will see an example of this later.

Comments Every programming language must provide a method to allow a programmer to annotate the code being generated, for self-preservation, if for no other reason. PostScript is no exception. Such annotations are called *comments*, and they are markers for the interpreter that indicate the end of PostScript-readable material and the beginning of text "for information only."

A PostScript comment begins with the character % and ends at the end of the line. This is quite different from C, where comments are started by the double characters /* and continue (including newlines and all) until the matching pair of characters */. The PostScript interpreter ignores all information after the % character and only begins processing again on the next line. This means that once you have begun a comment on any line, you can continue with any characters or words that you want, including more %'s, operator names, strings, or whatever. In all cases, the interpreter ignores everything until the next line begins. There is no method for continuing a PostScript comment onto a second line; each line of comment must begin with its own %. The only exception to this rule is that the % character can be used within a string without starting a comment. In this case, the interpreter does not recognize the % and continues to process the string until the ending) is read. It then continues to process the remainder of the line in the normal fashion.

These exercises use PostScript comments within the code itself for two reasons: to point out important issues within the code itself, and to number lines for reference.

Constructing Display PostScript Procedures

So far, you have only used the C procedures that called specific Display PostScript operators. This is fine and can be quite useful under some circumstances, but ordinarily you will want to combine more than one operation into a single function call. This makes your Display PostScript calls into something like C procedures; and, like those procedures, you make them up to perform specific tasks. In the next example, you will begin to write your own Display PostScript procedures and see how useful they are.

These procedures are called *wraps* because they are generated by the programmer to send Display PostScript code, in a special format, to a language preprocessor called *pswrap*. The *pswrap* preprocessor takes the Display PostScript code and turns it into a procedure that can be called by your C program and that can be sent to the PostScript interpreter. Chapter 2 covers the exact syntax and use of wraps in detail, but for now you need to know some basic information on how to create and read wrapped PostScript.

The *pswrap* translator creates C functions that associate PostScript source code with declarations of C functions. This allows you, effectively, to call PostScript language subroutines from within your C program. A sample *pswrap* procedure looks like this:

```
defineps PSWfirstExercise()
    /Helvetica 14 selectfont
    100 200 moveto
    (This is the first string to display) show
endps
```

This is a simple routine, which I have called PSWfirstExercise, that does exactly the same thing that the first exercise did. This would be called from a C program as

```
    PSWfirstExercise();
```

in the same way that you would call a C function.

Just a little more housekeeping, and then we can get to the meat of the subject. The wrap itself is translated into C code by the *pswrap* translator. Generally, you can invoke the translator by including the necessary commands in your **make** file. The actual wrap code itself (the **defineps-endps** code) is kept in a separate file, which usually must have a special file extension like ".psw" so the translator can find it. You might place all your wrap code in one file. The title of the file would be the name of the exercise, and whatever file extension is required by your system. Following that practice, this wrap might be called something like "first.psw". However, these external names are up to you.

With that out of the way, let's examine the structure of the wrap itself, ignoring the PostScript code for a moment. As you see, it consists of four basic parts. First, the keyword "defineps" signals the beginning of the wrap definition and must appear at the beginning of a line. Second is the procedure declaration, which consists of the name of the procedure, followed by a list of arguments; this is very much like a C function prototype declaration. Third is the *wrap body*, which consists of the PostScript code that you want to execute. Finally, the wrap ends with the keyword "endps", which terminates the wrap definition. Like the matching defineps, endps must appear at the beginning of a line. Each of these four elements must be present in this specific order for each acceptable wrap.

You should also review the PostScript code within the wrap body. It performs the same functions as the first example, but there are some subtle (and not so subtle) differences in the two presentations. Whereas the earlier set of library function calls required specific arguments for execution, the PSWfirstExercise procedure does not. The arguments are included in the procedure itself. Also, the arguments that you sent before had to be in C format: strings were delimited by ", numbers were float and so had decimal places, and so on. In this procedure, however, you're writing in PostScript: the strings are enclosed in the PostScript delimiters (and), and the numbers are simple integers that the PostScript interpreter will convert to the correct real format for coordinates. Finally, you notice that the font name, Helvetica, which you sent previously as a string, is now no longer in string format, but instead is simply preceded by a /. This makes it a PostScript *name literal*, which we discuss in more detail in Chapter 2. The important point here is that not all things that are represented in C as strings turn into strings when they are converted to PostScript.

TEXT AND COMMENTARY EXERCISE

With all that in mind, you can now proceed to create your third Display PostScript program. Once again, you should call these routines from a C application that opens a simple Display PostScript window. This time, you set two columns of text in the window, just as a text and commentary might be shown in a textbook or translation. This is just a convenient way to illustrate two-column text without generating enough text to fill one column before starting the next one.

Both columns have sentences consisting of several lines to show you how multiline text can be set. In addition, you set two different type fonts: one for the body of the text and another for the commentary.

Text Handling

You have already seen how to use the **show** operator, by means of a call to the PSshow library function, to display a single line of text. As we discussed during the first exercise, the **show** positions the current point to the end of the string being displayed when it paints the string onto the output page. However, it does not move automatically to the next line. You, as the programmer, must provide the necessary up or down movement. This is generally done by using the **moveto** operator with appropriate new coordinates.

Obviously the next question is how to determine these new coordinates. Remember that you scaled the type you were using to a particular size when you set the font with the **selectfont** operator. This size, the *point size* of the type, governs the height of the characters. Since we are using proportional fonts, the width of each character is scaled in relation to the height, but also varies according to the nature of the individual character (for example, the letter "w" is wider than the letter "l"). For readability, the minimum spacing between two lines of type is the point size, which is, by definition, the minimum spacing to avoid having the tops of letters on the lower line run into the bottoms of the letters on the upper line.

Generally, setting successive lines of type only the minimum distance apart makes a page look crowded and is difficult to read. This is particularly true for type sizes that are smaller than 14 points. For this reason, typesetters usually space lines of text slightly further apart than the point size of the type. This spacing is called *leading* and is also specified in points. Leading is proportional to the size of the type being set; as a guide, for type in the 10- to 12-point range, normal leading would be an additional one or two points. Therefore, with 12-point type (as we will use in the following example), the best line spacing would be 13 or 14 points. This means that the *y* coordinates must decrease (if you're moving down the page, of course) by 13 or 14 units for each new line of text. To illustrate this point and to keep computations simple, the example uses 12-point type with 14-point leading. This is usually expressed as "12 on 14."

Like so many other elements of display layout, the choice of font, size, and leading is essentially an aesthetic one. Very often, in advanced applications, the user is allowed to select whatever font and point size they want for the display, and sometimes they can choose the leading (usually called line spacing) as well. In any case, the object is to have a display that is beautiful because it is clean in layout, easily legible, and pleasant to the eye.

Design and Layout

First we need to define the procedures that we will use for this program. For simplicity, we use only two procedures: one to set the text column and a second to set the commentary. This requires that you make some decisions regarding layout within the window. This display is relatively simple, and the layout parameters are presented here in complete detail. In all of the following calculations, the coordinates used are the default PostScript coordinates, where 72 units equal 1 inch. If your window coordinates are different from this, you may want to change the exact calculations of the coordinates to match the window that you have created.

In this example, the display consists of a two-column text. The first column contains the commentary; the second contains the body text. The entire layout, with the dimensions in PostScript units, is shown in Figure 1-7.

Figure 1-7. Layout for text/commentary.

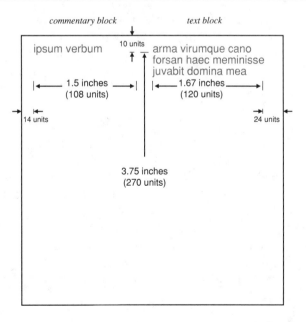

The commentary column is 1.5 inches (108 units) wide, starting a small distance inside the window border (14 units). The body-text column begins at 2 inches (144 units) into the window. The first line is 3.75 inches above the bottom of the window (270 units), assuming default coordinate orientation. This leaves a small, 18-unit top margin between the baseline of the first text and the top of the window (assumed here to be at 4 inches, or 288 units). We plan to leave a right margin of approximately 24 units; this makes the body-text column 120 units wide if the window's total width is 288 units. Note here that the text column is the derivative dimension. We have established all the other dimensions relative to the window and left the column width to be determined by the difference between the actual window size (which is also assumed to be 4 inches or 288 units) and the fixed amount of space taken up by the margins and the first column. In this way, if the window is larger than you expected, the remainder of the space is channeled into the body text, as you would want.

The example text is set in 12-point type with 14-point leading. The body text is Times-Roman, and the commentary text is set in Times-Italic (the italic version of Times-Roman) to set it apart from the body text, yet keep it in the same family for appearance' sake. Also for appearance and to enhance legibility, the beginning of each new paragraph is double-spaced, with 28 units between the paragraphs.

As a final touch, we align the commentary paragraphs to begin at the same vertical point as the corresponding body-text paragraphs. To do this, you must know where these paragraphs begin, which means that the body-text column (the second column physically) must be calculated first. Then the commentary column (the first physical column) can be set to match, aligning each paragraph with the body text. The example has only two paragraphs, but the principle is the same for multiple alignment points.

Sample Procedures

Now let's translate all this work into some Display PostScript. For this example, we will show you the actual code two times: first, in the same form as the first example, where all the Display PostScript is done with direct calls to the Client Library, and second, in a new form using *pswrap* to simplify the results. First, we will divide this into two C procedures, columnOne() and columnTwo(). Based on the preceding requirements and calculations, these would look something like the following:

```c
void columnTwo ( void )
{
    /* This is the procedure to set the body text
     *   paragraphs
     */

    float x, y;

    /* Note that this procedure will be called after
     *   the current font is already set
     */
    x = 144;
    y = 270;
    PSmoveto(x, y);
    PSshow("The quick brown fox");
    y -= 14;
    PSmoveto(x, y);
    PSshow("jumps over the lazy black");
    y -= 14;
    PSmoveto(x, y);
    PSshow("dog and then he jumps");
    y -= 14;
    PSmoveto(x, y);
    PSshow("over that lazy dog again;");
    y -= 14;
    PSmoveto(x, y);
    PSshow("but the dog is too lazy to");
    y -= 14;
    PSmoveto(x, y);
    PSshow("get up and do anything.");
    /* Now begin the second paragraph
     *   and note the number of lines
     *   (7 including double space below)
     *   for later use
     */
    y -= 28;
    PSmoveto(x, y);
    PSshow("Here is the quick fox");
    y -= 14;
    PSmoveto(x, y);
    PSshow("playing the same game again");
```

```c
        y -= 14;
        PSmoveto(x, y);
        PSshow("in a second paragraph.");
        y -= 14;
        PSmoveto(x, y);
        PSshow("You can easily see how");
        y -= 14;
        PSmoveto(x, y);
        PSshow("this could go on and on.");
        exit(0);

}   /* end of columnTwo */


void columnOne ( void )
{
    /* This is the procedure to set
     *  the commentary paragraphs
     */

    float x, y;

    /* Note that this procedure will be called
     *  after the current font is already set
     */
    x = 14;
    y = 270;
    PSmoveto(x, y);
    PSshow("This is a classic text");
    y -= 14;
    PSmoveto(x, y);
    PSshow("and commentary");
    y -= 14;
    PSmoveto(x, y);
    PSshow("layout.");
    /* Now set the second commentary paragraph
     *  based on the number of lines in the first
     *  column plus two for the inter-paragraph gap
     *  (total 7)
     */
    y = 270 - (14 * 7);
```

```
        PSmoveto(x, y);
        PSshow("using two fonts: ");
        y -= 14;
        PSmoveto(x, y);
        PSshow("Times Roman and");
        y -= 14;
        PSmoveto(x, y);
        PSshow("Times Italic.");
        exit(0);
}       /* end of columnOne */
```

These two procedures are quite similar to the ones you have already done, although a little longer. You should have no trouble in following them. However, these are supporting C procedures, and not suitable for running directly.

Programming the Exercise

Assuming that you have correctly named your procedures, let's look at the C code that you will use to call them. The overall function again is runPSInline, and it looks like this:

```
void runPSInline(void)
{
PSselectfont("Times-Italic", 12.0);
columnOne();
PSselectfont("Times-Roman", 12.0);
columnTwo();
}
```

When you execute this procedure from your application, you should get a window like the one shown in Figure 1-8.

Figure 1-8. Text and commentary display.

This is a classic text and commentary layout	The quick brown fox jumps over the lazy black dog and then he jumps over that lazy dog again; but the dog is too lazy to get up and do anything.
using two fonts: Times Roman and Times Italic.	Here is the quick fox playing the same game again in a second paragraph. You can easily see how this could go on and on.

Creating Wraps

When you examine the procedures above, however, you instinctively feel that this could be done more efficiently. You are correct; and that's where the *pswrap* translator comes into play. You have here a series of simple, repeated PostScript commands. Each of these commands must be sent from the server (your application) to the client (the Display PostScript system) in order to create the screen output. It is much easier, and more compact, to change these repetitive commands into a wrap. It is most efficient to keep the calculations of coordinates and so on in the C procedures, but the **moveto** and **show**, which are repeated so often, can be placed into a simple wrap PSWmovetoShow, as follows:

```
defineps PSWmovetoShow(float Xpos, Ypos; char *Str)
     % This is a simple wrap to clean up our exercise
     Xpos Ypos moveto    %1
     Str show     %2
endps
```

This wrap should be created with whatever editor is available in your C environment. It is produced like any other C procedure, and it should be placed into a single file that will be compiled with your C code. The exact conditions of naming and placement depend on the environment, but you will usually have to name all your wraps in some specific way for the C compiler to recognize them as PostScript wraps and invoke the *pswrap* translator to process them before the compiler creates the actual program. This involves setting a file extension, such as ".psw" so that the **make** function will know what wraps are to be sent to the *pswrap* translator. The translator itself usually must be invoked as part of the complete **make** function. In most environments, this is handled for you automatically once you have ".psw" files correctly included in the project. We assume here that the **make** function in your environment is prepared to handle the wrapped procedures and invoke the translator to process them. For an explanation of the various options available in the pswrap translator, you can look in the *Display PostScript System Reference, pswrap Reference Manual*.

Note that comments are used here both as line numbers and as full lines of commentary. This has nothing to do with either PostScript or Display PostScript; it is simply a convenient method of referring to lines in the text. You will see it again in other places in the book.

The PWSmovetoShow wrap takes three variables: the *x* and the *y* coordinates of the string to be shown, and the string itself. We will not discuss just yet all of the possible combinations of input and output parameters that can be sent to a wrap; those will be covered in detail in Chapter 2. The wrap here is presented to show you how easily you can simplify your Display PostScript code using wraps.

With this wrap, our two procedures now become much simpler. In fact, to simplify them still more, we will place the text into character arrays, which will allow us to produce the output quite easily and in a fashion that should seem very natural to a C programmer. Taking these two points into account, our new procedures look like this:

```
void columnTwo (void)
{

    float x, y;
    int count;

    static char *firstPar[] = {
        "The quick brown fox",
        "jumps over the lazy black",
        "dog and then he jumps",
```

```c
            "over that lazy dog again;",
            "but the dog is too lazy to",
            "get up and do anything."
            };

        static char *secondPar[ ] = {
            "Here is the quick fox",
            "playing the same game again",
            "in a second paragraph.",
            "You can easily see how",
            "this could go on and on"
            };

        x = 144;
        y = 270;
        for ( count = 0; count < 6; count++)
            {
            PSWmovetoShow(x, y, firstPar[count]);
            y -= 14;
            }
/* move down an extra line for the second paragraph */
        y -= 14;
        for ( count = 0; count < 5; count++)
            {
            PSWmovetoShow(x, y, secondPar[count]);
            y -= 14;
            }

        exit(0);
}


void columnOne (void)
{

        float x, y;
        int count;

        static char *firstPar[ ] = {
            "This is a classic text",
            "and commentary",
```

```
            "layout"
        };

    static char *secondPar[ ] = {
        "using two fonts: ",
        "Times Roman and",
        "Times Italic."
        };

    x = 14;
    y = 270;

    for ( count = 0; count < 3; count++)
        {
        PSWmovetoShow(x, y, firstPar[count]);
        y -= 14;
        }
/* move explicitly to the position of the second paragraph */
    y = 270 - (14 * 7);
    for ( count = 0; count < 3; count++)
        {
        PSWmovetoShow(x, y, secondPar[count]);
        y -= 14;
        }

    exit(0);
}
```

These two procedures can be run in the same way as the preceding two, using runPSInline. They produce the same output as you saw in Figure 1-8, yet they are much more compact and require fewer accesses across the client-server connection. This example illustrates the most common, and one of the most helpful, methods of using *pswrap*.

CONCLUSION

This completes the first set of exercises and shows you something about placing Display PostScript code into your C application. As you look back on these examples, particularly the last one, I'm sure you can see how these might be generalized for regular use. In Chapter 2, you will learn more about PostScript and how to use the various facilities in the PostScript language to create internal procedures to improve your coding efficiency.

We have actually covered quite a bit of ground in this chapter. You have been introduced to a variety of PostScript operators. These operators form the basic building blocks of PostScript procedures and programs and of Display PostScript operations.

You have completed two exercises. These have acquainted you with some simple Display PostScript coding. As a part of these exercises, you have been introduced to simple text operations and to how PostScript and its Display PostScript extensions handle text in a window. You have coded text displays, using procedures from the Client Library as well as procedures (wraps) that you have created yourself.

You have also met and used some basic PostScript concepts, which are essential to all PostScript and Display PostScript coding. The major points are stack operations, notation for PostScript—both for examples and for standard operator references—and a short discussion of how PostScript handles strings and comments. With all of this, you are well positioned to move on to Chapter 2 and find out about dictionaries and definitions in PostScript.

CHAPTER 2

Dictionaries and Procedures

This chapter is concerned with two basic issues. The first issue is how you can associate labels with PostScript objects through the mechanism of PostScript dictionaries. The second issue is how to create, name, and use PostScript procedures to build an application program.

These are clearly critical issues to understand in order to read and use any computer language. PostScript has some unique methods and unusual constructs in handling these points. In Chapter 1 you learned the basics of PostScript structure and a first group of PostScript operators. In this chapter we build on this information to fashion programs that begin to take advantage of PostScript's capabilities by using labels and procedures.

DICTIONARIES

Since PostScript uses a dictionary mechanism to implement all its processing functions, it's important to understand PostScript dictionaries in order to work effectively with the language. Dictionaries and stack operations are two of the most important concepts in PostScript processing. The dictionary concept is less common in computer work than stacks, but should be quite familiar from daily use. As with stacks, PostScript uses multiple dictionaries, such as font dictionaries and halftone dictionaries, to perform various functions; once you understand dictionary operations, you will use multiple dictionaries yourself in your work.

Definition

A dictionary, in everyday use, is a book that organizes and associates words with their definitions. In PostScript, a *dictionary* is a table that associates a *key*, usually a name, with a *value*. More precisely, a PostScript dictionary associates a pair of PostScript objects; the first object is the key, which is usually a name literal, and the second object, which may be of any type, is the value that is attached to the key reference.

Names and Literals PostScript has two types of nominal objects: names and name literals. The two different types allow you to distinguish between ordinary or executable "names," which the PostScript interpreter looks up in the dictionaries, and "name literals," which are the literal values of the names and which the interpreter places on the stack for subsequent processing, much as it would a string. This is an essential distinction. Somehow, the interpreter must distinguish the use of a name to reference an object already in the dictionaries from the use of a name as a literal to be enrolled in a dictionary as a key to associate with some other object. This distinction is the reason for all the references to "name literal."

A *name* in PostScript can consist of almost any sequence of characters. All alphabetic and numeric characters are acceptable; there are no restrictions (as there are in C, for example) on what characters can start a name. Like C, PostScript distinguishes between uppercase and lowercase letters; however, unlike C, most punctuation symbols are acceptable in PostScript names. Ten special characters, which are defined later in this chapter, cannot be used in valid PostScript names. Of these, the most obvious and the most important is the space; valid names cannot contain spaces. In general, if you follow the same rules that you would use in your C programming for PostScript, you shouldn't have any problems.

A *name literal* is any valid name preceded by the character /. As you might guess, the character / is one of the special characters that cannot occur in a valid name; it is reserved to distinguish name literals from all other objects.

Dictionary Stack PostScript uses dictionaries for a variety of important functions; for example, font access and use is through a series of dictionaries. However, the most important dictionaries are those provided by the PostScript interpreter for its own operations. The interpreter maintains a *dictionary stack* where all PostScript operations are defined. As you read in Chapter 1, all PostScript stacks work in exactly the same way, and the dictionary stack works just like the operand stack. There are several operators that specifically access and manipulate the dictionary stack.

Although the dictionary stack works like the operand stack, it is in no way connected to the operand stack. The dictionary stack is entirely separate and distinct. The two stacks only interact through the operators. Keep this in mind as we begin working with user-created dictionaries later.

Default Dictionaries The Display PostScript system provides three default dictionaries: *systemdict*, *shareddict*, and *userdict*. There are also other standard, internal dictionaries such as *errordict* that the PostScript interpreter uses. Since these dictionaries are not used in normal programming, they are not discussed further here.

systemdict is the bottommost entry on the dictionary stack, *shareddict* is directly above it, and *userdict* is above that. None of these can be removed from the stack. These are the only three dictionaries on the stack when PostScript begins operation.

PostScript provides three unremovable default dictionaries on the dictionary stack for a good reason. Certain PostScript operators, and the interpreter, implicitly reference the current dictionary, which obviously requires that there be a dictionary to reference. Moreover, the dictionaries are referenced in a particular order, which accounts for the ordering of these default dictionaries.

Because *userdict* is available for any use that you may want, you do not necessarily require any additional dictionaries. However, it is also sometimes required or useful to create individual dictionaries, which may then be referenced by the various PostScript operators.

In all cases, the topmost entry on the dictionary stack is called the *current dictionary* and is referred to by the name *currentdict*. Thus, when

PostScript begins operation, the current dictionary is *userdict*, and all references to the current dictionary refer to *userdict*. Although you can in fact do a substantial amount of work with just the default dictionaries, creating and using additional dictionaries is quite easy. This technique is also a useful addition to your PostScript vocabulary.

Dictionary Objects You use the **dict** operator to create dictionaries. This operator takes one operand, an integer that specifies the dictionary capacity, which is the maximum number of (key, value) pairs that can be placed in that dictionary. The operator returns an empty dictionary object with the specified capacity. Dictionaries are created with a specific capacity to hold pairs of objects. If you try to put more entries into the dictionary than the capacity specified at its creation, you get an error—and, more importantly, the (key, value) pair is not entered.

Note that this dictionary object is returned to the operand stack; it is not placed onto the dictionary stack. We use the notation *dict* to indicate a dictionary object that is on the operand stack in our discussion of operators. This is important because dictionary objects have certain specific characteristics that distinguish them from other PostScript objects.

A dictionary is placed onto the dictionary stack by the **begin** operator and is removed from the dictionary stack by the **end** operator. The **begin** operator requires a dictionary object on the operand stack and makes that object the current dictionary. The **end** operator does not affect the operand stack in any way. These operators can be summarized as follows:

    int   **dict**   dict

creates a dictionary *dict* with the capacity for *int* value pairs.

    dict   **begin**   —

pushes *dict* onto the dictionary stack and makes it the current dictionary.

    —   **end**   —

pops the current dictionary from the dictionary stack.

Now that you know how to create dictionaries and move them onto and off of the dictionary stack, we need to discuss how to enroll objects into a dictionary and how to get access to them once they're there.

Using Dictionaries

To understand how to use dictionary entries, you need to understand how the PostScript interpreter uses them. As the PostScript interpreter encounters an object, it takes one of two actions: either it places the object on the operand stack (as it would with a number or a name literal) or it looks the object up in the dictionary stack, using it as the key for the search. This process is how the interpreter handles all names that are not name literals—that is, that are not preceded by a / character. Specifically this is how the interpreter handles operator names, for example.

Up until now, the PostScript interpreter has been described simply as executing the various operators. In fact, this is a perfectly reasonable way to describe how the operators work. At this point, however, it is important for you to understand more precisely how the interpreter works overall. Operator names have no special significance to the interpreter. This means that they are not "reserved" in the sense that operator or system names are in other languages, such as C and BASIC. Even within MS-DOS, certain names such as CON and LPT1 are reserved for the operating system. In PostScript however, operator names are simply keys into the *systemdict*, where they are associated with the actual built-in function that performs the action specified by the operator name. This explains why the *systemdict* is always on the dictionary stack and cannot be removed.

When the PostScript interpreter encounters a name that is not preceded by the special character / (which would make it a name literal to be pushed onto the operand stack), it looks the name up as a key in the dictionary stack. The interpreter begins looking in the current dictionary. If it doesn't find the name as a key in the current dictionary, it continues to look down through the dictionary stack until it either finds a matching key or exhausts the stack. If there is no match, an error status is returned. When a match is found, the interpreter takes the appropriate action. If the value that matches the key is a procedure, the procedure is executed; if the value is not a procedure (so it's a string, literal, number, or so on), the value is placed onto the stack. The interpreter continues on in this way until it has consumed all the PostScript objects presented to it (or until it encounters an error, which forces it to stop).

Search Sequence The sequence used by the interpreter to search for names should be clear from the preceding discussion. Dictionaries are searched down through the dictionary stack. This process begins with the current dictionary and continues through the *userdict* (which may be the current dictionary) and ends with the *systemdict* at the bottom of the dictionary stack.

There are two exceptions to this default search sequence. These occur with operators that specifically reference a certain dictionary. This may be required for two reasons. The first reason is that the operator may require a dictionary specification by its nature; font manipulation operators are a good example of this (recall that fonts reside in a special set of dictionaries). The second reason is that the operator may be defined to provide specific access to dictionary values or operations. In either case, the important point to remember is that, although most PostScript operators that reference dictionaries deal with the current dictionary, certain operators can be explicitly directed to work with a specific dictionary.

Dictionary Access The most frequently used PostScript dictionary operators are naturally the ones that expect to access the current dictionary. Certainly the most common dictionary operation is the act of enrolling a (key, value) pair in the current dictionary. This is done with the **def** operator, which is defined as follows:

> key value **def** —
> associates *key* and *value* in the current dictionary.

The following example makes use of this operator:

> /abc 123 **def**

This process associates the name abc with the value 123 in the current dictionary. This means that, if you have placed the preceding definition earlier in a program, the following two statements produce identical results:

> 123 456 **add** -> 579
> abc 456 **add** -> 579

You see what the interpreter did here. In the second instance, the interpreter took the name abc and looked it up in the current dictionary, where it found the value 123. It then took that value and pushed it onto the stack, just as it did in the first instance, when it encountered the value directly. Hence the result of the **add** operator was the same in both cases. In other words, the dictionary lookup mechanism behaves in a completely natural way, with names being a substitute for their associated values and behaving just as if the value were inserted into the statement in place of the name.

A value is not limited to being a number; it can be any PostScript object. So we may write, for example,

> /string (this is a string) **def**

as a definition in our current dictionary.

In addition to the **def** operator, which always refers to the current dictionary, several other operators reference the dictionary stack as a whole, in a fashion similar to the interpreter. These operators (**load**, **store**, and **where**) are like **def** in that they do not reference a specific dictionary, but, unlike **def**, they do not stop with the current dictionary. Instead, they follow the search process of the interpreter and search the entire dictionary stack, beginning with the current dictionary, until they find the key they have been given.

TEXT AND COMMENTARY EXERCISE REVISITED

This seems like an appropriate time for a brief exercise using variable names in a program. To give you a flavor of what the use of variables does for a program, we will redo the second exercise, using the same text and format, but using variables in the program instead of constants. You should find this version of the exercise much cleaner and easier to understand.

This is still a very simple type of display and uses a relatively inefficient structure to make a specific point about PostScript variables and dictionaries. As such, it is not a style of programming that you would use in an ordinary application; instead, it is more suited to creating a "quick and dirty" prototype. Nevertheless, it should help you understand and use named constants and dictionaries.

Example Setup

The screen layout remains identical to that of the previous example. As a brief refresher, recall that there are two columns of text: the first column is a commentary column and the second is the body text. The commentary column has a left margin of 14 units and is 108 units wide. There is a space of 22 units between the first and second columns. The body-text column begins, therefore, 144 units from the left edge of the page. The second column is 120 units wide, with a 14-unit right margin. Both columns of text start 270 units from the bottom of the page. Remember that PostScript default measures are from the bottom of the page, with the origin in the bottom, left corner.

Each column of text has two paragraphs of several lines each. The text is set in 12-point type on 14-point leading, with double spacing between paragraphs. The commentary paragraphs are set to align with the text paragraphs, even though the text may be longer than the commentary.

This exercise still uses relatively simple wraps, but you will have six of them, instead of only one. Moreover, the structure of the display code has changed quite a bit. Where before you did all the computations and line control in the C application, here you are doing them in PostScript, but still taking advantage of the fact that all the moves to a following line are essentially identical. Let's first discuss how you might do that.

In general, in Display PostScript, you will have a series of short wraps, as we used earlier, rather than larger ones. In this way, each wrap can do some single thing and you can use the wraps again and again. It is a kind of macro definition. (In the next section, you will learn how to define and use PostScript procedures; note here that these are PostScript code wrapped into C procedures, not native PostScript procedures.)

You can see from the previous text and commentary exercise that most of the movement down the screen can be done in a single, identical step mechanism. This is an obvious candidate for a wrap in a prototyping environment. However, it's certainly not good programming practice to embed the text of a paragraph in a procedure; such "hard coding" of what is essentially variable data is a bad idea. To avoid that, you can use the PSshow library routine that you used in the first exercise to display the various lines of text and commentary. That means that you also need to set up for printing each column, and you need to save the paragraph location so that the commentary will line up with the text paragraphs. Finally, you should use named variables for the critical constants so that you can move things around without recoding.

This analysis leads us to the following six wraps, in addition to the use of PSshow and PSselectfont.

Wrap Name	Function
PSWnextLine	Advances to the next line of text, using the leading value in an external variable.
PSWstartBody	Starts the body text at the desired location on the display, using an external variable for the vertical coordinate.
PSWstartComm	Starts the commentary text at the desired location on the display.
PSWnextParBody	Advances to the next paragraph in the body text, using twice the leading value as spacing and saves the position of that paragraph in an external variable.

PSWnextParComm	Advances to the next paragraph in the commentary, using the external position variable set by the PSWnextParBody wrap.
PSWsetUp	Sets up all the variables that are required by the other wraps; called once before beginning display.

Example Wraps

Now that you know what the wraps are and something about their functions, let's look at them in detail. Here they are, presented in the same order as they were described earlier. Enter these into your project library and connect them to the project so that you can execute them.

```
defineps PSWnextLine()
    NowMargin
    currentpoint exch pop
    LEADING sub
    moveto
endps

defineps PSWstartBody()
    BODYMARGIN SavePara moveto
    /NowMargin BODYMARGIN def
endps

defineps PSWstartComm()
    COMMMARGIN VERTSTART moveto
    /NowMargin COMMMARGIN def
endps

defineps PSWnextParBody()
    BODYMARGIN
    currentpoint exch pop
    LEADING 2 mul sub
    dup
    /SavePara exch def
    moveto
    /NowMargin BODYMARGIN def
endps

defineps PSWnextParComm()
    COMMMARGIN SavePara moveto
```

```
        /NowMargin COMMMARGIN def
endps

defineps PSWsetUp()
    /BODYMARGIN 144 def
    /COMMMARGIN 14 def
    /VERTSTART 270 def
    /LEADING 14 def
%these are place holders — redefined in thewraps
    /NowMargin BODYMARGIN def
    /SavePara VERTSTART def
endps
```

Let's look at how each of these wraps creates the output display that we want.

The first wrap is PSWnextLine. This is the wrap that we first identified, based on the fact that most of the movement code in our previous exercise was identical: a single line that set the *x* coordinate for the desired margin and then calculated the new *y* coordinate for the next line by subtracting the leading spacing value from the current *y* coordinate. Our new wrap does exactly the same thing, but it uses two named PostScript variables instead of providing fixed values from the C application, as in the previous code. The first variable is named *NowMargin*, which is the current margin value. We need this so that we can use one procedure for moving both the text and commentary (which have margins of 144 and 14, respectively). This variable has to be set externally and is set to the current margin value by the procedures that set up each type of output—in this case, PSWstartBody and PSWstartComm. The second variable is the leading, called *LEADING*, which is a fixed constant and should be set in the setup procedure.

The next two wraps are PSWstartBody and PSWstartComm. These matching functions for the body text and the commentary perform similar functions. They move the current point to the top of the appropriate column, and they set the *NowMargin* variable to the desired value for subsequent use by PSWnextLine. They both use named variables for this process. In this way, the exact positioning of the columns is quite easy to modify; only the values in the single setup procedure need changing in order to make a move.

The *x* and *y* coordinates of the starting positions are named constants that are set in the PSWsetUp; the *y* coordinate is a named constant in the case of PSWstartComm, but it is the *SavePara* variable in PSWstartBody. This reflects the slightly different use that each of these functions has. PSWstart-Comm is only called once, at the start of the commentary, to set the first commentary position; after that, the position is set by PSWnextParComm. The PSWstartBody procedure, however, must be called before each body paragraph to reset the position from the last commentary display.

The next two wraps, PSWnextParBody and PSWnextParComm, again provide similar functions for text and commentary. This time these functions move down to the next paragraph position for each of the columns. Although the functions are the same, the mechanism is quite different.

PSWnextParBody moves the current point down by twice the leading value—since you want to double-space between paragraphs in the body-text column. It then saves the *y* coordinate of this point as the named variable, *SavePara*. How it performs this is worth some comment. The function proceeds in the same fashion as the previous procedure PSWnextLine and is equivalent up to the point of the **moveto**. At this point, the desired *y*-coordinate value is on the top of the operand stack. What you want to do is both save this value as the named variable, *SavePara*, and use it as a component of the subsequent **moveto**. You first duplicate the value on the top of the stack, using the **dup** operator. You then push the name literal of the variable onto the stack. All well and good, but the name must come before the value for a definition. The **exch** operator easily solves this small problem by swapping the top two operands on the stack. These are then removed by the **def** operator, which assigns the name literal, /SavePara, to the *y*-coordinate value. This leaves the operand stack in exactly the same condition as when you started, which is all set up for the **moveto** that follows. The last thing the function does is reset the *NowMargin* variable to *BODYMARGIN*.

The matching function for the PSWnextParComm commentary column takes the previously set variable, *SavePara*, and moves the current point directly to that position, so that the column in the commentary matches that in the body text. It then resets the *NowMargin* variable to *COMMMARGIN*.

There is one more point to notice here. You could, of course, have saved the paragraph position information in a variety of ways. Only one variable, *SavePara*, holds the starting position of the next body-text paragraph. This obviously implies that you will set one commentary text paragraph, then the matching body paragraph, and so on. This is a nice, general arrangement because it imposes no limit to the number of paragraphs that you can set. Because you are going to set the paragraphs in this order, however, each new paragraph (as established by the PSWnextParBody or PSWnextParComm functions) must reset the *NowMargin* variable so that the subsequent lines are correctly positioned. Also, you must call PSWnextParBody at the end of the previous body paragraph (to set the position for the new paragraph), then call PSWnextParComm to set the commentary, and finally call PSWstartBody to reset the beginning of the body-text.

The last wrap defines the constants and variables that the preceding wraps require. In this case, the four named constants, *BODYMARGIN*, *COMMMARGIN*, *VERTSTART*, and *LEADING*, are set to the same numeric values that were used in the earlier exercise. There are also definitions for the two named variables: *NowMargin* and *SavePara*. In this case, *SavePara* must be set here for the first call to PSWstartBody, but there is no requirement to set *NowMargin*. In general, variables don't actually need to be defined before their first use; PostScript has no requirement, as C does, that variables must be declared before they are assigned. The actual value of *NowMargin*, for example, is used in the functions that are set within other wraps.

It is good practice to define default values here for all variables, for two reasons. First, it places all the named constants and variables in one procedure, so that they can be easily identified. This is a poor substitute for a data dictionary, but it's all that's available. Second, it provides a default definition for these variables if, by some error in coding or structure, you use them without having set them correctly. In such a simple application as this, that's hardly likely; but in a more complex one, it would be quite easy to make an error and call a wrapped procedure that uses a particular variable before it had been set correctly by some other function. In such cases, if you have not preset these variables, you get a PostScript error that aborts the job; this can be both messy and annoying. It would be better to get some output, using the default values, than to have an error that aborts the job.

Displaying the Revised Exercise

With the wraps defined, you're ready to use them to create the display output. You still use the PSselectfont function to set the font, for the same reasons that you did before. Thus you can set the font to whatever is appropriate for this section of the application. We continue to use Times-Roman and Times-Italic. In addition, as we discussed earlier, you will use the PSshow function to show the strings of text at the current point.

The basic call is still to a single function called runPSInline. You should now enter the following changes to your function.

```
void    runPSInline( void )
{

PSWsetUp();    /* defines required variables */
/* now we set the first commentary paragraph */
PSselectfont("Times-Italic", 12.0);
PSWstartComm();
PSshow("This is a classic text");
PSWnextLine();
PSshow("and commentary");
PSWnextLine();
PSshow("layout;");
/* next we show the body text  */
PSselectfont("Times-Roman", 12.0);
PSWstartBody();
PSshow("The quick brown fox");
PSWnextLine();
PSshow("jumps over the lazy black");
PSWnextLine();
PSshow("dog and then he jumps");
PSWnextLine();
PSshow("over that lazy dog again");
PSWnextLine();
PSshow("but the dog is too lazy to");
PSWnextLine();
PSshow("get up and do anything.");
PSWnextParBody();
/* and then the second paragraph of commentary */
PSselectfont("Times-Italic", 12.0);
PSWnextParComm();
PSshow("using two fonts:");
PSWnextLine();
PSshow("Times-Roman and");
PSWnextLine();
PSshow("Times-Italic.");
/* now we do the second paragraph of body text */
PSselectfont("Times-Roman", 12.0);
PSWstartBody();
PSshow("Here is the quick fox");
```

```
PSWnextLine();
PSshow("playing the same game again");
PSWnextLine();
PSshow("in a second paragraph.");
PSWnextLine();
PSshow("You can easily see how");
PSWnextLine();
PSshow("this could go on and on.");
/* and you can see how this could be extended indefinitely */
}
```

This gives you the same screen display as we saw earlier, shown here as Figure 2-1.

Figure 2-1. Output from revised text/commentary.

This is a classic text and commentary layout	The quick brown fox jumps over the lazy black dog and then he jumps over that lazy dog again but the dog is too lazy to get up and do anything.
using two fonts: Times Roman and Times Italic.	Here is the quick fox playing the same game again in a second paragraph. You can easily see how this could go on and on.

PROGRAM STRUCTURE AND STYLE

PostScript is a remarkably flexible language with a large and powerful set of operators. But an inevitable result of that flexibility and power is an equal potential to generate unsatisfactory, unworkable, and unintelligible code. PostScript, as we observed before, has no specific structural requirements. Unlike C and most other computer languages, PostScript has no reserved words and no enforced data structures. PostScript allows any type of structure you find useful or entertaining—and it's the entertainment factor that you need to worry about.

PostScript programs generally consist of a large series of procedures, or "program fragments," as we have called them. Procedures can be—and most likely will be—used inside the definitions of other procedures and, as you have already seen, they are embedded into your C application code as well. This process is called *nesting*, and it is both an outgrowth of the PostScript language and a powerful tool for helping you accomplish complex display formatting tasks. The net result is that every PostScript program that you are likely to encounter, whether generated by an application program or created by yourself or someone else, will consist of multiple levels of nested procedures, usually culminating in a few powerful procedural definitions that accomplish major pieces of the final task.

Although nesting is a natural (at least in PostScript) and powerful process, it also can create a chaotic program when it is carried out in an undisciplined or uncoordinated way. You can imagine the difficulty and frustration in trying to discover an error in a procedure when you need to trace through five or six (or more!) layers of nested definitions in search of the source of the error. The frustration level rises rapidly if the definitions of the procedures are scattered throughout many pages of program text, and it will go into orbit if the names of the variables and procedures are short and cryptic or even completely nondescriptive. The only way to avoid the majority of these problems is to establish a style of programming and adhere to it tenaciously.

Selecting Names

Although the examples in the preceding section are somewhat complex and therefore possibly difficult to follow, you can easily see that they would certainly have been more opaque without the variable names that were used in them. Names like "LEADING" and "NowMargin" are an important part of creating readable code because they help you understand what function a program or program fragment is performing. You should make names that are descriptive of the function, not just to yourself, but also for others. You may think that no one else will ever see the programs and, anyway, who cares? You do. If the names are so cryptic that only you know what they mean, you will quickly discover that you have forgotten your clever abbreviations and cryptic symbols when you look at the program again after a few months—or even weeks. In the preceding example, imagine how much more difficult it would have been to understand (or explain) if the variable names were replaced by single letters or letter and number combinations, as they might well have been. Procedure and function names also need to be descriptive of what the procedure does, even more than variable names need to describe what the variable contains.

This also brings up another useful point for naming variables in particular, but also procedures. Using named variables in the preceding procedures, rather than using the actual numbers, means that changes to the margins, for example, would not affect the procedure itself. By the use of named variables the procedure is independent of the actual margins that have been set for the page. This is a nontrivial benefit that affects both independence and maintenance as well as readability.

Along these same lines, there is a tendency to reduce names to the smallest possible number of letters. This is particularly true for people (such as myself) who are accustomed to programming in languages where the maximum size of a name is only seven or eight characters. This habit is often rationalized by the programmer's reluctance to type out a long name, especially for a frequently used procedure or variable. There are several ways to use longer, more descriptive names and still avoid the repetitive typing, if that's the problem. You will, in the long run, be glad you used the longer names even if it means some additional work initially. PostScript is an unusually good language in this respect because the limits on length of a name are quite generous and there is almost no limit to the characters that can be used in the name.

One thing to keep in mind is that output from applications that generate PostScript code (such as PageMaker or Illustrator) does not contain very meaningful names. If you are going to modify much of that type of output, you are strongly urged to use a good editor with a global search-and-replace function to give descriptive names to the procedures and variables with which you are working. This doesn't usually take very long because you are almost always working with a small subset of the generated output.

Using Names

Names are an important ingredient in creating order out of the potential chaos of any program. Names and conventions about names—how they may be constructed, what they should look like, and so on—form an important part of program structure and style.

If you are familiar with programming at all, you have probably wrestled with the pitfalls and advantages that are associated with names in a programming environment. Basically there are two issues relating to names that you need to think about. The first is the issue of selecting names: how to make names meaningful in your particular environment. The second is the issue of naming practices, or conventions, which can be used to ensure that you use the same or similar structure for names of the same or similar type.

C, like PostScript, has very few forced naming conventions, but it has some that are so widely accepted as to be universal. I have adapted these here as part of the conventions for the names used in this chapter and throughout the book. In this way, the names used should seem somewhat familiar and should also translate easily and naturally between the C and PostScript environments.

Naming Conventions Besides making individual procedure and variable names descriptive of their purpose, you will find it extremely helpful to adopt some standard conventions for names in your programs. Your development and use of naming conventions is a matter of your personal style of programming; it really is an outgrowth of your experience and the requirements of the task at hand.

Although no one else can really define an appropriate set of conventions for you, as you begin to establish your personal approach, you should consider two points. First, PostScript, like C, treats upper- and lowercase letters as distinct characters. This allows you to use capital letters to help make your names both readable and distinctive. For example, you might decide to start every variable name with an uppercase letter and every procedure name with a lowercase letter, with subsequent words in both names being capitalized as appropriate. Following the C convention, you could also use all uppercase letters for constants and mixed upper- and lowercase letters for variables. For example, you would write:

reEncodeFont	(a procedure)
StringSize	(a variable)
average	(a procedure)
Average	(a variable)
LeftMargin	(a variable)
LEFTMARGIN	(a constant)

testMargin   (a procedure)

outsideMargin?   (a procedure)

The two names "average" and "Average" also illustrate why you might want to use case to indicate purpose or use. Using a convention like the preceding one, you know immediately which is a procedure and which is a variable; if you are haphazard in your capitalization, you would have to hope that the difference would be clear from context. In the same way, the choice of capitalization for the names "LEFTMARGIN" and "LeftMargin" tells you at a glance that one is a constant and the other a variable. The name "outsideMargin?" also illustrates that you can use almost any character in PostScript names; hence, the ? character is used to emphasize the testing intent of the procedure.

The second point to keep in mind is the use of standard names throughout your procedures for specific variables or types of variables or procedures. Certain variables recur throughout almost any PostScript program; for example, a current line (vertical position), a current horizontal position, and the margin settings. Similarly, certain types of variables occur regularly; for example, counters and strings. In all such instances, you will find that using a standard set of names during your programming provides enhanced portability and readability for your procedures. For common variables, you should establish common names. You might choose to record the names in some place where they may be readily referenced. The best situation, of course, would be to keep them in a dictionary file or a header that would be included at the beginning of each program. Some typical examples might be:

Xpos—the current position in the x direction (horizontally).

Yline—the current line position or position in the y direction (vertically).

and some similar variables and constants that can be easily imagined:

LEFTMARGIN

RIGHTMARGIN

TOPMARGIN

BOTTOMMARGIN

Prefixes or suffixes are often useful for distinguishing variable and procedure types. The most conspicuous example is using the "PSW" prefix for all wrapped functions. If you prefix all your wrap functions in this way, it is quite easy to select them all out of the other material in your C application; it is also consistent with the Display PostScript practice of naming the client library wraps (which we will discuss in more detail shortly) with the "PS" or "DPS" prefix. Internally, in your PostScript code, you can also use this same practice and even integrate it with the "PSW" prefix, by using combined lower- and uppercase words for procedure names. For example,

    testRightMargin

    testLeftMargin

These names follow the previous convention on capitalization and also lend themselves to being wrapped, if required. You would then use the following names, corresponding to the preceding procedures:

    PSWtestRightMargin

    PSWtestLeftMargin

In the same way, there is a real value to following common naming practices for variables as well, by using common elements for variables with similar functions, for example,

    StringSize

    ArraySize

    DictSize

These are only examples. You will notice that many of the exercises have not rigidly followed these specific practices, (although I have tried very hard to be consistent throughout the book), and I'm not necessarily suggesting that you adopt them. What I am suggesting is that you should be innovative and flexible and determine for yourself what works for you. Certainly you should consider very carefully whatever standard names and naming conventions you do choose to adopt. As was said earlier, the choice and use of conventions is a personal decision that, ideally, grows out of your experience and the requirements of the task to be accomplished.

REFERENCING OBJECTS

Up to this point, we have dealt rather intuitively with the concept of PostScript objects. This easy and rather straightforward approach has worked well for us, primarily because the intuitive concept is fairly accurate. Now, however, you are ready for a complete and precise definition.

A PostScript *object* is any syntactic entity that the PostScript interpreter can recognize. Generally, PostScript objects are created from a stream of data, which is normally a file, but may be a string or other source. The stream is analyzed into *tokens*, each of which represents a PostScript object. All data in a PostScript program as well as the procedures that form the program itself consist of PostScript objects. Neither the PostScript language nor the PostScript interpreter makes any formal distinction between data and procedures. Any PostScript object may be either data or program; some objects may be treated as one thing one time, and the other the next. This process is most noticeable in the handling of procedures, which are pushed onto the stack when they are first encountered but are executed when they are subsequently processed.

Special Characters

In addition to becoming familiar with PostScript notation, you need to become comfortable with a few format conventions in order to read both PostScript and Display PostScript easily. As we discussed in Chapter 1, most PostScript programs use only the printable subset of the ASCII character set, plus the characters space, tab, and newline (return or linefeed)—what we referred to as the ASCII encoding. This is the encoding format that is equally readable by the interpreter and by a human programmer.

When using this encoding, three characters—space, tab, and newline—are referred to collectively as *white space characters*. These characters serve as separators for other objects such as names and numbers. Any number of consecutive white space characters are treated as if there were just one. The only exception to this is within strings and comments where each of the white space characters has specific (and different) effects.

In addition, ten special characters serve as delimiters or markers for certain objects such as strings, procedures, name literals, and comments. These characters are as follows:

Character(s)	Function
{ and }	Begin and end a procedure.
/	Begins a name literal.
%	Begins a comment.
(and)	Begin and end a string.
<and>	Begin and end a hexadecimal string.
[and]	Begin and end an array.

Procedures

Procedures are operators and objects grouped together within matched braces, { }. Procedures are also known as executable arrays in PostScript. Some examples of procedures are as follows:

{Xpos 5 add}
adds 5 to the Xpos variable.

{add 5 div}
adds the top two operands on the stack and divides the result by 5.

Procedures may also be nested; for example,

{Ypos {Xpos 5 add} exec div}
adds 5 to the Xpos variable and then divides the Ypos variable by the result.

Name Literals

Name literals are just what their name implies, names of objects, usually procedures or variables. All characters except special characters and white space characters can appear in a name literal. A name literal begins with the character / (slash). The slash is not part of the name itself and is not included when reference is made to the name. The purpose of the slash, like that of the braces that enclosed procedures, is to notify the interpreter that what follows is a literal to be placed onto the stack. Some examples of valid names are

/name
/NaMe   (Note that this is different from /name.)
/Paragraph_12
/Times-Roman   (A name for a font.)
/$@#&&8**^   (An irrational name, but still valid.)

PostScript names used in the Display PostScript environment must not exceed 128 characters. Remember that the newline character is a white space character and is invalid within a name literal; therefore, a name literal cannot exceed a line in length. For obvious reasons, it is best to keep your names to a reasonable length. In particular, if you are passing names back and forth with your C program, it's best to limit yourself to the 31 maximum characters that C provides.

Comments

Comments begin with the special character % (percent). The comment consists of all characters, including special characters, until the next newline. PostScript treats a comment as if it were a single white space character. A couple of observations should be made about comments. First, since the comment begins with % and extends to the next newline, it is always the last element on a line or is on a line by itself—which is where you would normally code while programming. Note also that, since the only terminator for a comment is the newline, you cannot embed a comment in a line of code as you might do in C. Second, multiple comment lines must each start with a %.

The ability to include special characters means that, once you begin a comment, the interpreter does not process anything until the next newline. This can be extremely valuable in providing documentation within the program itself. Some examples of comments are

>/abc %this is all comment (including {abc add xyz}
>
>/abc%this is the same effect as the preceding line
>
>%this is %equally%%%[{] valid
>
>12%is just "12" as far as the PS interpreter sees
>
>%and so on - - you get the idea

As you see from the examples, a space is not necessary at the beginning of a comment; however, it is recommended since the comments are intended for the human reader. The single exception to this use of % to introduce a comment is when the character % is included within a pair of string delimiters. In that case (and no other), it is included by the interpreter as part of the string.

Strings

A PostScript string is a group of characters enclosed within matching parentheses, ( ). Within a string, the only special characters are the parentheses characters themselves and the character \ (backslash). Examples of valid strings are:

(this is a string)

(and so is !@#$%%^&*-__=+ this)

(and so is 1232 56677 45890)

(white space characters are NOT

excluded from

a valid string)

Parentheses may also be included as long as they are balanced. For example,

(this is () a valid (0) string)

And you can create a null string with ().

Like C strings, the \ character (backslash) signals a special requirement within the string. The character or characters immediately following the \ determines what that requirement is. The valid combinations, which are essentially the same as C codes, are as follows:

Character Combination	*Definition*
\n	Newline (return or linefeed)
\r	Carriage return
\t	Horizontal tab
\b	Backspace
\f	Form feed
\\	Backslash
\(	Left parenthesis
\)	Right parenthesis
\ddd	Character code ddd (octal)
newline	No character—both are ignored

Any other combination with \ is ignored.

You are probably familiar with most of these conventions from your C programming. The use of \(and \) is only required when these are not part of a matching pair within the string; however, you may use them whenever you place parentheses in a string. Many applications always use them within a string, and it is good programming practice to do so. This prevents any accidental missing parentheses from confusing the interpreter and crashing your program. (And a nasty and difficult-to-find bug it is, to be sure.)

The use of \ddd has a special value in PostScript that is identical to its use in C. Remember that PostScript is designed to use only the printable subset of the ASCII character set in its basic encoding. This enhances both readability and portability, as we have already discussed. Thus the \ddd notation provides a way to incorporate a character outside PostScript's normal range using notation that remains within the recommended subset. In this way you can include characters such as \010 (ASCII backspace) or \242 (the cents sign) in a string if you want. (We discuss use of these additional characters in more detail in Chapter 5 when we discuss advanced font handling.)

Finally, there is a special form of string, bracketed by < and >. A string within these two delimiters is a hexadecimal (base sixteen) string. The only valid characters are 0 through 9 and A through F (or a through f). Each pair of hexadecimal digits represents one character. Here are two examples of hexadecimal strings:

<1211a1f3>

<ab CD ef 1122 904f>

As you see, both upper- and lowercase letters within the correct range are equally acceptable. In the second example, you see that you can use white space characters—in this case, the space character—to break up the string without having any effect on the value. The interpreter ignores any white space characters in the string. If you have other characters outside the valid hexadecimal character set in the string, you get a PostScript error.

We can also illustrate the equivalence of pairs of hexadecimal digits to normal characters. Using the ASCII representation of characters, we can form the following example of a hexadecimal string:

<31355F4e616d65>

which is equivalent to the regular string

(15_Name)

This is quite different from the C representation of hexadecimal strings, and you should work a little bit with the PostScript variety to be sure you understand how they function. Also note that no hexadecimal escape encoding is available in PostScript; only the octal notation is used.

Because it is sometimes necessary to create empty strings, PostScript provides a **string** operator. This operator takes one operand, the size of the desired string, and returns a string of that length on the operand stack. This is often required for various PostScript string handling operators, which require an existing string as an operand to yield a place for their results. In our standard notation, the string operator looks like this:

    int   **string**   str

creates a string object, *str*, with length *int*, and fills each position in *str* with the binary value 0.

The **string** operator is used as follows:

    10   **string**   -> (   )

Note that the placeholders in the resulting string object are not spaces, but are binary 0; exactly the correct value to terminate a C string.

Arrays

A typical PostScript array is created by bounding a collection of PostScript objects with brackets, [ ]. When the Postscript interpreter encounters the [, it pushes a *mark* object onto the operand stack and then executes each subsequent object, placing the results onto the stack until it encounters the matching]. At that point, the interpreter removes everything down to the mark and creates an array out of the objects taken off the stack. Consider the following examples of PostScript arrays:

    [12 34 (abcd) 56 78]

This array consists of five elements: two integers, 12 and 34, followed by a string, abcd; and then two more integers, 56 and 78.

    [/name (name) .125 34]

This array consists of four elements: a name literal, "name"; a string, "name"; a real number, .125 and an integer, 34. Remember that the name object, "name", is not the same thing as the string, "name".

You may create empty and null arrays as required. The null array is quite straightforward; it may be created as follows:

[ ]

An empty array is an array of a fixed number of elements, all of which are initialized with the *null* object. To create such an array, you must use the PostScript **array** operator, which works in much the same fashion as **string**. In this case, the objects that fill the new array are the PostScript *null* object. In our standard format, the **array** operator looks like this:

   int   **array**   array
   creates a new array object, *array*, which is initialized to contain *int* null objects as entries.

The **array** operator is used in the following example:

   5   **array** -> [-null- -null- -null- -null- -null-]

where -null- indicates the null object. It is also possible to create a null array using the **array** operator, as follows:

   0   **array** -> []

As a final example, consider this array:

   [(div) 6 12 add]

This is an interesting and instructive example. This array contains only two elements: the string "div" and the integer result of adding 6 and 12, that is, 18. Note that the array construction does execute operators within it, before creating the array itself. This, of course, is what distinguishes the [ ] pair from the { } set that defines a procedure. When the interpreter encounters a [, it continues to execute operators; when it encounters a {, it stops.

OBJECT TYPES

The PostScript language has fourteen distinct types of objects shown in the following table.

Simple			*Composite*
Numeric	**Nominal**	**Special**	
integer	name	mark	string
real	operator	null	dictionary
boolean	file	save	array
		fontID	gstate

All syntactic entities recognized by the PostScript interpreter belong to one of these types.

All PostScript objects have certain common characteristics, including a type, attributes, and a value. In general, when you deal with a PostScript object, you need only be concerned with its type and value. The attributes of an object are primarily of interest to the interpreter, and, if they interest you, you will find a full discussion in the *PostScript Language Reference Manual* or in other complete PostScript language reference books. To deal with the combined issues of object type and value, we need to divide PostScript objects into two groups: simple objects and composite objects.

Simple Objects

Most PostScript objects are *simple* objects. This means that all their characteristics, type, attributes, and value are inextricably linked together and cannot be individually changed. This is certainly reasonable enough; you would hardly expect that the object 123 was the same as 456. The only way to change the characteristics of a simple object is to copy it to a new object that has the desired characteristic. All objects that are not composite objects are simple objects. Simple objects can be further subdivided, as shown in the preceding table, into numeric objects, nominal objects, and special objects.

Numeric Objects In PostScript there are basically two types of numeric objects: *integer* and *real*. Integer objects consist only of integer numbers between certain limits that are determined by the implementation. Real objects consist of real numbers within a wider range of limits. Real numbers are generally implemented as floating-point numbers and therefore have specific precision limitations. For that reason, when you access real numbers as arguments in your C routines, you must declare them as float. Numbers of both types may be freely intermixed in PostScript operations, except where an operator specifically requires an integer type. Where that requirement exists, you will find the notation *int* in the description of the operator to warn you that only an integer value is allowed.

You may also consider *boolean* objects as belonging to the numeric category. In this area, PostScript is quite different from C. In C, boolean values are, in fact, numbers, with 0 being false and any nonzero value being true. However, this is not the case in PostScript. Boolean objects have only two possible values: true and false. As you will read later in this chapter, they are produced by the comparison operators and are used by the conditional and logical operators. Although they are equivalent to the binary values, 0 and 1, these are distinct objects in PostScript; and 0 is not false, nor is 1 true. For this reason, the specific objects *true* and *false* exist within PostScript for those occasions when you need a direct reference to the values.

Nominal Objects Three types of PostScript objects can be thought of as names, or variants of names: *name* objects, *operator* objects, and *file* objects.

A name is an indivisible symbol uniquely defined by a set of characters. A name is a simple object; although it is referenced and identified by a string of characters, it is not the string of characters. The individual characters that make up the name are not in any sense elements of the name.

You need to notice two important points about names. First, they must be unique. Any specific sequence of characters defines one, and only one, name object. Second, names do not have values in the same sense that they would in other programming languages. Instead, names in PostScript are associated with values through the use of the dictionary mechanism, as you have already seen.

Operator objects represent the built-in PostScript actions; when the operator is encountered, the built-in action is executed. As we already discussed, operator objects are the value half of the pairing in *systemdict* with the key of the operator name. For most purposes, you will find it easiest to simply regard operators as being identical to their names. The purpose of this reference is simply to let you know that the operator and its name are not, in fact, precisely identical.

A file is a readable or writeable stream of characters, transferring information between PostScript and its environment. A file object refers to an associated, underlying file. PostScript provides two standard files: a standard input file, and a standard output file. The standard input file is where the PostScript interpreter generally receives programs, commands, and data to be worked on. The standard output file is the destination of the usual PostScript output, especially error and status messages and certain displays.

Many PostScript programs can run very satisfactorily with only the standard files. When these are not sufficient, however, PostScript does provide a full set of file operators, which allow you to open a file (which is the act that creates the file object) and to process the stream of characters in a variety of ways. It is almost never necessary to refer directly to the standard files, but there are names and mechanism for such reference if it is required. See the full discussion of file operators in the *PostScript Language Reference Manual* for use and limitations on these points.

Special Objects PostScript also has four special types of objects—*null, mark, save,* and *fontID*—each of which exists for a specific purpose. All of these special types are simple objects.

As its name implies, the null object is an object whose sole function is as a place holder. PostScript uses null objects to fill empty or uninitialized positions in composite objects (such as an array) when they are created. A null object can be referenced by the name "null". Most operators return an error if they are given a null object as an operand.

The mark is a special object used to mark a position on the operand stack. Several stack operators use the mark object in stack manipulation.

The PostScript interpreter uses the save and fontID objects for its various operations. Generally, you will not have to be concerned about them. The fontID object is, as you would expect, associated with creation and use of fonts; you will read more about this in the chapters regarding fonts and graphics.

Composite Objects

The *array, string, dictionary,* and *gstate* objects are *composite* objects. This means that each of these types of objects has components as well as an internal substructure that is both visible and accessible. The substructure of each of these types is discussed more fully later in the chapter, except for the *gstate* object, which is discussed in Chapter 3 when you will read about PostScript graphics.

There are two important points of difference that you should know about simple and composite objects. The first is that composite objects consume virtual memory within the interpreter. In other words, when you create a new dictionary or string or any other composite object, you use up some of the available memory resources. In ordinary PostScript programming, this is probably your most important resource, and it requires careful management. In Display PostScript, this is just as important but easier to manage, for three reasons. First, Display PostScript provides a "garbage collector" function that recovers the memory that was allocated to objects that are no longer in use. In regular PostScript, once you had allocated the memory, there was no automatic recovery to get it back. Second, in Display PostScript, the interpreter can usually access additional memory resources from within the workstation environment, like any other application. In regular PostScript devices such as laser printers, this is not an option; all the available memory is already allocated. Third, the Display PostScript system provides new operators that allow you to undefine composite objects and fonts individually; in regular PostScript, there is only a global mechanism for such management.

The second point of difference between simple and composite objects is more important and perhaps a bit more difficult to grasp. Composite objects have an internal structure. In the case of a string, for example, the characters in the string make up the internal components. If you duplicate a composite object such as a string, the original and the duplicate share the same components, and any change to one is reflected in all the other duplicates. Suppose, for example, that you have a long string, and you have a procedure to select a small portion out of it that matches some set of characters. If you now change that substring in your procedure, you are also modifying the original string. This is notably different from C, where strings and other arguments passed to a function, for example, are maintained as separate copies of the originals, and changes in the copies do not affect the original in any way. In PostScript, changing one version of a composite object is likely to change all the versions. It is possible to create true copies of composite objects that do not share components. This is done by using the **copy** operator, which we will discuss later. The points to remember here are that, in general, composite objects that were created from one another share internal values and that you can control this process, if you need to, by careful and selective use of PostScript operations.

String Objects You are already familiar, from Chapter 1 and the discussion earlier in this chapter, with the construction and use of strings in PostScript. A string object is simply a PostScript string. It is, as we said earlier, a composite object. That means that any operation that copies a string, or part of a string, results in a sharing of the string's value. String objects consist of a series of values, stored internally as integers from 0 through 255, and are conventionally used to store character data with one character being represented by each integer.

Individual elements within a string can be accessed by use of an integer index. In this, strings are very much like C strings, where a string is an array of characters. Also like C, PostScript strings are indexed from 0 if you want to access an element.

Dictionary Objects Dictionaries were also discussed earlier. A dictionary object is simply a PostScript dictionary; like a string, it is a composite object. Copying a dictionary to a new dictionary does not copy the values in the dictionary, it shares the values. That is, if you change a value in the old dictionary, you will retrieve the changed value in the new one.

Array Objects An array is an indexed collection of PostScript objects. PostScript arrays differ from arrays in C in two respects. First, a PostScript array does not have to be composed of only one type of object. A PostScript array might contain, for example, numbers, strings, names, and even other arrays. The second difference is that PostScript arrays are one dimensional. That is, access to individual elements in a PostScript array is always provided by a single index. Of course, since elements of a PostScript array may consist of other arrays, you can construct the functional equivalent of multidimensional arrays if you require them.

The index to a PostScript array must be a nonnegative integer. PostScript indices begin at zero, so a PostScript array with n elements would be indexed by values from 0 through n-1. Any attempt to access an array with an index that is invalid results in an error.

PROCEDURE DEFINITIONS

A procedure is an executable array of PostScript objects. As you learned in the preceding sections, procedures are enclosed in braces, { }. This distinguishes them from other PostScript arrays, which are enclosed in brackets. This is an important distinction. You may find the concept of an executable array to be somewhat strange. You may find it more convenient to think of procedures as a separate type of PostScript object, belonging to its own class and having its own properties. The main point to understand here is that the interpreter views procedures as arrays with the executable attribute.

Procedures are essentially small segments of PostScript programs. They are ordered collections—arrays—of PostScript objects that accomplish some task. These segments can be entered into a PostScript dictionary like any other PostScript and can be referenced by name. In fact, most of

PostScript program analysis consists of identifying a hierarchy of required procedures.

Transfer of Control

Since PostScript is a programming language, it necessarily provides several mechanisms for changing the order of execution of operations. Some such mechanism is essential for any type of programming. Interestingly enough, PostScript does not provide a traditional goto or branch operator nor does it have branch labels. In this sense, PostScript is a perfect example of a "structured" language. Since, however, most programmers have grown up with the notion of branching, you may find that you need to rethink some of your old habits.

Instead of branching, PostScript provides a variety of operators to perform procedures repeatedly or to execute them based on some condition. PostScript also provides a set of logical operators for creating, combining, and testing conditions. By using these facilities, a PostScript programmer can create very complex procedural variations to accomplish whatever the task is at hand. The essential requirement is to think of your task as a series of processes rather than as one, complex flow.

PostScript operators that control procedures can be divided into three groups:

1. Operators that execute a procedure repeatedly
2. Operators that execute a procedure conditionally, based on a test of some external object
3. Operators that PostScript itself uses to control flow

These groups are somewhat arbitrary and the first two groups, at least, will be very common in your work.

The first group is distinguished by being a simple, repeated operation. The operators in this group are as follows:

>{proc}   **exec**   —
>executes *proc*.
>
>int {proc}   **repeat**   —
>executes *proc int* times.
>
>init incr lim {proc}   **for**   —
>executes *proc* repeatedly, for values from *init* by steps of *incr* until reaching *lim*.

The second group of operators is a little more complex, being dependent on the results of a conditional test, either outside and independent of the procedure being executed, or within in. Note the new operand type, *bool*. This represents a boolean value, either true or false. These operators are as follows:

>bool {proc}   **if**   —
>executes *proc* if *bool* is true.
>
>bool {proc1} {proc2}   **ifelse**   —
>executes *proc1* if *bool* is true and executes *proc2* otherwise.

as well as the following pair of operators, which are used together:

>{proc}   **loop**   —
>executes *proc* an indefinite number of times.
>
>—   **exit**   —
>terminates an active loop.

Typically, some test or condition within the **loop** triggers the **exit** operation, so, in some sense, this is also a conditional execution structure. This grouping of operators shows very clearly how easy and natural structured programming is in PostScript.

The descriptions for each of these operators indicate that no results are left on the operand stack. This is quite correct, as far as the operator itself is concerned. However, each operator also executes an arbitrary procedure. Although the operator does not leave anything on the stack, the procedure may do so and the operator does not remove these items. In other words, it is up to the procedure to manage the stack however it wants; the operator does not "clean up" after it.

Perhaps at this point a short discussion of what constitutes "structured programming" is in order. Structured programming is a method of developing program logic according to a specific set of rules. Although this is not an appropriate place for a complete analysis of program structure and structured programming, a brief discussion should help you acquire the proper mental framework for writing PostScript code. The major rule of structured programming is that for maximum readability and logical clarity, program logic should use only three control structures:

- Sequential control structure
- Loop control structure
- If-then-else control structure

Each of these structures is used as required to form a group of computer instructions that both conforms to strict structural requirements and performs a single logical function, which makes such code easy to read and to understand.

The sequence control structure is just a fancy way of saying that the computer executes one instruction or operation after another. This is the ordinary sequential processing with which we are all familiar. The other two control structures, loop control and if-then-else control, correspond (more or less) to our first two groups of operators. The net result is that PostScript provides the ideal set of operators to create a structured program.

These structures are not as rich as the set of conditional execution operations that you are familiar with from C, but they are adequate. All of these can be related to the more familiar C operations. The **if** and **ifelse** operators are exactly similar to their C counterparts, *if* and *if-else*, differing only in syntax (which is the common difference between C and PostScript anyway). Similarly, the PostScript **for** operator is essentially the same as its C counterpart. The **exec** and **repeat** operators are most like the *while* or *do-while* operations in C. In both cases, the procedure body is executed for some period; the difference is that the PostScript operations are predesigned to execute a fixed (integer) number of times, whereas in C you would design an iteration loop counter to be tested during the *while*. The PostScript **loop** and **exit** construction is probably most similar to a *while* with a *break*, although, again, these are not quite identical in either approach or use since the C construction is more general. Finally, PostScript does not have any equivalent to either the C *case* structure or the *goto* operator.

We have already observed that the second group of control operators depends on testing some external object and changing control sequence based on the boolean operand that represents the results of that test. PostScript provides a complete set of relational testing and boolean manipulation operators to create the necessary values for these controls. The most basic of these are the operators that test for equality and inequality:

    any1 any2   **eq**   bool
tests *any1* equal to *any2*.

    any1 any2   **ne**   bool
tests *any1* not equal to *any2*.

Note that these operators accept any type of operands for a test of equality. The definition of equality depends on the types of the operands being compared. The objects do not necessarily have to be of the same type; for example, strings can be compared to name literals, and real numbers can be compared to integers, with correct results. The action here is very similar to C, where different types of argument values are cast into compatible forms for testing and use.

Comparison of dictionaries and arrays, however, is somewhat ambiguous. Remember that these are composite objects and that duplicate composite objects share values. Dictionaries and arrays are judged equal if, and only if, they share all values; that is, if the two objects being compared are duplicates of one another. Comparison of nonduplicate arrays or dictionaries always produces an unequal result even if the contents of the two objects are exactly equal. Thus you can have the rather unnerving experience illustrated by the following example:

    [1 2 3] [1 2 3]   **eq**   ->   false

In this case, the example creates two distinct array objects that have identical components; however, because the arrays are not duplicates of one another, they compare *false* when tested for equality. This can be especially important when you are passing values into a PostScript procedure in a wrap, and then expect to test them for equality. If the objects are arrays, it is best to test them outside the PostScript environment.

The one exception to this rule regarding comparison of arrays is illustrated by the following example:

    [ ] [ ]   **eq**   ->   true

Here you are comparing two empty, or null, arrays. These arrays always compare equal, so you can test for an empty array successfully, even though you cannot test directly for equal contents of other arrays.

Strings, on the other hand, do compare successfully in the expected way, even though they are composite objects. Two strings are equal if they have the same length and if each of their character elements is equal; the strings do not have to share values for this test. In other words, **eq** behaves on strings in the same manner as the C function *strcmp*. Therefore, the equivalent comparison to the preceding array comparison provides the correct and expected response, as follows:

    (asdfg) (asdfg)   **eq**   ->   true

because the two strings, although distinct, have identical lengths and components.

Besides tests for equality, which may involve any type of object, PostScript provides tests for other relations as well, but only for numbers and strings. This restriction is reasonable since defining ordering relations for other types of objects would be difficult and somewhat arbitrary. The ordering relationships are provided by the following operators:

    num1 num2 **ge** bool
    (str1) (str2) **ge** bool
tests *num1* or *str1* greater than or equal to *num2* or *str2*.

    num1 num2 **gt** bool
    (str1) (str2) **gt** bool
tests *num1* or *str1* strictly greater than *num2* or *str2*.

    num1 num2 **le** bool
    (str1) (str2) **le** bool
tests *num1* or *str1* less than or equal to *num2* or *str2*.

    num1 num2 **lt** bool
    (str1) (str2) **lt** bool
tests *num1* or *str1* strictly less than *num2* or *str2*.

Inequality relations for number are quite well defined, and PostScript numbers of both real and integer types and in any format can be freely mixed in these relational tests. Inequality testing for strings is done in the same manner as the C function *strcmp* by testing the character codes of the components of the strings. All strings are only tested to the point of first inequality, when the determination of the relationship is made. If two strings are of unequal length and are identical for the length of the shorter string, the longer string is reported as the greater.

PostScript also provides a series of boolean operators for combining conditions. These operators can be applied to both the boolean values *true* and *false* and also to integer values. The integer operands are treated as binary sequences, or bit strings. As bit strings, the numbers can have the same logical operations performed on them as the boolean values, by taking them in bitwise fashion, with 0 as the equivalent of false and 1 as true. The **not** operator, when applied to an integer, returns the one's complement of the number. These operators include:

    int1 int2   **and**   int
    bool1 bool2   **and**   bool
logical or bitwise and.

| int1 int2 | **or** | int |
| bool1 bool2 | **or** | bool |

logical or bitwise inclusive or.

| int1 int2 | **xor** | int |
| bool1 bool2 | **xor** | bool |

logical or bitwise exclusive or.

| int | **not** | int |
| bool | **not** | bool |

logical or bitwise not.

Finally, the following two operators allow you direct access to the boolean objects themselves, for testing and for other purposes:

| — | **true** | bool |

pushes boolean value *true* onto the stack.

| — | **false** | bool |

pushes boolean value *false* onto the stack.

The combination of these operators allows any form of testing on a PostScript object.

Procedures and Operators

The preceding section introduced you to the concept of procedures, as a part of the discussion of program control and related operators. Now you can begin to make more effective use of these operators by putting names on procedures and using those names as part of the control and flow process. As an illustration of this, let's revisit some of the procedural examples you saw before. If you don't remember any specific operators, just look one up at the end of the last chapter or you can find one in the operator summary in your language reference.

A procedure is named and entered into the current dictionary like any other PostScript object. For example,

/average { **add** 2 **div** } **def**

defines a procedure "average" in exactly the same way that

/str (this is a string) **def**

defines the string "str." All definitions are carried out in the same fashion. Procedure names can also be included in the definition of other procedures;

for example, if you have defined "average" as just shown, you might also define the procedure

/middlePage { 0 612 average } **def**

which would give you the average of the left and right edges of a standard (8 1/2 by 11 inch) page. Since the interpreter does not execute the procedure when the definition occurs, it is not necessary to have already defined "average" when you define middlePage. All that is required is that "average" be defined by the time you execute middlePage.

Notice that this procedural definition, middlePage, is different from the following definition of a named constant:

/MiddlePage 0 612 average **def**

Looks very similar, doesn't it? Other than the absence of the procedural braces { and } and the capitalization of the initial M to correspond to the naming conventions that we discussed before, it is similar, and it would, in this case, accomplish the same goal as the preceding definition. In both cases, the final result would be to leave the value of the middle of a standard-width page on the stack. The difference lies in how that result is obtained.

In the first definition, of a procedure, the calculation is carried out only at the moment the interpreter encounters the middlePage procedure. In the second case, the calculation is carried out at the moment that the definition is encountered, and the value of that calculation is stored under the name MiddlePage. These two cases have been constructed to illustrate to show you how these procedures work; the judgment of when to use one or the other must be made based on the requirements of each task or program. The point to note here is that in the one case (procedural definition), "average" does not have to be defined when the procedure is defined and that the calculation of the value occurs at the moment of use; in the other case (constant definition), "average" must be defined already because it will be executed to compute the value to be stored, and that value, once computed, will be fixed and used whenever the named constant is invoked.

Using these techniques, we can now revisit some of the examples from the last chapter. Let's begin by defining the following procedure:

/inch { 72 **mul** } **def**

This small procedure allows you to translate inches into PostScript coordinates, which you will recall are 1/72 of an inch in each direction.

Using this procedure, the following two program segments are identical in execution:

    7.5 inch

    7.5 72 **mul**

The first segment is, as you would expect, much easier to understand. Now you might define a variable, Xpos, to measure movement across the page, and a variable, Ypos, to measure movement down the page. Assume that you would like a 1-inch margin on both the left and the right edges of the page, and that you also want to start printing 1 inch from the top of the page. Then you would define

    /Xpos 1 inch **def**

and

    /Ypos 7.5 inch **def**

to begin each variable at the appropriate margin. Remember that the PostScript vertical coordinate system is positive up the page, and so a larger number represents a position higher up the page. You subtract from the Ypos variable to measure movement down the page. Then you could write the procedures

    /rightMargin { 7 inch } **def**

and

    /outsideMargin? { rightMargin Xpos **gt** } **def**

The first procedure defines a position that we call rightMargin at 7 inches, and the second procedure defines a test called outsideMargin?, which checks the Xpos variable against the rightMargin position. Using these definitions we can now test whether the Xpos variable has crossed the right margin by executing the outsideMargin? procedure.

Let us continue by supposing that you have determined that movement in the vertical direction will be at six lines per inch. Then you could define

    /linespace {1 inch 6 **div** } **def**

and

    /linedown { Ypos linespace **sub** } **def**

which define the six-per-inch line spacing as linespace and creates a linedown procedure to subtract a linespace from the Ypos variable. Now you can combine these procedures to accomplish in a more understandable way a simple task that you might need for any display: namely, to move down one line if the position across the page has crossed the right margin. This was written before as:

> 504 Xpos **gt** { Ypos 12 **sub** } **if**

but you can now write it as:

> outsideMargin? linedown **if**

which is much more intelligible, even if it still sounds somewhat like Pidgin English.

The important point here is that you have transformed a rather opaque piece of code into an understandable piece by the judicious choice of variable and procedure names.

Standard Error Handling

PostScript handles errors that it discovers during operation in a uniform manner which takes advantage of various PostScript language facilities. An understanding of PostScript's default error handling and reporting should help you read and modify PostScript code.

Every PostScript error has a unique name (sound familiar?) that is also intended to be somewhat descriptive of the nature of the error encountered, for example, stackoverflow, rangecheck, and undefined. Possible errors for each operator are clearly identified in the language reference materials. When the PostScript interpreter discovers an error during its own operation or while executing an operator, it looks up the name of the error condition in a special dictionary called *errordict*. The interpreter then executes the procedure associated with that name in *errordict*. In all of this, you see that the handling follows standard PostScript procedures.

Each name in *errordict* has its own associated error procedure. All of the default error procedures operate in a standard fashion. They record information regarding the error in a special dictionary called *$error*. This special dictionary contains information about what caused the error and about the state of the system and the interpreter at the time that the error occurred. Then the procedures stop the execution of the PostScript program and invoke the generic **handleerror** procedure. This procedure accesses the error data stored in *$error* and prints a text message on the standard output or standard error file.

For most PostScript environments, the text message that **handleerror** generates conforms to a standard status message format. This means that the text is bracketed by the strings %%[and]%% and consists of key: value pairs separated by semicolons. The standard format for an error message is as follows:

%%[Error: errorname; OffendingCommand: operator]%%

This rather formal structure allows user application programs to extract error messages (and other status messages) from other text or data being received over the communication channel and to provide additional processing, if desired. Generally it is considered good practice to screen errors and status information from the user of an application program; hence this method of reporting errors. If you are using the interpreter in interactive mode, you simply see the appropriate error message on your screen in the format shown (assuming you're using a standard PostScript printer, such as an Apple LaserWriter).

Display PostScript handles PostScript language errors in one of two ways. The normal, or default, processing invokes **handleerror** to report the error and forces the context to terminate, thus essentially flushing the application's Display PostScript connection. The application's error callback procedure is used to report the error, but there is no recovery except to terminate the display processing.

As an alternative, the context can be created to use the special **resynchandleerror** error handler. If this is done, then, if an error occurs in the context, the error is reported in the same fashion, but the context is not terminated. Instead, **resynchandleerror** and the application can work jointly to discard any buffered input and output, return to a known point, and resume normal execution.

Since this whole process uses standard PostScript facilities, it is possible to alter the standard error processing mechanism in various ways. Such advanced topics are beyond the scope of this book; if you want or need to take advantage of these facilities, a full discussion of the possible alterations is presented in the *Display PostScript System Reference* manuals. The PostScript default error processing provides better error diagnosis and messages than many computer languages; you should find it quite sufficient for your needs.

INTEGRATING C AND DISPLAY POSTSCRIPT

At this point, you are about ready to do another exercise. But, first, it is time to discuss in some more detail the exact nature of the connections between PostScript, Display PostScript, and your C application.

Before we proceed to that exercise, however, it would be appropriate to discuss how wraps are created, processed, and presented.

Accessing the Display PostScript Library

The first procedures that you used were from the Display PostScript Client Library, which was introduced very briefly. This is actually a series of header files of C procedures that your program can use to access various PostScript and Display PostScript functions. There are five common header files: *dpsclient.h*, *dpsfriends.h*, *dpsexcept.h*, *dpsops.h*, and *psops.h*, along with an additional, system-dependent header file. The Client Library and its associated *pswrap* translator provide the application programmer with full access to the PostScript interpreter. As is usual in C programming, you can access the procedures in the Client Library by including the appropriate header files in your C application code. The *Client Library Reference Manual* in the *Display PostScript System Reference* provides a complete discussion of the facilities and features of the Client Library. Later in this section, we will discuss both the Client Library and these header files in more detail.

Although the main access to the PostScript interpreter and to the Client Library function is through making and executing wrapped procedures (as you did in the last exercise), the Client Library also provides the *single operator procedures* such as PSshow and PSmoveto that we have used earlier.

Creating and Using Wrapped Procedures

The *pswrap* translator provides the application programmer with a means to compose a series of PostScript code sequences, or wraps, which can be called from a C language program. The wraps transmit the PostScript code, along with any defined arguments, to the PostScript interpreter and return any requested results to the calling program. The net effect, from the programmer's viewpoint, is to make the PostScript code just another C function. This is the most direct, understandable, and efficient way for an application program to communicate with the PostScript environment.

The *pswrap* translator is actually a preprocessor that reads a certain type of input file—the wrap code prepared by the programmer—and converts it into C procedures. Various options and features can be invoked when the translator is executed; these are fully described in the *pswrap Reference Manual*. In most environments, you only have to take two steps to have your wraps correctly processed. First, provide the correct file extension (usually .psw) to indicate that the file is a wrapped PostScript file. Second, list the file as part of the "make" procedure in your C environment—the exact method of doing this will be, of course, system dependent. Generally, looking at other code in the system is the fastest and easiest way to determine how to invoke the *pswrap* translator, and it is usually quite straightforward.

Procedure Definitions On the assumption that you have already been able to make the *pswrap* translator work—otherwise, you wouldn't have gotten this far—we want to look next at how to define general wrapped procedures. Up to this point, you have just input the wraps rather simply, as shown in the various exercises, and this has worked quite well. Now you should learn the full wrap structure and syntax so that you can design and create your own wraps.

As you might guess from your earlier coding, each wrap consists of four elements:

1. The keyword *defineps*, which starts the beginning of each individual wrapped procedure. This must appear at the beginning of a line, without any preceding spaces or tabs.

2. The *procedure declaration*, which consists of the name of the procedure and a list of input and output arguments, enclosed in parentheses. If the procedure does not require any arguments, the parentheses must still be present, with nothing between them. The procedure names created by these declarations are, by default, external names (in the C sense). As with other C names, if you want the name to be local, you may declare it *static*.

3. The *procedure body*, which is the PostScript program fragment that is to be transmitted to the interpreter. This should consist of standard PostScript code, separated (as usual) by white space characters.

4. The keyword *endps*, which ends each individual wrapped procedure. This must appear at the beginning of a line, just like the corresponding *defineps*.

Since the code within the wraps is PostScript, all comments in there must be PostScript comments, not C comments. In addition, you should realize that the *pswrap* translator removes all comments from its output before sending it to the PostScript interpreter. If you need to send comments through to the interpreter for some reason, you must use the Client Library procedures such as DPSWriteData, which can send arbitrary data to the interpreter.

Also, the *pswrap* translator does not actually understand PostScript code; therefore, the fact that a wrap compiles through the translator successfully in no way guarantees that it will function correctly (or at all) once it is sent to the interpreter. *pswrap* only checks basic syntax for matching parentheses, braces, and so on and makes the necessary substitutions for arguments.

Input and Output Arguments Arguments for a wrap consist of names in the procedure header. These names are defined using standard C types, with some additions for special objects that can occur in wraps. There can be any number of arguments, both input and output. Input arguments are listed first and are separated from output arguments by a single vertical bar. In both cases, the arguments are grouped by type, with argument names of the same type separated by commas and different types separated by semicolons. Here is an example:

 defineps PSWtestFcn(int a, b; float c, d; char *Str | float *Out; int *r, *s; char OutStr[24])

The standard C casts such as long and short are also valid in defining types for wrap arguments. Notice that the output from a wrap must be a pointer or an array in order to place the value back into the C program correctly, and it should, of course, be a pointer to or an array of the correct type.

Boolean values, in PostScript, are not integers as they are in C. If you declare an argument as type *boolean*, the translator expects a variable of type *int*. Following standard C practice, if the variable is 0, it is translated into the PostScript boolean object *false*, and it is translated into *true* otherwise. The same conversion, in reverse, is performed for output arguments: *false* is returned as 0, and *true* as 1. Arguments that are defined as unsigned integers are cast to signed integer since PostScript does not have any unsigned numbers. PostScript translates all numbers into either 32-bit integers or 32-bit real numbers. Real numbers are mapped into C float variables, and integers into long integers. Sending or receiving mismatched numbers, for example, a float for an integer or vice versa, generates an error.

Character input and output can be done by pointers to strings or by arrays of characters. Character strings must terminate in the standard C fashion, with a null (\0) character; on output, character strings are given a null character as a terminator. It is the application's responsibility to allocate sufficient room for the receiving string plus the terminator. Character arrays have a defined length, which must be a positive integer, and are not terminated with a null character. On output, the interpreter copies either all the characters in the output string onto an array (including the null terminator, if there is sufficient room) or it copies the number of characters specified as the array size. If the array is not long enough to receive all the characters, the null terminator is not included in the array and any characters that do not fit are discarded. Character input may be used as either names or strings; you will see examples of both as we proceed.

Exception Handling and Debugging

The Client Library provides some help and facilities for exception handling and debugging. Most of these facilities are beyond the scope of this book, but you should know that they exist and something about how they work. Chapter 6 discusses them in more detail, but here is a brief overview.

An *exception* is defined as an unexpected condition detected by a procedure that prevents it from running to normal completion. Instead of returning to the calling program directly, the procedure can exit by performing a function called *raising the error*. This returns control to a specified point in the application (not the calling procedure), which can then take appropriate action, including (but not limited to) reraising the error condition. There are a number of considerations in using these features; if you need them, you should review the *Client Library Reference Manual*.

BUSINESS REPORT EXERCISE

Now you are ready for another exercise. For this exercise, you will undertake to program a similar but distinct page of output. It is similar in that it is set in two columns in a text and commentary format; however, in this case it is text with marginal headings. The text represents a description of a company being analyzed; the marginal notations are subject headings.

The task here is to display a page of output about a company, Acme Software. The required format has a centered heading of two lines, with the remainder of the page set in two columns, in a fashion similar to the previous example. The exercise assumes that you have defined a window that is large enough to display the equivalent of an 8 by 6 inch page of output, or that you have defined a scrollable area for your window's use (if your interface support provides for automatic scrolling).

The two columns are set so that the first column has topic descriptions, whereas the second column contains the actual text itself. As before, the topic headings in the first paragraph are to be aligned with the paragraphs in the second column; this time, however, they are to be right justified. To do all this, you now need to analyze how such a page might be set up.

Simple Procedure Analysis

By now, you are probably becoming more familiar with PostScript's order of operands followed by operator and are finding it easier to read somewhat more complex PostScript statements. Because of PostScript's notational structure, complex PostScript statements are built up in concentric layers, somewhat like an onion.

The following example is a moderately complex PostScript statement that uses operators you are familiar with, but not any procedural definitions to simplify the structure of the statement. Note that this style of programming is not recommended; it is presented here only to make a point and as an illustration of the concentric nature of complex PostScript code. Such complex functions are generally not required in normal applications. For the sake of the illustration, let us suppose that the following constants and variables have been defined:

LEFTMARGIN	left margin position (in the *x* direction)
RIGHTMARGIN	right margin position
StringSize	width of some string (in *x* direction units)

Now suppose that we wish to position the current point in the *x* direction to display this string (the one whose width is given in StringSize) in the center of a line between the two margin values. The following code accomplishes that task:

```
LEFTMARGIN                          %1
RIGHTMARGIN LEFTMARGIN sub          %2
2 div                               %3
StringSize 2 div                    %4
sub                                 %5
add                                 %6
```

To analyze this program fragment, you first need to discuss how to accomplish the task at hand: namely, to determine the position, in the x direction, where a string must begin in order to center it between the left and right margins. A quick analysis tells you that this point will be one-half the distance between the margins less one-half of the size of the string. That is basically the same process most people would use to center a heading on a typewritten page, for example: space to the center of the line and backspace once for every two characters in the heading. The preceding example follows exactly the same process, although it may not look like it at first. The difference is the "onionization" of the procedure; let's analyze it by layers.

The last thing we want to leave on the stack is the absolute x coordinate for the display. We are assuming for the moment that movement to set the display operation will be invoked with the x coordinate as an operand on the stack, as it would need to be for a **moveto**, for example. This x coordinate is the left margin plus some calculated displacement.

So, the last line, line %6, adds the result of the calculations performed in lines %2 to %5 to the LEFTMARGIN constant in the first line, line %1. Here you see the onion effect, with the last line being connected to the first. Moving inward, you see that line %2 calculates the distance between the left and right margins by subtracting the left margin from the right and leaving the result on the stack. Line %3 then divides that result by 2, giving the displacement of the center of the line, which now remains on the stack. Line %4 divides the length of the string, given by StringSize, by 2 to give one-half of the length and pushes that result onto the stack.

Now the stack contains three numbers: on top is one-half of the string length, next is the position of the center of the line, and last is the left margin, still on the stack from line %1. All numbers are in x-axis units and the top two are calculated from the left margin, as we wanted. Now line %5 subtracts the top operand from the one below it on the stack and returns the difference on the stack. This difference is precisely the calculated distance that we want to add to the left margin, which (not accidentally) is now the second operand on the stack. Line %6, as we discussed before, now adds the two remaining operands to provide the final, desired result. From all this, you can see how this small program consists of several layers, one inside the other.

Text Manipulation

Simple text handling, such as that shown previously, is one of the most common features of all applications. In the normal course of showing text on a display, you will find that you need to make certain calculations in order to put the text where you want it; for example, you may want to center a string of text on the display, or justify a line of text. There are several important issues that you should understand to calculate text placement on your display. This section discusses text calculations and the functions that you use to make them.

As the previous section illustrated, most text manipulation involves calculating and using the length of a string of text. There are two basic methods for determining the length of any text string, whether it consists of a single character or an entire line. The first method is to use PostScript operations to calculate the length of the string. This method has two major drawbacks, however, which make it generally the least desirable option for text calculations.

To begin with, calculating the length of a string in PostScript requires a special operator, **stringwidth**. Let's take a moment to look at this operator in the usual format:

> (str1) **stringwidth**   wx wy
> calculates the width of the string *str1* in current units. Current units are determined by the current font and the current transformation matrix.

Note that the operator returns two distinct values, one a width in the x direction (**wx**) and the other a width in the y direction (*wy*). These are necessary because some fonts—Asian characters, like Japanese and Chinese, primarily—have width in both directions. In the case of all English fonts, there is no y direction width for a character, and hence the y-coordinate value is always zero. This provides the width value of any string in the units that are appropriate for the font and page coordinates you have set. Also note that you must have set a current font for **stringwidth** to work, otherwise you will get an error.

However, **stringwidth** calculates the width of the string by actually imaging the characters in the string and then measuring them. This can involve quite a bit of overhead, and is correspondingly slow. Moreover, once you have determined the width of the string you have to calculate all of the necessary adjustments to place the text where you want it in PostScript. PostScript is certainly capable of doing this, but it is not the ideal place for such calculations. The net result is that calculating string widths and making text adjustments is not usually done within the PostScript portion of an application.

Although it is possible to manipulate text in the form of strings from within the PostScript section of your application, this is not how text-setting calculations are generally done. PostScript is particularly good at graphics; however, it is not the optimal place for numeric calculations. A higher level application language such as C or Objective C handles numeric calculations more efficiently than the PostScript interpreter does. Moreover, an application—whether running in a Display PostScript environment or simply preparing output for a PostScript device—generally needs to maintain an internal picture of the current state of the page or display for a variety of reasons including line breaking and text adjustments such as kerning and tracking. For these reasons, your text calculations should generally be performed from within your application code and the calculated positions and controls passed to the PostScript functions that will create the output.

Display PostScript has some new, powerful operators that make text-setting calculations even more appropriate when you are working in a display environment. However, even in a standard PostScript environment, performing all the calculations within the application is more efficient than performing them in PostScript. The second method of calculating the length of a string of text is using font metrics from within your application.

Font Metric Files It is both possible and practical to generate the width of a string from a table of information that provides the width of each character in a font. This information, called *character metrics*, is available to an application as part of the *font metric* file for the desired font; the table can be accessed from your application by standard techniques. You will learn more about PostScript fonts and their associated font metric information in Chapter 5. For fonts from Adobe Systems and for most other commercially available fonts the widths that are kept in the font metric files are in a standard font unit, which is 1000 times the standard point size of the character—in other words, the size given is the size the character would be in standard PostScript units if you showed it as a 1000-point font.

In order to calculate the size of the character for a string, you will need the name of the font and the desired point size. The name of the font determines the correct font metric file to be used. The point size is used to adjust the standard units to the correct proportion for your application.

All this sounds very abstract, so let's look at some code that you can use in the next exercise. It shows two C functions, setFontWidth and strWidth, which provide simple access to string widths and character metrics. These functions are as follows:

```
float cwi[256];     /* a table to hold character widths */
float TMSBOLD[] =   /* actual values for Times-Bold */
    {
    250.0, 250.0, 250.0, 250.0, 250.0, 250.0, 250.0, 250.0, 250.0, 250.0, 250.0,
    250.0, 250.0, 250.0, 250.0, 250.0, 250.0, 250.0, 250.0, 250.0, 250.0, 250.0,
    250.0, 250.0, 250.0, 250.0, 250.0, 250.0, 250.0, 250.0, 250.0, 250.0, 250.0,
    333.0, 555.0, 500.0, 500.0, 1000.0, 833.0, 333.0, 333.0, 333.0, 500.0, 570.0,
    250.0, 333.0, 250.0, 278.0, 500.0, 500.0, 500.0, 500.0, 500.0, 500.0, 500.0,
    500.0, 500.0, 500.0, 333.0, 333.0, 570.0, 570.0, 570.0, 500.0, 930.0, 722.0,
    667.0, 722.0, 722.0, 667.0, 611.0, 778.0, 778.0, 369.0, 500.0, 778.0, 667.0,
    944.0, 722.0, 778.0, 611.0, 778.0, 722.0, 556.0, 667.0, 722.0, 722.0, 1000.0,
    722.0, 722.0, 667.0, 333.0, 278.0, 333.0, 581.0, 500.0,333.0, 500.0, 556.0,
    444.0, 556.0, 444.0, 333.0, 500.0, 556.0, 278.0, 333.0, 556.0, 278.0, 833.0,
    556.0, 500.0, 556.0, 556.0, 444.0, 389.0, 333.0, 556.0, 500.0, 722.0, 500.0,
    500.0, 444.0, 394.0, 220.0, 394.0, 520.0, 250.0, 250.0, 250.0, 250.0, 250.0,
    250.0, 250.0, 250.0, 250.0, 250.0, 250.0, 250.0, 250.0, 250.0, 250.0, 250.0,
    250.0, 250.0, 250.0, 250.0, 250.0, 250.0, 250.0, 250.0, 250.0, 250.0, 250.0,
    250.0, 250.0, 250.0, 250.0, 250.0, 250.0, 250.0, 333.0, 500.0, 500.0, 167.0,
    500.0, 500.0, 500.0, 500.0, 278.0, 500.0, 500.0, 333.0, 333.0, 556.0, 556.0,
    250.0, 500.0, 500.0, 500.0, 250.0, 250.0, 540.0, 350.0, 333.0, 500.0, 500.0,
    500.0, 1000.0, 1000.0, 250.0, 500.0, 250.0, 333.0, 333.0, 333.0, 333.0, 333.0,
    333.0, 333.0, 333.0, 250.0, 333.0, 333.0, 250.0, 333.0, 333.0, 333.0, 1000.0,
    250.0, 250.0, 250.0, 250.0, 250.0, 250.0, 250.0, 250.0, 250.0, 250.0, 250.0,
    250.0, 250.0, 250.0, 250.0, 250.0, 1000.0, 250.0, 300.0, 250.0, 250.0, 250.0,
    250.0, 667.0, 778.0, 1000.0, 330.0, 250.0, 250.0, 250.0, 250.0, 250.0, 722.0,
    250.0, 250.0, 250.0, 278.0, 250.0, 250.0, 278.0, 500.0, 722.0, 556.0, 250.0,
    250.0, 250.0, 250.0,
    };

void setFontWidth( char *name, float ps )
{
    /* the real function would access an AFM file
     * based on the font name,
     * collect the font width information in a table,
     * compute the actual character widths at the desired point size,
     * and store the result in the external array 'float  cwi[256]'
     */
```

```
        int i;

        for (i = 0; i < 256; i++)
                cwi[i] = (TMSBOLD[i] * ps) / 1000;

        /* now set the font and point size for the application's use  */
        PSselectfont(name, ps);
        return(0);
}

float strWidth( char *string )
{
        int i;
        float strw = 0;

        for (i = 0; i < strlen(string); i++)
                strw += cwi[ string[i] ];

        return(strw);

}
```

The first function, setFontWidth, performs several functions. In an application, it would access the external file system, find the requested font metric file, and load the character widths into a table for further processing. (Example code in standard C to perform this function can be obtained from Developer Support at Adobe Systems.) Since this code is dependent on the exact operating environment, we have substituted a simple table of character widths for the Times-Bold font. Because we are working with normal roman fonts, this table contains only x width values; if you were doing more elaborate calculations or using non-roman fonts, you could get a two-dimensional array that included both x and y values. This is exactly the type of table you would generate from the font metric files. Once the character width information is collected into an array, you can adjust the character widths to the correct widths for the given point size by multiplying the width by the point size and dividing it by 1000. The corrected widths are saved in an external array for use by the second function. The setFontWidth function sets the current font in the PostScript environment to the desired font, using the PSselectfont call.

The second function, strWidth, provides the length of a given string, based on the adjusted character widths provided by setFontWidth. This is a straightforward function that simply looks up each character in the width table, using the character as an integer index into the array, and accumulates the resulting widths into a variable that is then returned to the calling application as the desired result.

Simple Text Calculations Now that you see how to determine the string width from your application, it becomes quite easy to perform some basic calculations to position strings on the display or output page. Let's look at two common calculations that you will use in the next exercise: centering and right justifying a given string.

The first use of the string width is to center a string at a given point. This can be done using calculations similar to those you saw above for centering between margins; in this case, however, the trick is to calculate one-half the width of the string, subtract that value from the desired point, and then show the string at the calculated position. Once you know where you want to display the string, the actual display can be done with PSWmovetoShow. With that in mind, here is the code to center a string:

```
void centerText ( float xpos, y, char *string )
{
    float x;

    x = xpos - (strWidth(string) / 2);
    PSWmovetoShow(x, y, string);

    return(0);
}
```

Providing right justification to a defined margin point is a common and useful trick. Again, once you know the width of the string, the calculation becomes easy. You simply subtract the length of the string from the desired point and then show the string at the new location. The end of the string will be at exactly the specified right margin, as illustrated in the following code.

```
void rightJustify ( float xpos, y, char *string )
{
    float x;

    x = xpos - strWidth(string);
    PSWmovetoShow(x, y, string);
```

```
        return (0);
}
```

Now we proceed to use these new functions in another exercise.

Setup Analysis

This exercise might be analyzed in several ways; don't think that the approach given here is the only correct one. In fact, most reasonable tasks can be approached in a variety of ways, all essentially correct and yet each distinct. The approach shown here is especially suitable for prototyping displays. You would typically use other techniques for production applications; we will discuss these techniques in Chapter 4. You will develop your own methods as you become more familiar with page layout problems. This is only one successful approach to the problem.

You must now develop a layout of the page in sufficient detail that you can program it. I do this by working out the procedures required to actually output the page. Remember in all of the discussion that follows that we are assuming that you will be displaying a screen of output with dimensions of at least 8 inches wide by 6 inches high, either directly or by scrolling.

The first output is the heading. You will set this as Times-Bold, 16-point type on 20-point leading. There are two lines of heading, which are to be centered on the page, between the left and right margins. The left and right margins are to be 0.5 inch from either edge; this gives a left margin of 0.5 inch and a right margin of 7.5 inches, based on the left edge of the window. This portion of the layout is shown in Figure 2-2.

Figure 2-2. Heading layout.

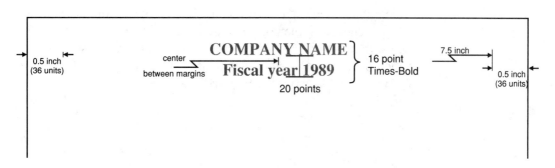

The paragraph titles are to be in the first column, as in the second and third exercises. The first column is to be right justified on a margin 2 inches from the left margin, which is 2.5 inches from the left edge of the window. There will be 0.5 inch between the paragraph titles and the text of the paragraphs. This means that the body-text begins at an offset of 3 inches from the left edge of the window. The second column will be 4 inches in width, ending at the right margin. These dimensions are illustrated in Figure 2-3.

Figure 2-3. Body layout.

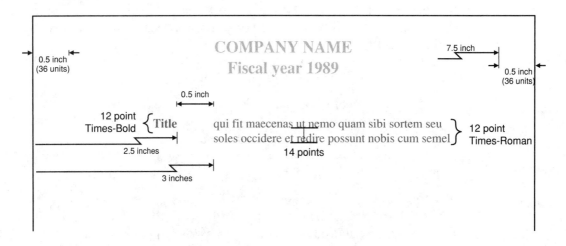

You will use Times-Roman for the body of the text and Times-Bold for the paragraph titles; both set in 12-point type on 14-point leading. Space between the paragraphs within the body-text is again two lines, or 28 points.

The heading on the page is to begin 0.5 inch from the top of the window, which is 5.5 inches from the bottom edge. The text and titles are to begin 1 inch below that, which is 4.5 inches from the bottom. All these numbers will be incorporated into named constants for the program. This final portion of the layout is shown in Figure 2-4.

Figure 2-4. Overall structure.

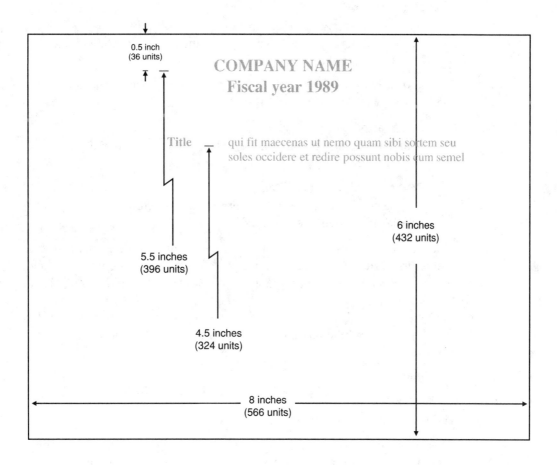

Wrap Definitions

For this exercise, we adopt the approach of doing a portion of the text-setting calculations in your PostScript code, although you do not generally want to perform such calculations in PostScript. However, this exercise illustrates some important points about how you can both send and return values from your PostScript wraps and shows you how to define and use procedures that are internal to your PostScript code. For these reasons, this exercise moves the line advance code into the PostScript application. In previous exercises you saw how to do this in C; here, you learn how you might do it in PostScript.

This method gives us one new wrap:

> PSWbodyText(char *Str)
> sets a text string (as an argument) for the body-text of the page. Then advances to the next line of text, using the leading value from an external variable.

Two additional procedures are required to perform functions supporting the PSWbodyText wrap:

> PSWsetUp()
> defines the constants and procedures that are required for the display wrap.
>
> PSWnextPar(| float SavPara)
> sets the position of the next body paragraph and returns the y coordinate for future reference.

Note the three major points of difference here. First, these wraps both take and return arguments. Second, since you can send and receive arguments, the y coordinate of each paragraph position is returned to the application, which is then responsible for setting the value correctly when it displays the heading and body-text. Third, the wrap PSWbodyText requires a PostScript function to advance to the next line; this function is defined as follows:

> advanceLine
> increments the current line position by the constant for leading.

and is delimited in the setup wrap.

This naturally leads us to the definitions of the wraps laid out above. Enter these wrap definitions into your project files as a single wrap procedure file:

```
defineps PSWbodyText(char *Str)
    (Str) show
    advanceLine
endps

defineps PSWnextPar( | float *SavPara)
    % first advance an additional line for double space
    advanceLine
    % then return the current y coord to calling program
    currentpoint
```

```
    SavPara pop
endps

defineps PSWsetUP()
    % first define auxiliary procedure
    /advanceLine
        {
        LEFTCOLUMN
        currentpoint exch pop
        LEADING sub
        moveto
        }
    def
    % now define constants
    /LEADING 14 def
    /LEFTCOLUMN 3 72 mul def
endps
```

Displaying the Report

With the wraps defined, you can proceed to the C code. You must include the C procedures that we developed earlier for string width calculations, text centering, and right justification. These can be combined with this function as one large file or compiled separately and included with this file when you run it. If you choose the second option, you will want to define a header file to pass the function's prototypes and the external constants to this file. In either case, the display mechanism is contained in the function runPSInline.

If you don't want to create and link the routines previously presented to calculate the width of a text string, use the code shown below, which contains the correct string widths as a comment. You can adjust the x coordinate for the display by these values and then use PSWmovetoShow instead of the routines shown to get the equivalent display.

```
void runPSInline(void)
{
    int i;
    float x, y;
    float save_y[4];

    char *textArray1[ ] =      /* first text block */
```

```
        {
                "Acme Software was founded in 1982 by Dippy and Daffy Acme",
                "    ...    ",
                "    ...    ",
                "    ...    ",
                "    ...    "
        };
        char *textArray2[ ] =        /* second text block */
        {
                "Acme Software sells exclusively to vertical markets",
                "  ...  ",
                "  ...  ",
                "  ...  "
        };
        char *textArray3[ ] =        /* third text block */
            {
                "Headquarters: Palo Alto, California",
                "  ...  "
        };
        char *textArray4[ ] =        /* fourth text block */
            {
                "$17 million in gross revenue for fiscal 1988.",
                "  ...  "
        };

        char *headings[ ] =        /* margin headings block */
            {
                "History:",              /* width is 42.66 */
                "Market Position:",      /* width is 86.988 */
                "Offices:",              /* width is 39.984 */
                "Financial Position:"    /* width is 96.348 */
        };

        PSWsetUp();
        setFontWidth("Times-Bold", 16.0);

        x = (((7.5 * 72) - (.5 * 72)) / 2) + (.5 * 72);
        y = (5.5 * 72);

        /* string width for "ACME SOFTWARE" is 144.448 */
```

```
centerText(x, y, "ACME SOFTWARE");

y -= 20;
/* string width for "Fiscal Year 1989" is 113.76 */
centerText(x, y, "Fiscal Year 1989");

PSselectfont("Times-Roman", 12.0);
for (i = 0; i < 5; i++)
    PSWbodyText( textArray1[i] );
PSWnextPar( &save_y[0] );
for (i = 0; i < 4; i++)
    PSWbodyText( textArray2[i] );
PSWnextPar( &save_y[1] );
for (i = 0; i < 2; i++)
    PSWbodyText( textArray3[i] );
PSWnextPar( &save_y[2] );
for (i = 0; i < 2; i++)
    PSWbodyText( textArray4[i] );
PSWnextPar( &save_y[3] );

setFontWidth("Times-Bold", 12.0);
for (i = 0; i < 4; i++)
    {
    x = (2.5 * 72) - strWidth( heading[i] );
    rightJustifyText( x, save_y[i], heading[i] );
    }

return(0);
}
```

You should now run this procedure as you have the preceding ones, and you should get an output something like Figure 2-5.

Figure 2-5. Business report output.

ACME SOFTWARE
Fiscal Year 1989

History:	Acme Software was founded in 1982 by Dippy and Daffy Acme ... ...
Market Position:	Acme Software sells exclusively to vertical markets ... ...
Offices:	Headquarters: Palo Alto, California ...
Financial Position:	$17 million in gross revenue for fiscal 1988. ...

Discussion and Review

Although runPSInline is rather long, it is quite straightforward. You have already looked at the wrap definitions in some detail, and the general outline of the C processing is quite similar (by design) to the previous exercise. However, you may still want to review a few points.

First, notice that this procedure uses the simple calculation of the design coordinates, which were in inches, multiplied by a constant, in this case 72, to give the correct PostScript coordinates. By changing the value of the constant, you can easily change the translation value. Of course, the best way to do this would be through a C *#define* in a header and a matching constant in the PSWsetUp procedure; however, here I have opted for the simplest form of constant.

Second, the first value of the float variable, x, is calculated as the difference between the left and right margins—as inches times 72 again—divided by 2. This gives the half-width of the space between the margins. This result is then added to the left margin to give the correct position for the center point. This seems more understandable than simply inserting the correct value. The same considerations apply to the calculations for y and for x later; in all cases, the calculations have been done in as obvious a fashion as possible. Also, as you can see in all the calculations, I am a great believer in parenthesizing to ensure the desired calculation order. Feel free to use your own C style if it is different—as long as you get the same result, of course.

The final point to note is that, in a real program, you would probably be getting your text input from some other procedure, which would be getting it from keyboard or file input streams. We have avoided all that here by using a lot of dummy lines in the display in order to focus on Display PostScript and not worry about the various C functions. Nevertheless, you should notice how these functions naturally fall into patterns that would easily integrate with such input functions.

MANAGING DISPLAY POSTSCRIPT RESOURCES

As you might imagine, the PostScript system involves a substantial amount of resources from the host system. To a great degree, the PostScript host manages these resources in a manner that is hidden from the application program. In basic PostScript programming, the only resource that is left for the application to manage is the use of virtual memory. In Display PostScript, however, things become somewhat more complex. Here, memory is joined with other resources such as processing tasking, and all of these may be subject to some control by the application. The system still provides a great amount of management, and for most purposes it is quite sufficient. In this section, you will learn about these resources and something about how they are managed.

Contexts

One obvious issue in resources is how the Display PostScript system supports many PostScript programs, which may be executing at the same, or virtually the same, time. This ability is essential for an environment where multiple application programs share a common window structure and display system. Using the same language features, it is also possible for a single application to use multiple, concurrent processes; for example, a text editing application might have several windows with different text files open at once. In either case, language features that allow such processes must be provided.

Display PostScript performs this small sleight of hand by using execution contexts, which provide the facilities for multiple, concurrent processes. A Display PostScript *execution context*—more usually simply referred to as a *context*—is a collection of all the objects and procedures that are visible to or affect an executing PostScript program. This includes the following items:

- An independent thread of control. Multiple threads can process concurrently.

- A complete set of all the PostScript stacks: an operand stack, a dictionary stack, a graphics state stack, and an execution stack. From these, a program can access all objects and conditions that are available to a PostScript program, for example, dictionaries, paths, and files.

- A private memory space, called *private Virtual Memory*.

- A shared virtual memory space, which is uniformly visible to all contexts.

- Standard input and output files, which are the primary means of communication between the Display PostScript system and the application program.

- Miscellaneous state variables, which are internal to the Display PostScript system. These include variables to control the garbage collection mechanism, the current view clipping path, array packing, and so on. When a new context is created, all these variables are set to their default values for that context.

Although contexts require resources to operate, they don't require management in the same way that, for example, memory resources do. In most Display PostScript programming, you can simply create a context for a display when you need one, and then free it when you are done. This is easily and naturally accomplished with the Display PostScript operators and procedures and does not generally require a lot of thought or concern on the part of the application programmer.

Usually, you have the situation of one application to one context, with Display PostScript managing the multiple executions. In such cases, each context has its own private virtual memory, or *space*, which is entirely separate from all other contexts that are executing. In this case, contexts can only interact by deliberately using the shared virtual memory area through such operators as **setshared**. Unless an object is deliberately placed into shared virtual memory, using such facilities, *userdict* and all composite objects that are created within the context remain only visible and accessible to that context. In this situation, you can simply regard a context as a private "virtual printer."

It is possible for an application, or several applications, to deliberately share one or several contexts, using special Display PostScript language facilities. Basically such coordination revolves around the use of synchronization operators and objects. Correct use of these features is quite advanced and is not generally recommended practice, and we will not discuss it here. Although some additional issues in this area are discussed in Chapter 6, the complete and definitive reference is contained in the *Extensions for the Display PostScript System* manual.

The context of operation is identified to the application by a *context identifier*, which is an integer value that uniquely identifies that context. Generally an application addresses the *current context* in all its operations unless it is specifically managing multiple contexts. The Display PostScript system does provide facilities for addressing contexts other than the current context.

The context identifier is used during communication between the application and the Display PostScript system. The context identifier is guaranteed to be unique during its own life and for the life of any currently executing context. A context can be created, suspended, or merged with another context. A context may terminate deliberately, or it may be terminated by an error. When a context terminates, all its stacks, dictionaries, and other private objects are destroyed. Its input and output files are closed, terminating communication with the application, and its context identifier can no longer be used.

The Client Library has procedures that allow you to send information to a specific context. It also has specific functions that can be used to create, manage, and terminate contexts.

Private and Shared Virtual Memory

The most interesting and important feature of contexts is the access and use of private and shared virtual memory. In a PostScript printer, managing memory was the sole responsibility of the application, and it was done in a very straightforward way. Memory was consumed by creating composite objects, and all memory used in this process was lost until the end of the program. This memory could only be recovered by the use of a **save**, **restore** pair of operators. The **save** operator took a picture of the virtual memory at a given point during the execution, and the matching **restore** returned memory to that state, effectively wiping out any composite objects created in between the two operations and recovering the virtual memory that they had used.

This approach was adequate for PostScript printers and still has some validity in the Display PostScript environment. However, Display PostScript provides additional facilities to handle the requirements of a display environment. The basic problem in a display environment is that the applications do not have such a structured life as they would in a printing environment. In a printer, the application creates its output and is done. In a display, the application potentially may create a part of a display, wait for some external event, and then continue with some subsequent display, and so on for some indefinite time. Although additional control of memory resources would be helpful in the printer, it is not required. In the display environment, however, such detailed control is required to allow the program to adequately manage the available memory in smaller and better defined units. The net result is that a display environment requires two additional facilities for managing memory and objects. These are *garbage collection* and *undefining objects*.

Garbage collection is the process of reclaiming the memory that was once used by composite objects that are no longer accessible to the current PostScript program. These are objects therefore that do not appear in the current stacks and are not connected to another composite object that is available. Garbage collection takes place independently of the application and is generally invisible to it. The application does exercise some control, however. It may specifically control the garbage collector through the **vmreclaim** operator, and it may adjust the automatic operation through the **setvmthreshold** operator. For our purposes here, the normal automatic operations are quite sufficient and effective; if you need to use these advanced features, they are fully described in *Extensions for the Display PostScript System*.

Of more interest to the ordinary application is the newly available **undef** operator. This operator works somewhat in the reverse fashion to the **def** operator that you met earlier. It removes a definition of a specified (key, value) pair from a specified dictionary. In this way, the space in the dictionary may be reclaimed. Here it is in the standard format:

    dict key   **undef**   —
    removes *key* and its associated value from the *dict* dictionary.

Note that, since the dictionary must be provided as an operand, it does not need to be on the dictionary stack. Conversely, just because it is on the dictionary stack doesn't enable **undef** to find the key; you must specify the correct dictionary as an operand.

This brings us to the original, and still available, process on memory management in PostScript. This is done through the matching operators, **save** and **restore**. These operators provide the means for the PostScript program to reclaim virtual memory in a static situation.

Consider the traditional basic PostScript program. In this case, the program keeps some indication of where it is in processing output. When a specific unit of output has been created and printed (usually a page), the application program recovers the virtual memory that was required to create that output. This can most easily be accomplished by invoking the two PostScript operators: **save** and **restore**. These operators have the following format:

    —   **save**   savestate
    saves the current state of the PostScript virtual memory as *savestate*.

    savestate   **restore**   —
    restores PostScript virtual memory to the state indicated by *savestate*.

Since the **restore** returns to the state presented to it as an operand, it is usually easiest and best to **save** the current state as a named variable and **restore** that specific variable. If a **save** is performed at the beginning of each output unit, and a **restore** is performed at the end of each to the state saved at the beginning, then each unit is necessarily independent of any other. In addition, all the virtual memory that was consumed by objects created in the process of making this output are recovered.

The **save** and **restore** operators are equally available in Display PostScript, but are not equally useful. This happens primarily because a unit of output is no longer so easily identified. Moreover, incorrect use of **save** and **restore** can undo the effects of some of the other memory management mechanisms. In particular, you cannot discard an object that may be recovered by a **restore**. Therefore, if you want to recover memory resources through the garbage collection mechanism, either explicitly through **undef** or automatically through recovery of composite objects that can no longer be referenced, you need to remain at a single save level throughout your program.

For example, suppose you create an array called "MyArray"—which is a composite object and so consumes virtual memory—and store it in the current dictionary. You save the state of virtual memory with a **save** operator, and then use an **undef** to remove MyArray from the current dictionary. Now, under normal processing, you cannot recover MyArray, so you might think that it would be reclaimed by the garbage collector. Not so, however, since you might execute a **restore**. Since the **save** took a picture of virtual memory at a time when MyArray existed, the **restore** can bring MyArray back. Since you can recover it in this fashion, the memory consumed by MyArray cannot be recovered. It can only be recovered if you **restore** and then perform an **undef**. In that case, since the object was created and undefined at the same save level, it can be recovered.

As you can see, this is quite a complex matter to delve into. Since the automatic mechanisms in Display PostScript work quite well, we will stick to them. In fact, all of these issues are very complex, and we have hardly skimmed the surface of them. You should take away from this discussion the following five points:

1. Each Display PostScript operation takes place in its own context, which means that it has its own set of critical variables and stacks.

2. Contexts may be referenced by their context identifier, which is a unique integer.

3. An application typically creates one context for all of its imaging, but it can create, manage, and coordinate multiple contexts if required.

4. You can share objects between contexts by using shared virtual memory.

5. You can remove definitions from a dictionary by using the **undef** operator. When properly executed, this can release virtual memory resources for recovery by the garbage collection mechanism.

Screen Management Concepts

The Client Library contains the procedures that provide access to the PostScript interpreter for an application. The Client Library also includes procedures for creating, communicating with, controlling, and destroying PostScript execution contexts. The Client Library system supports applications by functions that are available to the application through a series of C header files. We discussed these headers a little bit in the earlier section, where you began to create wraps with both input and output arguments. There are six procedure interfaces, or header files, five of which are standard and one of which is system dependent. These header files are as follows:

- *dpsclient.h* This header file provides functions that support managing PostScript contexts and sending data or programs directly to the PostScript interpreter. It is most often used by application toolkits, but can be used directly by an application.

- *dpsfriends.h* This header file provides a low-level interface for wrapped procedures and additional support for context management at the lowest level. The procedures in this library are not generally used by application programs, but are normally accessed indirectly by using *pswrap*, which uses them to send and receive information from the context.

- *dpsexcept.h* This header file defines the functions that support and implement the general exception and error handlers.

- *dpsops.h* This header file provides single operator PostScript functions that explicitly take a Display PostScript context identifier.

- *psops.h* This header file provides single operator PostScript functions that implicitly take the current context. These are the functions that you have been using so far.

The system-dependent header file contains procedures that are specific to the environment that you are working in. These are usually system-specific extensions for support of special system features. For obvious reasons, we will not be covering these features here.

The functions in *psops.h* and *dpsops.h* are essentially identical in function. You are already familiar with the functions in *psops.h* and how they are named. As you know, the names of these functions are the names of the associated PostScript operator, with the letters "PS" as a prefix. The functions in *dpsops.h* are named in a similar way, but with the prefix "DPS". Each one of these functions also requires a context identifier as its first argument. This means that all functions that begin with "DPS" require at least one input argument, which is the context identifier.

Finally, you should know that you also can write wraps that access a specific context, just like the wraps in *dpsops.h*. Such wraps are coded exactly like the ordinary wraps that you have written, but have the context identifier as their first (or only) input argument. The context identifier must be of type DPSContext, and it must be the first input argument. Also, unlike a regular procedure input argument, the context identifier is not directly referenced in the wrap body. It is used by the *pswrap* output to set the correct context for the wrap.

As an example, let's look at how the PSWsetUp wrap would be coded to use a specific context identifier. For consistency, you should change the name to DPSWsetUp. The result would look like this:

```
defineps DPSWsetUP( DPSContext ctx)
    % first define auxiliary procedures
```

and so on with the rest of the wrap, which would remain unchanged. The C code associated with this might look as follows:

```
#include <dpsclient.h>
/* required to access the context-specific functions */
...
DPSContext context;
...
context = DPSGetCurrentContext();
...
DPSWsetUp( context );
...
```

Alternatively, you can set the current context explicitly using functions from the Client Library, and then just use the procedures that we have defined. Finally, remember that most environments automatically set a default context for you, so that you do not necessarily need to specify a context value as long as you are working in the default context.

This completes our look at the support functions in the Client Library and our work in this chapter. In Chapter 3, we will use additional PostScript operations to create graphic output.

CONCLUSION

In this chapter, as in the preceding chapter, you have learned some important information and done some exercises. However, unlike Chapter 1, the exercises here have been subordinate to and in support of the process of learning the necessary concepts and definitions. The first concept presented here was the nature, creation, and use of PostScript dictionaries. This discussion, divided into two sections, told you what a dictionary is, what the various dictionaries do, and how to create and use them to store and retrieve objects.

The second concept in this chapter was that of PostScript procedure construction and use. This is directly related to dictionaries because procedures are named, stored, and executed from dictionaries. The ability to create and use procedures along with the ability to store and retrieve variables and constants makes your wraps much more useful, as the exercises showed you.

You have now been introduced to most of the basic PostScript concepts that you require to use Display PostScript. In all of this, you have only used text as an output vehicle, to show you how to create procedures, wraps, and so on. Chapter 3 allows you to branch out, building on these concepts, and produce pictures as well as text.

C H A P T E R 3

Text and Graphics

This chapter introduces a variety of PostScript graphics concepts and operators, including straight line segments and circular arcs. It also provides a formal introduction to PostScript fonts, which have so far only been used informally. The chapter also examines the intertwined issues of flexibility and independence, which are important aspects of PostScript programming.

DISPLAY POSTSCRIPT IMAGING MODEL

Display PostScript was designed to extend the powerful graphics capabilities of the PostScript imaging model to display devices. As such, it incorporates all the facilities of PostScript and provides a few additional touches that speed up and enhance graphics in a display environment. In the following sections, you will learn about how PostScript goes about creating images. Where the concepts apply to PostScript generally, the discussion will center on PostScript images, and where the concepts apply only to Display PostScript, I will mention that explicitly.

You have already been introduced to the PostScript graphics concept of "painting" a graphic image onto an output device. This is an intuitive way to think about graphics; and this conceptual model of graphic output is satisfactory because, to a great extent, it follows what graphic designers and artists actually do as they work. However, the computer and its associated output devices do not actually work in this way; being machines, they require precise mathematical directions.

I make this point simply to prepare you for the necessary intrusion of certain mathematical concepts into portions of the material presented here. By design, PostScript graphics operators insulate the user from most mathematical considerations. There is, however, an irreducible minimum of mathematics that must be taken into consideration in making particular graphics objects. Take a circle as a simple illustration. When an artist goes to draw a circle on a piece of paper, he or she need only pick the place and draw the circle. To create a circle on a computer screen, however, requires two pieces of mathematical data: a radius (or diameter) and a center. This is what I mean by an "irreducible minimum" of mathematics.

To continue with the circle as an example, the PostScript language does not have a simple operator that produces a circle. Instead, PostScript has operators that produce arcs, arbitrary segments of a circle, which are both more general and more useful than a circle operator would be. These operators can then be used to generate a circle, given the correct operands. In fact, even the arcs are special cases of the most general PostScript operators for making curved line segments, which you will learn about later in this chapter.

PostScript Graphics Concepts

At this point, you are familiar with the basic PostScript output structure and the output space coordinate system from your previous reading and exercises. Let's quickly review these concepts and introduce one new one that will help you master this material.

PostScript operates on an ideal output space, called the current page. Positions on the page are given by x and y coordinates that work like the standard mathematical coordinate system. The default origin, the point (0, 0), is in the bottom left corner of the page. Positive movement in the x coordinate moves horizontally to the right, whereas positive movement in the y coordinate is vertically up the page. The default coordinate units are 1/72 inch.

PostScript creates images on the page by tracing a current path, which can then be made visible on the page by "painting" it using one or more of the special painting operators. The end of the current path is the current point. So far in the exercises, you have not actually dealt with the current path; you have only moved the current point around the page to govern the positioning of text output. Working with a specific current path wasn't necessary because the **show** operator, which you have used to create the text output, handles these issues automatically. Now that you will be starting to produce graphics, you need additional information, along with more operators, to deal with the current path.

The current path can be composed of both straight and curved line segments. These segments may be joined together or they may be separate; a segment may even consist of a single point. The path may close or cross itself in any arbitrary way, creating enclosed areas or figures on the output space. Remember that the current path itself is never visible; it is only made visible when used by the painting operators to define an output area.

The current path may also be used to define other regions on the output page. The most important of these is the *current clipping path*. The clipping path controls where objects may be visible on the output display. All or part of an object that falls within the current clipping path is displayed; anything that falls outside is not displayed.

DISPLAY POSTSCRIPT BASIC GRAPHICS OPERATORS

You have already become familiar with several of the most basic PostScript operators that affect the current path; for example, **moveto** sets the current point to a given coordinate position, and **show** paints a given text string onto the page at the current point. You are also familiar with the Client Library single operator procedures that match these operators and with the wrapped versions of them. The operators and the procedure that you develop in the following sections are all quite similar to those that you have learned previously. Note, in particular, that all the new operators can also be used and are available in both forms. In the following exercises, we use the form that is most suitable for the operation at hand, without explicitly mentioning that the alternative form is available.

Using Line Operators

Obviously not all output is text; and, if text were all you wanted or needed to display, you could find many ways other than Display PostScript to create it. In this section, you begin to develop your PostScript vocabulary by learning to draw simple straight lines. Actually, as you will soon discover, even a simple straight line has its subtle points.

For the first exercise, open a window that is at least 4 inches by 4 inches. In this window, draw two lines at right angles. These lines begin at a point 1 inch from the left edge of the display and 1 inch from the bottom edge; the lines are to be 2 inches long. This can be easily done using the following C code and the procedures in the Client Library.

```
void runPSInline( void)
{
    float x, y;
    float width;
    /* first line begins at (72, 72) */
    x = y = 72.0;
    PSmoveto( x, y);
    /* and goes horizontally to ( 3*72, 72) */
    x = 3*72        /* 3 inches */
    PSlineto( x, y);
    PSstroke();
    PSnewpath();
    /* make second line thicker than first */
    width = 36.0;
    PSsetlinewidth(width);
    /* second line also begins at (72, 72) */
    x = y = 72;
    PSmoveto( x, y);
    /* and goes vertically to (72, 3*72) */
    y = 3*72;
    PSlineto( x, y);
    PSstroke();
}
```

This is really a very straightforward program; probably you have already been able to see how it works. It begins by defining the *x, y,* and *width* variables. These are all float values and are designated here primarily as mnemonic devices; as you see, you could replace them with the exact values if you wanted. This procedure uses all single operator functions to do its work. It begins with the familiar PSmoveto, using *x* and *y* set to 72.0 (1 inch) as arguments. It then resets *x* to a 3-inch value—since the line starts at 1 inch and goes for 2 inches—while leaving the *y* value the same.

Now you come to a new operator, **lineto,** and its associated single operator function, PSlineto. Like **moveto, lineto** takes two coordinate values, an *x* and a *y*. It then constructs a line segment from the current point to the designated point and adds that new segment to the current path. In this case, this is the first segment in the current path, and it extends from the point (72, 72) or (1 inch, 1 inch) to the point (3*72, 72) or (3 inch, 1 inch). At the end of this, the current point is left at the far end of the line, at (3*72, 72). If you wanted to add another line segment to the current path, you would not need another **moveto** to set the current point. In this example, once the line is constructed, you simply use the **stroke** operator by calling the single operator function, PSstroke, to paint the current path with its single line segment onto the display. This makes the line visible on the display.

Next you issue the **newpath** operator. This operator, as its name implies, clears the current path by erasing any old segments. In this case, there are, in fact, no line segments and no current path. This occurs because the **stroke** operator erases the current path as it paints it. Nevertheless, it is good practice to start new graphics with a **newpath** operation so that, if there has been some error or oversight, you still get only the output that you intend. Remember that a **stroke** paints all the segments of the current path, so if there are any additional, unwanted segments hanging around when it executes, you get unintended marks on your output. Therefore, starting with a **newpath** is generally good practice.

This is followed by setting the float variable width to 36.0, before calling another new operator, **setlinewidth,** through its single operator function, PSsetlinewidth. This operator sets the width of the current line to the given number in coordinate units. At first glance, it may not be at all clear why you do this. Let's examine the process of painting a line onto the display. The **stroke** operator marks or paints a line following the current path; in this example, a simple horizontal or vertical line. The current path, however, like any mathematical construct, has no width; effectively, the path is 0 units wide. When you **stroke** the path, it must have some width. The default width in PostScript is 1 unit, and this is the width that is used for the first line in the exercise. However, you can set the width to any positive number that you want, even to 0, by using the **setlinewidth** operator. In this case, you set the line width to 36 units, or 0.5 inch (assuming the default coordinate units of 1/72 inch are in use).

As an aside, if you do set the line width to 0, PostScript paints a line 1 pixel in width because that is the smallest line that it can create that still exists. This can be quite useful as a "hairline" for some applications. However, it does limit your output choices, since a 1-pixel line on a 72 or 94 dpi screen is quite a bit thicker, proportionally, than the same line on a 300 or 400 dpi printer, whereas a 1-pixel line on an imagesetter (at 1260 or 2540 dpi) is functionally invisible. Such device dependencies are lazy programming; if you want a hairline, specify a line of, say, 0.005 units (about 1/200 inch). This allows the interpreter to use a single-pixel line on displays, perhaps two pixels on a medium-resolution device, and a thicker line on higher resolution devices, so that the line remains about the same apparent size relative to other lines and remains visible on all devices.

After setting the line width, the program continues to draw the second line in a fashion similar to the first line, moving 2 inches vertically this time, instead of horizontally. The output on the screen should look something like Figure 3-1.

Figure 3-1. Line operator example output.

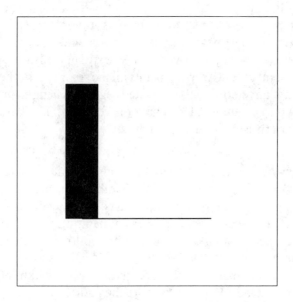

The next example is a variation on this same theme. It marks two X's on the display, along the same line, 1 inch from the bottom of the page. Both will be 1 inch high and 1 inch wide, with the first X starting 0.5 inch from the left edge of the display, and the second X starting 0.5 inch from the right edge of the first X.

Figure 3-2. Layout for first X.

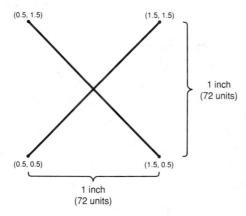

Before you begin coding, let's review Figure 3-2. This figure lays out the coordinates of each line of the first X. Rather arbitrarily, we draw the first line of the X from bottom to top, starting at the bottom left corner, and then top to bottom for the second line. Then we move over 0.5 inch and draw the second X in the same fashion. Note the coordinates for each of the lines that form the X. In inches, the first line has the coordinates (0.5, 0.5) for the bottom left corner to (1.5, 1.5) for the top right corner, whereas the second line goes from (0.5, 1.5) for the top left corner to (1.5, 0.5) on the bottom left. The choice of ends and order of drawing are, of course, almost arbitrary. As you will see, however, there is one reason to do the lines in this direction and order. The following code draws the two X's on the display.

```
void runPSInline( void )
{
    float x, y;
    float delx, dely;

    PSnewpath();
```

```
    x = y = 0.5*72;
    PSmoveto(x, y);
    x = y = 1.5*72;
    PSlineto(x, y);
    x = 0.5*72;
    y = 1.5*72;
    PSmoveto(x, y);
    x = 1.5*72;
    y = 0.5*72;
    PSlineto(x, y);
    /* don't stroke yet, first make second X */
    delx = 0.5*72,
    dely = 0;
    PSrmoveto(delx, dely);
    delx = dely = 72.0;
    PSrlineto(delx, dely);
    delx = -72.0;
    dely = 0;
    PSrmoveto(delx, dely);
    delx = 72.0;
    dely = -72.0;
    PSrlineto(delx, dely);
    /* now stroke all segments - both X */
    PSstroke();
}
```

The output of this two X example is shown in Figure 3-3.

Figure 3-3. Output from two X example.

As before, you start the path construction with the **newpath** operator. Then, as you probably gathered from Figure 3-2, you **moveto** the bottom left corner of the first X, draw a line up to the top right using **lineto,** move across to the top left corner, and draw a line down to finish the X. So far, so good.

Now you could lay out the second X in the same fashion as the first one, by calculating the coordinates and then **moveto, lineto,** and so on. However, this is not a very general method. Better, and more useful, would be to have a general wrap that creates a 1 inch by 1 inch X. But how to do it? The second X shows you the sort of code that can be reused and therefore easily moved into a wrapped procedure. It uses some new operators, for *relative movement,* which is movement relative to the current point instead of movement to a fixed coordinate on the page.

Notice, first of all, that you haven't stroked the first path. You don't want to because it would remove the current point and you would lose the basis for relative motion. There is no requirement that you stroke paths at any particular point; a path to be stroked—or for anything else—can consist of multiple, unjoined segments, as it does here. In fact, there is a significant performance improvement in delaying the stroke so that multiple subpaths are painted at one time. Naturally, all the subpaths must have the same characteristics of size, color, and so on. With the current point at the bottom right corner of the first X, you know from the specification that you want to move 0.5 inch to the right for the next X. So you issue the **rmoveto** (relative moveto) operator to move the distance given by the argument values *delx* and *dely*. In this case, you want to move 0.5 inch in the *x* direction and not at all in the *y* direction.

Next you make the two lines for the X in the same manner as you did earlier, only this time using relative displacements instead of drawing and moving to fixed coordinate positions. The results are the same, but the technique is much more general. This code could be used to draw an X at any point on the display, once you have moved the current point to the desired bottom left corner point.

To see how this works, let's rewrite the preceding functions using a simple PSWdrawX wrap. To make it a bit more interesting—and more general— we will make the wrap take three arguments, the *x* and *y* coordinates where you want to display the X, and one that sets the size of the X. Then the code for the wrap would look like this:

```
defineps PSWdrawX( float Xpos, Ypos, Size )
    Xpos Ypos moveto
    Size dup rlineto
    Size neg 0 rmoveto
    Size dup neg rlineto
endps
```

This looks very much like the preceding set of functions. Here the process begins by moving to the designated point and continues by pushing the *Size* argument onto the operand stack and then duplicating it. This gives the *x* and *y* coordinates for the relative motion in the first **rlineto.** Next the *Size* is again placed onto the stack and is then made into a negative number because you want to move in the negative *x* direction with a 0 *y* coordinate relative to the current point. Finally, the last line is drawn by moving the *Size* of the figure in the positive *x* direction while moving a negative *Size* in the *y* direction.

This negative movement may require a little explanation. The natural thought here might be to just place a minus sign in front of the *Size* variable, as you would in a C program, but that won't work. Normally the – (minus sign) that precedes a number is part of the number itself. However, *Size* isn't a number; it is a variable name. In such cases, languages like C use a unary minus operator to convert the variable to its negative numeric representation. PostScript, remember, does not have sign operators like + and –; PostScript operators have names and come after the value that they are operating on. And that is exactly what **neg** does: it takes a single numeric operand on the stack and converts it to the negative of that number. This gives you the negative value necessary for the coordinate movement that you want.

This wrap would then be combined with the following C code to produce the preceding figures.

```
void runPSInline( void )
{
    float x, y;
    float size;

    PSnewpath();
    size = 72.0;
    x = y = 72.0;
    PSWdrawX(x,y,size);
    x = 2.5*72;
    PSWdrawX(x,y,size);
    PSstroke();
}
```

This is obviously a cleaner, more understandable, and more general approach than that shown earlier.

To finish this section on simple lines, let's review the operators that have been introduced here and put them into our conventional format.

> num1 num2   **lineto**   —
>
> adds a straight line segment to the current path. The new line segment extends from the current point, (x, y), to the point ($num1$, $num2$). The current point at the end of the operation is the point ($num1$, $num2$).
>
> num   **setlinewidth**   —
>
> sets the current line width to *num*. This controls the thickness of the lines painted by subsequent **stroke** operators.
>
> —   **stroke**   —
>
> paints a line following the current path using the current line width.

— **newpath** —

initializes the current path to be empty and causes the current point to be undefined.

delx dely   **rmoveto**   —

moves the current point from the current point, (x, y), to the point $(x+delx, y+dely)$. Unlike the comparable **moveto** operator, the current point must be defined at the beginning of the operation.

delx dely   **rlineto**   —

adds a straight line segment to the current path. The new line segment extends from the current point, (x, y), to the point $(x+delx, y+dely)$. The current point at the end of the operation is the point $(x+delx, y+dely)$.

Creating Closed Paths

Now that you can draw straight lines, let's use those lines to make some figures. Closed figures are just a collection of lines (straight or curved) that finish at the same point where they began. Figures of this type are certainly some of the most typical graphic elements, and PostScript has several operators to help you construct and display them.

The first example in this section draws squares at various points on the page; and all dimensions, as before, are in inches. This example takes advantage of some of the features of your previous work to make the squares at different positions on the display.

In the first example, you draw a 1-inch square with its bottom left corner at the point (0.5, 0.5), that is, 0.5 inch from both the bottom edge of the window and from the left edge of the window. Then you move to the point (3, 0.5) and draw a box that is tilted toward the left, so that the bottom of the box is a line from (3, 0.5) to the point (4, 1.5), similar to the X that you drew earlier. Finally, you draw a square at the point (0.5, 2.5) that has a width of 1.5 inches. The layout of these three squares is shown in Figure 3-4.

Figure 3-4. Layout for square box example.

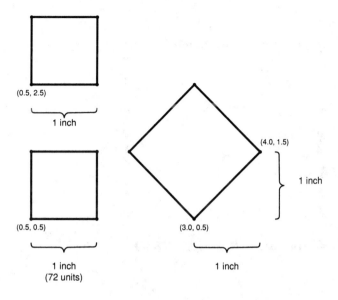

The essence of any closed figure is that the original line returns to its starting point. To close a figure, PostScript provides a special operator: **closepath.** There is a particular reason to use this operator to close a figure, but it is not entirely obvious. You saw before how PostScript paints a line with a stroke of some defined width. That width, appropriately enough, lies equally on both sides of the defining path line. In other words, the points that define the line are in the middle of the actual stroke. Since a line begins and ends precisely at designated points, which are in the middle of the stroke, if you simply return a path to its starting point and then paint it, you leave a small space at the end of the line—where it joins the original line—that is not filled in. This is illustrated in Figure 3-5.

Figure 3-5. Line join without closed path.

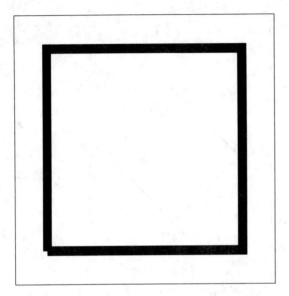

This problem is avoided by using the **closepath** operator. If you used **lineto** or any other operator to finish the figure and close the path, the interpreter assumes that these points simply fall on one another accidentally, and it does not fill in the junction. However, the **closepath** operator draws a straight line from the current point to the point where you started this part of the path and then fills in the join. The interpreter can do this because **closepath** tells it that you want to connect the first and last points explicitly. The initial point of this part of the path, called the *subpath*, is the point of the last **moveto** or the equivalent. Thus, for example, in the preceding exercise, each of the lines that formed an X would be a separate subpath since each began with a **moveto**. In your squares, each square is one subpath.

For purposes of this exercise, you will write a wrap for each of the first two squares; you will use a new PostScript operator for the third (and last) square. Each wrap begins by moving to the point that is the desired bottom left corner of the square. One wrap produces a normal square, oriented with its sides parallel to the axes; the other produces a square with its sides angled at 45 degrees to the axes. Each wrap takes a size argument in addition to the starting point coordinates. These two wraps might look something like this:

```
defineps PSWsquare( float Xpos, Ypos, Size )
    Xpos Ypos moveto
    Size 0 rlineto
    0 Size rlineto
    Size neg 0 rlineto
    closepath
    stroke
endps

defineps PSWangleSquare( float Xpos, Ypos, Size )
    Xpos Ypos rmoveto
    Size Size rlineto
    Size neg Size rlineto
    Size neg dup rlineto
    closepath
    stroke
endps
```

The bulk of these wraps should be quite familiar from the previous exercises. The first wrap, PSWsquare, simply moves the desired distance along three of the four sides; it then uses the **closepath** operator to finish the path with a straight line back to the starting point. Note here that the PSWSangleSquare wrap assumes that the current point has been correctly set outside of the wrap. In an actual program, this would be a dangerous dependency, and there are several ways you might avoid it. Here, for clarity, we will not worry about it.

With these two wraps you are now ready to write the C code to draw the designed figures.

```
void  runPSInline( void )
{
    float x, y;
    float delx, dely;
    float size;

    x = y = 0.5*72;
    size = 72;
    PSWsquare(x, y, size);
    /* back at the starting point of (0.5, 0.5) */
    delx = 2.5*72;
    dely = 0;
    PSWangleSquare(delx, dely, size);
```

```
        /* now the third square using rectstroke */
        x = 0.5*72;
        y = 2.5*72;
        PSrectstroke(x, y, size, size);
}
```

This produces the results shown in Figure 3-6.

Figure 3-6. Squares example output.

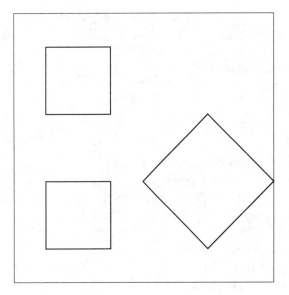

Most of this code should be quite transparent to you now. There are, however, one or two points to mention. First, note that the movement to the starting point of a subpath may be by an **rmoveto** as well as a **moveto**. Given the layout for the figures that you developed earlier, a simple **moveto** would have actually been a bit easier, but I wanted to demonstrate that you can use either form of the move to establish the starting point for the **closepath**.

This code also introduces a new operator: **rectstroke.** This operator, developed only in Display PostScript, provides a simple and fast way to draw a rectangle. As you see, the arguments required are the *x* and *y* coordinates of the bottom left corner of the rectangle, and the width and height of the rectangle—which are identical in this case because you are drawing a square. This operator, as its name implies, moves to the designated point, draws a rectangle of the desired width and height with sides parallel to the *x* and *y* axes, and then strokes that path. You can see that this is more general than the PSWsquare wrap since it takes both width and height to make an arbitrary rectangle, not a square. Because **rectstroke** and its associated Client Library procedure are optimized for this task, this is the fastest and most efficient way to draw a rectangle.

In this section, you have learned two new operators. These are summarized here in the standard format.

— **closepath** —
closes the current path by making a straight line segment from the current point to the starting point of this subpath (generally the point specified in the most recent **moveto** or **rmoveto**).

x y width height   **rectstroke** —
creates a path consisting of the rectangle whose bottom left corner point has coordinates (*x,y*) and whose size is *width* dimension parallel to the *x*-axis and *height* dimension parallel to the *y*-axis and strokes it.

Shading

Not all figures are simple line drawings. You might want to fill in the figure with a color or pattern. PostScript has a variety of operators to help you perform such tasks. As an introduction to these operators, let's begin with the simplest and most obvious operation: filling a figure with black.

Since, by this time, you may be getting tired of squares and rectangles, this exercise draws two triangles instead. Each triangle is different, with one being a right triangle and the other being an isosceles triangle. You will define two wraps, one for each type of triangle. The dimensions of the triangles that you will draw on the display are shown in Figure 3-7.

Figure 3-7. Layout for two triangle example.

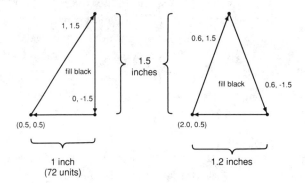

The wraps follow the basic structure that you have already seen for **rectstroke.** They do not assume that the current point has already been positioned. Instead, they are called with four arguments: the *x* and *y* coordinates of the bottom left corner of the desired triangle and its base and the height.

Finally, they fill the path with the desired color—in this case, black. The necessary wraps then look something like this:

```
defineps PSWrightTriangle(float Xpos, Ypos, Base, Hgt)
    newpath
    Xpos Ypos moveto
    Base Hgt rlineto
    0 Hgt neg rlineto
    closepath
    fill
endps

defineps PSWisoTriangle(float Xpos, Ypos, Base, Hgt)
    newpath
    Xpos Ypos moveto
    /HalfBase Base 2 div def
    HalfBase Hgt rlineto
    HalfBase Hgt neg rlineto
    closepath
    fill
endps
```

This time you begin the wraps with a **newpath,** which removes any previous segments from the current path. Then you use **moveto** to establish the first point on the new path. This combination guarantees that the final **closepath** will return to this point. Then you draw the first leg of the triangle, up and to the right of the base point, by moving the correct distance in the x and y directions. For PSWrightTriangle, this is simply the height and width of the desired triangle. On the isosceles triangle, however, the correct distance is one-half of the desired base because the apex of the triangle is directly over the middle of the base. To do this you calculate the temporary variable *HalfBase,* which is the correct value, and use that as the x coordinate value. For both triangles, the next step is to draw the second leg. For the right triangle, this simple means moving directly down by the negative of the *Hgt* variable to the base line. For the isosceles triangle, this is moving down by negative *Hgt* and across by the remaining *HalfBase*. Finally, you draw the base line by using the **closepath** operator. That completes each of the triangles.

The final step in each wrap is the fundamental, new process that brings us to this point. Remember that, in this exercise, you are not going to stroke the path to paint it on the display. Instead, you use the **fill** operator to fill the path completely with black. If you had wanted another line figure, you could have used the **stroke** operator again instead; nothing in the process of path construction determines how the path will be painted. This is just one of the positive features of the PostScript graphics model that creates a current path and then paints it using some general operator.

You see here that we have included the painting operation in the wrap itself. This has some advantages: it matches the use of the Display PostScript operators **rectfill** and **rectstroke,** and it also allows you to precisely control the path that is created and painted. However, as noted before, this is a less efficient method for painting paths than accumulating them and painting all path segments that have identical features with one operation. The difference in efficiency is not detectable in these examples, but in a larger application it can be quite noticeable. If you wish to get the higher level of efficiency, just remove the **fill** operator and the **newpath** and call them separately, using their Client Library functions.

With these wraps in hand, let's look at the C procedure to create the desired display.

```
void runPSInline(void)
{
    float x, y;
```

```
    float base, height;

    x = y = 0.5*72;
    base = 72;
    height = 1.5*72;
    PSWrightTriangle(x, y, base, height);
    x = 2*72;
    base = 1.2*72;
    PSWisoTriangle(x, y, base, height);
}
```

This produces the display shown in Figure 3-8.

Figure 3-8. Two triangles output.

All the code here should be quite easy for you to follow at this point; there is nothing here that you haven't seen before. The major difference between this procedure and the preceding one is that the resulting figures are filled, and not stroked.

There is no requirement that you stick to black and white, either. Let's do another exercise with varying shades of gray. These same techniques also work for color output, but, since we can't guarantee that you have a color display, we avoid that for now. Later we will discuss some things about color output and color procedures.

The exercise consists of three overlapping figures: two squares with a triangle in the middle. For this exercise, you will use the PSWisoTriangle wrap that you defined earlier, plus the **rectfill** operator, which works exactly like the **rectstroke** operator that you used before, with the single difference that it fills the resulting rectangle instead of stroking it—just like our earlier wraps. The exercise is laid out in Figure 3-9.

Figure 3-9. Layout for overlap and gray-scale example.

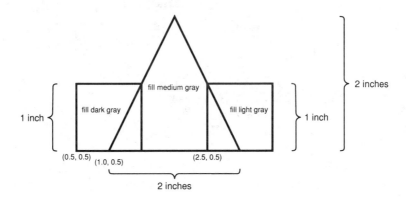

The layout shows several important features. First, it gives the essential dimensions for the program. Second, it shows each of the overlapping figures filled with a different shade of gray. The layout shows the starting point for each of the figures: (0.5, 0.5) for the first square, (1, 0.5) for the triangle, and (2.5, 0.5) for the second square. Both boxes have 1-inch sides, and the triangle has a 2-inch base and a 2-inch height. Each of the figures is filled with a different gray value: dark gray for the first square; medium gray for the triangle; and light gray for the last square. The figures are also produced in that order, left to right: dark square, triangle, light square.

You can adjust the gray level with the new operator, **setgray.** This operator takes a single numeric operand between 0 and 1 inclusive, with 0 being *black* and 1 being *white*. Values in between 0 and 1 set a level of gray proportional to the value; for example, 0.5 would be a medium gray, halfway between black and white. Any number outside this range causes an error. For this example, you will use gray levels of 0.33, 0.5, and 0.67, respectively.

The use of 0 for black and 1 for white may seem a little disconcerting at first. The best analogy is to think of a light falling on a page rather than ink on a page. With light, 0 represents no light, or black; whereas 1 represents full light, or white. Thinking of 0 and 1 as light may help you remember the two values.

There are no new wraps in this exercise; you simply reuse the PSisoTriangle wrap from the previous exercise, along with some single operator procedures from the Client Library. The C code then looks like this:

```
void runPSInline(void)
{
    float x, y;
    float base, height;
    float gray;

    /* first figure - dark gray square */
    x = y = 0.5*72;
    base = height = 72;
    gray = 0.33;
    PSsetgray(gray);
    PSrectfill(x, y, base, height);
    /* second figure - medium gray triangle */
    x = 1*72;
    base = height = 2*72;
    gray = 0.5;
    PSsetgray(gray);
    PSWisoTriangle(x, y, base, height);
    /* third figure - light gray square */
    x = 2.5*72;
    base = height = 72;
    gray = 0.66;
    PSsetgray(gray);
    PSrectfill(x, y, base, height);
}
```

The output from this exercise is shown in Figure 3-10.

Figure 3-10. Overlapping figures and gray-scale output.

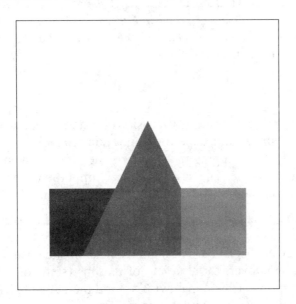

The important point here is that each of the figures completely obscures the preceding one, even though the preceding one was darker. This would remain true no matter what colors were used. The effect is that of opaque paint, or of solid, overlapping pieces of paper. There is no automatic mixing or bleeding of colors, nor are the colors transparent. On some devices, most notably at this time the NeXT system, it is possible to make the colors partially or fully transparent. This is done in a manner exactly analogous to setting the gray level; on the NeXT, it is by setting the *alpha* value. In that case, the figures underneath do show through, by the amount of transparency. However, since this is a system-specific feature, we will not discuss it further here.

Once again, here are the new operators in the standard format:

num **setgray** —
sets the current color to a shade of gray corresponding to the value *num*, which must be between 0, corresponding to black, and 1, corresponding to white. Intermediate values correspond to proportional shades of gray.

— **fill** —
paints the area enclosed by the current path with the current color and clears the current path.

x y width height **rectfill** —

creates a path consisting of the rectangle whose bottom left corner point has coordinates (*x,y*) and whose size is *width* dimension parallel to the *x*-axis and *height* dimension parallel to the *y*-axis and fills it with the current color.

Clipping

As we mentioned earlier in the discussion of general graphics concepts, the current path can be made to perform one additional role: to set the current clipping path. The clipping path restricts the area on the display where objects can be visible. This is a particularly important subject in Display PostScript and deserves some additional explanation.

Although the "ideal" PostScript page, like any ideal construct, is essentially unbounded, the real output device has quite specific limits on where graphics may be displayed. These limits are called the *imageable area* of the device. Moreover, for a variety of reasons (some of which we will discuss in a moment), you may wish to limit the output to a subset of the total imageable area. PostScript accomplishes both of these objectives by the use of a *clipping path*. The clipping path is the path that bounds that area where marks may be made on the output page. For example, suppose that you want to make a symbol on a piece of paper, and you want to limit where the paint goes on the page. You might do this by cutting out a mask and placing it over the paper, so that any marks would show on the paper only where the mask allowed access to the paper underneath. Even if the paint were splashed around all over the mask, only the amount within the mask would show on the finished output. This is how you stencil letters onto a page, for example.

PostScript works in the same way. When you start your program, the interpreter makes a rectangular mask that precisely matches the imageable area of the output device. In this way, no marks can be visible outside the masked area. This masked area is called the *clipping region,* and the path that outlines the masked area is the *clipping path*. The PostScript language provides operators that allow you to change the clipping path to any arbitrary region that lies within the imageable area, so that you can mask off parts of the output to prevent unwanted marks from showing. You will see some examples of this in the exercises later in this section.

Display PostScript adds one more feature to this. In basic PostScript, as you might expect, the current clipping path is a fixed feature that applies uniformly to all operations on the output. When you are working with display output, however, you often have to update (redraw) a portion of the display based on some action of the user. However, a large part of the display may remain the same. For such updates, the use of a clipping region is very useful. With that, you can simply make a clipping region that marks out the part of the display that is to be redrawn, and then redraw everything. The interpreter automatically changes only the part within the clipped area.

This would be a lovely solution, except that it often happens in real programs that one function is responsible for the display and another is handling path construction; in such cases, coordination of the functions could be quite difficult. Display PostScript therefore provides a special, quick, one-time clipping region called the *view clip* that can be set for such situations. This solves the display problem and allows the application to update only the required portion of the screen. Note that the view clipping path is set and controlled quite separately from the ordinary clipping path.

To illustrate these principles, let's do two quick exercises that use the clipping path in different ways. Note that both of these use the ordinary clipping path, not the view clip.

The first exercise creates a new wrap that produces a triangular clipping region and then paints a rectangle over that. First, let's make the new wrap, as follows:

```
defineps PSWisoTriClip(float Xpos, Ypos, Base, Hgt)
    newpath
    Xpos Ypos moveto
    /HalfBase Base 2 div def
    HalfBase Hgt rlineto
    HalfBase Hgt neg rlineto
    closepath
    clip
endps
```

This wrap is identical to the previous PSWisoTriangle wrap, except that it ends with a new operator, **clip,** rather than the previous **fill.** The **clip** operator takes the current path—here an isosceles triangle—and intersects it with the current clipping path to create a new clipping path that is the interior of both regions and makes that the new current clipping path. You should note how this works. The current path does not automatically become the current clipping path. Instead, the current path is matched to the existing current clipping path, and the area that is inside both paths becomes the new clipping region. Of course, if the current clipping path is the entire imageable area, as in our example, the current path—the triangle—becomes the clipping path. However, if the current clipping path were smaller than the current path, only the part of the current path that was inside the current clipping path would be part of the new clipping region. Look for a moment at Figure 3-11.

Figure 3-11. Examples of clipping paths.

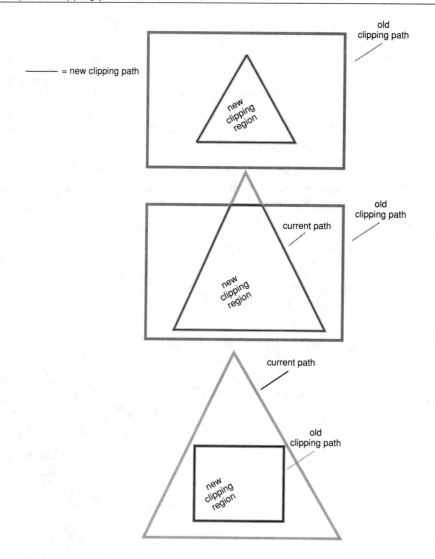

Figure 3-11 shows three different combinations of old clipping path, current path, and the new clipping region and its associated new clipping path. As you can see, only the points inside both the old clipping path and the current path are in the new clipping region; and the new clipping path is the path that outlines that region. This path is the intersection of the old clipping path and the current path.

This information is mostly cautionary because the general practice is to use a current path that lies entirely within the existing clipping region to set the new clipping path. Note that because of the clipping mechanism, you cannot use the **clip** operator to expand the clipping region; you can only make a new, smaller region. However, you can use the **initclip** operator to reset the clipping region to the maximum available, which makes the entire imageable area the clipping region.

The **clip** operator, unlike the **fill** and **stroke** operators, leaves the current path intact and does not erase it. Therefore, if you were careless enough to have procedures that do not start with a **newpath,** you might find some bizarre effects on your output.

The layout for the exercise is shown in Figure 3-12.

Figure 3-12. Layout for triangle clip.

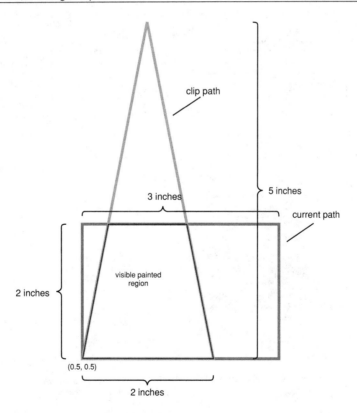

By now you can easily see how this translates into the following code.

```
void runPSInline( void )
{
    float x, y;
    float base, height;
    float clipx, clipy;

    /* set clipping region */
    clipx = clipy = 0.5*72
    height = 5*72;
    base = 2*72;
    PSWisoTriClip(clipx, clipy, base, height);
    /* now draw a rectangle */
    x = y = 0.5*72
    base = 3*72;
    height = 2*72;
    PSrectfill(x, y, base, height);
}
```

As you would anticipate, this produces the output shown in Figure 3-13.

Figure 3-13. Output from triangle clip.

Now let's reverse the procedure and use a rectangle clip with a triangle painted over it. In this case, you can use a special Display PostScript operator, **rectclip,** which sets a rectangular clipping region. In this way you can reuse your old PSWisoTriangle wrap and the new special operator, as follows:

```
void  runPSInline( void )
{
    float x, y;
    float base, height;
    float clipx, clipy;

    /* set clipping region */
    clipx = clipy = 0.5*72;
    base = height = 2*72;
    PSrectclip(clipx, clipy, base, height);
    /* now paint a large triangle */
    x = y = 0.5*72;
    base = 4*72;
    height = 2*72;
    PSWisoTriangle(x, y, base, height);
}
```

This produces the output shown in Figure 3-14.

Figure 3-14. Output from rectangle clip.

This time, I did not bother with a layout for such a straightforward example. You make a rectangular clipping region from (0.5, 0.5) with a width and height of 2 inches. Then you draw an isosceles triangle with a base of 4 inches and a height of 2 inches. The result, as you see, appears to be a right triangle, with base and height of 2 inches. The remainder of the triangle is outside of the clipping region and so isn't visible.

FONTS

You have already been introduced informally to fonts and text in the exercises and examples in the previous chapters. Up to this point, you have been given commands to control the fonts without any real explanation because you were concentrating on text handling, creating the correct wraps, and similar basic operations. You also needed some basic graphic information before you could become fully informed about PostScript fonts. Now you should be ready to proceed to a broader discussion of font management and use in PostScript.

This approach has meant that we have skipped over, but not ignored, PostScript font operations. You probably feel quite comfortable with the operations you have used so far, and you may have an intuitive feeling for how these work. PostScript font operators offer a natural approach to font access and use, and you have probably not felt that this informal approach was either difficult or distracting.

However, you will ultimately want to make more extensive use of fonts as the exercises become more complex and demanding, and you will need to understand more about the available choices and operations when working with PostScript fonts. In this section, you begin to explore these issues. This does not require introducing any new PostScript operators, but it does require a fuller discussion of fonts generally and a more systematic look at the PostScript font mechanism specifically.

Font Definitions

A *font* is defined as a complete collection of characters—including upper- and lowercase letters, numbers, punctuation symbols, and some additional symbols—in one typeface size and style. The easiest way to think about a font is to think of the type ball on a typewriter, which gives you a series of letters, numbers, and symbols in a specific size and style. Typewriter output is often in the Courier type style, which is a standard for office typewriter output. Just as the typewriter cannot produce any image on the page without the type ball, so the PostScript interpreter cannot create letter images without an active font.

In our discussion of general font issues, many topics apply to all fonts in any environment; some apply only to fonts on raster-output devices; none, however, is unique to PostScript. These general issues apply to the use of fonts, font construction and display on raster-output devices, families of fonts, and font names. Later we discuss font issues that specifically relate to PostScript and Display PostScript. These include access to and scaling of fonts, types of PostScript fonts, and font operators.

Before we examine the technical aspects of fonts, you should have some appreciation of type as a graphic element. The form of letters is one of the most ancient of graphic objects. As soon as humans began to write, they began to modify the shapes they used to convey language. Some languages, ranging from ancient Egyptian to modern Chinese, use stylized pictures to represent words and concepts. Our language, and others related to it, use characters to represent sounds that are then formed into the words of our language. The characters on a printed page were originally created in imitation of medieval calligraphy—meaning "beautiful writing"—and so embody the most familiar and yet complex graphics that we encounter every day. Each letter in a good typeface is a miniature work of art, a masterpiece of beauty and function harmoniously combined in one object.

For this reason, the best typefaces combine aesthetic qualities with utility. The beauty of a typeface is directly related to how well it performs its utilitarian functions of clarity, emphasis, and legibility. Each individual style of type has been designed to provide these virtues in a manner appropriate to a specific environment; Times Roman, for example, was designed as type in a newspaper. As a programmer, you should understand that the graphic designer has a real need for a variety of type styles as well as a matching need to see these beautiful objects precisely on the output, both display and print. These needs are one of the compelling reasons for Display PostScript.

Until most recent times, typefaces were designed for printing applications. In such applications, type produces solid and continuous lines of ink that form characters. The task, then, is to transform these solid shapes into dots in a way that preserves their beauty and readability. This task is neither easy nor trivial, especially on low-resolution devices like display screens.

The essential problem is to carry over all the fine nuances of the type style design into the series of dots that form the character display on the raster-output device. To do this, the characters are stored as mathematical representations of the outlines of the characters. Transforming these outlines into a specific set of pixels on the display is a special case of the general task of *scan conversion*. In many cases, in order to get the best and most appealing result, some adjustments must be made to the resulting set of pixels. For example, the strokes that make up an "E" might be 10 pixels wide on a 16-point font, but only 4 pixels wide on an 8-point font, 1 pixel less than you would expect by simple ratios. Such adjustments are essential to give the letter the correct visual proportions because our eyes do not always "see" in precise ratios. This adjustment process is known as *font tuning* and is an important, and jealously guarded, part of font technology. Obviously the adjustment is most required at small point sizes and on low- or medium-resolution devices, where the features of individual letters may be only a few pixels in size. In extreme cases of small point sizes and low resolutions, even with a tuning adjustment, letters may appear ragged and uneven; perhaps even becoming unrecognizable.

Using Fonts

Different fonts, which provide different typefaces and styles of type, are used in documents for three reasons. To begin with, fonts are used for legibility. This issue may seem obvious, but it is often overlooked or unacknowledged in selecting type. If you take the trouble to print something, you want it to be read and understood with minimal strain—as the saying goes, so that he who runs may read. Many fonts have been designed with exactly this requirement in mind, and they provide clear, readable characters that help convey the message embodied in the text. Fonts are also used to improve the quality of the finished output. Typeset output provides both visual appeal and impact.

These different fonts can also provide emphasis and create certain design effects. Sometimes design considerations are at odds with the requirements of legibility and clarity; use of old-fashioned gothic lettering or fancy script styles in block text would be an example of such a clash. Often, however, emphasis is provided by the use of different type styles and sizes within the same typeface, which avoids most of the problems. A common use of these techniques is to distinguish certain types of information within text; thus, for example, we have the conventional use of italics for book titles in a text block.

There are a variety of ways to group fonts. The simplest and most obvious, and therefore also the most common, is by design, or *typeface*. Most of these typefaces have names, which represent a complete range of fonts with a common design but in different sizes and styles. Such a set of fonts is properly called a *font family*. Remember that a font, precisely speaking, is only one size in a particular style of a single typeface design. You may have noticed that I have been using "font" for what is actually a much larger segment of a font family; namely, all of a particular design and style, such as Times Bold or Times Italic. For convenience, I will continue to use "font" in this way whenever there will be no confusion.

Font Styles Fonts within a font family generally also provide a variety of styles for output. The most common font styles are *italic*, where the letters slope to the right to provide a sort of handwritten effect; and *bold*, where the letters are heavier and darker to make them stand out. For any given typeface, there is also a wide variety of additional styles: condensed, extended, oblique, and others. In some cases, some styles may replace or substitute for others; for example, oblique is often used as a substitute for italic. Your font supplier will provide information regarding the exact variety of styles available for a given family and the differences between the styles.

Font Sizes Besides coming in different typefaces and styles, characters can be produced in varying sizes. Every character in a font has a certain height and width. The width of characters is called *pitch*. In some fonts, all characters have the same pitch; such fonts are called *monospaced fonts*. For most fonts, however, each character has a distinct width; such fonts are called *proportional fonts*. Fixed pitch fonts are very often associated with typewriter-style output since most typewriters cannot produce proportional spacing of letters. Courier, for example, is a monospaced font.

In a proportional font, the width of each character is carefully designed as a part of the overall shape. In traditional fonts, these widths are individually crafted to enhance the aesthetic appeal of the letters both in certain combinations and as a block. Proportions that are simply generated by mathematical ratios often lose this aesthetic quality when actually seen by the eye; arriving at the most pleasing proportions is a process involving equal measures of judgment and experience. One of the major advantages in using traditional fonts is that you have the benefit of many other people's craftsmanship.

Font height is also a consideration. In general, font height and width are connected by the *font metrics*, which are a series of measurements for each character in a font. The characters in a font are normally set along a straight line called the *baseline*. The part of lowercase letters such as "p" or "y" that extends below the baseline is called the *descender*, and the part that extends above the body height of lowercase letters such as a "k" or "t" is called an *ascender*, or riser. Font size is measured in *points,* which is the same measure used in the default PostScript coordinate structure that we discussed previously.

Since a point is 1/72 inch, 36-point type will be about 0.5 inch in height. More precisely, the font size is the distance that must exist between the baselines of successive lines of type if the ascenders of the bottom line are not to overlap the descenders of the upper line. Therefore, font height is measured from the top of the ascenders on tall letters to the bottom of the descenders on letters that go below the baseline. Thus, for example, 36-point type measures almost 1/2 inch from the top of a "k" to the bottom of a "p." Smaller point sizes indicate smaller type, with 4- or 5-point type being about the limit of legibility for most people. The PostScript language itself puts no limitation on the size of type; you may specify any size that can be stored and printed on your device.

PostScript Fonts

PostScript treats text characters as general graphic objects subject to appropriate operators, just like any other graphic object. A box or a triangle is conceptually no different to the interpreter than a "g" or an "R" and vice versa. Because PostScript does not distinguish between text and other graphics, it has no difficulty combining text and graphic objects on the same output. In a real sense, all output displays are graphic images to the PostScript interpreter. You could actually draw every character of a font on a display using PostScript commands, but that would be tedious. Instead, PostScript provides a variety of high-level operators to handle text conveniently and efficiently.

PostScript describes fonts through the means of a *font dictionary*. Each font dictionary is referenced by a PostScript name literal and provides information and procedures for building all the characters in that font. You have already seen the PostScript font mechanism in action in the exercises. The name of a font is used as a key into a special dictionary that returns the font dictionary for that font as the associated value. The PostScript interpreter then uses this font dictionary to define the process for rendering characters in a string onto the current page. The interpreter uses each character as an index to select the correct definition process.

There are two important points to remember here. First, PostScript actually does draw each character, using appropriate graphics operations; and, second, the PostScript interpreter creates characters through the use of a font dictionary that contains all the information required to produce a given font, including the appropriate procedures for rendering each character.

Most PostScript fonts contain characters that are defined as *outlines* in the font dictionary and that are processed by the interpreter and filled in to make the desired character. By using this process to create characters, PostScript can render all sizes of text with a minimum of distortion and can perform many other graphics operations on the characters or using the character's outline. Both Times-Roman and Helvetica are outline fonts.

It is also possible, and sometimes desirable, to stroke these outlines rather than fill them. Because PostScript fonts can be stroked or filled as required, they also are affected by the current color. Recall that the current color is set by the **setgray** operator. With the current color set, the text shows on the display in the usual range of black to white, as set by the results of the **setgray.** This provides an easy and effective way to change the coloring of a letter or letters on the output; for example, you can easily display white letters against a gray or black background.

Font Manipulation So far in the book, you have been using the single operator **selectfont** for all font-setting operations. This is fast and easy, and generally you will always want to use this operator for setting up fonts. However, it conceals three separate actions in its single operation. Using a PostScript font requires the following three steps:

1. The font name must be looked up in the master PostScript font directory to find the font dictionary and return it.

2. The character outlines in the font dictionary must be scaled to the desired size for output.

3. The scaled font must be made available to the interpreter and identified as the current font; that is, as the font to use for all subsequent text operations.

The **selectfont** operator performs all of these operations in a single step. In basic PostScript, however, each of these tasks has its own operator; and each operator performs in such a way as to leave the information for the next on the stack. In this way, the operations can be invoked in the preceding sequence. The three operators, in order, are **findfont, scalefont,** and **setfont.**

The first operator, **findfont,** identifies the font dictionary by its name. Taking a name literal as an operand, it looks the name up in a special directory and returns the associated font dictionary onto the stack. If you should give it a name it can't find, it returns an error; in most environments, it issues an error message and returns a system-defined default font. The **scalefont** operator performs the second task. This operator requires two operands: a number that represents the scaling factor and a font dictionary that is to be scaled. Typically you explicitly provide the scale factor when you call the operator; the font dictionary will have been left on the stack by a preceding **findfont** operation. The operator returns a correctly scaled font dictionary to the stack, where it can be used as an operand by the next operator in the series, **setfont.** This operator, as its name implies, takes a properly scaled font dictionary from the stack and makes it the *current font*. This is the font dictionary name that the interpreter uses for all subsequent text operations.

The **selectfont** operator, which you have been using, performs all three operations at once. It takes two operands: the name literal of the desired font and the scaling factor. Then it finds the correct font, scales it, and makes it the current font. **selectfont** has been optimized for this task in Display PostScript, so it is best to use it whenever it is available. Since printing PostScript devices do not yet support **selectfont,** I have spelled out the steps so you can use the individual operators where they are required.

At this point, you may notice that we have returned to our original definition of a font as a set of type in one style and one size. Now you know how to set up and use a PostScript font, how PostScript itself treats and works with fonts, and how Display PostScript differs from basic PostScript in this regard.

Let's recap these four font operators in the standard format.

name   **findfont**   font

obtains the font dictionary, *font,* specified by *name*.

font scale   **scalefont**   newfont

applies *scale* to *font* to create *newfont,* whose characters are enlarged in both the *x* and *y* directions by the given scaling factor when they are output.

font   **setfont**   —

establishes *font* as the current font, to be used for all subsequent character operations.

name scale   **selectfont**   —

finds the font dictionary corresponding to *name,* scales it to the size given by *scale,* and makes that scaled font dictionary the current font.

ADDITIONAL DISPLAY POSTSCRIPT GRAPHICS

So far in this chapter you have read about and worked with straight lines and characters as graphic objects. You have built a variety of shapes and figures, both stroked and filled, and you should be familiar and comfortable with basic PostScript operations.

With this background, you are now ready to extend your graphic vocabulary in two directions. First you will learn to work with arcs, circular shapes, and figures composed of both curved and straight line segments. Second, you will read about PostScript measurement and coordinates in more detail. This should prepare you for a final summary of PostScript graphics, which explains the conceptual and practical framework for all PostScript graphic operations. This summary also helps you formulate and use general graphics procedures that are independent of page and device structures and that do not affect other graphic operations.

Curves

Most interesting shapes and figures are not composed of just straight lines and character shapes. Curved lines are an important part of dynamic and visually attractive designs. Operations to create and use curved line segments are therefore essential in any comprehensive set of tools for rendering graphic objects.

By their nature, curved lines present more problems in a computer environment than straight lines do. By now, you are used to PostScript's ability to describe any point on a page as a pair of coordinate numbers (x, y). This type of coordinate system is called *rectangular* coordinates because it uses two dimensions that are at right angles to one another as a measurement system. Straight lines are a natural outgrowth of rectangular coordinates, as you have seen as you move around the PostScript output space. Curved lines, however, require more work to define and more information to use; unfortunately they also require more mathematics to understand. We begin with the easiest form of curved lines, circular arcs.

Making Circular Arcs Even in rectangular coordinates, the mathematics necessary to describe a circle precisely are relatively simple. You needed three items of information, or *parameters,* to define a rectangle and place it on the output. To use **rectstroke,** for example, you needed to set the coordinates of the bottom left corner of the rectangle, and you needed to provide a width and a height to give its dimensions. If the rectangle had been symmetrical—a square—you could have used only one dimension as a parameter, lowering the required information to two items. The circle, which is also symmetrical, also only requires two parameters in order to be positioned on the output display. These are the location of the center of the circle, which is equivalent to the corner of the square, and the radius of the circle, which is equivalent to the dimensions of the square.

Circular arcs are just portions of a circle. To define a circular arc requires two additional parameters: the beginning and ending points of the arc. Although there are various ways to specify the endpoints of an arc, PostScript uses a simple method that specifies the two angles that begin and end the arc, measured counterclockwise from the horizontal (positive *x*) axis. This measurement process is illustrated in Figure 3-15.

Figure 3-15. Circular arc mesurements.

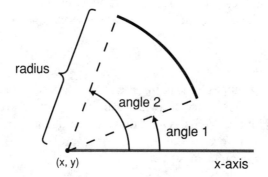

In this figure, the center of the circle is at the point (*x, y*) and the radius is *r*. The circular arc to be drawn begins at *angle1* and runs counterclockwise to end at *angle2*. These five values (two for the center point coordinates and one each for the radius and the beginning and ending angles) are the operands that are required for the PostScript **arc** operator and its associated Client Library procedure PSarc.

The **arc** operator takes these five values and adds a circular line segment to the current path that begins at the point specified by *angle1* and ends at the point specified by *angle2*. This endpoint, as is generally true when adding segments to the current path, becomes the current point at the end of the operation. The **arc** operator also may add a straight line segment to the current path, depending on whether the current point is defined or not. If the current point is not defined, the **arc** operator sets the current point to the point that begins the circular segment (the point defined by *angle1*) and makes the circular segment the first segment in the current subpath. If the current point is already defined, however, the **arc** operator adds a straight line segment from the current point to the beginning point and then adds the circular segment. In both cases, the endpoint is the new current point.

Let's do a simple exercise, using single operator wraps, to help you practice these operations. Like the first exercises using straight lines, this won't be visually exciting or artistically involving, but it will illustrate the possibilities. This example produces three arcs, one below the other, each progressively demonstrating potential uses of the operator. The three figures and their relative dimensions are shown in Figure 3-16. The solid lines on each figure are drawn onto the display; the dashed lines and the parameters are shown for reference.

Figure 3-16. Layout for arc examples.

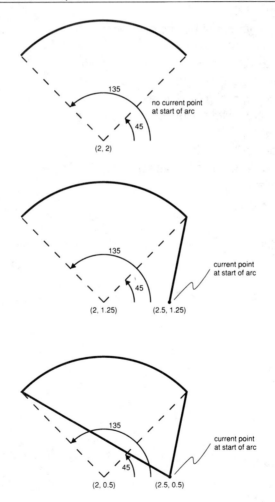

Chapter 3: Text and Graphics   171

With this information, you can easily work out the following code to draw the desired output:

```
void runPSInline( void )
{
    float x, y, r;
    float angle1, angle2;

    /* first arc - without current point */
    PSnewpath();
    x = y = 2*72;
    r = 1.5*72;
    angle1 = 45;
    angle2 = 135;
    PSarc(x, y, r, angle1, angle2);
    /* second arc - with current point */
    y = 1.25*72;
    PSmoveto(2.5*72.0, y);
    PSarc(x, y, r, angle1, angle2);
    /* third arc - with current point and added segment */
    y = 0.5*72;
    PSmoveto(2.5*72.0, y);
    PSarc(x, y, r, angle1, angle2);
    PSclosepath();
    PSstroke();
}
```

This produces the expected output as shown in Figure 3-17.

Figure 3-17. Arc examples output.

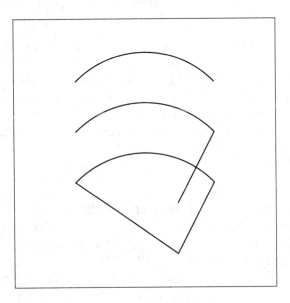

The program consists essentially of three **arc** operators. The first **arc** comes right after a **newpath,** which means that the current point is undefined. Therefore, the path that is created starts at the beginning of the curved segment. This arc has the parameters that you saw in the layout and are set up in the code as *x, y, r, angle1*, and *angle2*. For the second arc the program performs a **moveto** to the point (2.5, 1.25).

It is worth a moment to look at this PSmoveto since it is the first time you have sent arguments directly in the procedure call. In this case, you see that we have been careful to ensure that the value is cast to a float; the PostScript interpreter requires a float value as coordinates. The *y* coordinate is left as the variable *y* since this shows most clearly that the center of the arc and the current point are at the same vertical level. As mentioned earlier, you see the added straight line segment that connects the current point with the start of the curved segment. The third arc starts from a similar displacement from the designated center point, which has been set with a **moveto.** The difference here is that, at the end of the **arc** operation, you issue a simple **closepath** to connect the endpoint of the arc, which has become the new current point after drawing the curved segment, with the starting point.

Making Closed Curves PostScript has a matching operator, **arcn,** which draws the arc clockwise, rather than counterclockwise. This operator

Chapter 3: Text and Graphics   173

requires the same operands as the **arc**, and performs exactly the same way, but draws the reversed (clockwise) arc from the starting angle to the ending one. Let's use this, along with the **arc** to create a simple pie chart.

The setup for this chart is rather simple. The chart shows only the percentage of some whole that is represented by the entire chart. For the purposes of this exercise, suppose that the desired number is 28%; that is, the pie segment is to be 28 percent of the total circle. Here we will call our routine pieChart, instead of the usual runPSInline. In real programs, of course, this value would probably be calculated in some routine and passed to the pieChart routine as an argument. In the exercise, however, pieChart will take a void argument.

The segment lies on the right side of the display, placed symmetrically around the horizontal axis. This makes calculation of the angles quite easy. The center of the chart is at the point (200, 200), with each segment offset horizontally from that point by 5 units. Thus the center of one segment is (195, 200) and that of the other is (205, 200). The radius of the chart is 100 units. As you can see, for this example we use the default coordinates directly instead of using the previous calculations. No wraps are necessary for this version of the program; it can be done entirely with Client Library procedures as follows:

```
void pieChart(void)
{
    static float percent = 28.0;

    float x, y, r;
    float angle1, angle2;

    PSnewpath();
    x = 200 + 5;
    y = 200;
    r = 100;
    angle2 = ((percent / 100) * 360) / 2;
    angle1 = 360 - angle2;
    PSmoveto(x, y);
    PSarc(x, y, r, angle1, angle2);
    PSclosepath();
    /* displace for remaining segment */
    x = 200 - 5;
    PSmoveto(x ,y);
    PSarcn(x, y, r, angle1, angle2);
```

```
        PSclosepath();
        PSstroke();
}
```

This is really a very straightforward, but useful, routine and it produces the output shown in Figure 3-18.

Figure 3-18. Pie chart example output.

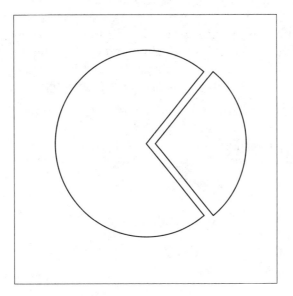

Let's just briefly review this procedure. It begins, as you expect, with the **newpath** operator to clear the current path. Then it calculates the *x* and *y* coordinates of the center of the first segment. The *y* position is just the coordinate value, but the *x* position is the desired center point plus the displacement value. The use of a displacement ensures that the two segments are visible as separate objects. The radius is set next. Then you must calculate the angle for the arc. Now this angle is some percentage; so the first calculation is to change the argument into a percentage by dividing it by 100. Then you multiply that percentage by 360 to get the total number of degrees in the segment. Finally, you divide that number by 2 since the arc is to be half above and half below the horizontal axis. This is the ending angle value for the arc. The beginning angle value is 360 minus the angle since 360 is equal to the horizontal axis. To draw the segment, first you move to the desired position. Then you can call the **arc** operator to draw the first two lines in the segment; and finally the **closepath** finishes the segment.

Now you proceed to the remaining segment. For this, you need only calculate the new *x* position, which is the coordinate value minus the displacement. All the other procedures and operands remain the same, except that you call **arcn** to draw the segment in reverse. Now that both segments are drawn, you paint them with one **stroke** operator. Of course, you could have filled either or both of them with a gray value if you had wanted.

Looking at this routine, you can also see how you might code a wrap that performed the same action. As a further exercise, let's look at a sample wrap to perform the same function. For illustration purposes, you can make this with five arguments: the *x* and *y* coordinates of the center position, the displacement of the two segments, the radius of the chart, and the percentage of the segment. The wrap then looks like this:

```
defineps PSWpieChart (float Xpos, Ypos, Disp, Radius,
Percent)
    % calculate angle from percent
    /Ang Percent 100 div 360 mul 2 div def
    % draw path for first segment
    newpath
    Xpos Disp add
    dup Ypos moveto
    Ypos Radius
    360 Ang sub
    Ang
    arc
    closepath
    % draw path for remaining segment
    Xpos Disp sub
    dup Ypos moveto
    Ypos Radius 360 Ang sub Ang arcn
    closepath
    % now paint the two segments
    stroke
endps
```

The C code to execute this with the same arguments is reduced to the following:

```
...
PSWpieChart(200.0, 200.0, 5.0, 100.0, 28.0);
...
```

This PostScript code performs the same functions as the previous Client Library calls, but internally it must perform some of the calculations that you did in C before. Remember that this trades off the efficiency of performing all the calculations in C for the simplicity that you see here. Let's review the differences.

To begin with, you calculate and store the angle value. This value is used several times, so you really do want to store it. Next you calculate the *x* position, as you did in C before, as *Disp* plus the *x*-coordinate argument *Xpos*. You need this twice, once for the **moveto** and once for the **arc,** so you duplicate the value on the stack. Then you place the *y*- coordinate argument *Ypos* on the stack and move to the desired point. Then you place *Ypos* onto the stack again—remember that the duplicate *x* value is on the stack already—followed by *Radius*. The beginning angle must be calculated as 360 minus *Ang,* and the calculated *Ang* is the ending angle. Now you can issue the **arc** operator, followed by the **closepath.** These two add the pie-shaped segment into the current path. Next you perform the same sequence of steps, but using the *Xpos* minus *Disp* instead of the sum, as before. The **arcn** operator draws the reverse path, and the **stroke** operator paints it. It's lean, tidy, and really rather general.

This gives you some sense of what you can do with circular segments. Let's now look at another useful operator that works with circular arcs, **arct.** This operator draws arcs connecting two lines, rather than using a center and a radius. As an example of how to use this operator, you will construct a new wrap, along the same lines as **rectstroke** and **rectfill,** that draws squares with curved corners. Since the result looks a bit like a television screen, let's call the wrap PSWscreenBox. You will do two examples with this wrap: one time to draw the box and stroke it, and one time to draw the box inside a square. The square will be filled with a dark gray (0.33) and the box with a light gray (0.8).

You will see here an alternative approach to paths and figures. In the Display PostScript operators such as **rectstroke** and in the wraps that we have made so far, the path is drawn and painted in one operation. This is the most general method of using paths because it allows the operation to leave no residue of segments or changed data in the PostScript environment. It is clean and neat. The drawback is that you have to have a different operator (or wrap) for each possible painting operator, or to make any other use of the path: thus we have **rectfill** and **rectclip,** for example. In this section, you create a wrap that does not automatically stroke or fill the path it creates; it leaves that for you. This has the advantage of requiring only one wrap and the disadvantage that the wrap itself must modify the current path. These are alternatives that only you, as the programmer, can effectively weigh and decide, although we will discuss these issues some more in the two following sections of the chapter.

Before you proceed to the examples, let's look at the **arct** operator that forms the heart of the wrap. To follow this discussion, look at Figure 3-19, which shows the key elements of the **arct** processing.

Figure 3-19. Operation of **arct** operator.

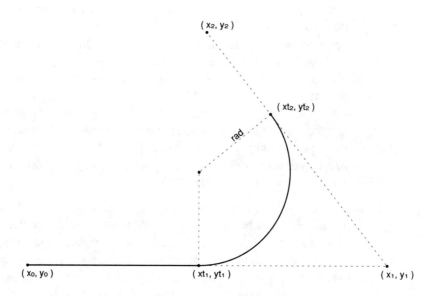

This operator, like **arc** and **arcn,** adds the arc of a circle to the current path, possibly preceded by a straight line segment. In this case, however, the arc drawn is defined by the radius r and two tangent lines. The tangent lines are from the current point—(x_0, y_0) in the diagram—to the point (x_1, y_1) and from (x_1, y_1) to the point (x_2, y_2). You can see that, like **lineto** and unlike the previous arc operators, **arct** requires a current point to start from.

The center of the arc is located at the intersection of the two lines that are perpendicular to the tangent lines at the distance r. (Recall from your plane geometry that there is only one such point.) The center always lies inside the inner angle formed by the two lines. The arc begins at the first tangent point (xt_1, yt_1) on the first line, from (x_0, y_0) to (x_1, y_1), and ends at the second tangent point (xt_2, yt_2) on the next line, from (x_1, y_1) to (x_2, y_2). Before constructing the arc, **arct** adds a straight line segment from the current point (x_0, y_0) to the first tangent point (xt_1, yt_1), unless the two are the same point. At the completion of the operation, the point (xt_2, yt_2) becomes the current point.

Let's now proceed to the PSWscreenBox wrap to see how the **arct** operator works in a concrete example. Suppose that you want to create a wrap that produces a general square with rounded corners. The arguments it requires are the coordinates of the bottom left corner of the square, the dimension of the square, and the radius of the corner of the square. This last item could, of course, be hard-coded into the wrap, but that is generally poor coding practice as it is much less flexible and harder to maintain. It can also be scaled to the size of the square, which is more general and more useful; we explore that option in the next section.

Now look at Figure 3-20.

Figure 3-20. Layout for the corner of PSWscreenBox.

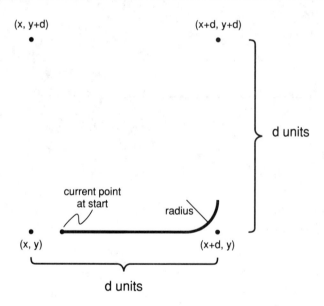

If the current point is (x, y), the four corners of a square with width of d are the points (x, y), $(x+d, y)$, $(x+d, y+d)$, and $(x, y+d)$. Because you want rounded corners tangent to the lines connecting these points, they represent the operands required for the **arct** operator.

Since you want all four corners of the square rounded, you must move some distance from the bottom left corner point before you start the **arct** commands. If you didn't do this, the first **arct** would draw a straight line at that point, which is also a corner of the box; and a small portion of the line would stick out when the corner was rounded on the finished figure. The result would have a bottom left corner that looks like the one in Figure 3-21.

Figure 3-21. Example of incorrect PSWscreenBox.

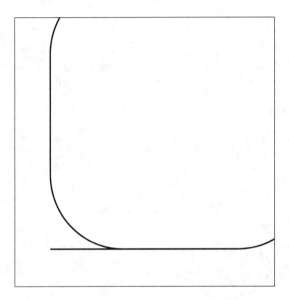

The best method to avoid this is to move a distance that is proportioned to the radius of the arc; if you move too short a distance, you will still get a part of the line, and if you move too far, you may run into the next corner. With that in mind, here is the design of PSWscreenBox:

- Move from the bottom left corner point by twice the radius value in the *x* direction to start.

- Perform four **arct** operations, using the following pairs of points:

    1. $(x+d, y), (x+d, y+d)$
    2. $(x+d, y+d), (x, y+d)$
    3. $(x, y+d), (x, y)$
    4. $(x, y), (x+d, y)$

- Finish by closing the figure to ensure that the end of the last **arct** operation meets the starting point.

This can then be translated into the following wrap code:

```
defineps PSWscreenBox (float Xpos, Ypos, Dim, Radius)
    newpath
    Xpos 2 Radius mul add Ypos moveto
    % create first side
    Xpos Dim add Ypos
    Xpos Dim add Ypos Dim add
    Radius arct
    % create second side
    Xpos Dim add Ypos Dim add
    Xpos Ypos Dim add
    Radius arct
    % create third side
    Xpos Ypos Dim add
    Xpos Ypos
    Radius arct
    % create fourth side
    Xpos Ypos
    Xpos Dim add Ypos
    Radius arct
    % and close up the figure
    closepath
endps
```

Using this wrap, you can now draw the round-corner square on the display, using our usual runPSInline as a base.

```
void runPSInline(void)
{
    float x, y, size, r;

    x = y = 0.5*72;
    size = 2*72;
    r = 20;
    PSWsquareBox(x, y, size, r);
    PSstroke();
}
```

This produces the output shown in Figure 3-22.

Figure 3-22. Stroked screen box.

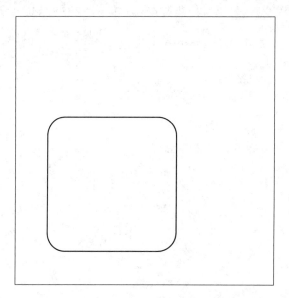

The procedure of just setting the operands for the wrap and calling it is quite simple itself. The screen box is located at (0.5, 0.5) and is 2 inches square. The corner radius is given in default coordinate units rather than inches; however, the choice is rather arbitrary and the number was chosen purely based on appearance.

As an illustration of how you can change the output but still use the same wrap, clear away that window and display a new one, using a changed runPSInline as follows:

```
void runPSInline(void)
{
    float x, y, width, height, r;
    float gray;

    x = y = 0.5*72;
    width = height = 2*72;
    gray = 0.33;
    PSsetgray(gray);
    PSrectfill(x, y, width, height);
    width = 1.5*72;
    r = 20;
```

182   Display PostScript Programming

```
    gray = 0.8;
    PSsetgray(gray);
    PSWscreenbox(x, y, width, r);
    PSfill();
}
```

This produces the output shown in Figure 3-23.

Figure 3-23. Second screen box example output.

This time you draw a 2-inch square, using **rectfill,** and then put a 1.5-inch screen box on top of it.

From this, you can easily see how you might generalize the wrap to produce a rectangle, instead of a square. This just requires another parameter and a small change to the wrap body. I have not done that here so that you can focus on the procedure and the new operator without any extraneous distractions.

One last point. The **arct** operator is new in Display PostScript. In basic PostScript, the same functions are performed by the **arcto** operator, which is available in Display PostScript as well. The only difference in the two operators is that **arcto** returns the coordinates of the two tangent points, (xt_1, yt_1), (xt_2, yt_2), on the stack after it creates the curved segment. In some rare cases, this can be quite useful because the points are otherwise quite difficult to determine. However, for the vast majority of operations, using **arcto** simply means adding four **pop** operators after executing it to remove the unwanted results from the stack. In addition, there are serious reasons why you want to use **arct** in Display PostScript environments, most notably when you are using user paths, which we discuss later in the book. For all these reasons, you should just use **arct** unless you really need the tangent points.

These examples show more complex procedures and wraps than the earlier ones. With them, you are getting near to what you want graphics procedures to look like. However, before you can produce completely independent graphics procedures, two topics remain to be covered: changing coordinates and the associated measurement issues, and PostScript graphics machinery.

Before proceeding to those topics, however, here are the four new operators for circular arcs. I have included **arcto** for completeness.

x y rad ang1 ang2   **arc**   —
adds a curved segment to the current path, possibly preceded by a straight line segment. The curved segment is an arc of a circle drawn counterclockwise in user space and has radius *rad* and the point (*x, y*) as a center. *ang1* is the angle of a vector from (*x, y*) with length *rad* to the beginning of the arc, and *ang2* is the angle of a vector from (*x, y*) with length *rad* to the end of the arc. If the current point is defined, the **arc** operator constructs a straight line segment from the current point to the beginning of the arc.

x y rad ang1 ang2   **arcn**   —
performs the same functions as **arc,** except in a clockwise direction.

x_1 y_1 x_2 y_2 rad   **arct**   —
creates a circular arc in user space of radius *rad,* tangent to the two lines defined from the current point to (x_1, y_1) and from (x_1, y_1) to (x_2, y_2). The **arct** operator also adds a straight line segment to the current line from the current point to the beginning of the arc if the current point and the beginning of the arc are not identical.

x_1 y_1 x_2 y_2 rad   **arcto** xt_1 yt_1 xt_2 yt_2
performs the same functions as **arct,** except that it returns the four coordinates of the tangent points on the stack.

Coordinates

PostScript provides a number of facilities to control and adjust coordinates. These operators make PostScript coordinate systems flexible and independent. The flexibility allows, for example, coordinates to be different on different parts of the display; and PostScript coordinates, which are independent of the device hardware, can also be made largely independent of the nominal display or window coordinates. This flexibility and independence come about because PostScript maintains a coordinate system, the *user space,* which is separate from the coordinates for the hardware, called the device space.

Recall the discussion in Chapter 1 of the PostScript coordinate system and the *default user space.* This is the coordinate system that you have been using for the exercises up to this point; it is the one that you are likely to use for most of your programming; and it is the one that you will continue to use regularly through the remainder of the book. It is not, however, the necessary or the only coordinate system for display or for PostScript. It is simply the *default* system: what you get when you start a fresh display. The default user space has no direct connection to the specific output device. It represents ideal coordinates and measures that always retain a fixed relationship to the current page.

Each individual output device has its own measure and coordinate system. Typically an output device uses a measure that corresponds to the device resolution and has some set of coordinates dictated by the motion of the output page through the device imaging system or by the scanning mechanism in the device. This device coordinate system is known as the *device space.*

The PostScript interpreter provides a method for transforming the default coordinates into the coordinates that the device uses. This process is normally transparent to the PostScript application and need not be considered in using PostScript operators. However, a program can access the device space and determine device coordinates if required for special purposes. Understand, however, that most PostScript programs, whether coded by hand or generated by an application, do not need to be concerned with device space. This freedom is a major contribution toward the device independence that is so important in PostScript.

Device space becomes an important concern when we are dealing with the related issues of scan conversion and device resolution. As we mentioned earlier, for devices of low- and medium-resolution, the human eye can often discern a difference in position or size of a single pixel. In these cases, graphics may need adjustment based on the characteristics of the device to avoid misleading the eye of the viewer. This is called tuning and is especially important, as you have already read, when dealing with character shapes and text output at sizes where the device resolution is a significant fraction of the size of the text characters. Tuning can and does take place in other circumstances, however, and can be an important part of display management. Display PostScript has introduced a *stroke adjustment* mechanism as a standard part of the PostScript imaging model. This provides automatic tuning for lines in the Display PostScript environment so that applications do not generally need to be concerned about this. If you want further information about this advanced topic, it can be found in the manual *Extensions for the Display PostScript System.*

Basic Transformations PostScript performs the conversion from one coordinate system to another by means of a mathematical process called *coordinate transformation*. This is a generalized mathematical process that changes points or distances in one coordinate system into another coordinate system by means of a *transformation matrix*. Every PostScript device comes with a built-in transformation matrix that is stored in the current graphics state and specifies how to transform user coordinates into device coordinates for that device. This matrix is called the *current transformation matrix,* or *CTM* for short.

The elements of the matrix actually specify the coefficients of a pair of linear equations in x and y that specify how to derive a new, transformed x and y. This is simply a convenient mathematical representation of the more natural and familiar concepts of geometric transformations such as rotation, translation, or scaling of coordinate systems. Most of the PostScript operators that implement these changes are organized according to this geometric model.

The form of transformation used most often does not replace the current transformation matrix, but rather modifies it. In this way, the mapping from the user space to the device space is preserved, but with the addition of some new features. The best way to visualize this is to think of the operators changing the user-space coordinate system in a sequence of transformations, with the last transformation always being the one from user space to device space.

Such transformations have many uses. The simplest are the coordinate transformations that affect the entire display. These might be a change in measure from points to inches, for example, or a translation and rotation of the coordinates to print graphics in the landscape mode (sideways) rather than in portrait mode. Basically any change in the coordinate structure that is useful can be accomplished using these facilities.

A more interesting use for these operations is to place individual graphics or portions of an output display within their own coordinate system. By doing this, the graphic can be moved, scaled, or otherwise transformed independently of its internal coordinates. In this fashion the graphic element is decoupled from its actual location on the display. This ability to move and transform properly formed graphics is the basis of PostScript's ability to embed page descriptions within one another. You will learn more about this in the next section, after we have discussed and practiced simple coordinate transformations.

PostScript provides operators that perform these simple geometric transformations. There are three coordinate changes that are most often needed, and each of these has a special PostScript operator. Here are each of these transformation operators in the standard format.

>   tx ty   **translate**   —
> moves the user-space origin (0, 0) to a new position with respect to the current page, while leaving the orientation of the axes and the unit length along each axis unchanged. The new origin is at the point (tx, ty) in the current user coordinates.
>
>   angle   **rotate**   —
> turns the user-space axes counterclockwise around the current origin by *angle,* leaving the origin and the unit length along each axis unchanged.
>
>   sx sy   **scale**   —
> modifies the unit lengths independently along each of the current x- and y-axes, leaving the origin and the orientation of the axes unchanged. The new units of length are sx times the current unit in the x direction, and sy times the current unit in the y direction.

These powerful modifications can be performed individually or in sequence to provide a wide variety of effect on the coordinate system. Let's look at some examples of these operations, using some of the wraps you have already developed.

Translation Translation is simply moving the coordinate origin around on the page. An example might look like Figure 3-24.

Figure 3-24. Example of translation.

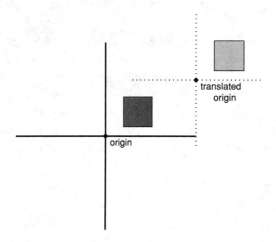

In this case, the origin of the coordinate system is translated to the point (7, 5). After the translation, the same code that produced the square at (2, 1) produces a square at (2, 1) in the translated coordinates, which would be (9, 6) in the original coordinate system. Both the old and the new coordinates and the two squares are shown in Figure 3-24.

This translation is of only limited use in drawing simple geometric figures; after all, **rectfill** can be placed anywhere on the page without any difficulties by simply giving it the desired coordinates for the bottom left corner. In the same way, most geometric figures, like **isoTriangle,** can be most easily repositioned by a simple **moveto.** The major use of translation is for more complex arrangements of objects, as you will learn later. Nevertheless, even simple geometric figures use simpler code with the help of a **translate.** As an example, let's rewrite the PSWscreenBox wrap using translation. The resulting code is as follows:

```
defineps PSWscreenBox (float Xpos, Ypos, Dim, Radius)
    newpath
    Xpos Ypos translate
    2 Radius mul 0 moveto
    Dim 0 Dim Dim Radius arct
    Dim Dim 0 Dim Radius arct
    0 Dim 0 0 Radius arct
```

```
        0 0 Dim 0 Radius arct
        closepath
endps
```

Note that this is quite a bit simpler to read, to convert (since it has fewer substitutions), to transmit, and to execute than the preceding wrap. Of course, this procedure depends entirely on the fact that the new **translate** has moved the coordinate origin to coincide with the bottom left corner of the figure; otherwise, this would produce rather strange results, or fail entirely.

Here is this new wrap used in a simple example:

```
void runPSInline (void)
{
    float x, y, r;
    float width;

    x = y = 0.5*72
    r = 20;
    width = 72;
    PSWscreenBox(x, y, width, r);
    PSsetgray(0.33);
    PSfill();
    PSWscreenBox(x, y, width, r);
    PSsetgray(0.66);
    PSfill();
    PSWscreenBox(x, y, width, r);
    PSsetgray(1.0);
    PSfill();
}
```

This produces the output shown in Figure 3-25.

Figure 3-25. Output of translated squares.

This result may surprise you, and it points out one problem of using translation directly. Looking at the code, you would most likely expect to draw three squares on top of one another, so that the last one would obscure the first. Instead you have them slightly offset, so that they look something like a fan. This occurs because the effects of the **translate** operator are cumulative, as are those of all the coordinate transformation operators, for that matter. That is, each translate sets the coordinates relative to the current coordinate system, not the default coordinate system. For this reason, each call to PSWscreenBox moved the origin another 0.5 inch and so caused the overlapping effect that you see.

I'm sure you are now wondering if there is ever a good reason to use coordinate transformations; after all, if the origin and other fixed parts of the system are repeatedly changed, how will you ever know where you are? There is, in fact, a simple technique that solves this problem which you will learn about soon. For now, let's continue with the remaining basic coordinate transformations.

Rotation Rotation is much like translation, except that it turns the coordinates counterclockwise around the current origin rather than moving them laterally. This process is illustrated in Figure 3-26.

Figure 3-26. Example of rotation.

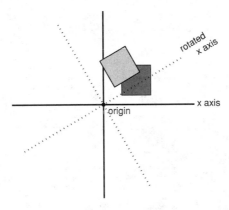

Let's use the single operator procedure for rotation from the Client Library and combine it with the previous example. The code might look something like this:

```
void runPSInline (void)
{
    float x, y, r;
    float width;
    float angle;
    x = y = 0.5*72;
    r = 20;
    width = 72;
    PSWscreenBox(x, y, width, r);
    PSsetgray(0.33);
    PSfill();
    angle = 30;
    PSrotate(angle);
    PSWscreenBox(x, y, width, r);
    PSsetgray(0.66);
    PSfill();
    angle = 15;
    x = y = 0;
    PSrotate(angle);
    PSWscreenBox(x, y, width, r);
    PSsetgray(1.0);
    PSfill();
}
```

This produces the output shown in Figure 3-27.

Figure 3-27. Output from combined rotation and translation.

The first square, of course, comes out just like the previous example. Then you rotate the coordinates through a 30-degree angle counterclockwise and translate them and draw another square. Finally, the axes are rotated through an additional 15 degrees. However, the square is not translated because the *x*- and *y*-coordinate values are set to 0. This illustrates that you can use these operators either alone or in sequence to provide a variety of effects.

Scaling The last of the basic transformations is scaling. The **scale** operator changes the size of the units of measurement on the *x* and *y* dimensions of the user space; that is, by means of the **scale** operator, you can make a distance of 1 unit be any physical distance you want. Moreover, you can make 1 unit in the *x* direction be a different actual distance than 1 unit in the *y* direction.

This can be a useful function, particularly if you would otherwise have to be making continual conversions from one coordinate system (say, the current mouse position, for example) to another. It also comes in handy for scaling objects up to a desired size, and for distorting an object in a standard way, for example, making a circle into an ellipse.

For this example you do not use any wraps at all, but just the appropriate single operator procedures from the Client Library. The example is a simple combination of functions as shown here:

```
void runPSInline (void)
{
    float x, y;
    float width, height;
    float sx, sy;

    sx = sy = 72;
    PSscale(sx, sy);
    PSnewpath();
    x = y = 0.5;
    width = height = 1;
    PSrectfill(x, y, width, height);
    /* now combine translate and scale;
       x and y have different scale factors */
    PStranslate(1.0, 1.0);
    sx = 1;
    sy = 2;
    PSscale(sx, sy);
    PSrectfill(x, y, width, height);
}
```

This produces the output in Figure 3-28.

Figure 3-28. Output of scaled figures.

This shows you, very graphically, the cumulative effects of the coordinate transformations. You begin by scaling the coordinates by a factor of 72; this makes every unit equal to an inch in the default coordinate system. Next you issue the standard **newpath** command; set the coordinates, width, and height for a rectangle (with the width and height identical to make the resulting figure a square); and call **rectfill**. Notice here that, because of the scaling, the units that you use are the position in inches where you want the graphic placed. Now you translate the origin to (1 inch, 1) inch—effectively making the new origin the center of the square. Then you scale the coordinates again, this time keeping the same scaling factor in the *x* direction but doubling the scaling in the *y* direction. Now you issue the identical **rectfill** with the identical arguments; however, this time the result is a rectangle that is exactly twice as high as it is wide. Also notice that the scaling has moved the corner of the figure—the *x* and *y* displacements of the corner from the origin are no longer identical.

Graphics State

Several implicit arguments are necessary for PostScript graphics operations to function successfully. You have now been introduced to quite a few "current" settings: current path, current point, current color, and so on. You have also learned, in the previous section, about coordinate transformations that allow you to change the default PostScript coordinates into virtually any configuration that you want. As you have seen, these translations are cumulative and can be combined. This makes them a very powerful tool that can be used to generate multiple shapes out of a single graphic object, but it also raises some questions and problems, which we touched upon when we discussed translations.

The very power and persistence of these operators causes some concern. How can you be sure that the output structure is what you expect and need when you start a procedure? You have already been using operators like **newpath** to ensure that you don't get unexpected results from leftover path segments. Basically the issue comes down to checking that the current state values are in their default condition or in some precisely defined state that you yourself set up. As the number of these current state variables increases—and there will be more of them as you proceed—we need to develop a standard method of controlling these values as a unit. Luckily the PostScript interpreter has similar issues to deal with and provides an elegant solution.

All of the current state parameters, which are necessary for the correct operation of the painting and other operators, are contained in a PostScript data structure called the *graphics state*. This structure defines the context for any painting operation. Most of the time, as you work on a unit of output, you want the same context for your graphics operations. Therefore, setting these parameters once globally and maintaining them in a standard structure makes writing PostScript easier and more straightforward than if you had to specify these arguments individually.

The graphics state is not directly accessible to the PostScript program. It is a collection of objects that form the control parameters for graphics operations; and these objects can themselves be accessed and modified by the proper PostScript operators. In this way the current context can be changed as necessary to produce the desired output.

The graphics state is a data structure that is maintained by PostScript in a separate graphics stack. There are two ways to control and set the graphics state, one common to both basic PostScript and Display PostScript, and one unique to Display PostScript. The way that is shared by both is also common in the sense that it is the way that you will use most in your code. This method uses the **gsave** operator to push the current graphics state, or context, onto the graphics stack and the complementary **grestore** operator to pop the topmost state on the stack and make it the current graphic state. This provides an effective method for controlling the current context for all graphics operations.

The alternative is to use the new **gstate** operator to generate a copy of the current graphics state and place it on the operand stack. Recall from Chapter 2 that one of the possible PostScript objects is the *gstate* composite object. This is the object that the **gstate** operator returns. This object can be treated like any other PostScript composite object and it can be named, saved, and returned. Applications that control a display may require the ability to move in one jump from one defined state to another. They need to respond to external events, such as a user action, without being too concerned with the exact number and placement of states on the graphic stack. The *gstate* object is ideal for this purpose. In Chapter 4, you will see how to save and use this to control the graphics state. For now, you will just use the first of these two methods.

The current graphics state is where all of these "current" values that we have been discussing remain. You can exert some control over the status of the graphics state by explicitly saving and restoring the graphics stack. This may seem to be just one more complication, but it's not; on the contrary, it is a source of freedom for your PostScript procedures.

Independent Graphic Objects You have seen some techniques that allow procedures to be somewhat independent of their placement on the output display: relative motion, translation of coordinates, and so on. However, you also saw that these various PostScript operations could persist and cause undesired side effects. Using **gsave** and **grestore,** you can now write procedures that have all the independence without the unwanted side effects. Does this sound like a commercial? It's not—it really works.

Using these techniques, procedures can be placed in their own coordinate system and then placed on the display at any desired point, without having any effect on other operations. Moreover, procedures designed to this standard can be sized and shaped independently of any internal constraint, making them much more powerful and useful than most such graphics procedures. Such independence is important when you want to develop a library of procedures that you can use repeatedly in different documents and with varied windowing systems and page coordinate structures. The best demonstration is to take the previous screenBox procedure and change it to the format just described.

The first step in revising the code is shown in the following segment:

```
defineps PSWscreenBoxFill (float Xpos, Ypos, Dim, Radius)
    gsave
        newpath
        Xpos Ypos translate
        2 Radius mul 0 moveto
        Dim 0 Dim Dim Radius arct
        Dim Dim 0 Dim Radius arct
        0 Dim 0 0 Radius arct
        0 0 Dim 0 Radius arct
        closepath
        fill
    grestore
endps
```

This is certainly a quite trivial change, and yet it has a major impact. Placing the **gsave, grestore** operators around the wrap body ensures that the procedure does not modify the graphics state at all. Let's see how it works. You save the current graphics state at the beginning of the wrap. This preserves, in particular, the current path and the current coordinate system, including the origin. Then you perform the wrap code, moving the origin, drawing the path, and filling it. Then you execute **grestore** to match the beginning **gsave** and return to the exact graphics state where you started.

The coordinates, the current path, and every other graphics state parameter are just as they were at the start of the wrap. The only difference is that you have placed the screen image onto the output display.

Note here that you must fill the path if you are going to use **gsave, grestore** because the **grestore** removes the current path. Once that happens, you don't have any path to stroke or fill (as the case might be). This is the issue that we discussed earlier, when we originally designed the screenBox procedure, about independence versus flexibility. Where before we opted for flexibility, in this section we are stressing independence.

This facility gives you the opportunity to modify the procedure to make it even more independent and to remove one argument that can be replaced. By adding a **scale** operator and using a standard radius for the curve, you can eliminate the *Radius* argument. In that case, you might choose to replace it with another dimension argument, thereby generalizing the procedure to a rounded rectangle instead of a square. Here is what that code would look like:

```
defineps PSWscreenRectFill (float Xpos, Ypos, Width, Hgt)
    gsave
        newpath
        Xpos Ypos translate
        Width Hgt scale
        0.5 0 moveto
        1 0 1 1 .2 arct
        1 1 0 1 .2 arct
        0 1 0 0 .2 arct
        0 0 1 0 .2 arct
        closepath
        fill
    grestore
endps
```

To see what this produces, let's once again run it in our standard manner.

```
void runPSInline (void)
{
    float x, y;
    float width, height;

    x = 100;
    y = 200;
    width = height = 72;
```

        PSWscreenRectFill (x, y, width, height);
}

This produces the output display shown in Figure 3-29.

Figure 3-29. Output of screenRectFill.

This is yet another variant of the independent graphics procedure. The basic features are the same as the earlier version; the new feature is the use of the **scale** operator to make the rectangle. Notice how this is done. The measures on each axis are set nonuniformly to the *Width* and *Hgt* arguments. Then a unit square with fixed radius corners is drawn. Because of the scaling, however, the actual object path that is created is the correct rectangle that you want. All the fixed units in the procedure are no longer genuinely fixed; instead, they are modified by the scaling factors to make them the correct size that you want. As before, the **gsave, grestore** ensure that these transformations have no impact on anything outside the procedure itself.

There is one caution to note here as well. You see that this is a filled object and is not stroked. You might suppose that it doesn't matter whether you fill or stroke this path—and, generally, you would be correct. Here, however, you have scaled the coordinate units and, moreover, have possibly scaled them nonuniformly. In such cases, you will find that the stroke is magnified by the **scale** just as any other graphic effect is, and so you will probably not get the result that you want. If you want to stroke the path, you are advised to use another technique to avoid this complication.

CREATING A LOGO GRAPHIC

This exercise builds on the concepts that you have been working with throughout this chapter. Although the examples in the text have illustrated the various points in the chapter and many of them have built on preceding work, this exercise is intended to integrate much of this material and allow you to see many of these ideas in a practical setting.

This exercise builds a logo for an imaginary company, Acme Software. The logo consists of a single, six-sided figure with a filled circle in the middle. The figure is not regular, but instead looks something like a triangle with the points cut off. Figure 3-30 shows you the exact layout and dimensions for the triangular figure, and Figure 3-31 shows you the layout and dimensions for the filled circle inside the triangle.

Figure 3-30. Layout for triangular element in logo graphic.

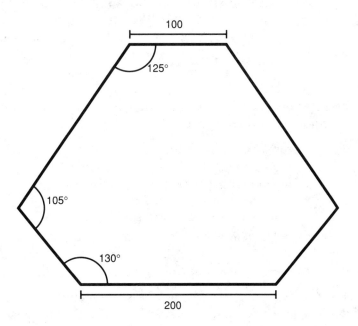

Figure 3-31. Layout for circle in logo.

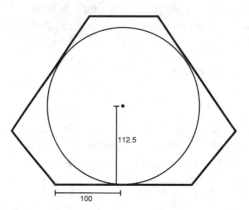

Note some differences between this figure and previous layouts that you have used. First, the dimensions are in units, not in inches. In fact, these units are not even necessarily tied to the coordinate system; they are simply intended to give relative dimensions for the logo graphic. All sides are either 100 or 200 units, so that the short sides are all the same length as the top line and the long sides are all the same length as the bottom line. The interior angles shown in Figure 3-30 are an important part of the overall layout, as you will see. The center and radius for the circle inside the figure were determined by a little geometry and empirical adjustment. The exterior figure is stroked at a line width of 4 units, and the center circle is both stroked with a line width of 1 and filled with 40 percent gray. The idea here is to produce this logo in a single wrap that can be placed and sized as required to display it correctly.

You are probably, by now, quite able to analyze such layouts for yourself and work out the necessary wraps to create such a figure. Let me just suggest a few points about the creation of such a graphic object. To begin with, you want to be able to position and scale the graphic as required. I would suggest that you pass the desired position and scale parameters to the wrap and let it do the work for you. Since all the measurements in the layout are relative, you could use any one of them; the exercise here uses the short side dimension as the argument for calculating convenience.

The next point, and possibly the most difficult to visualize, is how to draw the outline for the triangular figure. You could, of course, calculate the corner points, but that is tedious. Much easier and more comprehensible is to draw each side relative to the endpoint of the preceding side, using **rlineto**. Moreover, since the sides are in a fixed relationship to one another, the best way to do this will be to rotate the coordinates before you draw each side. In that way, each line will lie along a single axis, and can be easily drawn.

Logo Wrap

At this point you are ready to create the wrap function. We call this the PSWlogo wrap, and the code to generate the logo is as follows:

```
defineps PSWlogo ( float Xpos, Ypos, Short )
    gsave
    % first set up coordinates
        Xpos Ypos translate
    % then calculate variables
        /Radius 1.125 Short mul def
        /Long 2 Short mul def
    % next draw circle - stroke and fill it
        newpath
        Short Radius Radius 0 360 arc
        gsave
            .6 setgray
            fill
        grestore
        stroke
    % finally draw triangle figure and stroke it
        newpath
        0 0 moveto
        Long 0 rlineto
        50 rotate
        Short 0 rlineto
        75 rotate
        Long 0 rlineto
        55 rotate
        Short 0 rlineto
        55 rotate
        Long 0 rlineto
        75 rotate
        Short 0 rlineto
        50 rotate
        closepath
```

```
        4 setlinewidth
        stroke
    grestore
endps
```

Let's review the wrap together. You begin with a **gsave** operator to save the current graphics state, thus ensuring that any changes we make in the wrap are confined to it alone. Next you translate the origin to the bottom left corner of the base of the figure, using the argument values that were supplied in the call. Next you calculate the length of the radius—which is also the *y* coordinate for the center of the circle—and the length of the long side of the figure from the given short dimension. Note two things here. First, you could just as easily have used the long side dimension if you had wanted; it would be a divide operation instead of a multiply. Second, you could avoid these definitions if you wanted, by simply substituting the actual calculations into the wrap at the appropriate places. To keep the procedure as clear as possible, that is not done here.

Now you come to the meat of the wrap. You first draw and stroke the circle. The path is constructed by the familiar **arc** operator. Note here how you can save a path so that you can reuse it: you place a **gsave, grestore** pair around the **fill** and its associated **setgray**. This restores the path after the **fill** has wiped it out and allows you to reuse the path for the **stroke** operator. The circle must be drawn and filled first, before the outside figure, so that the lines that form the outside figure are not obscured by the filled circle. Remember that the last figure painted completely obscures whatever is beneath it.

Next you draw the triangular figure that forms the outside of the logo graphic. This is quite easy to draw with the tools now at your command. You begin, as always, with a **newpath** and then move to the origin, which you earlier translated to be the correct position for the base of the figure. You then move a long unit (twice the short argument, remember) along the *x*-axis. This draws the base of the figure. Next you rotate the coordinates through 180 degrees minus the interior angle of the figure; at this corner, that is 180 minus 130 or 50 degrees. This rotation now places the *x*-axis along the direction of the next side that you want to draw. Therefore, along this axis you now draw a short unit line. Then you perform the same trick again, this time using 180 minus 105 degrees. The next side is a long unit, but still directly along the *x*-axis, thanks to the rotation. And so you continue around the figure until you have completed all six sides. Of course, you could choose to not finish the last side, and let the **closepath** do it for you. In my experience, this is not usually a good idea because the **closepath** always finishes the figure back to the starting point. For a regular figure, I try to finish the path myself to ensure that I have calculated the points correctly; otherwise, you might have an error and only discover it much later. The final **closepath** is still necessary, however, to ensure that the path ends are joined correctly. Note that this same technique, of drawing the segment to the final point and then using a **closepath,** is essential when you are drawing curved line segments, since a **closepath** will add a straight line segment to the path if it is not at the final point.

The last thing you do is to set the line width and **stroke** the path. This completes the logo and allows you to issue the **grestore** that matches the original **gsave,** thus coming back to your application with the graphic state in exactly the same condition as when you left it.

To see the result on the display, let's insert this into our usual runPSInline procedure as follows:

```
void runPSInline(void)
{
    float x, y, dim;

    x = y = 72;
    dim = 60;
    PSWlogo(x, y, dim);
}
```

This produces the output shown in Figure 3-32.

Figure 3-32. Logo graphic output.

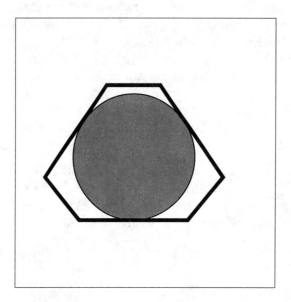

This exercise concludes the substantive portion of the chapter. This chapter has been full of new material and concepts that require some study and thought. Chapter 4 will help you digest this material because it is almost entirely exercises. You will construct a simple form using a variant of the logo graphic that you have just developed.

CONCLUSION

The chapter began with a section on the Display PostScript imaging model. This section, primarily a review of the previous concepts that you have worked with, leads naturally into simple PostScript graphics constructions. There are several examples here using straight line segments to illustrate both the old concepts and new operational issues. The examples proceed from straight line segments, to the creation of closed figures made from straight lines, to closed figures filled with shades of gray. The examples also illustrate how to create procedures that generate standard shapes and how such procedures can best be structured to be useful in a wide variety of circumstances.

The next section was concerned with fonts and PostScript font machinery. The section starts with some observations and definitions about fonts in general and then proceeds to specific information about PostScript fonts. This is an important topic because understanding and using fonts is one of the major issues in creating satisfactory display output.

The third section added curved line segments to the straight segments that you were working with earlier in the chapter and produced a similar set of examples based on simple circular arcs. This work leads into an examination of PostScript coordinate structure and the various transformations that can be used to modify the default user coordinate structure. The three most common transformations, translation, rotation, and scaling, were each discussed in detail.

The chapter ended with a final exercise that integrated all the preceding techniques and processes into a coherent, practical unit. This exercise created a simple, stylized logo for an imaginary company, which will also be used in Chapter 4 as part of a complete document display.

CHAPTER 4

Window Operations

This chapter integrates the processes and procedures that you have developed thus far in the book by means of a long exercise. The purpose of this exercise is to display a basic screen of both text and graphics.

The exercise consists of laying out a common form and filling it out. As always, the data entry part of the program is left to you; this is the device- and environment-dependent portion. Once you have the required pieces of information, however, you still must know how to display it. This is exactly the task that the exercise sets out to perform.

You will design and display a simple, basic document such as might be used in any accounting or money-related system. This document is a single-page form, a simple two-section check, and it is designed to be filled out by text and numeric data coming into the application from the screen. The form is a business check, with an attached stub on the bottom that allows you to enter a description of the purpose and so on. It is quite a standard form, one that is common to many typical business and personal systems. For this reason, it seems quite appropriate to use here.

The assumption here is that you have already received the necessary information to fill out the check—possibly from keyboard input, but it might just as easily come from a database or a transmitted file. The form itself is displayed blank, as a unit. The appropriate data is then added to the form and displayed in blocks that might approximate those that you would receive in ordinary processing. This is intended to demonstrate the ordinary processes and complexity in creating window and page output.

A form is particularly illuminating, not only because forms are a regular part of ordinary life, but also because they are conceived and displayed as an output unit. In this respect, they are different from many other output applications where the division of output into units—windows, or pages, or whatever—is essentially arbitrary.

This form is presented as a quick approach to putting together a prototype display for an application. The wraps and other functions developed in the body of the chapter trade ease of programming and debugging for speed and efficiency. This seems very reasonable here. First, this allows you to try a variety of PostScript and Display PostScript methods so that you will learn new techniques for your future work. Second, the display here is quite short and simple; the gains available from alternative approaches are minuscule, at best, for such a simple display. Finally, these techniques minimize the problems you may have in porting this display onto a standard PostScript output device.

However, it is important that you understand and have available more efficient techniques when you need or want to use them. For that reason, this chapter ends with a discussion of the alternative techniques that you could use in this exercise to speed up the display and make it more efficient. Once you have created the prototype, you will see that this conversion is quite easy, if you want to do it.

SETTING UP THE EXERCISE

Before you can proceed to any other problems in designing and displaying this form, you must consider the overall structure of the task at hand; that is, to create a check and fill it with appropriate information. A number of points need to be resolved before you can complete this job successfully. This section of the chapter presents a simple but effective approach to this, or any similar, task.

The form in this exercise needs to be structured to accommodate both the fixed display of the form and the display of the variable information that fills in the check. Both the fixed and the variable parts of the page have their own requirements that impose constraints on the design and display, and yet each must also fit into the other. In addition, the variable information may come in pieces, not necessarily in any given order. The solution is to consider the design of each segment of the display separately.

In a sense, the exercise is designed as two separate displays. The first part of the display is the blank form, and the second part is the various fields of variable information that must be displayed. The final display is created by overlaying all these elements onto one output. You might think of this as two transparent overlays on top of the window. The one is a fixed display of the form; the other, a sheet where the user can write the variable data that is required. The technique is to place one image onto the display, and then lay the other data on top of it, displaying both as a single composite graphic.

Overall Design

At this point, you should take a look at what this form will be like. You don't need, just yet, to get too detailed. This is just an overview to give you an idea of what we need to program and how it will be laid out. Here, as would normally be the case in a real application, I have laid out a check form in blocks, based on an actual check design that was prepared for computer output. The block design is shown in two pieces, in Figures 4-1 and 4-2.

Figure 4-1. Block design for overall check form.

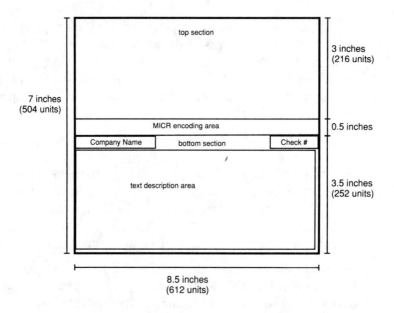

Figure 4-2. Block design for upper part of check form.

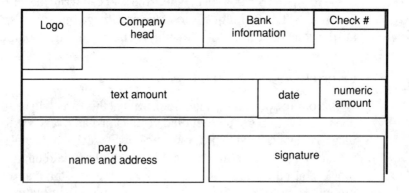

This is presented in two parts so that you can see the various elements in a clear and unambiguous way. The first design, in Figure 4-1, shows the upper and lower parts of the check, separated by the MICR coding region. The overall dimensions of each of the sections of the check form is also shown. The entire form is 8.5 inches wide, as you might expect. The upper section of the form is what we might call the check proper; it is 3 inches high and contains the amount, payee, and so on. A more precise block layout of this top region is shown in Figure 4-2. The bottom section is 3.5 inches high and is quite a bit simpler. These two regions are divided by a third region of 0.5 inch that is set aside for the MICR encoding required for bank processing.

The top section is broken down into several components. These can be best set out in the following table.

Component	Description
logo	The company logo, basically the same logo that you prepared at the end of Chapter 3.
company head	The name, address, and telephone number of the company in a standard format.
bank info	The name, address, and bank number of the issuing bank.
check num	The check number, such as 1225.
text amount	The amount of the check in words, such as "Three hundred forty-two and 50/100".
date	The date of the check as a text string, such as "3 Nov, 1989".
numeric amount	The amount of the check as a text number, such as "342.50".
pay to	The area for the name, and possibly address, of the payee of the check. This region is set up so that the check can be placed directly into a window envelope.
signature	The area where the check will be signed, either manually or automatically.

Note that the date field is presented as a text string so that alternate formats such as 11/3/89 or 3/11/89 can be used to accommodate whatever the system date format may be. This allows easy and central customization and internationalization. The same logic is used in the numeric amount field as in the date field. The conversion to text is done outside the display routines for easy internationalization.

The second part of the check is the bottom half of the form. This part is quite simple compared to the top, and it shows only three blocks. The company name and the check number are derived from the information in the top of the check. The text description area consists of a region of data that can be filled in to provide a description of the transaction. This is essentially free-form, except that it is a text area and is divided into lines for easy text entry and display. The actual number of lines that can be displayed is determined by the leading value for the text that has been set outside the display routines, as we will discuss in the following event sequence.

The third segment of the check form is the MICR encoding area. The exact contents and layout of the MICR codes and of this entire region is precisely laid out by interbank regulations, and we only discuss it briefly here. In real life, you would most likely acquire a MICR font for display of the account number here; indeed, it would be required if you were going to actually output this onto plain paper, using a magnetic toner to make a real check. For our purposes, however, this is simply another part of the form, and we will use the Symbol font to display the account number here so that it can be shown on the screen. If you have a MICR font, you may wish to substitute it.

Before you work out exactly what the form and data will look like, however, you need to think about how this is going to be presented to the user and how the user is going to respond. Since this is presumably an application, let's follow a typical scenario for selecting this form and filling it in with data. These actions are shown as a series of related, but not necessarily sequential, events that would normally take place. They are initiated by the user and responded to by the application. This forms the basis of our further analysis of the required procedures and wraps to support these actions. The following table shows the user actions and the application responses.

User Action	Application Response
Selects font, point size, and leading for variable information display.	Records choices in global variables.
Selects menu item for check form.	Opens new window and displays check form in it.
Enters data on form displayed in window.	Determines location of text entered, selects correct display procedure for given location, and makes any required data conversions.

The application must also take some of the following actions to make this application display correctly, based on external values and user input.

212   Display PostScript Programming

- The application must associate a context with the display window and save the context value as a global variable.

- The application must coordinate the window size and the display size to ensure that all the display elements fit inside the created window.

- The application must convert the numeric amount presented by the user into a string of words; for example, from "342.50" to "Three hundred forty-two and 50/100".

- For payee data, the application must determine what line the data is being entered on, based on the current cursor location and the global leading value.

- For text in the bottom section, the application must determine a line number for display purposes, based on cursor location and global leading.

- For all text display, the application is responsible for determining when text strings exceed the correct display location dimensions; for example, when the date or amounts cross over into other blocks of the displayed output.

For text in the bottom section of the form, we invert the display coordinate system, so that the origin is at the upper left corner of the text display area, and the positive y-axis is directed downward. This speeds up and improves the text display, and it also shows you a useful technique for handling text generally, especially, unlike this case, where you allow the user to control the exact location of the text. Here you are constraining the user to some degree by forcing the text into lines.

Before you can define a final layout for this form, you must still perform several more steps:

1. Determine the overall size of each graphic element.

2. Position and scale each element onto the final form layout.

3. Identify specific information (data elements) that will be required for each graphic element.

4. Decide on the size and placement of the data elements in each graphic element.

As you can see from this list, you are not yet finished with the blank form design and layout; you still need to detail out the exact location and positioning of the various elements that make up the blocks.

Layout Set Detail

In this case, the layout is made to match a typical business check from a major bank. No single layout can present all the information that you need to code this form; therefore, you must divide it into four parts:

1. *Layout of graphic elements*   Shows the various graphic elements—the logo, the company heading, and so on—in correct relationship. It also shows the designated coordinates for each element.

2. *Specification of the type*   Determines what type fonts, sizes, and styles are to be used for the fixed type elements. Also determines the exact placement for these elements on the form.

3. *Color specifications*   Specifies the colors and gray values to be used on the form, by graphic element.

4. *Variable data specification*   Shows the layout and placement of the variable data fields within the overall form. There is no type or exact placement because this is at least partially under user control.

These four layouts put together show you how to display this form.

The layout for the graphic elements of the check form is shown in Figure 4-3.

Figure 4-3. Form layout by graphic element.

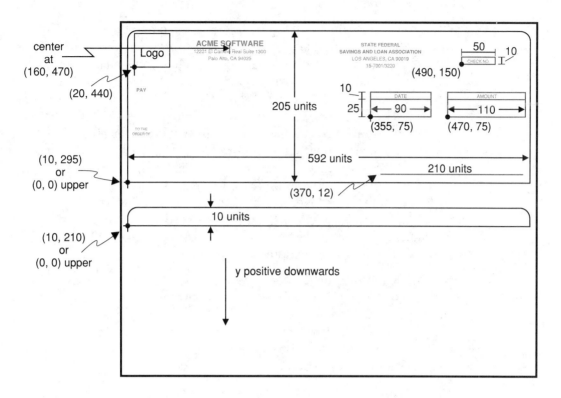

This figure does not present all the detailed information that you need, but it does give you the first look at the overall form. Let's review some of these specifications. You see that there is one repeating graphic element. This is a rectangle with a square bottom and rounded top corners, which we refer to as the *outline rectangle*. This figure is used in two places. It outlines and colors both the top of the check and a small area on the bottom of the check. The bottom left corner of each of these areas determines an origin for the top and bottom, respectively, of the form, each of which has an independent coordinate system.

These independent coordinate systems and their coordinate dimensions deserve some discussion. For now, you are laying this out as an 8.5-inch (612-unit) wide by 7-inch (504-unit) high space. The window need not correspond to these dimensions, which are the dimensions of the actual form. However, we are assuming that the relative dimensions of the window, its *aspect ratio*, which is the ratio of the width to the height, are the same as those of the form. If you create a window with the correct aspect

Chapter 4: Window Operations   215

ratio, you can easily scale the form display to fit into it and still retain the full-size coordinate system.

The form, as you can see in Figure 4-3, is divided into three parts. There are actually three coordinate grids used in this form, for good reason. The first grid is the one you have been using right along, and it has its origin at the bottom left corner of the window. The other two grids are set to provide convenient coordinate structures for the top and bottom, respectively, of the form. The top section has a coordinate origin at the point (10, 295) on the first grid. Other than the change of origin, these coordinates are exactly like the default coordinates. The coordinate grid on the bottom, however, is somewhat different. It has its origin at the point (10, 270) on the first grid, and the direction of the y-axis is set so that increasing values move down the form, not up. This helps set the text for display on the bottom of the form. All the graphic elements on the top, except the logo and company heading, are specified in the top coordinate system. Similarly, the elements of the bottom are specified in the bottom coordinates.

Finally, the logo and the company heading are shown in the original grid coordinates. The idea here is that the wraps that draw the logo and place the heading would be independent of the other drawing procedures. By making them independent, they can be reused on other forms and in other places. Therefore, they require separate placement on the check form from the other graphic elements.

All these placement coordinates share certain common elements. Each of the figures shows the coordinates of the bottom left corner of each graphic element. For left-adjusted text, the given coordinates are those of the left corner of the baseline. For centered text, the x coordinate is the center point of the string and the y coordinate is the baseline. For multiline text, this is the baseline of the top line; the following lines are spaced according to the leading value shown in the type specification layout below.

Most of these coordinates and the associated elements require little or no explanation. As you can see from the coordinates, the date and amount boxes are actually drawn as two separate elements: the bottom is a stroked rectangle and the top one is filled, with the base of the top being the same line as the top of the lower rectangle. The company heading consists of four text lines, centered on the point (140, 470). This point was chosen visually; it is not tied to any other specific element.

Finally, in the upper left corner, we have a space reserved for the logo graphic. Recall from Chapter 3 that the logo is drawn by calling a procedure with the x and y coordinates of the lower left corner of the logo and the short-side dimension. Here, you want to position the logo graphic as a rectangle, with the bottom left corner of that rectangle at the point (10, 440). This rectangle is the rectangle that exactly encloses all points of the logo and is called the *bounding box*. Using a short-side length of 100, Figure 4-4 shows the relationship between the graphic and the bounding box.

Figure 4-4. Logo bounding box.

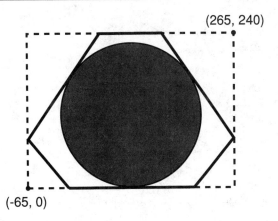

As you see, the bottom left corner—point (-65, 0) in Figure 4-4—and the upper right corner—point (265, 240) in the figure—completely and exactly define the bounding box. In fact, bounding boxes for graphics are quite common in PostScript, and they are always defined in this manner by giving the four coordinates of the lower left and upper right corners of the box. Encapsulated PostScript graphics are always defined in this way, and it would not require too much additional work to turn our logo into a graphic element that could be placed and manipulated in that fashion. Here, however, for simplicity, we have avoided this additional coding. Instead, the C program that calls the logo procedure adjusts the position and dimension coordinates so that the logo fits into the desired box.

Notice on the layout that only the height dimension is given. Either the height or width could have been specified, but only one of the dimensions was needed since you want the logo to appear in correct proportion. The aspect ratio, which in this case is 330:240, automatically determines the other. Since the height of the logo is set at 50 units, the width becomes ((50/240)*330), or 68.75 units. You want to use the height here since the vertical dimension is the critical one for fitting the logo onto the form; in other circumstances, where the horizontal positioning required more precise alignment, you might use the width.

The next layout, Figure 4-5, specifies the type fonts, sizes, and styles to be used for the fixed data elements in the form.

Figure 4-5. Type layout.

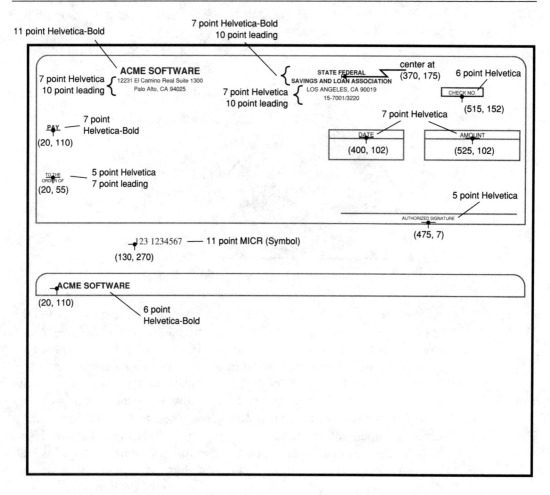

The font here is simple Helvetica, with the only change of family being for the MICR account number. If you have the MICR font, you would use that; here, for commonality and simplicity, we use the Symbol font. This doesn't look anything like a MICR font, but it does provide some special characters that we can use here to simulate the special MICR dividers. The layout also gives the positioning information for the text items. The coordinates follow the rules that we discussed earlier.

218   Display PostScript Programming

The third layout, shown in Figure 4-6, is quite simple visually, but may come as something of a surprise. This form is designed in two colors: dark blue and black. The text and many of the elements are in straight black. The date, amount, and the box around the check number label are in dark blue, as is the stroke around the outline rectangle in both parts of the form. In addition, the interior of the outline rectangle is painted with a 10% gray fill as a background.

Figure 4-6. Color layout.

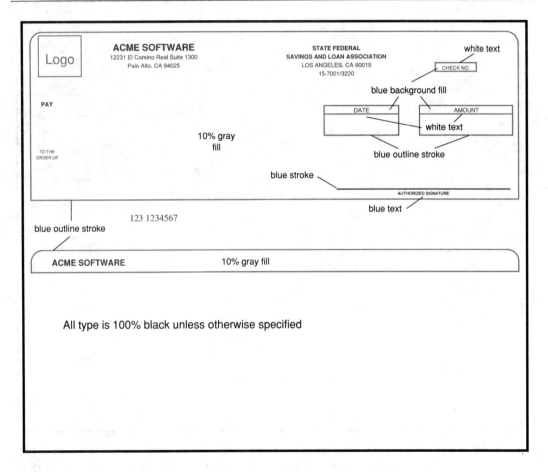

The last layout, shown in Figure 4-7, specifies the beginning locations of the variable data on the form. For the most part, the user determines the font, size, and style for this information. The next section discusses how to take care of this. The sole exception here is the check number. This is in a defined font and size, like the captions on the check form; however, because the check number is not a predefined value, it has also been laid out in this specification. Also note that the coordinate values for the check number are shown in the original window coordinates, not in the revised ones provided for each section of the form. This is done so that the wrap that prints the check numbers will not have to readjust the coordinates for each section because the number must appear on both sections.

Figure 4-7. Variable data layout.

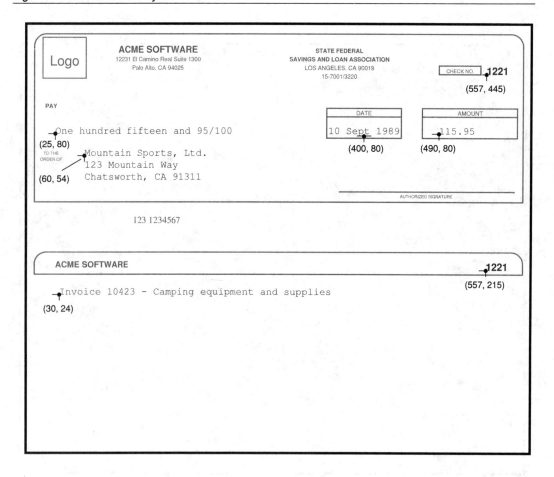

The changed coordinates are intended to facilitate the drawing; if they become a hindrance, don't use them. How this works may not be obvious at first. The point of the special coordinates is that each area of the form can be laid out and displayed independently of the other. This allows, for example, the routines used here to be reused in some other context or for another form. However, this requires that the coordinates be set up before each display. When you are displaying one item on both sections of the form, as here, swapping coordinates is an unneeded complication. You can use the simpler original coordinates to place the two check numbers and so avoid all the coordinate changes that you would otherwise have to make.

CREATING A BLANK FORM

Now that you have seen the various components of the check form laid out in detail, we need to consider how to actually create these elements in Display PostScript. The first thing to consider is the information used to fill out all the parts of the form. This data is of various types, and each needs to be integrated into the form.

Data Requirements

The data required for the check comes from several sources and represents several distinct types. The first type is the fixed information for the form that is programmed into the system. This might be presented in a data structure, from a file, or—least satisfactory—it may be hard-coded into the program. Although the hard-code is the least flexible and therefore would be avoided for some or all of these items in an actual application, it suits our requirements here perfectly, and so we will use it. The fixed information includes the following items: company logo; company name and address; bank name, address, and bank number; and bank account number. To give some flexibility, this information is set as global PostScript variables in the setup routine.

The second type is what might be thought of as system-generated variable information. These are the date and the check number fields. These fields are variable in the sense that they will change regularly; but they are normally provided by the system or the application. The application ordinarily fills in the date for the user by calling a system function, and it usually provides the check number from some external file or memory, based on the last previous check written on this account. In both cases, real, working applications would allow the user to override the default values. Here, however, for the sake of simplicity, we restrict these displays to the preprogrammed values. Nevertheless, these must be established outside of the PostScript environment and passed as parameters to the wraps that will display them.

The third type of information is the simplest to handle for display, although it is not the easiest to generate in practice. This is truly variable information, generated by the user, normally by keyboard input. As always, no attempt is made here to show you how to get or edit these keystrokes. The assumption here is that this data has been gathered into strings, ready for display. In addition, the presumption is that the application has determined, from the selected line spacing (or leading) value and from the cursor position, exactly where this string is to be displayed.

Text display here takes two formats. In one form, the position of the text determines what routine is called. No further positioning information is required. This occurs for the amount fields. The second form of data requires a position as well as the string. This form is used for the payee name and address data and for the text information block on the bottom half of the form. In both cases, the application determines a line number for the display and passes it to the PostScript wrap. It is up to the application to determine whether the text string "fits" onto the defined area, either in width or in length, and to take appropriate action if it does not fit.

For purposes of this exercise, all of these data items are determined by the selection of the strings to be displayed in the body procedures or in the wraps. This is necessary so that the exercise can be complete and self-contained. This analysis is still required, however, so that you can determine what functions to place in wraps, what to place in auxiliary C procedures, and what to do in the main procedure coding. The code that is produced here will run correctly as it stands; the coordinates and text strings are correct and correctly measured. However, this is actually all variable information that could be generated in a variety of ways in a more complete application.

The application must set and keep certain global variables. These are as follows:

- Check number
- Context
- Font name
- Font size
- Line spacing, or leading

Normally, these would be defined in a header file and used in all the separate procedures. Here, they are simply shown as global variables, and it is up to you to make them accessible to the various procedures. They are initialized here with the values that they will have for our exercise. You may wish to change them, or, if you have a more complex, working application, you may wish to connect them to actual external objects and let the user set them. The context, of course, is not initialized; it would be set by the routine that creates the window and gets the associated context. I assume that your window creation routine (or routines) have done so.

You may be wondering why we are concerned at this point about the context, whereas in the previous exercises we had been able to ignore it. The answer is both simple and illustrative. In the earlier exercises, only a single window was used to display the output you created. In this case, at least conceptually, there may be other windows, holding perhaps invoice forms, or statements, or purchase orders, and so on. Moreover, multiple checks might even be displayed. The application must be able to direct its output to the correct window to ensure that the data is in the right place. Generally this requires a connection with the window, either through the context or through some other environment-dependent variable.

The context is also required for another reason. In some environments, it is your responsibility to ensure that the interpreter has successfully processed all of the information that you wish to display before you continue. This coordination job is important enough that you must provide for synchronization at critical points if it is not done automatically. Here you see how to do this task if it is required in your operating environment.

Form Display

With these necessary preliminaries out of the way, let's proceed to the actual form. In this exercise, unlike the preceding ones, you start with the main procedure and work down to the required wraps. Obviously some work has already been done; for example, you have determined what global data is required, that the coordinates will be independent for the two sections, and so on. Nevertheless, you have not yet defined enough information to actually design or code the wraps. Instead of analyzing this any more, let's start out with the components and the layout that we have and work from the top structure down to the more basic elements.

The first part is to set out the global variables that you have already identified. These are as follows:

```
/* Global Variables */
char *font = "Courier";
float size = 12;
```

```
float leading = 14;
float chknum = 1221;
DPSContext ctx;
```

Next, you code the main procedure. At the main procedure level, this is envisioned as one of possibly several forms that the user might choose. A common way of handling this would be in a case structure. Using that approach, you would have the following code:

```
char *date;
/* initialize for example - normally from system */
date = "6 Nov 1989";
case CHECK:
    ctx = makeWindow();
    drawCheck(ctx);
    PSselectfont(font, size);
    PSWdispDate(date);
    DPSWaitContext(ctx);
break;
```

As yet there is, of course, no display since you haven't created the support procedures. However, the basic flow is fairly straightforward. The user selects the check form, which is equivalent to the case constant, CHECK—which was presumably set in a header or somewhere. This case starts by creating a window to hold the check form; the procedure returns the context value associated with the new window. The next procedure, drawCheck, creates the blank check form into the given window. It sets the current context to that provided by the first procedure and does not reset it. Once that has been done, it is no longer necessary to reference the context in the remaining calls. After the form is drawn, the next process is to set the current font to the display font and size chosen by the user. Here, the default selection of 12-point Courier is used. Then you display the date in the chosen font, using the wrap procedure PSWdispDate. Notice that this takes the date as a string, as we discussed earlier. Finally, you issue a DPSWaitContext so that the application does not proceed until the display is complete and ready for further processing.

As always, the makeWindow procedure is not covered here, being directly dependent on the system environment. However, we do need to discuss the size of the window before proceeding. The check form itself is designed to be 8.5 inches by 7 inches. This is quite wide for most displays and probably not necessary on the screen. However, when you print, you do want it to be that size. This can be easily handled by creating a window of the same aspect ratio as the check form but somewhat smaller, and then scaling the check display down to the window size. In this way, the display is entirely in full-size coordinates, but the display is adjusted to the desired smaller size. Here we assume that the window is 60 percent of the full-size form, or 5.1 inches wide and 4.2 inches high.

Setting that aside then, you have identified so far one auxiliary C procedure and one wrap. In addition, you have used the Client Library functions PSselectfont—an old friend by now—and the new DPSWaitContext.

C Support Procedures

Obviously most of the work here is in the auxiliary procedure, drawCheck. This procedure calls the wraps necessary to draw the check form. It might look like this:

```
/* drawCheck */
void drawCheck (DPSContext ctx);
{
    float x, y;
    float dim;

    DPSSetContext(ctx);
    PSscale(0.6, 0.6);
    PSWsetupCheck();
    x = 10;
    y = 295;
    drawChkTop(x, y);
    y = 210;
    PSWdrawChkBottom(x, y);
    x = 140;
    y = 470;
    drawHead(x, y);
    /* calculate starting point and dimensions */
    /* ratio is 50/240 */
    /* bounding box corner is (10, 440) */
    y = 440;
    /* corner (10) plus offset of 65 * ratio */
    x = 10 + (65 * (50/240));
    /* size is 100 * ratio */
    dim = (100 * (50/240));
    PSWlogo(x, y, dim);
```

```
        PSWcheckNo(checknum);
}
```

This procedure contains several wraps and functions and deserves careful study. It begins by setting the current context to that provided as an argument, using the DPSSetContext procedure from the Client Library. This allows the remainder of the procedures to ignore the context issue and simply draw into the current context, as usual. The next procedure is the **scale,** which fits our form into the window. Then the real work of the function begins.

Jumping a bit out of sequence, let's first look at the function to draw the top of the check.

```
void drawChkTop ( float xpos, ypos )
{
    /* save current graphics state
     * since the following code modifies it
     */
    PSgsave();

    /* first set background for top */
    PSWdrawBkgnd( xpos, ypos);

    /* then add black elements
    PSsetgray(0.0);

    /* first all bold */
    setFontWidth("Helvetica-Bold", 7.0);
    /* bank heading */
    /* stringwidth for "STATE FEDERAL" is 57.946 */
    centerText(370, 175, "STATE FEDERAL");
    /* stringwidth for "SAVINGS AND LOAN ASSOCIATION" is 120.953 */
    centerText(370, 165, "SAVINGS AND LOAN ASSOCIATION");
    /* labels */
    /* stringwidth for "PAY" is 14.392 */
    centerText(20, 110, "PAY");

    /* next the regular font */
    setFontWidth("Helvetica", 7.0);
    /* bank address */
    /* stringwidth for "LOS ANGELES, CA 90019" is 84.042 */
    centerText(370, 155, "LOS ANGELES, CA 90019");
```

```
/* stringwidth for "15-7001 / 3220" is 47.089 */
centerText(370, 145, "15-7001 / 3220");

/* payee heading */
setFontWidth("Helvetica", 5.0);
/* stringwidth for "TO THE" is 18.335 */
centerText(20, 55, "TO THE");
/* stringwidth for "ORDER OF" is 26.340 */
centerText(20, 48, "ORDER OF");

/* set color elements */
PSWdrawColor();
/* and text (blue color and same font as last text) */
/* stringwidth for "AUTHORIZED SIGNATURE" is 63.060 */
centerText(475, 7, "AUTHORIZED SIGNATURE");

%and last the white text
PSsetgray(1.0);
setFontWidth("Helvetica", 7.0);
/* stringwidth for "DATE" is 18.669 */
centerText(400, 102, "DATE");
/* stringwidth for "AMOUNT" is 30.331 */
centerText(525, 102, "AMOUNT");
setFontWidth("Helvetica", 6.0);
/* stringwidth for "CHECK NO." is 33.336 */
centerText(515, 152, "CHECK NO.");
PSgrestore();

%return to standard coordinates and set MICR data
PSselectfont("Symbol", 11.0);
PSWmovetoShow(130.0, 270.0, "\130002055\130
\300121000148\300");

}
```

This function is long but not really very complex, and it uses auxiliary functions that are quite familiar by now. The only C auxiliary functions that you need to update for this are those that calculate the string width. For these, you need new font width tables. Of course, if you have implemented the font widths from the font metric files, you don't need to make any changes. However, if you are using the functions that we defined in Chapter 2, you will need the new tables for Helvetica and Helvetica-Bold.

These are shown below, along with an updated version of the setFontWidth function that allows selection of any one of several font width tables.

```c
/* STRWID2.C
 *   creates AFM tables for font metrics
 *   also defines algorithms for getting and setting string widths
 */

#include <string.h>
#include <stdio.h>
#include <conio.h>
#include <dos.h>
float cwi[256];        /* a table to hold character widths */
float HELVBOLD[ ] =    /* actual values for Helvetica-Bold */
    {
    278.0, 278.0, 278.0, 278.0, 278.0, 278.0, 278.0, 278.0, 278.0, 278.0, 278.0,
    278.0, 278.0, 278.0, 278.0, 278.0, 278.0, 278.0, 278.0, 278.0, 278.0, 278.0,
    278.0, 278.0, 278.0, 278.0, 278.0, 278.0, 278.0, 278.0, 278.0, 278.0, 278.0,
    333.0, 474.0, 556.0, 556.0, 889.0, 722.0, 278.0, 333.0, 333.0, 389.0, 584.0,
    278.0, 333.0, 278.0, 278.0, 556.0, 556.0, 556.0, 556.0, 556.0, 556.0, 556.0,
    556.0, 556.0, 556.0, 333.0, 333.0, 584.0, 584.0, 584.0, 611.0, 975.0, 722.0,
    722.0, 722.0, 722.0, 667.0, 611.0, 778.0, 722.0, 278.0, 556.0, 722.0, 611.0,
    833.0, 722.0, 778.0, 667.0, 778.0, 722.0, 667.0, 611.0, 722.0, 667.0, 944.0,
    667.0, 667.0, 611.0, 333.0, 278.0, 333.0, 584.0, 556.0, 278.0, 556.0, 611.0,
    556.0, 611.0, 556.0, 333.0, 611.0, 611.0, 278.0, 278.0, 556.0, 278.0, 889.0,
    611.0, 611.0, 611.0, 611.0, 389.0, 556.0, 333.0, 611.0, 556.0, 778.0, 556.0,
    556.0, 500.0, 389.0, 280.0, 389.0, 584.0, 278.0, 278.0, 278.0, 278.0, 278.0,
    278.0, 278.0, 278.0, 278.0, 278.0, 278.0, 278.0, 278.0, 278.0, 278.0, 278.0,
    278.0, 278.0, 278.0, 278.0, 278.0, 278.0, 278.0, 278.0, 278.0, 278.0, 278.0,
    278.0, 278.0, 278.0, 278.0, 278.0, 278.0, 278.0, 333.0, 556.0, 556.0, 167.0,
    556.0, 556.0, 556.0, 556.0, 238.0, 500.0, 556.0, 333.0, 333.0, 611.0, 611.0,
    278.0, 556.0, 556.0, 556.0, 278.0, 278.0, 556.0, 350.0, 278.0, 500.0, 500.0,
    556.0, 1000.0, 1000.0, 278.0, 611.0, 278.0, 333.0, 333.0, 333.0, 333.0, 333.0,
    333.0, 333.0, 333.0, 278.0, 333.0, 333.0, 278.0, 333.0, 333.0, 333.0, 1000.0,
    278.0, 278.0, 278.0, 278.0, 278.0, 278.0, 278.0, 278.0, 278.0, 278.0, 278.0,
    278.0, 278.0, 278.0, 278.0, 278.0, 1000.0, 278.0, 370.0, 278.0, 278.0, 278.0,
    278.0, 611.0, 778.0, 1000.0, 365.0, 278.0, 278.0, 278.0, 278.0, 278.0, 889.0,
    278.0, 278.0, 278.0, 278.0, 278.0, 278.0, 278.0, 611.0, 944.0, 611.0, 278.0,
    278.0, 278.0, 278.0,
    };
float HELV[] =     /* actual values for Helvetica */
    {
```

```
        278.0, 278.0, 278.0, 278.0, 278.0, 278.0, 278.0, 278.0, 278.0, 278.0,
        278.0, 278.0, 278.0, 278.0, 278.0, 278.0, 278.0, 278.0, 278.0, 278.0,
        278.0, 278.0, 278.0, 278.0, 278.0, 278.0, 278.0, 278.0, 278.0, 278.0,
        278.0, 355.0, 556.0, 556.0, 889.0, 667.0, 222.0, 333.0, 333.0, 389.0, 584.0,
        278.0, 333.0, 278.0, 278.0, 556.0, 556.0, 556.0, 556.0, 556.0, 556.0, 556.0,
        556.0, 556.0, 556.0, 278.0, 278.0, 584.0, 584.0, 584.0, 556.0, 1015.0, 667.0,
        667.0, 722.0, 722.0, 667.0, 611.0, 778.0, 722.0, 278.0, 500.0, 667.0, 556.0,
        833.0, 722.0, 778.0, 667.0, 778.0, 722.0, 667.0, 611.0, 722.0, 667.0, 944.0,
        667.0, 667.0, 611.0, 278.0, 278.0, 278.0, 469.0, 556.0, 222.0, 556.0, 556.0,
        500.0, 556.0, 556.0, 278.0, 556.0, 566.0, 222.0, 222.0, 500.0, 222.0, 833.0,
        556.0, 556.0, 556.0, 556.0, 333.0, 500.0, 278.0, 556.0, 500.0, 722.0, 500.0,
        500.0, 500.0, 334.0, 260.0, 334.0, 584.0, 278.0, 278.0, 278.0, 278.0, 278.0,
        278.0, 278.0, 278.0, 278.0, 278.0, 278.0, 278.0, 278.0, 278.0, 278.0, 278.0,
        278.0, 278.0, 278.0, 278.0, 278.0, 278.0, 278.0, 278.0, 278.0, 278.0, 278.0,
        278.0, 278.0, 278.0, 278.0, 278.0, 278.0, 278.0, 333.0, 556.0, 556.0, 167.0,
        556.0, 556.0, 556.0, 556.0, 191.0, 333.0, 556.0, 333.0, 333.0, 500.0, 500.0,
        278.0, 556.0, 556.0, 556.0, 278.0, 278.0, 537.0, 350.0, 222.0, 333.0, 333.0,
        556.0, 1000.0, 1000.0, 278.0, 611.0, 278.0, 333.0, 333.0, 333.0, 333.0, 333.0,
        333.0, 333.0, 333.0, 278.0, 333.0, 333.0, 278.0, 333.0, 333.0, 333.0, 1000.0,
        278.0, 278.0, 278.0, 278.0, 278.0, 278.0, 278.0, 278.0, 278.0, 278.0, 278.0,
        278.0, 278.0, 278.0, 278.0, 278.0, 1000.0, 278.0, 370.0, 278.0, 278.0, 278.0,
        278.0, 556.0, 778.0, 1000.0, 365.0, 278.0, 278.0, 278.0, 278.0, 278.0, 889.0,
        278.0, 278.0, 278.0, 278.0, 278.0, 278.0, 222.0, 611.0, 944.0, 611.0, 278.0,
        278.0, 278.0, 278.0,
    };
float NULLFNT[256] = { 0.0 }; /* null font - initialize to all zeros */

void setFontWidth( char *name, float ps )
{
        * the real function would access an AFM file
        * based on the font name
        * then collect the font width information in a table
        * and then compute the actual character widths at the desired point size
        * and store the result in the external array 'float cwi[256]'
        */

        int i;
        float *pw;

        pw = NULLFNT;
        if (strcmp(name, "Helvetica-Bold") == 0)
```

```
              pw = HELVBOLD;
    if (strcmp(name, "Helvetica") == 0)
              pw = HELV;

    for (i = 0; i < 256; i++)
         cwi[i] = (*(pw + i) * ps) / 1000;

    return(0);
}
```

The other auxiliary functions, centerText and strWidth, are the same as before. Remember to either compile all the C functions together or place the common elements into a header file and make them external variables that can be referenced from all of the functions.

The positioning and graphic elements are all as defined by the layouts that you have already seen. Be careful that the elements are drawn in the correct painting order. Since PostScript uses opaque paint, it is essential that the background be painted before anything that is to appear on top of it; otherwise the background will obscure anything underneath. Similarly, the white text on the blue background must be set after the boxes are drawn.

The drawChkTop function saves and restores the current graphics state, using the Client Library functions PSgsave() and PSgrestore(). This is exactly analogous to what you would do in a standard PostScript environment and illustrates that you can easily translate code from one language environment to another. It uses our familiar PSWmovetoShow procedure to display the MICR date on the check. It also uses two custom wraps, PSWdrawBkgnd and PSWdrawColor, to create the background and to draw the colored elements on the top of the check. As you will see, the first wrap also contains some essential setup work.

Next let's look at the auxiliary function, drawHead, which draws the headings for the top of the check. This function uses the standard coordinates so it does not require any special wraps to function. It looks like this:

```
void drawHead ( float xpos, ypos )
{
    setFontWidth("Helvetica-Bold", 11.0);
    /* stringwidth for "ACME SOFTWARE" is 98.384 */
    centerText(xpos, ypos, "ACME SOFTWARE");
    setFontWidth("Helvetica", 7.0);
    /* stringwidth for street address is 107.387 */
```

```
        centerText(xpos, ypos - 10, "12231 El Camino Real, Suite 1300");
        /* stringwidth for city, state is 64.981 */
        centerText(xpos, ypos - 20, "Palo Alto, CA 94025");
}
```

This function simply places the correct text in the correct font at the positions already determined in the layout. The support functions are identical to those for drawChkTop.

Form Wraps

There are six wraps that are used in this process of drawing the blank check form. They can be described as follows:

PSWsetupCheck
sets the procedures and variables required for the subsequent check processing.

PSWdrawBkgnd
draws the background for the top of the check and sets the graphics state for the components of the top of the check.

PSWdrawColor
draws the colored elements of the top of the check.

PSWdrawChkBottom
draws the fixed elements of the bottom of the check.

PSWcheckNo
shows the check number at the desired position on the check.

PSWlogo
draws the logo graphic onto the top of the check. This is identical to the PSWlogo wrap that you created in Chapter 3.

To use PSWlogo, you have to set the corner point and the dimensions for the logo. This is done in a series of calculations in the procedure body. Although there are other approaches to creating and using a graphic such as this, the one here, with the coordinate calculations in C, is quite fast since C handles such calculations quite well. To follow the calculations, refer back to Figure 4-4.

The positioning on the layout gives a point for the lower left corner of the bounding box and a height for it. As you see from Figure 4-4, when the short side of the logo is 100 units, the height is 240 units. Since we want the height here to be 50 units, you need to make the short-side dimension

(100 * (50/240)). In the same way, when the short side is 100, the offset for the lower left corner of the bounding box is -65 units in the *x*-axis; the *y*-axis remains the same. So, to position the lower left corner of the actual logo, you must add a distance of 65 units to the corner of the bounding box. In this case, that displacement is (65 * (50/240)). This is added to the 10 position for the corner of the bounding box and gives the correct offset for the logo.

Let's look at the code for these wraps individually. Since the setup is a derivative of the other procedures, let's do that last. Begin with the simplest of the wraps:

```
defineps PSWcheckNo ( float CheckNum )
    /Helvetica-Bold 12.0 selectfont
    % convert check number to string for display
    CheckNum 5 string cvs
    dup
    557 445 moveto show
    557 215 moveto show
endps
```

This wrap simply shows the check number in the positions that you established earlier. The number comes into the wrap as a float value; the assumption here is that this is kept as a numeric value in the application. Since PostScript only displays a string value, you must invoke the **cvs** (convert to string) operator to change the number into a string. This is done by using the **string** operator to create an empty string five spaces long; the **cvs** uses this to store the result of the conversion. Notice that this limits the check number to a maximum of five digits.

PSWlogo is identical to the procedure in Chapter 3.

```
defineps PSWlogo ( float Xpos, Ypos, Short )
    gsave
    % first set up coordinates
        Xpos Ypos translate
    % then calculate variables
        /Radius 1.125 Short mul def
        /Long 2 Short mul def
    % next draw circle - stroke and fill it
        newpath
        Short Radius Radius 0 360 arc
        gsave
            .6 setgray
```

```
            fill
        grestore
        stroke
    % finally draw triangle figure and stroke it
        newpath
        0 0 moveto
        Long 0 rlineto
        50 rotate
        Short 0 rlineto
        75 rotate
        Long 0 rlineto
        55 rotate
        Short 0 rlineto
        55 rotate
        Long 0 rlineto
        75 rotate
        Short 0 rlineto
        50 rotate
        closepath
        4 setlinewidth
        stroke
    grestore
endps
```

Next let's look at the two wraps that help set up the top of the check in the function drawChkTop, which we designed earlier.

```
defineps PSWdrawBkgnd ( float Xpos, Ypos )
    FormDict begin                                  %1
        newpath                                     %2
    %set up adjusted coordinate system
        Xpos Ypos translate                         %3
    %save for future use
        /TopState gstate def                        %4
    %draw background first
        .9 setgray                                  %5
        ChkBkgnd ufill                              %6
    end                                             %7
endps

defineps PSWdrawColor ( )
    FormDict begin
```

```
            %now set blue elements
                0 0 1 setrgbcolor                                    %8
            %stroke outline
                ChkBkgnd ustroke                                     %9
            %data boxes
                355 75 90 25 rectstroke
                355 100 90 10 rectfill
                470 75 110 25 rectstroke
                470 100 110 10 rectfill
                490 150 50 10 rectfill
            %signature line
                370 12 moveto
                210 0 rlineto
                stroke
        end
endps
```

These two wraps are not unusual; however, they do have two features that are new to you: the use of a graphics state object to store the revised coordinate system for later use, in line %4, and the use of user paths to help draw graphics for the background, in lines %6 and %9.

The wrap PSWdrawBkgnd begins, on line %1, by establishing the private dictionary, FormDict, as the current dictionary. This is the same dictionary that you have met before. It is removed at the end of the procedure, in line %7. The second wrap, PSWdrawColor also sets and removes this dictionary.

Line %8 introduces you to a new color operator, **setrgbcolor.** This operator works in a manner exactly analogous to the **setgray** operator, except that it sets red, green, and blue light instead of white. The three operands are values for red, green, and blue, respectively. If the operands are all set to 1, then the result is exactly the same as **1 setgray** since the result will be white light. Here you have set 100 percent blue and no red or green.

Note two things. First, the PostScript interpreter automatically converts the value from blue into a gray level if your system does not support color output. Second, this value carries over into your output file and can be used to create color separations and other printed output.

Graphic Objects

You were introduced to the concept of graphic objects earlier; here you have a concrete use of them. In this case, you need to save the coordinate transformation that you have made so that it can be used later in the display of the variable text on the check. You could, of course, have saved the x and y coordinates that you have passed into the wrap and sent them again and again for each variable that you display. It is easier and faster, however, to set up the coordinates once and then save the graphics state. Lines %3 and %4 perform this task. Line %3 moves the origin to the new point that you want. Then line %4 returns the current graphics state (which includes the redefined coordinates) as a graphics state object and saves it. Note that it is saved in your private dictionary FormDict so that it can be retrieved by the other procedures without any difficulty.

The PostScript graphics state consists, as you know, of many individual parameters that are accessed implicitly by the imaging operators. Although it is possible to set each of these individually—as you have done repeatedly in the past—it is often more useful to save and use them as a unit.

The traditional way to do this is by the **gsave, grestore** operators that you have been using. However, in a display environment, these are not always sufficient. The situation here is a good example. A **gsave** only pushes the current graphics state onto the graphics state stack. The problem is that, when you enter one of the variable display routines, since they are executed in an arbitrary sequence, you won't know where that state is on the stack or even whether it is still there. The solution is to save this specific state, using the **gstate** operator as you do here, and then restore that state when you are ready to do the display.

User Paths

The other new concept here is that of the *user path*. This is a new feature in Display PostScript that allows you to create arbitrary paths and save them in a compact form for repeated use. These paths can be preprocessed and saved for even faster recovery, if they are going to be reused in exactly the same form many times. Here, we have saved the outline rectangle as a user path and can now use it for both filling, with the light 10 percent gray background, and stroking, in the default blue color. The fill is done by the new **ufill** operator in line %6; this takes a user path and fills it with the current color. This must be the first graphic element created since it is the background for all the other elements. The stroked path, however, is held until line %9, when the user path ChkBkgnd is stroked in the current color—set to blue at this point—using the new **ustroke** operator. The user path must be created in the setup process and stored in the private dictionary.

A *user path* is a new PostScript language concept. It is a procedure consisting entirely of path construction operators and their coordinate operands expressed as literal numbers. This means that the path is a completely self-contained description of a path in user space; it has no external references at all. The idea here is that the desired object can be drawn by executing the user path and then filling or stroking the result. This is very fast. However, the definition is quite restrictive; there are no dictionary lookups for variable names allowed, for example. Also the path description must conform to rather strict standards. There is a way around all these restrictions—one that allows you the full freedom of the Post-Script interpreter and yet retains the speed and other benefits of the user path. It is based on the new **upath** operator, which takes the current path and turns it into a correctly formed user path. You will see this operator in action in the setup procedure where it is used to good effect to create this path.

Remaining Wraps

With the top out of the way, here is the similar, but much shorter, wrap that draws the bottom of the check form:

```
defineps PSWdrawChkBottom ( float Xpos, Ypos )
    FormDict begin                              %1
    gsave
        newpath                                 %2
    % set up adjusted coordinate system
        Xpos Ypos translate                     %3
    % draw small background
        .9 setgray
        SmallBkgnd ufill
        0 0 1 setrgbcolor
        SmallBkgnd ustroke
    % return to black
        0 setgray
        /Helvetica-Bold 10.0 selectfont
        35 5 moveto
        (ACME SOFTWARE) show
    % now reverse y axis coordinates
```

```
        1 -1 scale                                      %4
    % and save for future use
        /BottomState gstate def                         %5
    grestore
    end
endps
```

This wrap is very similar to the preceding one. It begins again by setting the private dictionary. Then it translates the coordinates to the desired position. Next it uses these, in their normal orientation, to draw the small outline rectangle and to display the name of the company. It reverses the coordinate structure in line %4, by doing a **scale** operation with a negative unit value for the *y* scaling factor. This simply reverses the direction of the *y*-coordinate axis without changing the actual values on it. This new coordinate system is now saved as the BottomState gstate for future use.

The last, but by no means least, of your wraps is the setup wrap called PSWsetupCheck. You can now see why we deferred creation of this wrap until now; you needed to see the other wraps in order to understand what this wrap has to do. Let's look at the tasks it must accomplish.

- It must create and store a private dictionary with enough room for the two gstate objects and for the additional variable definitions created by the working procedures.
- It must define and save the two user path objects to draw the check background, ChkBkgnd, and the small background, SmallBkgnd.
- It must define an auxiliary procedure, outlineBox, which will be used to create the backgrounds.

With these tasks in mind, here is the setup wrap:

```
defineps PSWsetupCheck ()
    % first define the dictionary
    /FormDict 25 dict def                               %1
    FormDict begin                                      %2
    % next the auxiliary procedures
    /outlineBox                                         %3
    {
        /Hgt exch def
        /Width exch def
        currentpoint translate
        0 0 moveto
        Width 0 lineto
```

```
            Width Hgt 0 Hgt 10 arct
            0 Hgt 0 0 10 arct
            closepath
        }
        def
        % now make user paths
        gsave                                           %4
            /ChkBkgnd
            10 295 moveto
            590 205 outlineBox
            false upath
            def
        grestore                                        %5
        gsave                                           %6
            /SmallBkgnd
            10 210 moveto
            590 25 outlineBox
            false upath
            def
        grestore                                        %7
    end                                                 %8
endps
```

This setup does just what we set out to do. It begins on line %1 by defining a new, private dictionary, FormDict, which is created with room for 25 (key, value) pairs. It begins to use that dictionary for all its definitions by pushing the new dictionary onto the dictionary stack with the **begin** operator in line %2. Line %3 begins the auxiliary procedure to help you create the user path objects later in the wrap. As we discussed earlier, both of these objects have a similar shape, although they are different in size. The procedure here, outlineBox, draws an outline box—one that has square bottom corners and rounded top corners—of the given dimensions, with the bottom left corner at the current point. The calculations necessary for this operation are made possible by translating the coordinates to that bottom left corner. In most wraps, this would be enclosed in a **gsave, grestore** pair to avoid having the change persist after the procedure. Here, however, you want to save the path and you also need the coordinates translated for that path. Therefore, the procedure does not protect the following code; you have to do that outside the process. The actual drawing is quite straightforward, using the **arct** operator to draw the rounded corners as we saw in Chapter 3.

The exact process of saving the path is shown in the two sets of procedures from line %4 to line %5 and from line %6 to line %7. These are essentially identical processes. The first line provides the **gsave** that was missing in the outlineBox procedure. The name for the final definition is added to the stack and then you do a **moveto** to the desired point. Then you draw the outline box of the desired size, leaving the current path intact at the conclusion of the procedure. Notice that the coordinates are now translated into their new positions. This current path is processed by the **upath** operator into a user path object, which is now able to be defined, using the name from the beginning of the process, into the private dictionary. The **false** operand is used to disable caching of the user path. Magic.

And finally, you must prepare the PSWdispDate wrap that displays the date. If you look back, you will see that this was called in the main procedure, after DrawCheck. We have delayed looking at this wrap because it requires the setup process from the previous procedure to be complete before it can execute. Now you can code it, like this:

```
defineps PSWdispDate ( char *Date)
      FormDict begin                              %1
      currentfont                                 %2
      TopState setgstate                          %3
      setfont                                     %4
      380 80 moveto                               %5
      (Date) show                                 %6
      end                                         %7
endps
```

This is a short procedure, but quite instructive. It begins, as you might expect, on line %1 by setting the private dictionary FormDict as the current dictionary. This ensures that all the required definitions and associated procedures are available. Next, in line %2 it calls up the current font and places that on the operand stack. Remember here that you have set the font to the user's current setting by calling the PSselectfont procedure immediately before this. That set the current font in this context to the one that the user currently has selected for display. However, you are about to replace the graphics state with the one you saved earlier, to match the coordinates set previously. This will also replace the current font, as well as the current coordinates.

To transfer the desired font into the new graphics state, you need to pass it forward into the new graphics state. You can do that, as here, by saving it on the operand stack. Then you use the **setgstate** operator in line %3 to replace the current graphics state with the gstate object that you saved earlier, in the setup process, as TopState. Once that has replaced the current graphics state, you take the previous font, which is still on the operand stack, and make it the current font by using the **setfont** operator in line %4.

With the font set, you can now simply move to the location set out on the layout and display the text string. Then you pop the private dictionary off the dictionary stack in line %7 and exit the wrap.

This completes the wraps and all the C procedures for the blank form. At this point you can execute this code, assuming that you have taken care of the housekeeping issues discussed earlier and that you have structured or modified the main line program to execute correctly. If you have, you should get an output that looks something like Figure 4-8.

Figure 4-8. Blank form display.

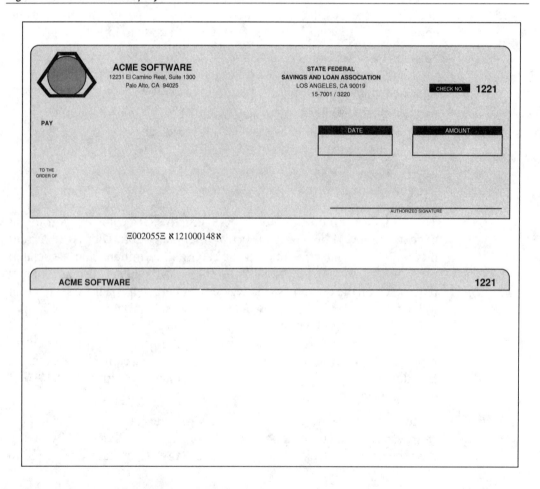

ENTERING TEXT

Once the blank form is built, placing and displaying text on it for this exercise requires only a very few procedures. You will display the text in two groups, the top and the bottom, corresponding to the divisions of the form itself. Of necessity, this set of functions is somewhat less realistic than the form procedures. In a running application, the user would enter this information. Here, to illustrate the wraps and processes required, we use fixed strings to represent the user input. In the next section, we discuss in some detail what might be done in an actual application.

The data for the top of the form consists of three items:

1. The amount as a string of words
2. The amount as a number string
3. The name and address of the payee

The first two are actually the same data presented in two different forms. This suggests that you should display both in one wrap, using the two text strings as arguments. The name and address data, on the other hand, although one group of data, must provide for multiple lines. In this case, the best approach is to use a single wrap with a position argument.

This suggests the following code for the section of the main procedure that is displaying this data:

```
/* ctx, font and size are global variables */
/* string definitions for this exercise */
char *num = "115.95";
char *text = "One hundred fifteen and 95/100";
char *name = "Mountain Sports, Ltd.";
char *addr = "123 Mountain Way";
char *city = "Chatsworth, CA 91311";
/* also a single internal variable */
float y;
    .
    .
    .
DPSSetContext(ctx);
PSselectfont(font, size);
PSWdispAmount(num, text);
PSWdispPayTo(0, name);
y = 1 * leading;
```

```
PSWdispPayTo(y, addr);
y = 2 * leading;
PSWdispPayTo(y, city);
DPSWaitContext(ctx);
   .
   .
   .
/* string definition for bottom text */
char *btext = "Invoice 10423 - Camping equipment and supplies";

DispBottomCheck(ctx, 1, btext);
   .
   .
```

Two methods of display are used here. The first, used in the first group, is to set the context and then call the individual wrap procedures from the main code. In this case, this is quite easy since the complete body of variable information for the upper section can be set at one time. This approach minimizes the number of times you have to set the various global parameters, such as the context and the font.

Let's review the first group of code for display of the data on the top of the form. It begins by setting the context for the display. This is required, remember, because there may be multiple displays. Once this is set, you select the font for the display, using the global variables that the user has established—here, they are the default values that you set up initially. Next you display the amount in two forms, both strings: first, as a number, and second, as a text. The presumption is that the application has made the conversion from the number "115.95" to the words "One hundred fifteen and 95/100." This conversion could be done in the PostScript routine, if required. However, PostScript is clumsy and slow at handling text strings, whereas C is fast and flexible. Generally you want to allow C to do this type of work. Since it is likely that the numeric amount has been typed in, making it a text string as it enters, you probably do not need to convert it into a string as you did earlier with the check number. If you did need to do that, PostScript would be the better choice since the code is easy and efficient.

The display of the payee name and address is just a repeated call to a single wrap, with different position offsets. It would be up to the application to be sure that there is room on the form, both horizontally and vertically, for the display. Here we have chosen to display three lines of text, which fit quite comfortably onto the form.

Let's look at the wraps that support this code:

```
defineps PSWdispAmt ( char *Number, *Text )
    FormDict begin
    currentfont
    TopState setgstate
    setfont
    490 80 moveto
    (Number) show
    25 80 moveto
    (Text) show
    end
endps

defineps PSWdispPayTo ( float Line; char *Text )
    FormDict begin
    currentfont
    TopState setgstate
    setfont
    60 54 Line sub moveto
    (Text) show
    end
endps
```

These are both quite simple wraps, just as you would expect. They display the given text values at the locations set out in the layouts. The only slight complexity here is the PSWdispPayTo wrap, which calculates the y position for the display by subtracting the displacement, provided by the application, from the starting y coordinate on the layout. This means that the first line to display will always have a displacement of 0, whereas subsequent lines have a displacement equal to the line number times the current leading value. This is exactly as calculated in the application code.

An alternative method is used for display of the bottom information. Here, the context and the variable data are passed to another C procedure, which actually handles the display. This procedure looks something like this:

```
/* DispBottomCheck */
void DispBottomCheck (DPSContext ctx, float line, char *text)
{
    DPSSetContext(ctx);
    PSselectfont(font, size);
```

```
        PSWdispLine(leading, line, text);
        DPSWaitContext(ctx);
}
```

To make this intelligible, you must remember that you have set the font, size, and leading variables in a global header, as we noted earlier when we discussed the first C main procedure. With that, you see that this is not much different from the main procedure code, except that the leading and the line value are passed to the PostScript wrap as external arguments. The complete wrap looks like this:

```
defineps PSWdispLine ( float Line, Lead; char *Text )
    FormDict begin
    currentfont
    BottomState setgstate
    setfont
    30 24
    Line 1 sub Lead mul
    add
    moveto
    (Text) show
    end
endps
```

In this case, the calculations that were done before in the C application are now done within the PostScript routine. In general, this is not the preferred way to handle this; calculations like this should be done in PostScript only if there is some good reason to do them there—for example, if the line number or leading were most conveniently (or only) available in the PostScript environment. Nevertheless, I have used this here to show you how it can be done if you need it, and because it simplifies the code that you have to produce to display the bottom of the check. Note also that the displacement is positive, and therefore added to the starting point, even though the lines move down the page. Placing this into your C application, you should be able to run it now and get an output display something like Figure 4-9.

Figure 4-9. Form with variable data.

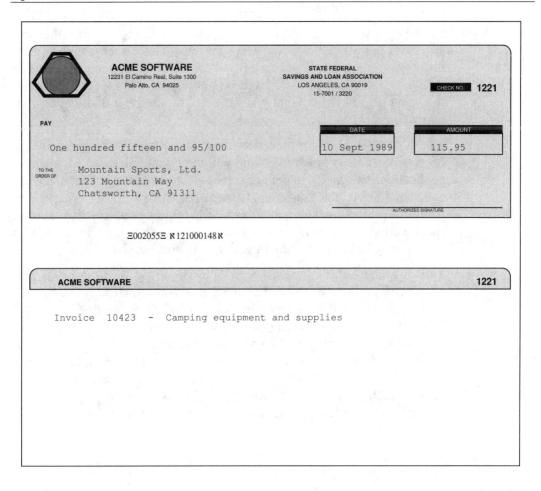

This completes the basic exercise that we set out to accomplish. It creates a blank form and fills it with variable data and displays the result. This is good, but there are still more issues and techniques that we might discuss as part of this chapter.

INTEGRATING THE EXERCISE INTO AN APPLICATION

This output provides a fine display and it gives you a feeling of accomplishment to have completed this exercise; but you probably still have some questions about how this would be used in an actual application. After all, the preceding discussion repeatedly warned that the code, particularly the main procedure code, is not quite "realistic." The issue, then, is what might have to be changed to integrate this into a real application.

Let's begin with what doesn't have to change. To start with, the case statement is probably exactly what you would use in an application to display a form that was selected from, for example, a menu choice. The exact method would depend how the system signaled the application about the menu selection; but what you see here is quite typical and in no way unrealistic.

The same can be said for the procedures that create and display the blank form. All of this is much like what you might actually use in a working application. The choice of default values—fonts, point sizes, logo, layout, and so on—is inevitably arbitrary to some degree. In a typical scenario, you would be reproducing an actual form or laying one out to some external specification. That is effectively what you have done here and it is quite easy to translate into Display PostScript, as you can see.

The area where this exercise becomes less realistic is in the wraps that support the procedures and in the handling and presentation of the variable data. Here you needed to set strings of variable data so that you could complete the exercise and have some useful output. Now you need to look at efficiency. That means examining how to take advantage of the special operators that are available in the Display PostScript system. In an actual application the user and display requirements would probably necessitate changes in these procedures: tuning the blank form display for efficiency, managing the display font, handling the event sequence, and displaying the variable data.

Efficient Display Coding

You must keep three principles in mind to get the maximum performance from your display code:

1. Minimize the number of operations in your PostScript code.
2. Use the most efficient location for each type of code.
3. Minimize the communication between your application and the Display PostScript system.

Let's examine each of these principles in turn to see how they improve efficiency in your application.

The reason for the first, and most important, principle—to minimize the number of operations in your PostScript code—is that the PostScript interpreter, which performs the operations that you send, represents an additional layer of software overhead. Every time you execute something in PostScript—an operator or procedure, for example—the interpreter must parse, analyze, and execute that object. Although the interpreter is quite good at this, it stands to reason that the fewer operations it has to do, the faster your code will execute.

There are three ways to minimize the work that the interpreter must do. First, use the smallest number of operators and procedures that you can to do the job. In particular, do not make auxiliary procedures that are stored within the PostScript interpreter unless you absolutely require them. Even the best procedures require multiple lookups in order to execute correctly. Second, use the new Display PostScript operators and features such as **rectfill** and **selectfont** whenever possible. These operators have been optimized to make less use of the interpreter than previous PostScript operations did. For example, each of these operators combines several previous operators into a single new one. Finally, **fill** or **stroke** the paths you create only when it becomes necessary. We have already discussed this issue, but it bears repeating. If you group all your paths by common characteristics such as size and color and then stroke or fill them, you will save a substantial amount of processing time. If you make all the common segments into a user path, you will speed up the process even more, as the user path operations are optimized for speed and efficiency.

The reasons for the second principle—place processing functions in the part of your application code where they are most efficient—are to simplify your PostScript code and to help you use the fewest PostScript operations. The primary instance of this is to place all calculations into your C code. We have followed this principle in most of the example code, and it is a useful point to remember.

The reason for the third principle—to minimize the communication between your application and the Display PostScript system—is that every command sent to the Display PostScript system takes some time on a bus or communications link, which inevitably slows down processing. You can reduce this time by using arrays and encoded structures to send information to Display PostScript. When you use the Client Library, you are already doing this to a great degree. However, you can do more if you want by building your own user paths or arrays of data to pass to those operators that can use them, such as **rectfill**.

You make certain tradeoffs to achieve these benefits. First, the application code becomes more complex, as more information structures must be maintained in the application itself. This is why I used a more casual, prototyping approach in the examples; sacrificing some efficiency for ease of programming and simplicity in the C code. This approach has also allowed us to ignore problems of compiler and system differences and concentrate on the Display PostScript system.

An additional concern is that the techniques that gain you maximum efficiency in a display are new to the Display PostScript system. The current installed base of ordinary PostScript devices does not support these new operations. In some cases, the new operators are specific to a display and present no problems. Others can be easily mimicked in an ordinary PostScript device. In such cases, you will not gain any speed from using them, but you won't lose any either. Some features, however, have no counterpart in PostScript and can only be emulated at some cost in speed and performance. Therefore, using these features to speed up your display output, may slow down the printed version to some degree. In any case, using these new features means that you must have printer driver software that can convert the new operators and processes into current PostScript operators if you want to run your code on the present set of installed PostScript devices.

Font Settings

First, is the question of setting and using a user-defined font, style, and point size for the display. Also associated with this is the question of line spacing, or leading. Let's look at each of these in turn. In most applications, you would enable some feature in the environment, either through a menu or some other standard feature, to set a current font, style, and point size. All of these settings would then be communicated back to the application by some event report. When the user changes the settings, the application is expected to change the display accordingly. Usually these changes apply only to new text, but under some circumstances—which are up to you, as the programmer—they may also apply to previously displayed data. Since PostScript has no separate style settings, the application must translate any selection of a style, such as bold or italic, into the necessary font name.

The leading is a bit different. This might be chosen by the user directly, or it may be generated by the application in response to the setting of the point size. In either case, however, this is a variable that is external to the display routines and is associated, in a natural fashion, with the font and size.

In the preceding processing, you have handled this by setting some global variables, font, size, and leading, that are then referenced as required by the display routines. Another possible way to handle this would be to have a separate procedure that you called whenever a change to these parameters was signaled to the application. The procedure would determine the required font name and if it was available—an issue we have avoided in these exercises—and then set these variables where they could be referenced by all the associated PostScript procedures. I chose not to use this method here because it seems to me to leave too much out of the picture, making the display depend on invisible external events when that isn't necessary. The method used here, saving these values as global variables, has the advantage that it can be used from within a variety of processes. Nevertheless, storing this information in private data structures would work quite well. The choice should be dictated by your application requirements and by your personal programming style.

Event Sequence

This raises the issue of the sequence in which events happen in the real world. Since you are responding to users' input, it can easily happen that users do not do things in the sequence that you expect. In fact, the routines here already protect the application to a great degree from the random intrusion of user events. For example, the routines wait for the context to finish processing and displaying before they proceed to create more output or transition to some other part of the application, or even to another application. The display for each of the sections of the form is also divided by some arbitrary code (that's what the vertical dots are supposed to represent), both from the code that creates the initial display of the blank form and from each other.

However, the code that displays the data on the top of the form is quite dependent on being done in sequence. Here, this is acceptable since the data is in strings and can be displayed as a unit. In more usual circumstances, however, the display of each line would have to be separated; in fact, you would probably separate the display of the number and the words for the amount. Similarly, each of these would require a separate setting of the font to ensure that the current and correct font was being used. The important point here is that these displays must be made independent of one another and independent of being executed in any particular order.

Adjusting the Text Display

The best way to handle this issue, and also the most general, would be to have a simple text display routine that shows a single character, or a string of characters if more convenient, at a given point. This, in fact, is one of the most common ways to display text on the screen. With such a routine, you would not have any special calls to wraps to set specific text items. Instead, you would simply call a single wrap with the exact *x* and *y* coordinates that you wanted to use for placement. Since these would be coordinate values in user space, you might wish to have separate, but similar, routines for the upper and lower sections of the form. Then each routine would be able to start using the private dictionary, restore the correct graphic state, and display the text.

Display PostScript has some special operators that can help in this process: the **xshow, yshow,** and **xyshow** operators. The **xyshow** is characteristic of these new operators, and it works as follows:

> textstring numarray   **xyshow**   —
> prints successive characters from *textstring* in the same way as **show** would print them, but instead of moving to the end of the character after the display, it selects a pair of values out of *numarray* to use as the *x* and *y* coordinates, in user space, of the next character origin.

In other words, the values in *numarray* are used to position each character instead of the internal coordinate measurements. This allows the application very precise control over the placement of each character and allows a full range of text controls, such as character pair kerning, to be easily implemented. The **xshow** and the **yshow** operators perform a similar function, but only move in the *x* or *y* directions, respectively.

Obviously, to make this work, the application must have available the actual width of each character. These are generally provided by font metric files, which an application can use to determine the exact width of each character. The programming required to use these techniques is not shown here, but you should know that such techniques are often used, and, if they were applied here, could replace the wraps that you have created with much more powerful and general procedures.

Changing the Form Code

All these techniques can be applied to our form exercise to make it more efficient. The actual code would take up more room than we have here and would require much more interaction with the operating environment than I can provide specific information for in this book. Nevertheless, the changes are not too hard to follow once you have completed the prototype application. They fall into two major categories.

First, make all of the paths into user paths. Group the path segments by size and color and whether they are filled or stroked. Then convert these elements into user paths within the C application code by simplifying them into **moveto**s and **lineto**s and so on. Pass all of the common segments to the Display PostScript system as a single user path and **ustroke** or **ufill** it with one command.

Second, you must build, or access from the font metric files, the character widths of all of the fonts that you use. (You have already seen how to do this for centering and justification). With this information, you can build a data structure in your C application that precisely locates every character that you wish to display. Group all characters by font, point size, and color, and send the characters, along with their associated positions in both the x and y dimensions to the Display PostScript system. Use an **xyshow** operator to display the characters. In this way, all the characters in a single font and color will be displayed at once. Elements in the same font but different colors must be displayed separately, since the display will be in the current color for all the elements.

This last change may not be worthwhile for displaying fixed data, such as a form, in any application. There is little that the user is allowed to change on the display or on the output and, therefore, creating and maintaining the required data structures is quite a bit of effort and code to no visible purpose. In text processing applications, however, the overhead is less and the need is greater. In such cases, the user is often allowed to perform tasks such as kerning letters or adjusting line spacing, which require the application to maintain all or much of this data anyway. In these cases, using **xyshow** will be both faster and easier than the older methods.

USING FORM SETS

Another natural question that arises is what changes might be necessary to integrate form processing, such as illustrated here, into a more general environment where the application was creating and using multiple different forms, which we might call form sets. If you were implementing a set of forms in an application, there are several points to consider.

First, you can expand the private dictionary to include processes for all the forms. In that case, you would most likely have a global setup procedure and wrap that was executed once at the start of the application. Then each form might add some more variable definitions or procedures to that dictionary in a specific setup wrap. If you think in this way, you begin to see how useful a private dictionary can be.

The same type of thinking can be used to create and reuse user paths. Many companies have common graphic elements in their forms. If you are implementing a set of forms, such common elements make ideal candidates for user paths. By creating them once and reusing them again and again, you have both speed and flexibility—necessary qualities in a practical application.

There is an additional consideration when you start to create these user paths. Should you cache the resulting paths or not? This is not a black-and-white issue. Adobe System's documentation warns us of the overhead in caching a user path. Therefore, if the path is not going to be used often, you should not cache it. On the other hand, if it appears on every form, and you are doing primarily forms processing, it probably should be cached. For the in-between cases, you will have to calculate the tradeoff between the time to cache the object—and the possible loss of previously cached items—against the need to process the same path repeatedly. Note here that it is not the path that is cached; it is the filled or stroked version of the path. Therefore, in our exercise, caching would not speed up the use of the same path because the first time, the path was filled, and the second time, it was stroked. The cache would only help if the same, filled background were used several times, in the same form or on others.

Finally, there is the issue of the logo. As you could see from the calculations that we used and the problems in layout, it would be much easier if the logo were already set to be used according to its bounding box coordinates. This is actually quite easy and is a common task in using Encapsulated PostScript (EPS) graphics. I have not done so here, as we discussed, because the code to control and process such graphics is not germane to the subject here and would only distract from the Display PostScript issues. However, in an actual program, you would be well advised to take the trouble to make your logo into a graphic object that could be placed and sized by its bounding box, rather than by its actual corners or specific dimensions, as you have done here.

CONCLUSION

In this chapter you have created a working form, a check, and filled it with data. This is the type of work that is done by applications every day. The chapter starts out by laying out a design for the check form in blocks. These blocks help you to get an overview of how the check form is put together and what you must provide on the display. The next part of the design is a detailed layout of the check in four sections: the layout of the graphic elements in the check, the layout of the type for the check, the layout of colors used on the check, and the layout of the variable data elements onto the form. Along with this, you are introduced to graphic placement and bounding boxes for graphic elements, using the logo graphic that you developed in Chapter 3. These techniques are very common and useful in many contexts, so they are discussed in some detail.

With the design done, you can proceed to drawing the blank check form. This is done from the top down, by starting with the main procedure calls that would be used and working down, through the auxiliary C procedures, to the wraps themselves. At each level, the code is presented and analyzed in some detail, so that you can understand how the elements fit together and match the layouts that you prepared earlier. This allows you to produce a finished, blank check form.

In these wraps, two major new concepts are used to speed up and facilitate the drawing process. First, the coordinates of the check are modified and saved as a graphic state object. This allows you to easily reuse the changed coordinates. Second, portions of the check background are drawn and saved as user paths, which allow significantly faster processing for common graphic elements. Both of these are techniques that you will use repeatedly in your future work.

Then the variable data is placed into the blank form. This is not a difficult task, but it still requires some care and work, which is shown in the procedures and wraps that display this output. The only new process is the conversion of the check number into a string for display, which is accomplished by the PostScript wrap. The wraps used here employ two similar but different techniques for display of variable data so that you will be familiar with both.

The chapter ends with two sections that discuss efficiency and integration of actual variables into a display and creation of multiple forms in one application. These sections have no code, but they discuss these issues from the viewpoint of an actual application, as opposed to the more restricted version that you have worked with in the exercise. Overall, the chapter gives you valuable practice in creating and displaying a relatively complex document and covers some new concepts that will be especially valuable to you in actual application programming.

CHAPTER 5

Font Creation and Modification

This chapter provides additional information on how fonts work in PostScript and on how you can control and affect the font machinery. It contains detailed information on how PostScript fonts work, including a look at the internal structure of the PostScript font dictionaries. It provides techniques for modifying fonts in several ways, all of which are both common and useful in PostScript programming. Along the way, you are introduced to new techniques for displaying and handling text that are sure to be useful in your applications.

FONT MECHANICS

Up to this point in the book, you have been using PostScript fonts that are supplied with almost every PostScript device. You have been using these fonts to set text in the font and then to display that text on an output. All the work that you have done so far with fonts has been oriented toward this typical type of text output. There have been enough challenges in producing typeset-quality documents without getting fancy about type itself.

Now you have mastered the basic font operations and should be quite comfortable with positioning and displaying text on an output page. This enables you to move beyond simple text and begin to do some exciting work using PostScript fonts more creatively. PostScript is a language that has a natural affinity for graphics; and PostScript treats characters in fonts as graphic objects. This concept allows you to make interesting and useful modifications to PostScript fonts and, indeed, even allows you to create your own fonts.

Your first response to that thought may be to wonder why you would ever wish to modify or create a font. After all, the fonts are already provided, and they work quite well. There are two reasons. First, PostScript fonts actually contain characters that can be difficult or impossible to access from the keyboard. There are 256 available characters in a PostScript font, whereas there are fewer than 100 keys on your keyboard. Obviously the keyboard contains the most often used characters: the alphabet, both upper- and lowercase, numbers, and common punctuation. Adding special function keys allows you to access additional characters from the keyboard. But there are characters, less frequently needed, that are still included in the standard PostScript fonts. These additional characters include the tilde, the symbols for the British pound and the Japanese yen, the cents sign, upside-down exclamation point and question mark (used as punctuation in Spanish), and many others. Moreover, these special characters are generally provided in a range of ASCII codes that may not transmit successfully across a network or serial connection. The issue, then, is how to access these characters in a simple device-independent way that is also transparent to communication lines.

These additional characters can be referenced by using the *ddd* notation, which we mentioned when we discussed strings in Chapter 2. Let's expand on that notation. The form *ddd* is used within a string to indicate to the PostScript interpreter that you wish to reference the character indicated by the octal value, *ddd*. Appendix A of the *PostScript Language Reference Manual* shows you that each character has an octal code assigned to it.

When you want to include in your string a character that isn't on the keyboard, you can look up the octal code in this table and use that code, in the form *ddd,* to reference the character. For example, the paragraph symbol is shown as octal code 266, so you would code \266 to insert a paragraph symbol into a string. An entire string including such a code would look like this:

(This string has a paragraph symbol, \266, included in it)

When you perform a **show** on that string, the paragraph symbol would appear between the commas. Since every character has a code, you could use all octal numbers to create a string, but that would be a waste of time for characters that already exist on the keyboard and are represented by codes of less than octal 177 (decimal 127). You should understand that this isn't an exclusive arrangement; you could choose to reference every character by number. For the interpreter, there isn't any difference between "a" and \141.

Adobe Type Library fonts also retain an additional 56 characters available to you for special work. These special characters make up all accented characters that are used in various languages. PostScript can create these on command. This is different from the process of referring to characters not on the keyboard that we outlined earlier. In that case, you really don't have to do anything special to the font to access the characters; in this case, someone does have to modify the font to get PostScript to make these characters. These are general techniques for font modification that systems commonly use to create the exact character sets they require.

There is a second reason why you might want to modify fonts. Fonts have their own measurements, called *metrics,* included within them. You can access and change these metrics in several ways to produce new fonts with interesting and valuable properties.

You can also create your own fonts. Before attempting anything so difficult, you should be aware that fonts have to be tuned and formed to present a satisfactory graphic image on a screen or other low-resolution device. Creation of even decent fonts, therefore, is not an easy or a quick job. The task is complex and requires a good understanding of PostScript font machinery. In addition, there is the essential but indescribable requirement for aesthetic quality. Nevertheless, a particular application, or even an unusual document, may sometimes require a created font. The actual creation of a new font is beyond the scope of this book, but we will go through font concepts and machinery in sufficient detail that you will be well equipped to undertake such a task if you wish.

The important point here is to understand the workings of PostScript fonts in some detail. Effective and efficient use of PostScript fonts requires that you have a good, working knowledge of font structure and font mechanics. Even if you never modify a font—much less create a new one—you will find it invaluable in creating PostScript documents, whether you are programming PostScript directly or using an application program, to understand good font handling practices and be able to distinguish them from those that are poorly conceived and poorly executed. You will apply these techniques here; you will understand why you are applying them; and you will be able to distinguish them in other PostScript programs.

Font Operation Review

Before you plunge into the new material, we should review two aspects of PostScript operations. These are operations involving fonts and operations involving dictionaries. The font operations are clearly important, but you may wonder why dictionary operations should be included. The answer is that PostScript fonts are implemented by means of dictionaries. In all aspects of using fonts, you are constantly working with dictionary objects. The fonts themselves are dictionaries; and, as you will see, they contain subsidiary dictionaries as well.

PostScript provides a simple method for accessing and using fonts. This method was referred to in the earlier chapters where you first met font use, but it is not the method that you have been working with during the previous examples and exercises. You may remember, when you were first introduced to fonts, that we described the three steps required to access fonts. However, in Display PostScript, these three steps are combined into one new operator, **selectfont,** which is what you have been using. The three individual steps are still available, however, and each has its own operator. Let's review these individual steps and their associated operators.

The first task is to identify the font to be used. This is done by putting the name of the font onto the stack and invoking the **findfont** operator. Next the font must be set to the correct point size that you want to use. This is done by the **scalefont** operator, which requires the desired size on the stack as a numeric operand. Finally, the font must be identified to the PostScript interpreter as the current font, that is, the font to be used for all subsequent text operations. This is done with the **setfont** operator. After the font is made, the current font operators such as **show** can be invoked to use that font to display strings onto the output device. The alternative, of course, is to simply use the single **selectfont** operator to do all these at once. The three-step sequence normally looks like this:

/Helvetica **findfont** 12 **scalefont setfont**

whereas the equivalent sequence that you have been using looks like this:

/Helvetica 12 **selectfont**

However you accomplish this sequence, you must remember that these are each three separate and independent, but related, operations. They are combined in Display PostScript for speed and convenience, but each one has a place and a purpose, and they sometimes must be separated to do certain tasks. An excellent example of this occurred in Chapter 4, where you had to save the current font, restore a specific graphic state, and then reset the current font. In that case, the font operator used was a simple **setfont** since you did not know, or care, what the previous setting was. You only cared to save that setting and restore it in the new graphic state. This is a good example of using each of these operations independently.

The other subject that we need to review, dictionaries, is an essential component of PostScript generally and the major implementation mechanism for fonts in particular. Most of the dictionary work that you have done up to now has been defining and retrieving objects from the default *userdict*. But since PostScript fonts are themselves dictionaries, you now have to refresh your memory about general dictionary operations and particularly those operations that help you access and use the font dictionaries.

This refresher isn't intended to be a full recapitulation of what you already know; instead, it is meant to be more like a series of one-liners, to recall certain aspects of dictionary operations. If any of this isn't clear, or doesn't come back to you, don't hesitate to review the topic in Chapter 3 and then return here when you're ready. This isn't a classroom, and you're under no compulsion to forge ahead before you feel comfortable. The new material, of course, will be fully covered and presented in the usual way.

A dictionary is a PostScript object that contains (key, value) pairs. The key is used to access the value from the dictionary. Two standard dictionaries are always present: the *systemdict* and the *userdict*. PostScript works with a dictionary stack, and you may have more dictionaries than just these two. The topmost dictionary is called the current dictionary; in your work so far, the current dictionary has typically been *userdict*. The normal search method for dictionaries is for the interpreter to take a key, usually a name, and search downward through the dictionary stack until it finds a match to the key. When it finds a match, it retrieves the value associated with the key and returns that value to the stack or executes it as appropriate.

Values are associated with keys and entered into the current dictionary by the use of the **def** operator. No special operator is required to retrieve a value from the dictionary. When the interpreter receives a name, it looks up that name in the dictionary stack. Operators are no different from any other PostScript name in this respect; the main difference is that operators are defined in the *systemdict*.

Fonts themselves are PostScript dictionaries and can be handled and accessed with the appropriate dictionary operators. Each font dictionary also contains additional internal dictionaries, making up a set in a hierarchical order. All this will become clearer when you begin to work with the font dictionaries. Each font has its own dictionary, whose key is its name, like Helvetica or Times-Roman. The list of all available fonts is maintained in a master dictionary, called the **FontDirectory**.

The font handlers actually take care of most of the manipulation of the font dictionaries for you, but, for investigative and debugging purposes, you need to remember how to begin using a new dictionary—in other words, how to add it to the dictionary stack—and how to stop using it. These two operations require the two operators: **begin,** which places a dictionary onto the dictionary stack, making it the current dictionary, and **end,** which removes the top dictionary from the dictionary stack. You were first introduced to these operators in Chapter 2, and you used them in the exercise in Chapter 4 as part of creating and using a private dictionary.

Finally, as you recall from Chapter 2, the *systemdict* and *userdict* dictionaries are permanently installed on the dictionary stack, and any attempt to pop them, by using an **end** operator without having issued a **begin,** for example, causes an error.

Font Dictionary Entries

Every PostScript font dictionary follows a set format. Certain specific keys must be present in the dictionary, and other keys may be present. The values associated with each of these keys may vary, but the type of object associated with a specific key is invariably the same. This should make perfect sense because the PostScript font machinery cannot work without certain special and specific information.

Other than the set format, there is nothing special about a font dictionary. It is created and manipulated by all the same operators that work on regular dictionaries. The only special handling comes when you want to identify a specific dictionary as a font dictionary. That is done by using the **definefont** operator, which checks the new dictionary for the correct format, and then enrolls the name that you give the dictionary into the master font directory, **FontDirectory**. The **definefont** also adds a special fontID object with the name **FID** to the new directory.

A font dictionary is required to have a certain set of (key, value) pairs defined in it. Some of the (key, value) pairs must be present in a properly formed PostScript font dictionary, whereas others are optional and can be defined by the user. The following table lists the keys that are required in any PostScript font dictionary, with associated values that must be the type of object shown in the table and contain the information described next to the key.

Key	Type	Information
Encoding	array	An array with 256 elements; normally, the elements are names associated with the character glyphs (shapes) and these elements are accessed by using the character codes as indexes into the array.
FontBBox	array	A four-element array that defines two pairs of x, y coordinates that represent the lower left and upper right corners of the font bounding box in the character coordinate system.

The *font bounding box* is the smallest rectangle that would enclose all the characters of the font if they were printed on top of one another at the same point. The font bounding box may be used to provide font size information for caching and clipping operations. If any part of any character falls outside the defined bounding box, you may get incorrect results. If all four components of the **FontBBox** are zero, the bounding box information is ignored.

Key	Type	Information
FID	fontID	A special entry that is required by the font machinery and is generated and maintained by the PostScript interpreter.
FontMatrix	array	A standard transformation matrix that maps the character coordinates into user coordinates.

Chapter 5: Font Creation and Modification   261

Characters are usually defined in their own, independent coordinate system. The **FontMatrix** maps this character coordinate system into a 1-unit square in the user coordinate system. When the font is called for use, it is normally scaled or otherwise transformed to map into the desired size and orientation. That process concatenates the new transformation with the **FontMatrix** to yield the correctly transformed font.

Key	Type	Information
FontType	integer	An integer value that indicates where to find the character descriptions and how these are represented.

A value of 3 indicates a user-generated font; a value of 0 indicates a composite font (a member of a hierarchical font group). A value of 1 indicates an encoded font; the built-in PostScript fonts have a value of 1. Any other value is either undefined or implementation dependent.

In addition to this required information, information is provided or may be provided for built-in PostScript fonts, as follows:

Key	Type	Information
CharStrings	dictionary	This dictionary associates character names (as defined in the **Encoding** array) with the glyph descriptions, generally stored in strings with a protected, proprietary format. This dictionary is required for certain **FontType**s.
FontInfo	dictionary	This dictionary contains text data regarding the font. (The specific contents are described later in this section.)
FontName	name	The font's name as it would be used for access within a PostScript program. This information is for the application's use only; it is not used by the font machinery. An example would be "/Times-Roman".
Metrics	dictionary	This optional dictionary associates the name of characters (as defined in the **Encoding** array) with character metric information. When this dictionary is present, the values in it override the metrics that are encoded as part of the character definitions.
PaintType	integer	An integer value that indicates how the characters in a font are to be painted onto the output.

The possible values for **PaintType** are as follows:

Value	Function
0	The character descriptions are to be filled.
1	The character descriptions are to be stroked.
2	The character descriptions, which are designed to be filled, are to be outlined instead.
3	The character descriptions are responsible for controlling their own painting process.

Generally, changing the value of **PaintType** for a font does not give acceptable results. The only change that you should consider is from 0 (filled) to 2 (outlined).

Key	Type	Information
Private	dictionary	This dictionary contains protected and proprietary information about a font.
StrokeWidth	number	The stroke width, in character coordinate units, for outlined fonts (**PaintType** 2).

This field is not initially present in the font dictionary; it must be added if you change the **PaintType** from 0 to 2.

Key	Type	Information
UniqueID	integer	An identification integer that uniquely identifies the font.

That is, every font or every different version of the same font, even if there is only a minor difference, should have a different value of this entry. The only exception is for changes that only affect the **Encoding** array; such changes do not require a new **UniqueID**. This entry is not necessarily present in every font; when present, it is used by the font machinery to speed up the caching process. Every **UniqueID,** if it exists, must be a truly unique 24-bit number, and the font creator is responsible for ensuring this.

In addition to these entries, user-created fonts (**FontType** 3) must also provide a **BuildChar** entry. The **BuildChar** entry is associated with a PostScript procedure that takes the character code of the character to be created and builds the character pixel outline from that code, using the arrays and procedures defined in the font dictionary. When the PostScript interpreter goes to display a character from a user-defined font, it first looks in the font cache to see if the character is already there. If it is not, the interpreter calls the **BuildChar** procedure defined in the font dictionary to create the character. Depending on the procedures implemented in **BuildChar,** the resulting character may or may not be placed into the font cache before it is placed onto the output. The decision to cache a character shape is controlled by the **BuildChar** procedure for the user-defined font and the standard caching parameters, both of which can be controlled by the PostScript application.

The **FontInfo** dictionary contains a variety of information that the application may use. This information is for reference only and is not used by the font machinery. It has the following format:

Key	*Type*	*Information*
FamilyName	string	This string provides the family name of the font. For example, "Helvetica."
FullName	string	This string provides the full text name of the font. For example, "Helvetica-BoldOblique."
isFixedPitch	boolean	This boolean value is *true* if the font is a fixed-pitch (or monospace) font, and *false* otherwise.
ItalicAngle	number	This is the angle in degrees of the dominant vertical strokes of the font, measured counterclockwise from true vertical. As a result, the **ItalicAngle** values for most italic or oblique fonts are negative numbers because the fonts slope to the right (clockwise) rather than to the left. For example, the **ItalicAngle** value for the Helvetica-Oblique font is -12 (degrees).
Notice	string	This string gives the font's trademark or copyright information, if applicable.
UnderlinePosition	number	This number is the distance from the baseline to the underline stroke, in units of the character coordinate system.
UnderlineThickness	number	This number is the thickness of the underline stroke, in units of the character coordinate system.
version	string	This string contains the version number of the font, in the format 0.0.
Weight	string	This string gives the "weight" of the font strokes; for example, Bold, Medium, Light, and so on. Note that this is a descriptive string value, not a number.

Once a font is created, with all the necessary information in its dictionaries—here, the font information is a dictionary that contains several other layers of dictionaries within itself—it must still be made available to the interpreter by a **setfont** or **selectfont** operator. This process is done by maintaining all the currently available font dictionaries in a separate dictionary, called the **FontDirectory**. The **FontDirectory** is itself a dictionary where the keys are the font names, the same name reported by the **FontName** entry in the font itself, and the associated values are the font dictionaries. Remember that, although the name in the **FontDirectory** should be the same as the name reported and stored in the **FontName** field, there is no intrinsic connection between the two.

Most of this information has little or nothing to do with the average PostScript programmer; it is useful to know, some of it is interesting, but generally it doesn't affect how you handle the PostScript fonts. Some of the entries must be modified to create certain effects or to change the characteristics of the font. Most of the time, however, manipulation of the font dictionary outside of the prescribed methods is dangerous and potentially disastrous.

Two components do lend themselves to modifications, however. These are the font **Encoding** and the **FontMatrix.** Both of these provide you with some powerful change mechanisms that you can use to great advantage.

In addition, you might want to change the **PaintType** font. This is one way to derive character outlines; there is an alternative method for showing strings in outline format. We discuss both methods and work with the alternative method in Chapter 6. The general process of font modification is discussed later in this chapter and some examples of common modifications are given. After you have completed the examples in that section, you should be able to make other changes, such as changing the **PaintType** from filled to outlined, without much difficulty.

The normal operation of PostScript fonts uses the information in the font dictionary to create the images of the characters that are to be painted onto the output device. Let's consider exactly how this three-step process operates.

You begin the process by putting a name literal that represents a font name onto the operand stack and invoking the **findfont** operator. That operation, done as a single step, looks like this:

    /Helvetica **findfont**

This operator takes the name literal off the operand stack and looks it up in the **FontDirectory**. If it doesn't find the name, it returns an error. If it does find the name, it returns the associated value to the operand stack. This value is a pointer to the named font dictionary.

It may surprise you to get a pointer back, and not the object itself. Remember that a dictionary is a composite object, and that values of composite objects are shared, not duplicated, as we discussed in Chapter 2. This sharing is done by using pointers to the objects, instead of moving around the objects themselves.

Next, to set the point size for the font, you would issue the following command:

    12 **scalefont**

The **scalefont** operator takes the value on the operand stack and uses it to scale **FontMatrix** from one unit to the number of units given. The result is stored back into a new **FontMatrix,** and the pointer to the modified font is returned to the stack. Now you issue the **setfont** operator. This takes the pointer off the operand stack and stores it in the graphics state as the current font. Once that has been done, the modified font can be retrieved from the graphic state by execution of the **currentfont** operator, as you saw in Chapter 4. Remember that all of this has been done using pointers, not the actual objects themselves. This way is both quicker and more efficient than manipulating entire dictionaries.

Note that you can't retrieve the font information we listed earlier—**FontType**, **FontName**, **Encoding**, and so on—simply by executing the name of the desired object and then retrieving it from the operand stack, as you might with any typical object. The information is unavailable because the font dictionary—whether it is the current font or not—is not on the dictionary stack, where the interpreter is looking for the information, but is either saved in the graphics state as the current font or referenced through the **FontDirectory**. To retrieve this information, you must move the desired font dictionary onto the dictionary stack and make it the current dictionary.

Let's look at how you can gain access to this information to display it in your programs. Note that we are not discussing how to access the font, as a font; we are talking here about access to the font information in the font dictionary, which is quite a different matter. You already know how to access the font in the usual way; you now want to be able to examine items in the font dictionary such as the **FontName**.

We will start with a short example, designed to show you how you can access and display the font information. Once again, you will return to the familiar runPSInline procedure, using the standard Client Library single-operator calls. As always, you are expected to have set up a window and a procedure to create and access that window; then call the runPSInline procedure from there to see the results. You will look at the Helvetica built-in font to begin with. This code provides a good example of how you can access PostScript font information, starting like this:

```
void runPSInline (void)
{
    DPSContext ctx;
    char *name = "Helvetica";

    /* return current context for display work */
    ctx = DPSGetCurrentContext();

    /* set up to print font dictionary entries */
    PSselectfont("Times-Roman", 10.0);
    PSmoveto(18.0, 100.0);

    /* now retrieve and display font information */
    PSfindfont(name);
    /* the font dictionary is now on the operand stack */
    /* now place that onto the dictionary stack */
    PSbegin();
    /* and display it at the location set by the moveto */
    DPSPrintf(ctx, "FontName 36 string cvs show");

    /* do another level of display */
    PSmoveto(18.0, 86.0);
    DPSPrintf(ctx, "FontInfo");
    PSbegin();
    DPSPrintf(ctx, "Notice show");
    PSend();
}
```

This should give you a display something like Figure 5-1.

Figure 5-1. Display of font internal information.

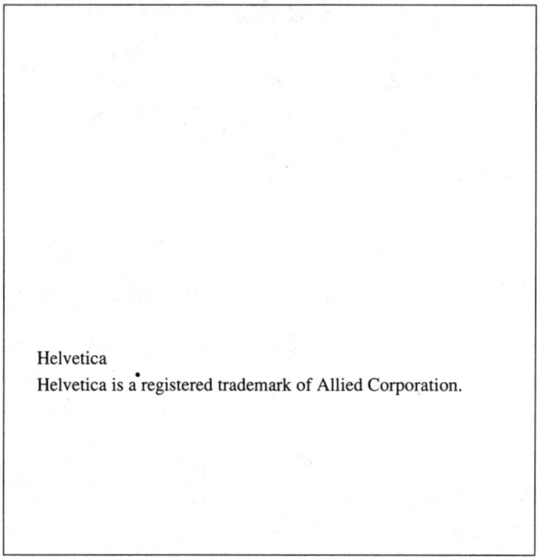

Helvetica
Helvetica is a registered trademark of Allied Corporation.

This procedure tells you something about font structure and illustrates one or two new coding tricks to help you get information to and from the Display PostScript environment.

The program starts by getting the current context information. You may already have this; if so, it isn't necessary to do it again here. However you get it, though, you will need it later in this procedure. The next two lines set a font for display of the font information you will be getting, and then move to a defined spot on the screen so that you can display the information from the font dictionary. Here you are using Times-Roman as the display font to make a specific distinction between the font information and the font used for the display.

Now you arrive at the heart of the procedure. You begin by sending a **findfont** command to the interpreter. This retrieves the Helvetica font dictionary, based on the name stored in the *name* argument, and returns the pointer to the dictionary (for our purposes, the dictionary) on the operand stack. Normally in this process you would continue with **scalefont** and **setfont**, but not this time. Instead you continue as shown, with a **begin** operator. This takes the dictionary off the stack, puts it onto the dictionary stack, and makes it the current dictionary. That's just what we said before would be necessary for you to retrieve information from the font dictionary as though it were a regular dictionary. The Helvetica font dictionary is now on the dictionary stack, and you can retrieve information from it by giving the interpreter the name, or key, and getting the associated value back on the operand stack.

Here, however, you encounter a small difficulty. You don't have any Client Library function to access these names in the dictionary, and you don't know any general way to send an arbitrary string to the interpreter. You could, of course, write a special wrap to send a single line of code to the interpreter, but that's rather a nuisance and not necessary. Instead you are introduced here to the Client Library procedure DPSPrintf, which sends an arbitrary string to the interpreter using the same format conventions as the standard C procedure, printf. This makes the procedure easy to use, and yet allows you full flexibility for sending information to the PostScript environment. The only catch here is that there is no comparable PS function, so you must have the current context as an argument for this procedure. This is why you have to get the context information at the beginning of the processing—so you can use it in this procedure.

With the context, you send down a standard string that starts with the name of the item that you want along with the additional commands to display the item. When the interpreter receives this string, it executes it just as if the string had been encountered in the ordinary course of PostScript processing. In this case, this means that the name **FontName** is looked up in the dictionaries on the dictionary stack. It is found in the Helvetica font dictionary that you placed onto the dictionary stack in the preceding **begin.** Executing the name places that item onto the operand stack for further processing.

If you look back at the list of names in a font dictionary, you see that this item, **FontName**, is an actual name. Before you can display it, you have to make it into a string. There are several methods of doing so, but the easiest is to convert the name directly into a string. This removes the / from the front of the name and displays it as an ordinary string. This action is taken by the next sequence of operators in the string. The first of these creates a string of 35 blank characters as a place for the converted string; the second issues a **cvs** (convert to string) command and changes the name into a string. Only the converted part of the string, which holds the name, is left on the stack. You can now issue a **show** command to paint this information on the page. Notice that you have already set the font and current point so that the **show** can execute correctly.

Going down another level in the dictionary hierarchy inside the font is just the same technique applied again. For example, suppose you now want to access the **FontInfo** dictionary. The next section of code in runPSInline shows how you can do that.

With the Helvetica dictionary still on the dictionary stack, you send down a string that is only "FontInfo". This causes the interpreter to get the associated value, which is the **FontInfo** dictionary contained within the Helvetica dictionary, and place that onto the operand stack as before. Then you can again issue the **begin** command to place that dictionary in turn onto the dictionary stack and make it the current dictionary. You now use the same mechanism as before to display the **Notice** information, after moving down the display window a bit to place this string on another line. In this case, the **Notice** information is already in a string, so no conversion is required.

Finally you use the **end** operator to pop the **FontInfo** dictionary off the dictionary stack when you are through with it. Remember that you can't access the **FontInfo** dictionary until you have performed the earlier step of getting a font dictionary and putting it onto the dictionary stack. If you try to access **FontInfo** before that, you will get an error; the **FontInfo** dictionary is included within the font dictionary, just like the other font information.

Character Metrics

Before you can understand how fonts work, you need to know how the characters within fonts are measured. Figure 5-2 shows two typical characters, a "g" and an "h," positioned one right after the other. The figure also shows some of the important measurements, called *character metrics*, that affect characters and character placement.

Figure 5-2. Character metrics.

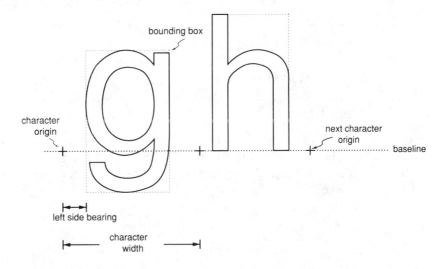

All the measurements for characters are done in a separate *character coordinate system*. This coordinate system is distinct from the coordinate in the user space and can use any scale that you want. For built-in fonts, the characters are usually scaled in a coordinate system of 1000 units by 1000 units. This works in the same way that the graphics procedures that you defined before work; that is, each character has its own *character origin* (0,0) that is separate from any page reference at all. This is the same method you used to create, scale, and position the logo graphic in Chapter 4. It also explains why the character widths from the font metric files must be divided by 1000, as you have been doing in your string width procedures. The widths given in the metric files are in character coordinate units.

The character origin is also called the *reference point* and is the point that **show** (and other text painting operators) positions on the current point of the user space when the character is painted onto the page. This is the connection between character coordinates and user coordinates.

The *width* of the character is the distance between the origin of the character and the origin of the next character, when printing consecutively on the page. In other words, the *next character origin* shown in Figure 5-2 is the character origin plus the width; and this is the point that **show** returns to you as the current point if this is the last character in the string. As you noticed in the exercises where you used the **stringwidth** operator, character width is a vector in the character coordinate system. That's a fancy way of saying that it has both *x*- and *y*-coordinate values. For our purposes, the *y*-coordinate value is always zero; but you should remember that it's there.

The character is enclosed in a *bounding box*. Like the bounding box that we discussed in Chapter 4, around the logo graphic, this bounding box represents the smallest rectangle that completely encloses all the marks that make up the character. You will remember the **FontBBox** entry in the font dictionary; that is just the largest of all the bounding boxes for all the characters in the font.

Finally, there is the *left side bearing* of a character. This is the distance from the character origin to the left edge of the character's bounding box. This distance, like all the measurements for characters, is in character coordinate units. Note also that it may be negative; that is, the character may start on the left of the character origin.

Using Character Encoding

The preceding section discussed and reviewed the operations required to select a font and put it into use. Now you are going to explore the operations that place a character onto a page using a font. This is an important issue for working with and modifying fonts. It is in the process that actually paints characters on the page, called *font encoding,* that you can have a marked effect on the efficiency of PostScript programs. This is also the first process that we will modify (just slightly) to create a revision to an existing font.

We use the **show** operator as the example since you have already worked with this operator, but the same process applies to all the character painting operators. In the ordinary course of work in PostScript, **show** is called with a string as an operand. Let's use (abcd) as the example string; then you would write:

    (abcd) **show**

to paint the string onto the output page. This assumes, of course, that the current font and the current point are set to what you want them to be. For the rest of this section, we will take the existence of a current font and a current point as already provided.

The **show** operator is going to work on each character in the string in an identical fashion, so we will only look at the process for one character. **show** takes the first character and uses the character code, which is the numeric value of the character as defined by your system environment, as a key into the **Encoding** array. This array matches the value of the character with a name. You notice that this is a straightforward indexing process, where the character value—as a number—is the index to retrieve the element at the designated position in the array.

In this case, the character "a" has the numeric value of 97. The **show** operation therefore indexes into the **Encoding** array and pulls out the ninety-eighth element (remember that indices run from 0 in PostScript), which is a name literal. In this case, this name literal is /a. If the Helvetica dictionary is on the dictionary stack, this process is exactly equivalent to the code

> Encoding 97 **get**

Names of simple alphabetic characters in the **Encoding** array are just the single letters themselves, but other characters have names that are complete words, such as "plus", "comma", and "cent". The names of all the characters are given in the Codes and Names section of Appendix A of the *PostScript Language Reference Manual,* right alongside the octal codes. Notice particularly that the numbers also have word names, like "one", "three", and so on. Each **Encoding** array has 256 entries, corresponding to the 256 possible character codes. Naturally, not all positions in the array correspond to valid character codes. Positions in the array that do not have a character code with a corresponding entry in the **CharStrings** dictionary contain the special name /.*notdef,* which indicates that the position does not correspond to an existing, encoded character.

The name found in the **Encoding** array is then used as a key into the **CharStrings** dictionary for the current font. Once again, if the Helvetica dictionary is on the dictionary stack, this can be represented by the simple code

> CharStrings /a **get**

The values in **CharStrings** are, effectively, procedures that tell the interpreter how to construct the given character. This is done by normal PostScript graphic operations, just as you might draw a character using PostScript procedures. In actual practice, the values in **CharStrings** are encrypted and locked so that the character outline, which is proprietary, cannot be stolen. Unlike most forms of copy protection, this one is virtually invisible, and generally not a nuisance, to the user. The encryption method can also be used to provide special processing that makes these operations faster than simple native PostScript.

When the character is fully formed, at the correct size, it is imaged onto the page at the current point. Then the current point is moved by the appropriate distance for positioning the next character.

The formed character is also placed into the *font cache*. The font cache is an area that is set aside to help speed the process of rendering characters. Once a character has been used in a page, it stays in the font cache for a period of time. This means that the next occurrence of that same character doesn't have to go through the entire process just outlined. Instead, the interpreter uses the image of the character that has already been created and stored in the font cache. This makes the process of printing the character on the order of a thousand times faster than executing the entire procedure again.

This completes the processing cycle for the letter "a." Now the **show** returns to the string, picks the next character code, and starts again, until the string is exhausted.

Now that you have seen how a typical character is transferred to the output device, we should look at the various types of PostScript fonts that provide these character descriptions. In PostScript, three types of fonts, corresponding to the three types of graphic images that PostScript can represent, can be created. These are as follows:

- Outline fonts
- Stroked fonts
- Bitmapped fonts

Outline fonts are the most common form of fonts in a PostScript environment and may be rendered onto the page either as stroked outlines, or, more commonly, as filled shapes. In either case, they behave exactly like a box or a circle on a page. Stroked fonts, on the other hand, are made up of single lines, rather than shapes. In this, they resemble the straight lines you have produced in earlier examples. Just as you could not fill a line, you cannot fill a stroked font. The distinction, then, is that outline fonts may be either filled or stroked along the outline; stroked fonts can only be stroked, and not filled. Both of these types of fonts use PostScript operations to render the fonts onto a page.

The third type of font, bitmapped, is somewhat different. We are not going to deal here in any great degree with bitmapped fonts, but I want to mention them for the sake of completing the list, and because you will probably hear them mentioned from time to time. Bitmapped fonts are direct pictures, as it were, of a letter. They are a series of dots (the bits) that are turned on to make up a letter—sort of like the pictures of Christmas trees made up in computer departments by printing zeros and ones on a page. Generally such fonts do not provide a nice typeset quality to output that is being created on medium- or higher resolution devices. These fonts require a lot of coding and design, and examples of bitmapped fonts are beyond the scope of this book.

In Display PostScript there is an additional aspect of font handling and bitmapped fonts that deserves some mention. On low-resolution devices such as display screens, the PostScript scan conversion process that turns the outlines into bitmaps for display does not necessarily produce characters that are as clean and readable as bitmaps that have been especially created for the device, particularly at typical text point sizes such as 10 to 12 points. This has been, in the past, a source of annoyance and is one reason why different images have been used for screens and printers.

Character images that have been especially tuned for screen display are called *screen fonts*. Display PostScript has a facility that automatically uses such screen fonts, if available. This guarantees that your display is of the highest possible quality, without any additional work on your part. This is done by the interpreter at the time that the **show** operator is displaying the character. The first source for the character is the font cache—as we discussed earlier, the font cache is the fastest and most efficient source of characters. If the character is not in the cache, the interpreter asks the system if there is a bitmapped version of the font/size/character available. If there is, that character is displayed and placed into the cache for future use. If not, the interpreter continues in the ordinary way to create the character from the outline, displaying the result and placing it into the font cache according to the normal processing rules.

This singular exception aside, characters in PostScript fonts are generally created by the equivalent of the path construction and painting operations. This is entirely consistent with the design of PostScript and the notion of type as a graphic object. This approach offers the user several benefits that may not be obvious at first glance.

First, this approach to creating characters preserves the quality of the fonts. Since PostScript effectively draws each character at the correct point size, it preserves the relative size and weight relationships down to the finest available resolution. Many electronic fonts, on the other hand, are simply reductions or enlargements of a fixed size of characters. This means that the font becomes coarse and unappealing at sizes quite different from the design size. This doesn't happen with PostScript fonts.

In addition, this process of drawing the characters also forms an important part of the device independence that PostScript provides. Because PostScript is independent of device-specific qualities like resolution, the way it represents characters must allow it to place the characters in precisely the same relative positions on different devices and yet allow the maximum resolution that the device can produce.

Displaying the Font Encoding

With all this discussion about things that cannot be seen, you may think that we have approached the theological; so it's time for an exercise to show you how these pieces look. For this exercise you will display the **StandardEncoding** vector in your system. The advantage of using the standard encoding vector is that it is both readily available in *systemdict* without pulling it out of a font, and it is quite standard, so the results are predictable. The techniques that we develop here, however, can be just as readily applied to any encoding vector in the system, whether retrieved from a font or accessible from the *systemdict*.

This is a very practical exercise, and one that you may well wish to extend after you have finished with it here. The majority of the work in this exercise is done by PostScript routines that are created during the setup procedure and are stored in a private dictionary as you have done before. The intention here is to display all the elements in an **Encoding** array that are defined; that is, that do not contain the special name /.*notdef*. These are displayed in a window at least 4.5 inches by 5.5 inches. You will use the same technique (scaling) as you did for the check form to allow you to display a complete 8.5 inch by 11 inch page within the window. Because of the number of entries, you will display these listed in three columns, down the page. There is a 1-inch margin at the top of the page, a 0.5-inch margin at the bottom, and so on. By now, most of this is quite easy for you.

Starting with the top process, here is the runPSInline procedure that will do the job for you:

```
void runPSInline (void)
{
    int begin, end;

    /* scale to fit full page in window */
    PSscale(0.5, 0.5);
    PSWsetupDisplay();
    PSselectfont("Times-Roman", 12.0);
    /* remember that PostScript indexes from 0 */
    begin = 0;
    end = 255;
```

```
        PSWencodeDisplay("StandardEncoding", begin, end);
}
```

As you see, this is quite simple. You begin, as you did in the check display, by scaling the output to the window size. Then you run the setup functions. Next you select the font and font size for the display—remembering not to make it too small because you are scaling the window display down, anyway. Then you set the beginning and ending elements for the display. In this case, you intend to display all 256 of the elements; note, however, that you could choose to display a subset if you wanted. Finally, you call the display wrap with the name of the array—in this case, **StandardEncoding**—and the beginning and ending positions as arguments. The wraps do the rest.

Let's get into the heart of the process and look at the wraps that are going to do the actual work. In fact, as you saw earlier, there are only two: one to set up the required procedures and variables, and one to display any requested segment of an encoding vector. The code is as follows:

```
defineps PSWsetupDisplay ()
    %set up private dictionary
    /PersDict 50 dict def                                              %1
    PersDict begin                                                     %2

    %now define procedures
    /dispElement
    %display a single element out of the array
    %called as: number array dispElement —
    %where number is the index number of the desired element in array
    {
        1 index get                                                    %3
        showEntry
    }
    def

    /showEntry
    %actually shows a given element
    %called as: element showEntry —
    {
        {currentpoint}                                                 %4
        stopped                                                        %5
            { XMar TopMar moveto /Index 0 def }                        %6
            { pop pop }
```

```
            ifelse
            dup /.notdef eq                                    %7
            {
                pop pop                                        %8
            }
            {                                                  %9
                exch
                dup Tstr cvs                                   %10
                gsave                                          %11
                    show                                       %12
                grestore
                25 0 rmoveto                                   %13
                dup 8#10 lt                                    %14
                {
                    (\\00) dispOctal                           %15
                }
                {
                    dup 8#100 lt                               %16
                    {
                        (\\0) dispOctal
                    }
                    {
                        (\\) dispOctal
                    }
                    ifelse
                }
                ifelse
                15 0 rmoveto                                   %17
                Tstr cvs show                                  %18
                nextLine                                       %19
            }
        ifelse
    }
    def

    /dispOctal
    %display a number in octal notation (\ddd)
    {
        show
        8 Tstr cvrs                                            %20
        show
    }
```

```
    def

/nextLne
%move down one line and test for end of column
{
    currentpoint
    LL sub
    dup BotMar lt                              %21
        { nextCol }
    if
    exch pop                                   %22
    XMar exch moveto
}
def

/nextCol
%move over to next column
{
    pop TopMar                                 %23
    /XMar                                      %24
    Xarray                                     %25
    dup length Index ge not                    %26
        { /Index 0 def }                       %27
        { /Index Index 1 add def }             %28
    ifelse
    Index get def                              %29
}
def

%now define required variables
/Tstr 40 string def                            %30
/TopMar 10 72 mul def
/BotMar 0.5 72 mul def
/XMar 36 def
/LL 13 def
/Xarray [36 216 396] def%31
/Index 0 def

end %PersDict
endps
```

```
defineps PSWencodeDisplay (char *Array; int Begin, End)
    PersDict begin
    Begin 1 End
    {Array dispElement}
    for
    end %PersDict
endps
```

Putting these together with the earlier C procedure generates a display that looks something like Figure 5-3.

Figure 5-3. Listing of the StandardEncoding array.

32	\040	space	85	\125	U	172	\254	guilsinglleft
33	\041	exclam	86	\126	V	173	\255	guilsinglright
34	\042	quotedbl	87	\127	W	174	\256	fi
35	\043	numbersign	88	\130	X	175	\257	fl
36	\044	dollar	89	\131	Y	177	\261	endash
37	\045	percent	90	\132	Z	178	\262	dagger
38	\046	ampersand	91	\133	bracketleft	179	\263	daggerdbl
39	\047	quoteright	92	\134	backslash	180	\264	periodcentered
40	\050	parenleft	93	\135	bracketright	182	\266	paragraph
41	\051	parenright	94	\136	asciicircum	183	\267	bullet
42	\052	asterisk	95	\137	underscore	184	\270	quotesinglbase
43	\053	plus	96	\140	quoteleft	185	\271	quotedblbase
44	\054	comma	97	\141	a	186	\272	quotedblright
45	\055	hyphen	98	\142	b	187	\273	guillemotright
46	\056	period	99	\143	c	188	\274	ellipsis
47	\057	slash	100	\144	d	189	\275	perthousand
48	\060	zero	101	\145	e	191	\277	questiondown
49	\061	one	102	\146	f	193	\301	grave
50	\062	two	103	\147	g	194	\302	acute
51	\063	three	104	\150	h	195	\303	circumflex
52	\064	four	105	\151	i	196	\304	tilde
53	\065	five	106	\152	j	197	\305	macron
54	\066	six	107	\153	k	198	\306	breve
55	\067	seven	108	\154	l	199	\307	dotaccent
56	\070	eight	109	\155	m	200	\310	dieresis
57	\071	nine	110	\156	n	202	\312	ring
58	\072	colon	111	\157	o	203	\313	cedilla
59	\073	semicolon	112	\160	p	205	\315	hungarumlaut
60	\074	less	113	\161	q	206	\316	ogonek
61	\075	equal	114	\162	r	207	\317	caron
62	\076	greater	115	\163	s	208	\320	emdash
63	\077	question	116	\164	t	225	\341	AE
64	\100	at	117	\165	u	227	\343	ordfeminine
65	\101	A	118	\166	v	232	\350	Lslash
66	\102	B	119	\167	w	233	\351	Oslash
67	\103	C	120	\170	x	234	\352	OE
68	\104	D	121	\171	y	235	\353	ordmasculine
69	\105	E	122	\172	z	241	\361	ae
70	\106	F	123	\173	braceleft	245	\365	dotlessi
71	\107	G	124	\174	bar	248	\370	lslash
72	\110	H	125	\175	braceright	249	\371	oslash
73	\111	I	126	\176	asciitilde	250	\372	oe
74	\112	J	161	\241	exclamdown	251	\373	germandbls
75	\113	K	162	\242	cent			
76	\114	L	163	\243	sterling			
77	\115	M	164	\244	fraction			
78	\116	N	165	\245	yen			
79	\117	O	166	\246	florin			
80	\120	P	167	\247	section			
81	\121	Q	168	\250	currency			
82	\122	R	169	\251	quotesingle			
83	\123	S	170	\252	quotedblleft			
84	\124	T	171	\253	guillemotleft			

Really, all of the complexity in this process is handled in the setup process. Before we get to that, however, let's briefly review the display wrap, PSWencodeDisplay. As shown, you start by establishing the private dictionary as the current dictionary—an absolute necessity as you are going to be accessing many items from the dictionary. The elements of the array are accessed by using the **for** operator, which you learned about in Chapter 2. (If you are not familiar with it, you may want to review its requirements in Appendix A of this book.)

To start the process, you push the beginning element number, passed as an argument, on the operand stack. This is followed by a 1, which is the increment value of the loop variable, and completed with the ending element number, also an argument. These are the beginning, increment, and ending values for the **for** loop. The **for** executes a defined procedure for each value of its internal looping variable, placing the current value of the variable onto the stack before executing the procedure. The variable begins at the first operand value, it is incremented by the second, and the whole process stops when the internal looping variable exceeds the ending value given. In short, quite a standard for loop, such as you are familiar with from C programming.

The difference here is in the procedure to be executed repeatedly. This consists of two objects: the array itself and the dispElement procedure, which displays one element out of the array. The **for** loop variable, which is also on the stack each time the procedure is executed, is the index of the element to be reported. So each time dispElement is executed by the **for** operator, there will be two objects on the stack. On the top of the stack is the array, and underneath that is the current value of the looping variable.

This leads quite naturally into the PSWsetupDisplay wrap, where this procedure and all the ancillary procedures and variables are defined. Let's go through these one at a time. By this time, much of this code is quite familiar to you, and I will not trouble you with explanations of the processes that you have already studied. However, some issues still need to be discussed.

The wrap begins in lines %1 and %2 by defining and using a private dictionary, PersDict. The next section of the setup defines a series of procedures, beginning with the procedure dispElement. This is a short, two-line procedure that accesses the desired element from the array, in line %3, and then executes the showEntry procedure, which displays the element that has been retrieved. To follow the operation in line %3, remember that two operands are on the stack: the element number and the array itself. Line %3 retrieves the second operand (the element number) from the stack and duplicates it on the top of the stack—remember that all PostScript indices begin with 0, so the top element on the stack is element 0, the one below it is 1, and so on. This sets the stack up for the **get** operator, which retrieves the single designated element from the array, leaving that element on the stack. The stack now contains, from the top down, the element of the array and the number of the element.

The showEntry procedure comes next. It starts with a useful trick, in lines %4 to %6. Since you are going to need to have a current point, and since you will define variables for the page layout, you can use this method to avoid having your wrap exit ingloriously with an error if the current point is not set. You start by creating a procedure, in line %4, that consists only of the **currentpoint** operator, which, as the name implies, returns the current point coordinates onto the operand stack if the current point exists. If the current point does not exist, the procedure raises an error. This procedure is executed by the special operator **stopped** in line %5. This operator executes the procedure operand and returns *false* if the procedure executes correctly and *true* if it does not. What does that mean here? It means that, if the current point is set, you will get the two coordinates on the stack with a *false* boolean on top of them; if the current point is not set, you will get the *true* boolean and nothing else. The important point, however, is that in any case, processing continues as normal without raising any error that could return to trouble your application.

Now in line %6 you can set the starting coordinates for the display process if the current point is not set, that is, if the **stopped** operator returned *true*. You use the (as yet undefined) variables for the left margin, XMar, and for the top margin, TopMar, for the coordinates. You also set the Index variable to its starting value so that the display process continues in the correct column. (You will discover exactly how this works in a moment, in the nextCol procedure.) If **stopped** returned *false,* the current point is already set, and you simply pop the two extraneous values off the stack and continue processing.

Line %7 tests for the element /.notdef in the array. The intention here is to not print any element that is not defined; this keeps the size of the display down and doesn't clutter it with a series of undefined entries. Line %8 disposes of the items on the stack if the entry is, in fact, /.notdef. If it is a valid entry, processing continues in the procedure beginning at line %9.

At this point, you want to display three items in a line: the element number in decimal, the element number in octal, and the element itself. You know that the elements are all names, and you have both these items on the operand stack. What you need to do is to convert this information to a displayable form and position it along the line for display. At the end of all this, you need to move down a line on the display to be ready for the next line.

You start by switching the operands on the stack. Since you are going to display the element number first and then the element itself, you want them on the stack with the number on top. Then, in line %10, you duplicate the element number—since you want to display it two times, once as decimal and once as an octal number—and you convert the number to a string representation. Remember that this is the same technique you used to display the check number in Chapter 4. Here you use a temporary string variable, Tstr, for the conversion. Since you will be performing several conversions in the course of this display process, you should save virtual memory by creating only one string and reusing it throughout the process.

The problem is that the number returned may be one, two, or three digits, depending on the magnitude of the number converted. (You know that the maximum element number is 255, so it will never be larger than three digits.) Nevertheless, how can you position the remainder of the display to account for the varying width of the string? You can't simply move to a specific *x* position on the page because you are creating a multicolumn display. In a word processing program, you would use a tab; here, you can perform the equivalent maneuver by moving a defined distance from the beginning of the column. To do so, you save the graphics state with a **gsave** in line %11, do the **show** of the string in line %12, and then restore the graphics state. This returns the current point to the beginning of the column and allows you to do a relative move in line %13 by a fixed amount to position the display for the next item.

Here you have the converse of the previous problem. You want to display the number in the standard octal format, \ddd, using leading zeros after the backslash if the number contains fewer than three digits. The tests and procedures from line %14 down to, but not including, line %17 provide this service. Most of this should present no problem for you; the only exception may be the form of the numbers for testing in lines %14 and %16. Here you use the radix form of the number, 8#10 (or 8#100). This form of number is a base value—here, 8—followed by the number in that base. Since you want to test for one, two, or three digits in octal, using base 8 for the tests makes more sense than trying to understand the process if you used 8 and 64 (the base 10 variants of the same numbers). As always, the intention here is to write code that is both correct and easy to follow, and therefore easy to maintain.

The procedure dispOctal, called in line %15, is simply a convenience procedure that avoids coding a repetitive sequence of instructions. You could simply insert the three lines of code represented by dispOctal here. In fact, that would be slightly more efficient because it would avoid an additional dictionary lookup of the procedure. However, here we have chosen clarity over efficiency instead. The only interesting line in the procedure is line %20, which uses a new conversion operator, **cvrs,** to convert the number into a string. **cvrs** (convert to radix string) works in a manner similar to **cvs,** but it works only on numbers, and it takes two arguments. Here it is in the standard format:

> num base string   **cvrs**   substring
> converts *num* into a string representation according to the number system whose base number, or radix, is given by *base*. The string equivalent of *num* is placed into the first part of *string* and is returned to the stack as *substring*.

In this case, as you see in line %20, the base is 8, and you use the usual temporary string, Tstr, to hold the result for display.

Since the octal number is displayed in a string of fixed size, the next move, in line %17, can be from the end of the string. Having printed the element number in both forms, you can now display the name itself in line %18, using the same techniques that you used earlier for the numbers. Finally, the position on the display is moved down a line by invoking the nextLine procedure on line %19.

The nextLine procedure is very straightforward and uses techniques that are quite familiar to you from the previous exercises. It takes the current point, subtracts the leading value LL, tests for the bottom of the column, and moves to the next line. The test on line %21 simply compares the new *y* coordinate of the display with the bottom margin variable. If it is less than the bottom margin, the nextCol procedure is executed; otherwise, line %22 swaps the *x* and *y* coordinates, pushes the correct *x* coordinate, XMar, onto the stack, swaps them again, and moves to the new line coordinates.

Which brings us to the last procedure, nextCol. This is a bit more complex, but still quite understandable once you see how the processing is being done. The procedure begins at line %23, which throws away the previous *y*-coordinate value and replaces it with the TopMar variable. Next you need to determine what the *x* coordinate for the next column will be. This has been set up in an array, Xarray, which has one entry for each column, with the value of the entry being the *x* coordinate of the column. You start the process by pushing the name of the *x* margin variable onto the stack in line %24. This is used later by the **def** operator in line %29. Then you retrieve the array. The basic idea here is to pull the next element out of the array and define it as the *x* margin variable. All well and good, but first you have to determine how many elements are in the array so that you don't try to access more values than are in it. This little chore is done in line %26, where the length of the array—the number of elements in it—is calculated and compared to the current value of the index variable Index. As long as the index value is not equal to or greater than the size of the array, you can bump the index value by 1 (in line %28) and get the next element in the array in line %29 and define it as XMar. Line %27 provides (rather inadequately, if this were a real commercial application) for the situation where you have run out of columns: it starts over at column one.

The remainder of the setup process is just defining the variables that you have used in these procedures. The temporary string, which is defined in line %30, is made fairly large because any overflow causes an error, and the element names might be fairly long. The Xarray array, defined in line %31, contains the margin positions for three columns; note that the XMar variable must be initialized at the same value as the first element in Xarray.

Even with all this work, there are still several improvements that would be nice for this process. Column headings would improve the display, for example, and showing the actual character as well as its name would improve the display quite a bit. In addition, a real application should not hard code the column positions or the leading for the display. All of these should be set from the application code, where the information about the window is available and where the point size of the font is set and kept. Indeed, as you saw in the check form, the leading should be able to be changed by the user; and you might want to handle the column positions in some way that also allows the user to control them.

FONT MODIFICATIONS

Now that you have covered the operation of PostScript fonts in detail, it's time to use this deeper knowledge to help you make some changes to the available fonts. This section shows you how to modify fonts and characters within fonts to provide some effects that you may not be able to get in any other way. Remember that the font machinery is quite complex, for all its ease of use, and that you have to be careful when you work with the fonts. Arbitrary or unplanned changes are likely to result in poor quality output at best and may cause a disaster at worst. Be sure to read the exercises carefully before you do them, and follow the explanations so that you know what is intended. With that small caution, you will find that modification of characters and fonts is both useful and fun.

The first type of modifications are of individual characters. These are the easiest modifications to make as well as the most common. You should find this work interesting because it allows you additional freedom to use characters as graphic objects. Of course, all modifications to a font ultimately come down to modification of characters. What character modification means here is modifications to specific individual characters within a font, rather than global modifications to a font that change all the characters uniformly. Such global modifications are covered in the next section.

The first character modifications that you will do are those that change the font encoding to allow you to access characters that otherwise may be unavailable to your program.

The use of the **Encoding** array may have seemed to be a rather indirect method to produce the desired result of imaging a character onto the page. So it is, but it offers some substantial benefits as well. One of these is the ability to render characters that are not in the standard encoding; another is that standard characters may be rearranged into an alternative encoding scheme if necessary. In this example, you will modify the standard encoding vector, **StandardEncoding,** to add some more characters. The additional characters that are available are listed under "Unencoded Text Characters" in Appendix A of the *PostScript Language Reference Manual*.

You now have enough information to follow where these characters come from. These characters have names and procedures in the **CharStrings** dictionary for the built-in fonts, but do not have names in the standard **Encoding** array. What you have to do is make entries for those characters that you want to use in a new **Encoding** array with the names of the characters at the positions that you choose. This should suggest that another method to determine the list of characters unavailable in your current environment is to dump the **Encoding** vector, as we did earlier, and compare it to the keys in the **CharStrings** dictionary. The keys that do not have entries in the array are the ones that you cannot retrieve with that version of the array.

Let's do an example assuming that you are using the **StandardEncoding** vector. (If you have a different encoding vector, the process would be the same, but the choice of characters might be different.) This example is a portion of a menu for a rather fancy dinner that presents some interesting combinations of food and wine. You want to produce a menu with correctly accented letters where required. After reviewing the food and wine, you make a list of the additional letters, with accents, that you need for the wording on the menu. Now you look in Appendix A of the *PostScript Language Reference Manual* to determine the correct name for each of these letters. The complete list of letters that you will use, along with the correct name is shown in Figure 5-4.

Figure 5-4. Accented letters for menu example.

Character	Name
â	acircumflex
à	agrave
è	egrave
é	eacute
û	ucircumflex
ü	udieresis
ó	oacute

Execution of these names in **CharStrings** causes the interpreter to build the accented characters shown in the appendix. The task now is to include these character names into an encoding vector so you can use them in your menu.

You must first decide what character codes you want to use to make these letters. Theoretically you might choose any character that is coded from 0 through 255; however, that really isn't practical. Your document is already using ordinary text and punctuation, so you don't want to substitute any of these special characters for the regular ones. The special characters aren't on the standard keyboard (although they may be accessible through optional keycodes), but we have already discussed how you can use the octal codes to call out characters that are not on the keyboard. So now you need to determine what octal codes you want to use for these characters.

You have identified seven accented characters that you want to use on the menu. If you look back at your display of the **Encoding** array, you can see a continuous block of unused codes from \330 to \336; you will use these codes for your additional letters.

There is one more point to discuss before you get to the example. That is the choice of font for the menu, and the method for changing the encoding vector for that font. In this example, you will use a 10-point Times-Roman font for all the type. You certainly don't want to modify the encoding vector for Times-Roman in any permanent way. Therefore, the correct method to produce a temporary modification of the encoding vector is to duplicate the font before you make the modification.

Here are the steps that you need to take in the program to produce the menu output:

1. Duplicate the Times-Roman font.
2. Reset the encoding vector to include the new codes and the associated character names.
3. Set the menu text using the appropriate octal codes for the accented characters.

As before, you can start at the procedure level and work down to the wraps, or vice versa. Here we again start with the runPSInline procedure, which looks as follows:

```
void runPSInline (void)
{
    float x, y;
    float pointsize, leading;
    char *basefont, *newfont;
    int done;

    pointsize = 10;
    leading = 11;
    PSWsetupMenu(pointsize, leading);

    basefont = "Times-Roman";
    newfont = "Times-Menu";
    /* use return value to ensure completed execution
    PSWreEncode(basefont, newfont, &done);

    /* processing does not continue until return value
```

```
/*   so re-encoding is complete at this point
PSselectfont("Times-Menu", pointsize);

x = 36.0;
y = 5*72;
PSWshowFood(x, y)

x = 5*72;
PSWshowWine(x, y);

x = 2.5*72;
y = 2*72;
PSWshowAfters(x, y);
}
```

The wraps necessary to perform this process are then defined as follows:

```
defineps PSWsetupMenu ( float PointSize, Leading )
    %— — — — —Variables— —
    /Ps PointSize def    %set point size                    %1
    /Lead Leading def    %set leading                       %2

    %— — — —Modified Encoding Vector— —
    /MenuVec                                                %3
    [
        8#330 /acircumflex                                  %4
        8#331 /agrave                                       %5
        8#332 /egrave                                       %6
        8#333 /eacute                                       %7
        8#334 /ucircumflex                                  %8
        8#335 /udieresis                                    %9
        8#336 /oacute                                       %10
    ]
    def                                                     %11

    %— — — —Procedures— —
    /ss                                                     %12
    {
        Xpos Line moveto show
        /Line Line Lead sub def
    }
    def
```

Chapter 5: Font Creation and Modification   289

```
    /nextblock                                          %13
    {
        /Line
        Line Lead 2 mul sub def
    }
    def
endps
```

```
defineps PSWreEncode ( char *BaseFont, *NewFont | boolean *Done )
    %— — — —Re Encode Font— —
    /ReEncodeDict 12 dict def                           %14
    ReEncodeDict begin                                  %15

     /BasefontDict /BaseFont findfont def               %16
     /NewfontDict BasefontDict maxlength dict def       %17

     BasefontDict                                       %18
     {
        exch dup /FID ne                                %19
        {
            dup /Encoding eq                            %20
            {
                exch dup length array copy             %21
                NewfontDict 3 1 roll put                %22
            }
            { exch NewfontDict 3 1 roll put }           %23
            ifelse                                      %24
        }                                               %25
        { pop pop }                                     %26
        ifelse                                          %27
     } forall                                           %28

     NewfontDict /FontName /NewFont put                 %29
     MenuVec aload                                      %30
     length 2 idiv                                      %31
     { NewfontDict /Encoding get 3 1 roll put }         %32
     repeat                                             %33
```

```
        /NewFont NewfontDict definefont pop          %34
        end                                          %35
        true Done                                    %36
endps


defineps PSWshowWines ( float X, Y )
        %— — — —Program (Wines)— —
        %Position and show wines
        /Xpos X exch def                             %37
        /Line Y exch def                             %38

        (Louis Roederer Cristal 1979 ) ss            %39
        ( Brut ) ss

        nextblock                                    %40
        (Ch\330teau Clerc Milon 1970) ss             %41
        (Ch\330teau La Gaffli\332re 1970) ss         %42

        nextblock                                    %43
        (Ch\330teau Cheval Blanc 1970) ss
        (Ch\330teau Haut-Brion 1970) ss
        ( ) ss

        nextblock
        (Ch\330teau Les Forts de Latour 1970) ss
        (  (en magnum) ) ss
endps


defineps PSWshowFood ( float X, Y )
        %— — — —Program (Food)— —
        %Position and show courses
        /Xpos X exch def
        /Line Y exch def

        (Oxtail Rillettes) ss
        ( with Catalan-style Tomato Bread) ss
```

```
        nextblock
        (6-Lily Risotto) ss
        ( with Black Sesame Seeds) ss

        nextblock
        (Saffron-flavored Rago\334t of Chicken,) ss
        ( Chicken-of-the-Forest Mushrooms,) ss
        ( and Parsnips) ss

        nextblock
        (Roast Triangle Tip of Beef with Bordeaux Basil Butter,) ss
        ( Pencil-thin Asparagus,) ss
        ( and Stuffed Baby White Eggplant) ss
endps


        defineps PSWshowAfters ( float X, Y )
        %— — — —Program (Dessert)— —
        %Position and show after-dinner courses
        /Xpos X exch def
        /Line Y exch def

        (Assorted Cheeses \331 la Red Smith) ss

        nextblock
        (Marc de Gew\335rztraminer (Gilbert Miclo),) ss
        (Marc Mascar\336, and other alcohols) ss

        nextblock
        (Caf\333 Demi-decaf\333in\333) ss
endps
```

This program produces the results pictured in Figure 5-5.

Figure 5-5. Menu example output.

```
Oxtail Rillettes                                    Louis Roederer Cristal 1979
  with Catalan-style Tomato Bread                     Brut

6-Lily Risotto                                      Château Clerc Milon 1970
  with Black Sesame Seeds                           Château La Gafflière 1970


Saffron-flavored Ragoût of Chicken,                 Château Cheval Blanc 1970
  Chicken-of-the-Forest Mushrooms,                  Château Haut-Brion 1970
  and Parsnips


Roast Triangle Tip of Beef with Bordeaux Basil Butter,   Château Les Forts de Latour 1970
  Pencil-thin Asparagus,                              (en magnum)
  and Stuffed Baby White Eggplant



                    Assorted Cheeses à la Red Smith


                    Marc de Gewürztraminer (Gilbert Miclo),
                    Marc Mascaró, and other alcohols


                    Café Demi-decaféiné
```

This is not an easy program to follow, so we will go through each portion of it in detail. We will begin with the wraps, which have been numbered consecutively for easier reference.

First of all, the program begins with the PSWsetupMenu wrap. This sets the variables and PostScript procedures used by the remainder of the wraps. It begins by defining the two variables, Ps and Lead. These two determine the point size for the output and the line leading. The point size is just used in the C program, whereas the leading is just used internally by the PostScript procedures. For debugging and clarity, they have been made variables in both parts of the code and set here to provide an easy method for changing and adjusting the output.

Next, in line %3, the program defines an array, MenuVec, which has the revised encoding in it. Specifically this array consists of pairs of entries: an octal number specifying the code, and the name of a character from the list in Figure 5-4. This introduces you to the use of [and] as delimiters for arrays; this was mentioned in Chapter 3, and the use is precisely like the use of { and } for procedures. The array itself consists of lines %4 to %10. Each line contains a pair of objects: a number and a name literal. The number is an octal number, denoted by the prefix 8#, followed by the three digits of the character position. In this case, the positions represented by the numbers are those chosen earlier, 330 to 336. The name is the name for the character that you want to image when you invoke that character code; the names are taken from Figure 5-4. These names must correspond to the keys in the font's **CharStrings**, remember.

Then there are two simple, short procedures. The first procedure, ss, shows a given string at the point specified by the variables, Xpos and Line, and moves down the page by the size of the Lead variable. The second procedure, nextblock, moves the vertical place variable Line down the page by a fixed distance, which is defined to be twice the Lead variable. These procedures are used to display the text on the page at appropriate locations.

Line %14 begins the interesting portion of the program—the part that reencodes the font. The section begins by defining a working dictionary, so that nothing that you define here will hang on or affect the permanent dictionaries. It uses the **dict** operator, which takes an integer operand, to create an empty dictionary big enough to hold the number of entries equal to the integer value of the operand and then the process returns the new dictionary to the stack.

Line %15 issues a **begin** to push this new dictionary onto the dictionary stack and make it the current dictionary. Line %16 defines BasefontDict to contain a copy of the font dictionary name that has been designated for reencoding, and which was retrieved by the **findfont** operator. It is this dictionary, the copy, that you will use everywhere in the following code to ensure that you can't damage the original font.

Line %17 uses another new operator, **maxlength,** to determine the maximum size of BasefontDict. This number is used as an operand by another **dict,** and the resulting dictionary—which is still empty, remember—is defined as NewfontDict. This is the dictionary that will become your new font. Notice that NewfontDict is exactly the same size as the original font dictionary.

Lines %18 through %28 perform the function of filling in the new font dictionary with entries from the original font dictionary, represented by BasefontDict. This is done by the **forall** operator on line %28, which executes the procedure defined in lines %19 through %27 for every element in the BasefontDict dictionary.

Basically this procedure copies each element of BasefontDict into the new NewfontDict. This is done by a rather clever use of two new operators, **put** and **roll**. To begin with, you want to insert (key, value) pairs into a dictionary that is not on the dictionary stack. You can do this by using the **put** operator. This operator takes three operands: a dictionary, a key, and a value—in that order. The value must be on the top of the stack, followed by the key, followed by the dictionary. Remember this order, as it is key to what you have to do next. You retrieve each entry from the BasefontDict, and the key for that entry is put onto the stack by the **forall** operator followed by the value. That would be perfect for **put,** except somehow you need to get the NewfontDict dictionary onto the stack below the key. You can do this little trick with the **roll** operator. Let's look at the stack after **forall** has done its work. For the purpose of this example, we'll use the **FontName** entry, but remember that **forall** is going to get each and every entry in the dictionary. The stack at this point is as shown in Figure 5-6.

Figure 5-6. Stack entries after **forall**.

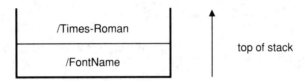

Now you push the NewfontDict dictionary that you want to work with onto the stack, which now looks like Figure 5-7. Note the small numbers off to the right; these are not part of the stack, but they are essential to understand how **roll** works.

Figure 5-7. Stack entries after NewfontDict.

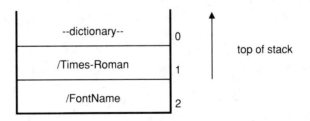

Now you invoke the **roll** operator, which takes two more operands, 3 and 1. These two numbers tell **roll** that you want to affect the top three operands on the stack, and you want to move them all up one position. That means that the key, in this case, the name literal /FontName, at position 2 rolls up to position 1; and the value at position 1 rolls up to position 0. Of course, that action can't be continued because the dictionary, at position 0, has no position above it to go to. So **roll** does what you might have suspected from its name: it puts the top element, the dictionary, marked 0 in Figure 5-7, after the lowest element that you moved, the key from the old font dictionary, marked 3. This rolls all the operands into the new positions shown in Figure 5-8, which are just what you need for the **put.** Now, when you execute the **put,** you get an entry into the NewfontDict dictionary that matches the original entry from BasefontDict.

Figure 5-8. Stack after roll.

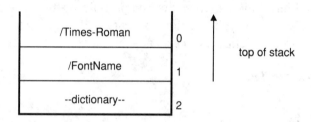

You do want exactly the same entries, but with two exceptions. (Naturally, nothing could be that simple.) These two exceptions are handled by a pair of **ifelse** conditions within the larger procedure.

The first exception is the original **FID** entry. Recall from our previous discussion that this entry is created by the **definefont** operator; therefore, you can't copy it into the new font. This exclusion is handled by the first **ifelse,** which has the conditional test on line %19 matching the **ifelse** on line %27. Let's analyze this process.

First, you have to identify the **FID** entry. You can do that by testing for the key, the name /FID. That's great, except that you know that the key went onto the stack first, followed by the value; therefore, you have to reverse the order on the stack by using an **exch** before you can do the test. So that's what you do first on line %19. Then you need to test for the name literal /FID. When you perform the test, using the **ne** operator, it consumes the two objects on the stack used for the test and returns a boolean value *true* or *false.* Because you use up the key by doing the test, you first must use a **dup** operator to get an extra copy. Then you push the name literal, /FID, onto the stack and make the comparison. If the comparison is *true,* the **ifelse** operator executes the first procedure, from lines %20 to %25; if it is *false,* it executes the second procedure, given on line %26. Since the test is whether the entry is not equal to /FID, it executes line %26 if the key is /FID and lines %20 to %25 for all other keys. That works fine because line %26 consists of two **pop** operators, which simply throw away the **FID** entry from the original dictionary. Notice that this leaves one unused entry in the new dictionary, since the new dictionary was created to hold the same number of entries as the old one. **definefont** uses this space for the new **FID.**

Lines %20 to %25 form the second **ifelse** test. In this case, you are looking for the **Encoding** array. The first question is why not just copy the original **Encoding** array and then modify it? For the answer, recall the discussion of composite objects in Chapter 3. An array is a composite object, and when you duplicate a composite object, you share the values between both copies. That means that, if you were to simply **put** the old **Encoding** array into the new font dictionary, the two arrays would be sharing the same values. This would mean that when you modify the **Encoding** array, you would affect the old array as well as the new one, and you don't want to do that. Instead, you want a new version of **Encoding** with the same values.

PostScript provides one operator that copies values from one composite object to another; that operator is called **copy.** You use the **copy** operator to generate the new **Encoding** array to go into NewfontDict.

You must first test for the **Encoding** entry. This is done just like the test for the **FID,** except that you don't have to swap the top two operands on the stack first because you already did that for the previous test. You just duplicate the key on the top of the stack and test whether it is equal to the name literal /Encoding. If it is not equal, the **ifelse** on line %24 executes the second procedure, which is on line %23. This procedure is basically the same routine that we analyzed earlier, using the **put** and **roll** operators. However, it has to be preceded by another **exch** operator. This is necessary because you took the key and the value from the original dictionary and reversed them to perform the **ifelse** tests on lines %19 and %20. Now you have to put these back the way they came off BasefontDict originally.

If the test is *true*, and the entry is the **Encoding** array, the **ifelse** executes the procedure on lines %21 and %22. This procedure starts out by swapping the operands on the stack again for the same reasons that the procedure on line %23 had to, namely, to put the key and value back in their original order. This also, not coincidentally, places the actual **Encoding** array on the top of the stack for further work.

The last part of the procedure is also familiar since it consists of the same sequence of **put** and **roll.** The new part is on line %21, where you have to provide a new copy of the **Encoding** array. You begin this task by duplicating the array on the stack, and then using the **length** operator to determine how many entries it has. **length** takes the array and returns an integer value, the size of the array, to the top of the stack. This value is the operand for the **array** operator, which generates an empty array of the given size. So the operand stack now contains the following items, from the top down: an empty array that is exactly equal in size to the original **Encoding** array, the original **Encoding** itself, and the name literal /Encoding. Now you can apply the **copy** operator, which moves the values from the original array to the empty array, one by one, and returns the new, filled array to the top of the stack. This leaves the new array, followed by the name literal on the stack. Then you perform the same exercise to enroll this object in the new font dictionary.

Now you have created a new font dictionary, NewfontDict, which has an independent copy of the original encoding vector and does not yet have a **FID** entry, but has room for one. Having enough room is essential because when you eventually issue the **definefont** command, in line %34, there must be a place to enter the new **FID** entry in the font dictionary. In line %29, you change the **FontName** entry in the new font to the new name that you want to use; in this case, /NewFont, which is the name supplied externally for the new font.

Now you have to modify the encoding vector to add the entries for the additional characters that you want to use. This is done in lines %30 to %33. This is another tricky piece of code, but in fact it is very similar to the preceding task in lines %18 to %28. First you put MenuVec on the stack. Since MenuVec has seven pairs of entries that have to be added to the encoding vector inside the new font dictionary, your next task is to unravel MenuVec into its component parts so they can be placed into the new encoding array in the correct locations. This can be done by the **aload** operator, which takes an array on the operand stack and converts it into all its parts. It places all the parts onto the stack in order, with the last element on the top. Finally, **aload** pushes a copy of the original array onto the stack. Applying this operator to MenuVec results in the stack looking like Figure 5-9.

*Figure 5-9. Stack after **aload** of MenuVec.*

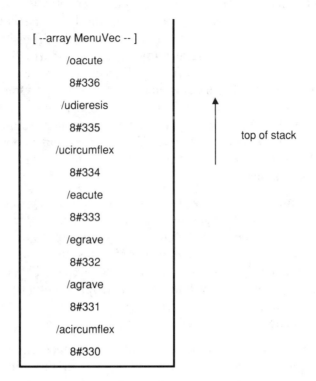

Now you have to insert these values into the **Encoding** array in NewfontDict. This task is done by the **repeat** operator in line %32, which needs to execute the procedure on line %31 once for each pair of entries in the new vector. The number of times to execute the procedure is calculated on line %30. First, the **length** operator is used to determine how many entries there are in the array that was on the top of the stack after the **aload** as shown in Figure 5-10, and is now replaced by the results of the **length.** This number is twice the correct number since the entries come in pairs. Therefore you divide the number by 2. Well, almost. The **repeat** operator requires an integer number on the operand stack; the **div** operator returns a real number in all cases, even if the actual numbers used in the division are integers. The answer here is to use a variant of divide that solves this problem, **idiv.** This operator returns only an integer result; any remainder is discarded. Using this, you get the integer 7 being pushed onto the stack as a result of the operations at line %30.

Now look at the procedure in line %31. This uses the familiar **roll** and **put** sequence to insert the entries in MenuVec into the new **Encoding** vector. It retrieves the new **Encoding** vector from the new font dictionary, NewfontDict, by executing the **get** operator. This operator takes two operands: first, a string, an array, or, in this case, a dictionary; next, an index (for a string or an array) or a key (for a dictionary). Here you give it the key, the name literal /Encoding, and the dictionary NewfontDict, and it returns the value associated with the key in the dictionary, the encoding array itself, on the operand stack. This is just what is required for the insertion of the new encoding values. When the **repeat** is done, the new values have been transferred from MenuVec to the new **Encoding** entry in NewfontDict.

You may wonder why you don't have to issue a **put** to match the **get** and restore the encoding array to the font dictionary. This is again a situation created by the shared values of composite objects. An array, as we observed earlier, is a composite object and therefore two duplicate arrays share values. In this case, the array on the stack that you are working with is a duplicate of the actual array in the font dictionary, and the two copies share values. So, when you change the values in the copy on the stack, you are changing the values for the copy in the font dictionary at the same time.

Now you have constructed a well-formed font dictionary in NewfontDict and are ready to use it. It is enrolled in **FontDirectory** by the **definefont** operator in line %34, using the same name that you inserted into the dictionary before. That definition does not automatically affect the name that you use here; it's up to you to keep the two names the same. Finally, the whole set of definitions is cleaned up by popping the temporary dictionary, ReEncodeDict, from the dictionary stack. As a last step, the return value Done is set to true in line %36.

The rest of the program follows the usual form and is quite straightforward. The new font is used, like any other font, in a **findfont** operation in line %36. Since the font has all the normal characters, you can use it for all the text on the page.

The text for the menu is printed in two columns, wine on the right and matching food courses on the left. The two procedures, ss and nextblock, position the text as you want it on the page. The only further point for comment is the use of the special characters. As we discussed earlier, these characters do not appear on the keyboard. Therefore, they have to be placed into the display strings by use of the \ddd convention. A typical example appears in line %42, where the *acircumflex* and *egrave* characters are printed using their octal codes, \330 and \332, in the output string.

There is one more point to make regarding these additional entries in the encoding vector. Recall that these characters exist in the PostScript font but are not contained in the standard **Encoding** array. If you look at the list of the standard **Encoding** for a PostScript font, such as the display that you prepared earlier, you will see, besides all the alphabet and the punctuation, a series of individual accent marks. These marks, together with the appropriate letters, make up the additional accented letters that you called for when you reencoded the font. These accented character are called *composite characters* because they are made up of two other characters. For example, the acircumflex that you used in the preceding exercise (\330) is actually built up out of the letter "a" (\141) and the circumflex accent in the font (\303). Both characters that make up the composite character must be available in the new **Encoding** array for the encoding of the composite character to work properly.

This completes your exercise in reencoding a font. You can see here how flexible and powerful PostScript font machinery is, and how you can work with it to take maximum advantage of its features. You have been introduced to a number of new operators in this exercise. All of these operators are included in Appendix A (Operator Review) of this book, where they are presented in the standard format that we have been using. You should review them there to see their full range of capabilities.

Modifying Font Metrics

The most common global change made to a font is to change its size. Actually, you have performed this operation every time you have used a font, by using the **scalefont** operator. In this section, you will learn how to adjust the size of the font in a more general way. The measurement of size in a font and the coordinates used by the font are distinct from those used in user space; these characteristics are called *font metrics*.

The changes to a font work analogously to changes in the coordinate system in general. The main difference is that you can change the font coordinates without making any change to the page coordinates as a whole. In fact, this is what **scalefont** does; it works on the font coordinates in exactly the same way that the **scale** operator works on the entire page.

We have already discussed the most ordinary change that you might make to a font's size, namely, scaling it to the correct point size by using the

scalefont operator. This is fast and convenient, but it doesn't even have the flexibility that **scale** has because you can only scale a font uniformly in both *x*- and *y*-coordinate units using **scalefont.**

The **scalefont** operator works by changing the **FontMatrix** array in the font dictionary. This array gives the transformation required to change the character coordinates into user coordinates. Since characters in the built-in fonts are typically sized in 1000 units, the typical **FontMatrix** divides all the character coordinates by 1000, by multiplying them by 0.001. The **FontMatrix** array contains six numeric entries that represent mathematical coefficients for the transformation. That really sounds more formidable than it is. Let's examine the typical **FontMatrix** array, which looks like this:

[.001 0 0 .001 0 0]

The first element of the array is the multiplier for the *x* coordinate. As you would expect, the multiplier is 0.001 to change from the 1000-unit character coordinate system into 1 unit in the user coordinate system. Similarly, the fourth element of the array is the multiplier for the *y* coordinates. The remainder of the six entries affect the font coordinates in other ways that we won't discuss here.

When you execute a **scalefont** operation, the following revised matrix would appear in the font dictionary if you scaled the font to 12 points:

[.012 0 0 .012 0 0]

You have simply multiplied the *x* and *y* coordinates by the scale factor of 12.

This suggests how you can scale fonts in unequal proportions; all that you need to do is change the *x*- and *y*-coordinate multipliers in the **FontMatrix** by different amounts. This can't be done by **scalefont,** but PostScript has thoughtfully provided another, more general, operator that allows you to do just that. This operator is called **makefont** and it works like this:

font matrix   **makefont**   newfont
applies *matrix* to *font,* and produces *newfont* whose characters are transformed by the values in *matrix* when they are printed. The operator first creates a copy of *font,* then replaces the **FontMatrix** in the copy with the result of combining the original **FontMatrix** and *matrix*. The resulting *newfont* is returned to the stack.

This operator is used in the same place and in the same way as the **scalefont** operator, which isn't surprising since **scalefont** is simply a special case of the more general **makefont.** In addition, the matrix that you use for the operation must have all six elements, not just two. However, it looks just like the **FontMatrix** that we discussed earlier, so the first element is the x-scaling factor and the fourth element is the y-scaling factor.

The same process can be used with the **selectfont** operator. Just as in the **makefont,** the process is to replace the single scale factor with a matrix. The **selectfont** then proceeds to scale the font accordingly, performing the equivalent of a **scalefont** if the second operand is a single number and the equivalent of a **makefont** if it is an array.

Now you can make extended and condensed fonts using this operator. Let's do a short example. This example simply shows an arbitrary string in both expanded and condensed Helvetica down the display. For this example, make a window that is at least 4 inches high and 6 inches wide. The usual runPSInline procedure calls a single wrap to do the entire process. The procedure and the wrap would go like this:

```
void runPSInline (void)
{
    PSWsampleText();
}
```

```
defineps PSWsampleText ()
    %first define the new condensed font
    /Helvetica-Condensed
        /Helvetica findfont
        [ 10 0 0 12 0 0 ] makefont
    def

    %then define normal Helvetica for comparison
    /Helvetica-Normal
        /Helvetica findfont
        12 scalefont
    def

    %now make test strings
    /StrCond
        (This is a test of Helvetica condensed font - units 10 on 12)
    def
    /StrExp
        (This is a test of Helvetica expanded font - units 15 on 12)
```

```
        def
        /Str
            (This is a test of Helvetica normal font - 12 point)
        def

        %now use each font
        %first the normal 12 point
        Helvetica-Normal setfont
        18 144 moveto
        Str show
        %next condensed 10 on 12
        Helvetica-Condensed setfont
        18 120 moveto
        StrCond show
        %next expanded 15 on 12
        /Helvetica [ 15 0 0 12 0 0 ] selectfont
        18 96 moveto
        StrExp show
    endps
```

This program produces output as shown in Figure 5-10.

Figure 5-10. Output using condensed and expanded fonts.

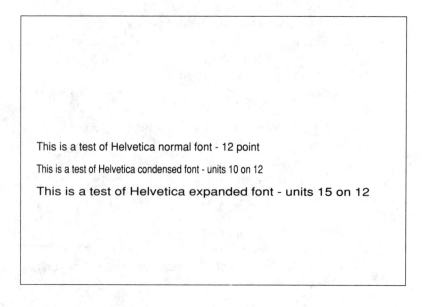

The program itself is quite simple. You start by defining each of two fonts: one condensed and one the normal Helvetica. These definitions both follow the same pattern. First, you push the name for the scaled font onto the stack. Then you use **findfont** to get the basic font and put it onto the stack. Then you issue either **makefont** or **scalefont** with an appropriate operand.

The expanded font is handled in a slightly different manner, in the body of the wrap. Here I wanted to show you the use of the **selectfont** operator with a matrix operand. Since the **selectfont** automatically makes the new font the current font, it was placed in the body of the wrap instead of making it into a definition, The following section, about multifont documents, discusses these options more thoroughly. The important point here is that you can use any of these methods.

In the case of the condensed font, the matrix provides a scaling of the font by 10 units in the x direction and 12 units in the y direction. Since point size is a measurement of the font in the y direction, this is a 12-point font. Since the x-scale is 10 points instead of 12, this results in a condensed font; that is, the characters take less room in the x direction than in the y direction. In the case of the expanded font, the reverse is true. Here the scaling is 15 units in the x direction, but still 12 units in the y direction. You still have a 12-point font, but it is expanded by about 25%. Finally, you have defined a normal version of Helvetica, scaled to 12 points for comparison.

Now you create three separate strings to test each of the fonts. The first portion of each string is the same to help you see the differences and similarities in the letters; the last portion of each string is unique to identify the different strings. Then comes the meat of the program. First, you use the normal font, showing the normal string left justified on a line 9 inches from the bottom of the page. Next, you do the same thing for the condensed font, moving the new text line 24 units below the previous normal text. Finally, you show the expanded text in the same way, 24 units below the condensed font.

This is an interesting and instructive little program. It is the first time that you have defined fonts in this way and saved them for use in a multifont document. You will see more of this, and a discussion of the most efficient ways of handling fonts, in the next section.

Note that typographers distinguish between *condensed* fonts and *narrow* fonts. Condensed fonts, in this terminology, are fonts that have been designed to have tighter spacing than the normal font, whereas narrow fonts are mathematically reduced versions of the normal font. A condensed font, therefore, has a **FontMatrix** that shows no scaling effect, that is, [.001 0 0 .001 0 0], whereas the narrow font shows different numbers as the *x*- and *y*-coordinate multipliers. By that definition, the font that you have just created is a narrow font, not a condensed font. In fact, it closely approximates the Helvetica-Narrow font that is part of the LaserWriter Plus.

Displaying Multiple Fonts

Text representation is one of the most time-consuming and resource-intensive activities that is normally performed in creating page descriptions, yet it is also one of the most common. PostScript has an efficient and well-designed mechanism for dealing with text, as you already know. Nevertheless, there are things you can do to aid the interpreter in working on your pages and things you should avoid so you don't slow the output.

Here are some points to be sensitive to in handling PostScript fonts. Using a lot of different fonts on a page is a potential problem. Setting aside the aesthetic considerations, there is a limit to how many fonts will fit into PostScript memory at one time. Note that this is not a limitation of the PostScript language; this is a limitation of the realization of the language in a specific device. Each device has more or less room for fonts to be stored and used internally. Some devices, of course, store the fonts externally, in cartridges; and some fonts, like the built-in fonts that you have been using in the examples and exercises, are often stored permanently in the device to increase font handling speed. All such efficiencies are device-dependent, however, and should not be relied on for most PostScript pages.

To ensure that you have reasonably quick font handling, you want to use a minimum of font changes on a page. This is not intended to inhibit you from changing fonts; just be aware that every font change—and a change in point size is a font change for our purposes here—has a cost in terms of performance and page output.

Because font character conversion is so resource intensive, PostScript uses the font cache to speed up text processing. You saw earlier how the process works to insert characters that you are putting onto the page into the font cache for reuse. This is an important consideration in designing efficient PostScript code.

Minimizing the number of font changes is also an important issue. Every character that is different from a preceding one in either size or style causes the interpreter to convert it from the font; whereas every character that is reused can be, and is, taken directly out of the font cache, rather than being reconverted. The process of retrieving a character from the cache is almost 1000 times faster than the process of conversion. Whatever you can do to minimize the changes that cause more conversion work for the interpreter will improve your performance measurably.

To improve font handling, you might also consider the method you use to generate multifont documents. Unlike most of the preceding techniques, this is not an issue that you can control if you are using an application to generate most of your PostScript text. If, on the other hand, you are generating your own text, as you have been in the preceding exercises and examples, you can use this technique to improve performance for your documents.

The technique was used earlier to create the form with fill-in data. In that exercise, you created two separate, but matching, pages and overlaid one on top of the other. Consider how this technique can speed up the processing of the page. First, you can minimize the font changes required for page processing by putting all of one font on one overlay. In that way, the font cache can efficiently store the required characters even if you have a large page of text. In addition, you can reduce the number of font accesses to limit the overhead lost to the font machinery.

You should realize that this technique may not be practical, or even possible, in all cases. For pages of mixed text—say, italic and regular text intermixed irregularly throughout many lines, for example—it would be a major task to compute or otherwise store the position of each different font. In this case, you should use the other techniques that we have discussed as the best answer for maximum performance. Where you can delimit the different fonts, however, as you could on the form and fill-in, you can use this overlay technique to good effect.

ADDITIONAL FONT TECHNIQUES

Besides adding fonts that are supplied by others, such as the Adobe Type Library fonts, you can also create fonts of your own. The entire font creation process is quite a bit of work and requires design and layout skills (not to mention PostScript procedures) that are beyond the scope of this book. However, we will look into the types of fonts that you might want to create and give you an overview of the process you would have to follow to create a new font.

The fonts that you have been using and all fonts that are supplied by Adobe are fonts where the characters in the font, the letters, numbers, and punctuation, are drawn using PostScript operations as we have discussed. We also mentioned bitmapped fonts. These fonts are not drawn, but are a collection of dots that closely approximate a character in all aspects: point size, typeface, rotation, and so on. Generally, bitmapped fonts are significantly lower quality than drawn fonts, except in situations where the font has been tailored for a specific output device at a specific point size.

You can also use a combination of reencoding and drawing to associate alternative shapes with various codes. You might use this technique to create bullets or small open circles to be used as part of an outline in your text. You could associate any arbitrary figure in place of a code. For example, you could take the logo graphic that we created in Chapter 3 and associate it with an arbitrary code or even replace a letter code, say, L (for Logo) and have the graphic print out when you entered the code or the letter. Needless to say, I don't recommend replacing letters (or any keyboard character) in such a way; it could be quite confusing unless you had a specific purpose in mind. The point here is that you can, if you wish, associate arbitrary graphic procedures with any character code, as well as the usual letter shapes. After all, the letters and other characters in a font are just graphic shapes themselves.

Creating fonts in PostScript is very similar to modifying the encoding vector. In fact, it uses all the same techniques and adds a few. Let's briefly look at the process of font creation.

A user-defined font must follow all the rules laid down by PostScript for fonts. In particular, all the required entries for the font dictionary must be in place and be correct. This can be done using the same procedures that you used in the example of reencoding a font. The **FontType** must be set to 3 to indicate that this is a user-defined font. In addition, the font dictionary must contain a procedure named **BuildChar,** which is used to create characters in the new font.

When a PostScript program invokes an operator that displays a character, for example, **show,** the interpreter looks first to see if the character is in the font cache. If it is, the image in the cache is used; but if it isn't (and no character of the new font will be at first), the interpreter pushes the current font dictionary onto the operand stack, followed by the character code (an integer number, remember, from 0 through 255), and then executes the font's **BuildChar** procedure.

This procedure must use the supplied information to construct the requested character. This involves determining what character has been requested, usually by using the character code as an index into the **Encoding** array; taking the key from the **Encoding** and looking up a procedure to create the character; supplying character metric information; and finally constructing the character and painting it by executing the procedure.

The **BuildChar** procedure must work within a **gsave, grestore** pair, so that changes to the graphics state do not affect other operations. It can assume that the coordinate system has been properly set to reflect both the font matrix defined in the current font and the current user coordinates. It should then use ordinary PostScript operators to construct the desired character and paint it.

Once the **BuildChar** is done, the interpreter takes the completed character and transfers it both onto the output device and into the font cache. The character is included into the font cache only if that was requested within **BuildChar** by use of the appropriate operator.

This is all that we will present here regarding the creation of new fonts in PostScript. If you want more information, the appropriate methods and procedures, including the requirements for **BuildChar** and even a short example, appear in the *PostScript Language Reference Manual*.

CONCLUSION

The chapter started out with a very detailed discussion of the PostScript font mechanics. The detail is necessary if you are going to adjust the fonts in the ways that we have discussed, but the detail can also help you use PostScript fonts efficiently. The first topic covered was the structure of a font dictionary. This is the place where PostScript stores all the information related to a given font. The second topic was how the interpreter uses the dictionary to create characters and how those characters are treated when you place them on an output page.

With this information as a guide, you proceeded to the first real task at hand: displaying an encoding vector. The encoding vector is an important part of the font machinery, and this exercise provided techniques and tools for displaying any encoding vector. As part of the process, you created a multicolumn display with an arbitrary number of columns and you learned about error trapping for single lines of code to prevent recoverable errors from aborting processing. Both of these are useful techniques in many diverse circumstances.

After displaying an encoding vector, you moved on to modifying a PostScript font. The next exercise had you access some of the accented characters that are available in most PostScript fonts and use them in a display. This particularly interesting exercise introduced you to some real, effective code such as you might find in an actual application program. Each step of this complex exercise was examined in some detail.

The next section dealt with two related but different topics. The first topic was global modification of fonts. Up to this point in the chapter, all the modifications had been done character by character; now you are to modify all the characters in the font at once. The most common, and the most useful, global change that you make to fonts is in the size of the characters. This section showed you how to make size changes in two different ways. Then you used the techniques you read about in an example where you created and displayed both condensed and expanded versions of a PostScript font. The second topic was the efficient use of PostScript fonts in a multifont display.

The chapter ended with a short section on creating your own fonts. Although presenting the techniques required to create a complete font is beyond the scope of this book, you did learn, in general terms, what would be required for making a new font.

CHAPTER 6

Advanced Screen Handling

This chapter covers a variety of advanced graphics operations that are available in PostScript. You will see only some examples in this chapter, and the ones here are, for the most part, relatively simplified. To adequately explore the potential of the operations discussed here would require almost a separate chapter for each operator. The chapter, therefore, is primarily devoted to letting you know what these operations are and how each works in general. In any case, you are now familiar with Display PostScript programs and programming and are able to work out examples and experiment with these new features on your own. If one or another of these operations seems interesting, try to create your own examples and work out the exact requirements and possibilities. This chapter provides you with a basic framework for these operations, and you can then use the *PostScript Language Reference Manual* and the *Display PostScript System Reference* to guide you in the detailed requirements.

HANDLING THE SCREEN

One of the major points of difference from the basic PostScript environment when working in Display PostScript is in the interaction between the user and the application. Generally this is done through a mouse (or other pointing mechanism) and a keyboard. However it is accomplished, the application must usually respond to the user input by changing the display in some fashion—by displaying new data that has been entered, for example, or by refreshing the display. Display PostScript provides a number of new operators that help you perform these tasks.

View Clips

One of the most common actions that happens in a display environment is that the user changes some part of a window, causing the application to redraw that portion of the window. Typically this happens for one of two reasons. First, the user has caused objects not previously visible in the window to become visible, for example, by resizing the window. Second, the user has made some change to a displayed graphic element that requires a change in the display of that element. Since a window may contain any arbitrarily complex set of graphics, it is quite inconvenient and cumbersome to redraw the entire window contents if only a small area of the display has been affected by the change. To help you deal with such situations, Display PostScript has implemented a new addition to the PostScript graphics model.

This is called the *view clipping path*. This path is independent of the current clipping path in the graphics state, and, indeed, is not part of the graphics state at all. When you draw objects on the display, only those objects, or parts of objects, that lie within both the current clipping path and the view clipping path are actually shown.

This could be accomplished by changing the current clipping path. However, if that were done, you would have to communicate the new clipping path to all the procedures and processes that might have to be executed to redraw the screen. This would not be convenient, particularly in processes such as you developed in Chapter 4, where, for example, you switched into a new graphics state to display portions of the form. If this process used the current clipping path, all the graphics states that you had saved might have to be changed to get the display correct. Clearly this would be an excessive chore. Instead, you can set the view clipping path and then execute the display operations, knowing that the view clip will function correctly without regard to the current graphics state settings.

Think about this for a moment, and you will see what a valuable tool this is. You can set the view clipping path independently of the graphics state, so you can set it at the point in the application where you know the area to be covered. Now you can redisplay the screen, knowing that the display will be correct. Moreover, since the current clipping path and the view clip interact, if any specific clipping is being done within one of the displays, that clipping will still work correctly, and only the area that falls inside both the current clipping path and the view clipping path will be shown.

This feature of the Display PostScript environment is defined by the new operator **viewclip,** and its associated operator **rectviewclip,** which provide a fast and easy method for redrawing only the new sections of the display. In our standard format, these two new operators look like this:

—   **viewclip**   —
replaces the current view clipping path with the current path in the current graphics state. After setting the view clipping path, the current path is undefined.

x y width height   **rectviewclip**   —
replaces the current view clipping path with the rectangular path described by the operands. The path of the rectangle begins at the point (*x, y*) and extends for *width* distance parallel to the *x*-axis and *height* distance parallel to the *y*-axis, all in the current user coordinate system. The result of using **rectviewclip** is exactly identical to constructing the rectangle described by the operands and then invoking the **viewclip** operator.

As you see, you can create an arbitrary path and make that the view clipping path by using the **viewclip** operator. However, the new area to be displayed can often be easily described as a rectangle. You have seen before, in previous exercises, how useful the new special rectangle operators—**rectfill** and **rectstroke**—can be; here is another rectangle operator to join that set. By using **rectviewclip,** you can create the path and make it the view clipping path all in one action. In the exercise later in this section, you will use **rectviewclip** in exactly that way.

Locating the Cursor

Another common task in display management is relating the current cursor position on the display to the image on the screen. For example, the user may move the cursor to some arbitrary position in a text display and start typing. The application must display the new type at the location of the cursor and move any subsequent text down the display to make room for it. As another example, the user may move the mouse pointer to a graphic object that is being displayed, click on the object to select it, and then drag it to some other position on the screen. This is a good example of both of the situations that we are discussing. First, the application must know that the mouse click matches some object that is displayed. Second, the previous display of that object must be erased, and a new display of the object must be done at the new location.

Here we want to focus on the first action: recognizing that a given coordinate is on or within a given graphic object. Consider this problem for a moment. A display or windowing environment normally handles mouse operations in some standard fashion and passes the current mouse pointer coordinates back to the application when an event, such as clicking the mouse button, happens. The application then must handle the actual display response to the click. In the situation just described, this would be to change the display of the given object in some way to show that it was selected. The trick is, how do you tell that the mouse position falls on or in a given graphic? For simple shapes such as rectangles or circles, it isn't too difficult for the application to determine for itself, given the current mouse coordinates, whether the point is within the shape. But the display may consist of some arbitrary graphic such as a complex curve, where this calculation is not at all easy or straightforward.

For these circumstances, Display PostScript has implemented several new operators that allow you to determine whether a given coordinate point is in or on a given path. Generally the operators take the desired point as a pair of operands and test it against the current path. Some of the operators take both the point coordinates and a user path and perform the test. In any case, this provides the application with a quick, convenient, and standardized method of detecting whether a mouse click hits a given graphic.

Let's look at the most common versions of these new operators, presented in our standard format.

    x y   **infill**   bool

returns the boolean result *true* if the point (x, y) in user space would be painted by a **fill** of the current path in the current graphics state; otherwise, it returns *false*.

    x y   **instroke**   bool

returns the boolean result *true* if the point (x, y) in user space would be painted by a **stroke** of the current path in the current graphics state; otherwise, it returns *false*.

In both cases, the operation does not change the current path; nor does it make any marks on the output page. These operations simply tell you whether or not any given specific point lies inside or on the current path. These operations do not take any account of the current clipping path or of the view clipping path; in other words, they don't care whether the given point would actually be displayed if the **fill** or **stroke** operation were carried out. If you want to know whether or not the given point would be actually painted, you can combine these operators to test the point jointly against the current path and the current clipping or view clipping paths.

If you have stored a path as a user path, as you did in Chapter 4, you can test that user path directly against a given point without converting it to the current path. The operators to do that are a natural extension of the preceding ones. They are defined as follows.

> x y userpath   **inufill**   bool
> returns the boolean result *true* if the point (*x, y*) in user space would be painted by a **ufill** of the *userpath*; otherwise, it returns *false*. Except for the manner of determining the path, **inufill** behaves in the same manner as **infill.**

> x y userpath   **inustroke**   bool
> returns the boolean result *true* if the point (*x, y*) in user space would be painted by a **ustroke** of the *userpath*; otherwise, it returns *false*. Except for the manner of determining the path, **inustroke** behaves in the same manner as **instroke.**

As before, these operators do not make any marks on the page, and they do not change or alter either the current path or the user path objects that they test.

These operators allow the application to test a given pair of coordinates against any particular graphic. Then you can take action at the application level, at the level of the wrap that you are executing, or at both levels if necessary.

Exercise in Drawing Arbitrary Curves

Let's put these concepts to practical use in an exercise. This exercise is designed to render arbitrary curved line segments onto the display. Displaying such segments is a fairly typical use of graphics in an application. As in previous exercises, we have simplified the actual processing somewhat to clarify the concepts involved and to keep the code to a reasonable size.

In Chapter 3 you were introduced to circular arcs, and you have used those arcs in several examples and exercises throughout the book. PostScript also provides an operator that draws arbitrary curved segments, called **curveto.** The difficulty in using the **curveto** operator is that describing an arbitrary curved segment mathematically is not a very intuitive process. Although a circle can be easily described in terms of its center and radius (or diameter), arbitrary curves in PostScript are described by the rather advanced mathematics of Bézier equations. The person drawing a curve need not understand the actual mathematics, but he or she must have some sense of where the curve will fall, given a certain set of parameters. Even in this less demanding sense, the description of an arbitrary curve is not at all intuitive. This exercise allows you to display arbitrary curved segments in some detail, including the controlling parameters that shape the curve.

To understand what information ought to be displayed, you need to know how the **curveto** operator behaves. Here is the description of the **curveto** operator in our standard format.

> dx_1 dy_1 dx_2 dy_2 ax_2 ay_2 **curveto**   —
> adds a curved line segment, described by a pair of Bézier cubic equations, to the current path. The curve begins from the current point, which is called the first *anchor point,* with the coordinates (ax_1, ay_1), to the second anchor point, whose coordinates are given by the operands (ax_2, ay_2). The shape of the curve between the two anchor points is determined by two additional points, called *direction points,* whose coordinates are given by the operands (dx_1, dy_1) and (dx_2, dy_2). The entire curved segment lies within the box connecting these four points.

The shape of the curve is determined by the direction and distance of the direction points from the anchor points. The curve is drawn tangent to a straight line connecting the first anchor point and the first direction point, and it finishes tangent to the straight line connecting the second direction point and the second anchor point. The curved segment ends at the second anchor point, which becomes the new current point.

All of this is rather difficult to visualize, so this exercise provides a method to display the curve, along with the associated anchor and direction points, and the control lines that connect the anchor and direction points. This is usually done in graphics programs, which then implement additional methods for allowing the user to move these points and see the resulting changes to the curved segment. However, we won't provide these additional features here. As always, our approach here is to produce a simple prototype that can be used in a variety of ways.

To avoid cluttering up the display with multiple points, only one curved segment at a time should show the complete set of points; any other segments on the display should just show the curved line itself. When the user clicks on a curved segment, that segment should display its complete set of points; if the user clicks off of any segments, no segment should display the complete set of points. In short, this behaves quite like most graphics programs with which you are familiar.

As usual, you do not implement any mouse (or whatever the pointing mechanism might be) procedures here. We assume, for this exercise, that all that is already handled. Also, the controls of the curve are simplified so that the complete curve can be drawn in a single wrap.

Before you start creating the code for this exercise, we should discuss the strategy that you will use to accomplish all these tasks. For our discussion, there will be two types of display for any curved segment. The first type has all the points and controls showing: dots at each of the anchor points and the direction points, dashed black straight lines connecting associated pairs of anchor and direction points, and the curve itself painted in the current color. This is called the *fancy curve* display. The second type simply displays the curved segment itself, as it would be painted normally.

When a curve is created, it is displayed as a fancy curve. You want to be able to redisplay a curve in the fancy mode at any point if the user clicks on it. To do that you will keep each curve as a user path, stored in an array, so that it can be redisplayed as a fancy curve at any time. The user path provides a convenient storage unit for later use.

You also want to be able to display any curved segment in the ordinary fashion at any point. To do that, you first need to erase any fancy display that is presently on the screen, and then you need to redraw the display. As we discussed earlier, the best way to do this is to set a view clipping path and use that for controlling both the erase and the redisplay. To make sure that you erase the correct area, each time a curve is displayed in the fancy mode, the path bounding box for that curve is returned to the application. Then you can use that bounding box as the clipping path for the erase and redisplay.

When you erase the screen, any portions of other graphics that lie in the area that you erase will also be erased and therefore need to be redrawn. To do that, you add the curve as a segment to a large user path that represents all of the graphics that have been created on the display so far. By using this user path for the redisplay, you get all of the graphics at once, limited only by the view clipping path. That fits perfectly with the requirements of the situation.

Now that you have established your strategy for the display, let's look at the procedure that does all this. We will start at the top level, with our old friend runPSInline.

```c
float bbox [4];

void runPSInline (void)
{
    extern float bbox [];

    float ax1, ay1, ax2, ay2;
    float dx1, dy1, dx2, dy2;

    /* start by setting up the private dictionary */
    PSWsetupCurves;

    /* now display the first curved segment */
    ax1 = 36;
    ay1 = 72;
    ax2 = 270;
    ay2 = ay1;
    dx1 = 130;
    dy1 = 130;
    dx2 = 200;
    dy2 = 10;
    PSmoveto(ax1, ay1);
    PSWdrawCurve(dx1, dy1, dx2, dy2, ax2, ay2, &bbox);

}
```

This procedure is continued later, as we proceed with the creation, display, and redisplay of more curved segments. For now, let's look at the wraps that you have specified so far.

```
defineps PSWdrawCurve ( float DX1, DY1, DX2, DY2, AX2, AY2 | float BBox[4] )
    PersDict begin                                             %1
    currentpoint                                               %2
```

```
            newpath
            moveto
            gsave                                               %3
                DX1 DY1 DX2 DY2 AX2 AY2 fancyCurveto            %4
            grestore
            %add 1 element to path array

            /PathArray                                          %5
                PathArray                                       %6
                dup length 1 add array                          %7
                dup 3 1 roll copy                               %8
                pop                                             %9
            def                                                 %10
            %fill new element with userpath for curve
            PathArray                                           %11
            dup length 1 sub                                    %12
            DX1 DY1 DX2 DY2 AX2 AY2 curveto                     %13
            false upath                                         %14
            put
            %get path bounding box for return
            pathbbox BBox                                       %15
            %and add path to full screen path set
            /ScreenPath                                         %16
                ScreenPath uappend                              %17
                false upath
            def
            end %PersDict
endps
```

This wrap has several new features and some interesting code. It starts by defining the six input arguments and then adds an array of four elements as an output. This is the bounding box array that you require for the application, as we discussed earlier. This is the first time you have used this method to return an array of values; as you see, it is quite consistent with the return mechanism that you have used before. The definition of the return is also quite familiar since it looks quite a bit like a C definition.

The wrap code itself starts at line %1 by establishing your private dictionary as the current dictionary, thus making all the required procedures and variables available for reference. Then line %2 pushes the coordinates of the current point onto the operand stack. This is done to save them while you clean up the current path with the **newpath** operator that follows. Then you reset the current point by doing a **moveto,** using the coordinates that you saved on the stack. This little operation guarantees you that the only thing in the current path is the current point. You need to ensure this so you don't add extraneous elements into your user path objects or paint something that's accidentally left over from some previous operation.

You then save the graphic state in line %3. This ensures that the fancy curve drawing routine doesn't change anything in the current graphics state—in particular, that it doesn't add anything to or remove the single current point that is set here. Line %4 executes an auxiliary procedure, fancyCurveto, that draws the fancy curve with all the points and so on, and then the graphic state is restored. So, at this point, you have imaged the complete curve onto the display, including all the control points and so on, and are now back with the single starting point as the current point.

The display is done, but you still have to save the path and the path bounding box. You can do this in several ways. You start by adding another element to the PathArray array. This array is defined in the setup processing, and it contains all the paths that have been drawn onto the screen as user paths. However, since any arbitrary number of paths might be created, how do you provide storage for them? There are two approaches to this problem. First you could allocate some fixed amount of elements for the paths. Then, when you come to store the next path here, you would test whether there was room in the array. If not, you could either enlarge the array or raise some sort of error flag. Alternatively, you could enlarge the array by one element each time, thus always having just enough room. In the standard PostScript environment, this latter approach would be quite poor since each array is a composite object and consumes virtual memory. In such a situation, a large number of iterations might exhaust the virtual memory, with dire consequences. The Display PostScript environment, however, has a mechanism that reclaims memory that is no longer in use, so this technique is acceptable. Moreover, it simplifies the handling of the array, both here and later in the hit processing, since there are no unused entries in the array to worry about.

Finally, in a production application you would probably choose to store the bounding box coordinates and the path components in a C data structure. Then, when you need them, you can simply refer to the data structure for the correct components and send the complete set of data to the Display PostScript system. This is by far the most efficient method of doing this, but it is the least obvious and requires the most C programming. For our prototype here, we will work in the Display PostScript system exclusively.

So, line %5 pushes the literal name of the array onto the stack to be used by the final **def** operation in line %10 after you have expanded the present array. The actual array itself is placed on the stack in line %6. Line %7 creates an array with a size that is one greater than the current array, by taking the length of the current array, adding one, and creating a new array object with this length. Next you duplicate the new array, in line %8, and rearrange the elements for the **copy** operation. This is similar to what you did in Chapter 5 to copy the font dictionary. Since the **dup** operation makes a true duplicate, the new array, with all the elements of the old array, is on the stack twice—the part of it that matches the old array is on top of the stack and the complete version is beneath that. You don't need the partial version, so line %9 removes it from the stack, leaving only the complete new array and the name literal, which the **def** then uses. So here you have expanded the PathArray by one element, which is the last element in the array.

Line %11 returns the array to the stack. Line %12 calculates the index for the last element of the array—remember that the indices run from 0, so that the last element has an index of one less than the length of the array. The actual curved segment is created in line %13, and then it is turned into a user path in line %14 and placed into the array with a **put.** Note that the **upath** does not erase the current path, so the curved segment is still there for further processing. Since the path is still there, line %15 determines the bounding box for the path with the **pathbbox** operator and then sends the output back to the application by using the BBox output argument.

You could also determine the bounding box information entirely in your C application, rather than getting it from the PostScript operator as we do here. This calculation depends on the fact that every point on the path created by a **curveto** lies inside the quadrilateral formed by the anchor points and the direction points. Therefore, to calculate the path bounding box, you can simply compare the coordinates of each of the points. The minimum *x* coordinate and the minimum *y* coordinate are the lower left corner of the bounding box, while the maximum *x* and *y* coordinates form the upper right corner. This technique is very useful if you are maintaining independent data structures in your C code.

The path is still in place since the **pathbbox** does not erase it. This allows you to add it conveniently to the master user path, called ScreenPath. The process starts by pushing the ScreenPath name literal onto the stack in line %16. Then the old ScreenPath is retrieved from the private dictionary and the path is added to the current path, using the **uappend** operator in line %17. This makes the current path consist of the new curved segment, plus all the segments that were in the ScreenPath before. This entire path is converted into a user path by the following **upath** operator and the result is stored as the new ScreenPath. With that done, the private dictionary is removed from the dictionary stack and the wrap is completed.

However, the setup wrap still requires some work. At this point, the setup looks like this:

```
defineps PSWsetupCurves ()
    /PersDict 30 dict def                                   %1
    PersDict begin                                          %2

    %procedure definitions
    /fancyCurveto                                           %3
    %use curveto operands but show all points

    {
        /ay2 exch def                                       %4
        /ax2 exch def
        /dy2 exch def
        /dx2 exch def
        /dy1 exch def
        /dx1 exch def
        dot                                                 %5
        gsave                                               %6
            dx1 dy1 lineto                                  %7
            dot                                             %8
            [5 5] setdash                                   %9
            0 setgray                                       %10
            stroke                                          %11
        grestore                                            %12
        dx1 dy1 dx2 dy2 ax2 ay2 curveto                     %13
        dot                                                 %14
        gsave                                               %15
            dx2 dy2 lineto
            dot
            [5 5] setdash
            0 setgray
            stroke
        grestore
        stroke                                              %16
    }
```

```
        def

        /dot
        %utility function to draw a dot at the current point
        %   dot is 4 times current line width
        {
            gsave                                       %17
                currentpoint                            %18
                newpath
                moveto
                1 setlinecap                            %19
                currentlinewidth 4 mul                  %20
                setlinewidth
                currentpoint lineto                     %21
                [] 0 setdash                            %22
                stroke                                  %23
            grestore
        }
        def

        %initialize global variables
        /PathArray [] def                               %24
        /ScreenPath                                     %25
            newpath
            0 0 moveto
            false upath
        def

    end %PersDict
endps
```

This wrap, as you no doubt anticipated, creates a private dictionary, PersDict, in line %1 and begins using it in line %2. The first procedure in the setup—and in the dictionary—is the auxiliary procedure fancyCurveto that you invoked in the preceding wrap to draw the curve with all the points, lines, and so on. This procedure begins on line %4 by defining all the operands. Remember that, since the operands are on the stack, you must remove them in the reverse order that they were placed onto the stack. Here this is the reverse order from the **curveto** operator since that's how the procedure was called. Next, in line %5, you call another auxiliary procedure, **dot**, that places a dot at the current point without making any permanent change in the graphics state.

At this point you are at the first anchor point for the curve and have painted a dot at that point. The next sequence of seven lines, from line %6 to line %12, creates the line associated with the first direction point. The process begins by saving the current graphics state in line %6. It draws a line from the current point to the first direction point in line %7 and places a dot at that point in line %8. Next it sets the dash configuration for the line.

This is a new operator, and it has the following definition.

> array offset   **setdash**   —
> sets the current dash setting in the current graphics state according to the *array* and *offset* operands. The current dash pattern is defined by the *array,* which consists of nonnegative numbers that represent the alternating length of dashes and spaces along the path to be stroked, and the *offset,* which is the starting point of the dash pattern along the line. An empty array, [ ], generates a solid line.

The combinations of array and offset provide a powerful method for specifying a variety of dashed line effects; the number of possible combinations is much larger than we have space to go into here. For this exercise you are using, in line %9, one of the simplest dashed patterns—one that is on for 5 units and then off for 5 units, repeating for the length of the line. The offset is zero, so that the dash pattern begins at the start of the line. Line %10 sets the current color to black. Then the dashed line is stroked in line %11, and the graphics state is restored to the condition at the start of the process in line %12.

You construct the actual curved line segment in line %13. This leaves the current point at the end of the segment; now, at line %14, you place a dot there. The seven lines of code beginning at line %15 duplicate, for the second direction point, the same process that you performed before in lines %6 through %12, which we have already discussed. All that remains, after the dashed line and the additional dot have been inserted, is to paint the actual curved path in line %16. Notice that this is done in the current color since no color setting is done here—or, for that matter, anywhere in the procedure outside of **gsave, grestore** pairs.

That still leaves you with one more auxiliary procedure, **dot**, whose definition immediately follows fancyCurveto. This procedure is intended to create a dot at the current point and leave the current graphics state unaltered. You ensure this by starting, in line %17, with a **gsave**. At the end of the procedure, a matching **grestore** restores the graphics state.

Let's consider the process of drawing the dot. You could, of course, make a small circle and fill it, but that requires more work than is necessary. You can use a shortcut to make a small dot. The trick is to set the graphics parameters so that all lines end with a half-circle, and then draw a line that is only a single point. This gives you two half-circles, back to back, since the two ends of the line are identical, and the diameter of the circle is the width of the line.

The actual processing begins on line %18 with the same set of operators that we looked at before, and for the same reasons. You wish to eliminate every component of the current path except the single current point. That done, line %19 sets the line cap parameter of the current graphics state to 1, which sets round line caps. The line cap parameter determines how PostScript finishes off the ends of a line: 0 means that the lines are finished off square to the line end; 1 means that the lines are finished with a half-circle; and 2 means that the lines are finished with a half-square. The results of these settings are shown in Figure 6-1.

Figure 6-1. Line cap parameter values and results.

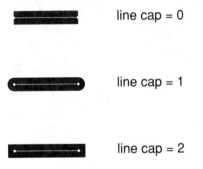

line cap = 0

line cap = 1

line cap = 2

If this is not familiar to you, you can read the description of this operator in Appendix A of this book, or you can refer to a more complete discussion in the *PostScript Language Reference Manual* or in any other PostScript reference book.

Next, in line %20 and the subsequent line, you retrieve the current line width, multiply it by 4, and reset it. This makes the circle four times the size of any line extending from the point, which is a good size for visibility. Then, in line %21, you make a line from the current point to the current point. Naturally this line does not have any length and if you painted it with a line cap of 0, it would not appear. Here, however, you have set the line caps to half-circles, and so you can now stroke the "line"—which is a single point—in line %23. Before that, in line %22, you set the dash to a solid line by setting the dash array to [], the empty array. This ensures that the point is actually painted. The result is a perfect circle, at the current point, which has the diameter that you set in the **setlinewidth** operation.

The last thing in the setup procedure is to initialize the global variables, PathArray and ScreenPath. The PathArray is simply initialized as an empty array. The ScreenPath is a little more complex; it is initialized by creating a user path that consists of a single element: a **moveto** command to the origin. This is so simple that you could actually create the path yourself, but it seems safer to let the interpreter do the work. This way ensures that the form of the path is always correct.

With these wraps done, you can now compile and run the procedures so far. You should see something like Figure 6-2.

Figure 6-2. Output of first fancy curve.

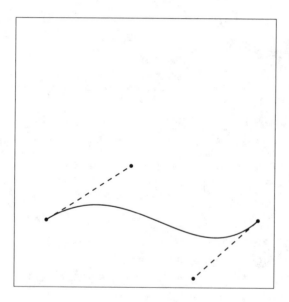

So that's how you can draw the curve and label all the fancy bits. Next, let's add to the runPSInline procedure to erase the first curve, redisplay it without the fancy bits, and draw a new curve. This involves adding the following lines of code to the runPSInline that you created earlier:

```
/* continue with more code for runPSInline */
float rect [4];

/* set up coordinates for rectangle from bounding box */
/* make this a function in a real application */
rect[0] = bbox[0];
rect[1] = bbox[1];
rect[3] = bbox[3] - bbox[0];
rect[4] = bbox[4] - bbox[1];

PSWreDraw(rect);

/* now display the second curved segment */
ax1 = 100;
ay1 = 170;
ax2 = 200;
ay2 = ay1;
dx1 = 30;
dy1 = 230;
dx2 = 280;
dy2 = 250;
PSmoveto(ax1, ay1);
PSWdrawCurve(dx1, dy1, dx2, dy2, ax2, ay2, &bbox);

}
```

This introduces two new elements: the calculations for the rectangle and the new wrap, PSWreDraw. The intention here, as you already know, is to create a rectangular view clipping path, using the **rectviewclip** operator, to control the area of the display that is actually erased and reimaged. To do this, you must pass the coordinates of the rectangle as *x, y, width, height*. You have stored the bounding box information, which also contains four elements—however, those elements are the coordinates of the lower left and upper right corners of the bounding box. You can readily see that this is the same information in a different form. The rectangle's *width* is just the difference between the *x* coordinates of the two corners, whereas the *height* is the difference between the *y* coordinates. You could have passed the bounding box information to the wrap and let it calculate the correct values. However, C is generally more efficient at such calculations than PostScript, so we have done the calculations here, before calling the wrap.

This leaves us with the new wrap, PSWreDraw, which should be added to your wrap file. Here is its code:

```
defineps PSWreDraw ( float RectSize [4] )
    PersDict begin                              %1
    gsave                                       %2
        RectSize rectviewclip                   %3
        gsave                                   %4
            1 setgray                           %5
            RectSize rectfill                   %6
        grestore                                %7
        ScreenPath ustroke                      %8
    grestore                                    %9
    initviewclip                                %10
    end %PersDict
endps
```

The wrap begins by establishing your private dictionary as the current dictionary in line %1. Then, in line %2, you save the current graphics state on the graphics state stack. This ensures that you will not disturb any path segments or other graphics setting that may have been made externally to the wrap. Line %3 sets the view clipping region to exactly the rectangle that you calculated in the application. This just surrounds the curve that you want to erase and redraw. Now you know that you will not affect anything outside that rectangle. Next you save the graphics state again in line %4, so that you can restore the current color after the erase. Line %5 sets the current color to white, and line %6 erases everything inside the rectangle by overpainting it with white.

Line %7 returns you to the previous graphics state settings, so that the current color is now whatever the application has set. You see the point here—by saving and restoring the graphics state, you don't need to worry about what the current graphics parameters are; you can just restore them to the previous state and proceed with your work. The real work of restoring the image is done in line %8, where you stroke the ScreenPath user path. Recall that this represents all the elements that you have placed on the display. The view clipping path restricts the reimaging to only the area that you have just erased, and the fact that you are reimaging every path ensures that any path that crosses that space will be correctly and accurately redrawn.

This point is worth reviewing for just a minute. You could have simply redrawn the specific curve; for example, by selecting it from the PathArray and restroking it. However, you don't know exactly what you may have erased. Other curves, or parts of other curves, may fall within the bounding box for this curve and therefore within the rectangle that was painted with white; they are now equally erased from the display. By setting the view clipping path and then repainting all the paths, you guarantee that all path elements that were previously erased are now redrawn and match their previous images exactly. The sole exception is the fancy bits on the curve that you wanted to erase. Those are not redrawn because you have to make a special effort to show the dots, lines, and so on; the **ustroke** is only going to draw the basic paths, just as you want.

At line %9 you restore the graphics state to its original condition, resetting all the graphics parameters that were in effect when you called the wrap, except one: the view clipping path. Remember that the view clipping path is not a part of the current graphics state, for all those good reasons that we discussed earlier. Yet, if you do not do something, every display that you attempt after this wrap will be confined to the rectangle that you just redrew. This would be, I assure you, most disconcerting. So, how to reset the view clipping path? There are two possible choices. The first is the one shown here, which resets the view clipping path to its initial value using the **initviewclip** operator. The second method would be more cumbersome and more time consuming; it would save the current view clipping path at the beginning of the wrap and restore it at the end. This is not exactly easy since the view clipping path is not easily accessible and storable. However, it can be done by converting the view clipping path into a current path and storing that. Then you would restore the current path at the end of the wrap and use the **viewclip** operator to make that the current view clipping path again.

There is, however, one catch to using the first method: you must promise yourself that you will never set the view clipping path in one place and expect to use it in another. You must establish, as a personal programming convention, that all view clipping will be set and used within a single wrap and the view clipping path reset to the initial value at all other times. If this works for you, well and good. If it does not, for any reason (such as managing multiple windows or multiple display regions), you will have to go the longer but more general route of saving and restoring the view clipping path.

With this new code in place in both the application and the wraps, you can rerun your test and you should end up with a display that looks like Figure 6-3.

Figure 6-3. Output of second fancy curve.

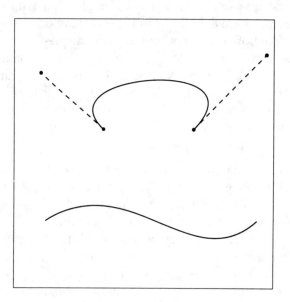

You still need to address several points in this application. The first one involves determining when a mouse click lies on one or another of the curves that you have drawn. Let's continue to add code to runPSInline to solve that problem. Here is the additional code:

```
/* continue with more code for runPSInline */
float x, y;
int hit;

/* reset rectangle coordinates from new bbox */
rect[0] = bbox[0];
rect[1] = bbox[1];
rect[3] = bbox[3] - bbox[0];
rect[4] = bbox[4] - bbox[1];

/* now simulate a mouse hit at (100.0, 100.0) */
x = y = 100;
PSWisAhit(x, y, &hit);
if (hit)
{
    PSWreDraw(rect);
    PSWredrawFancy(hit, &bbox);
```

330   Display PostScript Programming

```
        }
    else
    {
        PSWreDraw(rect);
    }
```

This code is quite clear. You have defined a wrap—as yet not coded—called PSWisAhit, which takes two coordinate values and returns a number, *hit*, which indicates whether these coordinates lie on any of the existing paths. The variable *hit* returns a 0 if there is no hit and a number (basically the index number into the PathArray indicating the hit path) if there is a hit. This makes the C coding very convenient because it allows you to test *hit* conventionally for the redisplay function.

The test and its consequences are also quite clear. If *hit* is not 0—that is, one of the paths was hit—the application redraws any current curve normally and then redraws the curve that was hit with the fancy bits. If *hit* is 0, no curve was hit and the application just resets the currently highlighted curve to normal display.

The PSWreDraw is the same wrap that you used earlier, and the calculations for converting the bounding box coordinates into rectangle coordinates are also identical to those done earlier. In a real application, as noted in the first occurrence of this routine, you would most likely set up a simple C procedure to perform this transformation and then you could call the procedure whenever you needed it.

The two new wraps here are PSWisAhit and PSWredrawFancy. Since these coordinates (100.0, 100.0) are not on either of the curves, you won't execute PSWredrawFancy this time. Let's look at PSWisAhit for this part of the code.

```
defineps PSWisAhit ( float X, Y | int *Hit )
    PersDict begin                              %1
    gsave
        0                                       %2
        0 1 PathArray length 1 sub              %3
        {
            X Y                                 %4
            PathArray                           %5
            3 index get                         %6
            inustroke                           %7
            {
                exch pop                        %8
```

```
            1 add                                    %9
            exit                                     %10
         }
         {
            pop                                      %11
         }
         ifelse                                      %12
      }
      for                                            %13
      Hit                                            %14
   grestore
   end %PersDict
endps
```

This wrap provides the essential test for whether any given set of coordinates matches any point on one of the paths. The wrap is designed to return a result, Hit, of 0 if there is no match, and an index number 1 greater than the actual index if there is a match. You can't return the actual index value because the first valid index is 0, which would conflict with the "no hit" return. Using the value that is one greater than the actual value is just as convenient and can be restored to the correct index just as easily.

The wrap begins, predictably, with the establishment of the private dictionary in line %1. Then the current graphics state is saved, so you won't cause any unexpected errors in other routines. It is particularly important in such routines to preserve the graphic state because in a real application this would likely be the sort of routine that might be called at any point in time, caused by some user action.

The 0 in line %2 is the default return value that must be placed onto the stack now. It will be all that remains on the stack if the search for a match fails, and thus it fulfills your requirement to return a 0 value if there is no match. Line %3 sets up the operands for the **for** operator in line %13. This is the heart of the wrap. You are going to run through all the elements of the PathArray in order, testing each user path in the array to see if the given coordinates are within that path. To do this, you start at element 0, using increments of 1, for the length of PathArray minus 1—since the indices start at 0, and the length starts at 1. The procedure to be executed by the **for** is contained in lines %4 through %12. It begins in line %4 by pushing the coordinates to be tested onto the stack. Next, in line %5, it places the PathArray itself on the stack. This makes three operands on the stack above the loop variable itself. You want to use the loop variable as an index into the array, so in line %6 you retrieve that variable and place it on the top of the stack. This sets you up to **get** a single element from the array. This user path is now on the top of the operand stack, with the two coordinates, *x* and *y*, below it.

This brings us to the Display PostScript operator **inustroke,** which is one of several operators that allow you to test for hits on graphic objects. This whole process was discussed in the earlier sections of this chapter and won't be repeated here.

With this operation in hand, the result from line %7 is quite clear. If the point specified by *x* and *y* is within the user path that you have retrieved from the PathArray, you execute the code in lines %8 to %10; if it is not, you execute line %11. The stack at this point contains two values: the current loop variable and the 0 that you placed on the stack in line %2. If you get a hit, you exchange these two values and throw away the 0, add 1 to the loop variable (which is also the index count), and **exit** the loop immediately. In this case, processing continues on line %14. If there is no hit, line %11 discards the loop counter and the loop continues with the next element of PathArray until the loop is finished. If the loop terminates without ever getting a hit, the only thing left on the stack is the 0 that you started with. In either case, line %14 assigns the value on the stack to the output argument Hit. Then the wrap closes with a **grestore** and ends the use of the private dictionary.

The issue of the new wrap, PSWredrawFancy, remains. This really shouldn't be too hard since you already have all the pieces in place to make it work. The actual wrap looks like this:

```
defineps PSWredrawFancy ( float Hit | float BBox [4] )
    PersDict begin
    gsave
        newpath
        PathArray
        Hit 1 sub
        get
        uappend
        redrawFancy
    grestore
    end %PersDict
endps
```

This type of code should be quite clear by now. The wrap sets up the private dictionary and saves the graphic state. Then it clears the current path, accesses the correct element in PathArray (remembering to subtract one from the argument value to compensate for the 1 that was added in PSWisAhit), and adds this user path to the current path (which is empty, remember). Next it calls a new auxiliary function, redrawFancy, to redraw the path with the required elements. The wrap ends by restoring the graphics state and terminating the use of the private dictionary.

Only one piece is left: the new auxiliary procedure redrawFancy that must be added to PSWsetupCurves. It looks like this:

```
/redrawFancy
{
    {moveto}
    {}
    {fancyCurveto}
    {}
    pathforall
}
def
```

Add this into PSWsetupCurves anywhere before the **end**; I prefer to place it after the definition of **dot** and before line %24 where the definitions of the variables begin.

This procedure interacts with the **uappend** in the PSWredrawFancy to recreate the previous curve, using the procedures that you have already defined. It does this by invoking the **pathforall** operator. This very useful PostScript operator has the following definition:

mvproc lnproc cvproc csproc   **pathforall**   —

enumerates all the elements of the current path, using the procedure operand *mvproc* to process any **moveto** or equivalent operations, the procedure operand *lnproc* to process any **lineto** or equivalent operations, the procedure operand *cvproc* to process any **curveto** or equivalent operations, and the procedure operand *csproc* to process any **closepath** operations. Each procedure operand is called with the appropriate coordinates for the associated operation, based on the current element of the current path being enumerated.

In the processing here, you have carefully tailored the path to match the requirements of the **pathforall.** You have cleared the current path and ensured that the only thing on it is the desired curve. The curve, as you know from building it earlier, is a simple **moveto** followed by a **curveto.** This allows you to create the redrawFancy procedure here, which has only two procedure operands: a simple **moveto** to set the current point at the start of the processing and a call to fancyCurveto to redraw the curve with the extra points displayed.

You can now execute runPSInline as far as it goes. This generates the result shown in Figure 6-4.

Figure 6-4. Output after no hit test.

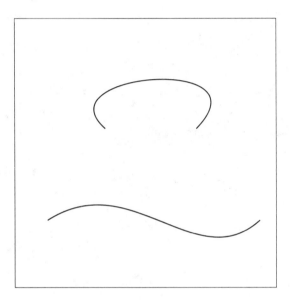

Let's add just one more section to runPSInline to show the results if you do have a hit. To simulate this, add the following code to runPSInline:

```
/* final code for runPSInline */

/* reset rectangle coordinates from new bbox */
rect[0] = bbox[0];
rect[1] = bbox[1];
rect[3] = bbox[3] - bbox[0];
rect[4] = bbox[4] - bbox[1];

/* now simulate a mouse hit at (270.0, 72.0) */
x = 270;
y = 72;
PSWisAhit(x, y, &hit);
if (hit)
```

```
        {
             PSWreDraw(rect);
             PSWredrawFancy(hit, &bbox);
        }
        else
        {
             PSWreDraw(rect);
        }
}
```

Running this all together, or at least the first and last sections, generates an output something like Figure 6-5.

Figure 6-5. Output after actual hit.

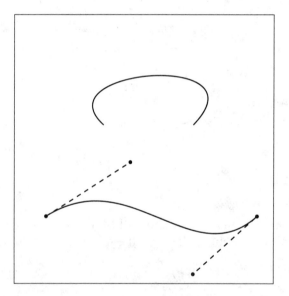

This completes this exercise, showing how you can control your graphics and test for user events on the screen. As is true in most programming, this represents only one way to solve the problem. Indeed, because of the constraints of the exercise, this is not precisely the solution anyone would adopt in a real application. Nevertheless, it does give you a sense of some useful approaches to these problems, and it demonstrates the tools that Display PostScript has provided for you in these areas. Now it is up to you to combine the tools in any given application to solve these problems.

DISPLAYING SAMPLED IMAGES

An image is a representation of the outward appearance of something; in other words, an image is a form or shape that represents some object. Obviously PostScript provides many facilities for creating and manipulating certain common types of images, in this general sense. Not all representations of forms or shapes can be easily described by the PostScript operators that you have used up to now, however. Complex images such as photographs or even intricate, shaded line drawings are the sort of image that requires alternate handling and processing. Generally you can handle such complex images by scanning the original that you plan to include in your display or output and turning the image into a series of numeric values.

Besides being able to create graphics from outlines, PostScript can also accept, process, and output sampled images of all kinds. A *sampled image,* which we will just call an *image,* is a rectangular array of values, with each value representing some color, and the whole array comprising a representation of some scene or object. The values may be generated artificially, as they are in a computer graphic, or they may represent some actual scene, as you would get on a television or video display device.

An image in PostScript is described by a sequence of values obtained by scanning the image in some organized fashion. The scanning process usually divides the image into rows or columns to create a rectangular grid and assigns a value to each element as it is processed. Each element becomes a pixel on the output image. One, three, or four values may be assigned to each element in a row or column, representing a gray value, or three or four color values, depending on the scanning technique and the color model. Color images may be scanned into the environment either by providing multiple values for each element (one for each color component) as the scanning takes place, or by making multiple passes over the scanned image, providing one set of values per pass for each component. The PostScript language supports any of these options.

You can picture this grid of elements as a series of squares, with each one representing a section of the image. At the simplest level, each square can be either black or white, with no intermediate shades. In this case, the color of each square can be represented by a 0 or a 1; if we follow the PostScript conventions, we would use 0 for black and 1 for white (like **setgray**). Each square could also be given some range of gray values to provide additional shading of the image, or it could have a range of values representing appropriate color components of the original image, as described earlier.

Each value is represented internally by one, two, four, or eight bits of data, providing up to 256 shades of gray or any color component. Devices that use 8-bit data representations for each pixel are called *full gray-scale devices*; on such devices, no halftoning technique is necessary or provided. Devices that have 1 bit per pixel are *binary devices*; such devices always require halftoning to provide shades of gray or color tints. Devices with intermediate numbers of bits per pixel use a combination of varying intensity and halftoning to represent the complete range of grays or colors. For now, let's look at the simplest case, where each square is black or white.

The properties of an image are entirely distinct from those of the raster-output device on which it is to be displayed, but they are similar in character. Images have an orientation based on the scanning orientation, a resolution based on the resolution of the scanning device, a scanning order based on whether the scan was done by rows or columns, and so on. All these parameters must be properly transformed into whatever form the output device requires. PostScript provides controls for all these parameters. Generally the PostScript graphics machinery tries to render the image as accurately as possible, using sampling and halftoning as appropriate, subject to the limitations of the given output device.

Four data items must be supplied in order to allow the PostScript interpreter to render an image correctly:

1. *Source image format*: image width in number of rows; image height in number of columns; and number of bits per sample element.

2. *Image data values*: a stream of binary data that is *width* x *height* x *bits/sample* bits long.

3. *Transformation matrix*: transforms the image coordinates to the user coordinates in order to map the image into the user space correctly and also defines the shape and size of the user region that is to accommodate the image.

4. *Mapping*: maps the color values in the image into the color values in the printed output.

It may be helpful, at this point, to look at Figure 6-6, which represents a simple image that is rendered into a grid format.

Figure 6-6. Example of a sampled image.

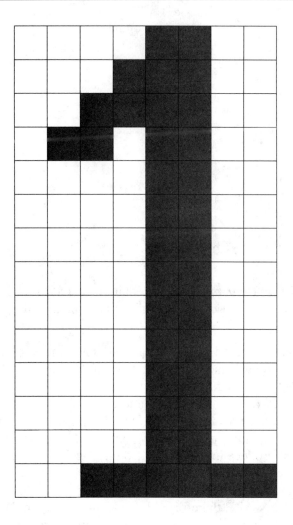

Figure 6-6 shows the image of the number 1 transformed into a grid. This is a very simple image and could easily have been generated with ordinary PostScript operands, but it serves to illustrate the processing mechanism. In actual practice, images being used might represent the appearance of some natural scene or a complex, generated graphic. The simplicity of our example is a virtue because it allows you to focus on the concepts involved.

The entire image is enclosed in a box that is 8 squares wide and 14 squares high. As was said earlier, you can represent this image as a series of 0s and 1s (where 0 is black and 1 is white); it then looks like Figure 6-7.

Chapter 6: Advanced Screen Handling   339

Figure 6-7. Bit representation of sampled image.

```
1 1 1 1 0 0 1 1
1 1 1 0 0 0 1 1
1 1 0 0 0 0 1 1
1 0 0 1 0 0 1 1
1 1 1 1 0 0 1 1
1 1 1 1 0 0 1 1
1 1 1 1 0 0 1 1
1 1 1 1 0 0 1 1
1 1 1 1 0 0 1 1
1 1 1 1 0 0 1 1
1 1 1 1 0 0 1 1
1 1 1 1 0 0 1 1
1 1 1 1 0 0 1 1
1 1 0 0 0 0 0 0
```

This image is a *bitmapped* representation of the number 1. Using this figure, we can now discuss the PostScript mechanism for processing such images.

Each image is defined by three numbers: the number of columns in the image, or the *width*; the number of rows in the image, or *height*; and the number of *bits per sample*. In our example, these are 8, 14, and 1, respectively. The number of rows and columns is easily understood; the number of bits per sample may be less clear. This is a value for the gray level in the square represented by the sample. As we have discussed, devices that produce images range from full-gray scale devices to binary devices. The value for bits/sample tells the PostScript image machinery the nature of the originating device. In the example, you have chosen to use either black or white; therefore, 1 bit is all that is required to represent the color value. Using more bits per sample, of course, carries the obvious cost that you must process 2, 4, or 8 times as many bits to generate the image.

The sampled data that makes up the image is represented by a stream of characters. PostScript image processing obtains this data by executing a procedure that delivers the data, normally through reading a file stream that contains the data. This file may be the standard PostScript input file or it might be some external file stream, depending on the facilities in the system environment and the source of the data. The data are represented as a stream of characters, which is basically a stream of 8-bit integers in the range from 0 through 255. Each set of 8 bits represents from 1 through 8 sample squares, depending on the number of bits per sample. In this example, each character would represent 8 sample squares since each sample is only 1 bit. At the other extreme, if the samples were the maximum of 8 bits, each character would represent 1 sample square. Since the example in Figure 6-7 has 8 columns and only 1 bit per sample, each row can be represented by 1 character.

Image data must be presented in a defined order for processing. Each image is produced by the PostScript image operators within its own independent coordinate system. This system mimics the default PostScript user coordinates, with the origin (0, 0) in the left bottom corner of the image, and with the *x* coordinates ranging from 0 through *width,* and the *y* coordinates ranging from 0 through *height*. Thus the image is contained in a rectangle that is *height* high by *width* wide, with each sample value occupying 1 unit square in the image coordinate system.

In addition, the PostScript graphics machinery assumes that the sample values to fill the image rectangle are presented in columns from left to right, and the rows are filled moving up the rectangle from bottom to top. In this format, the first sample data value fills the position (0, 0), the next fills (1, 0), and so on until the entire bottom row is filled. The next row up is filled, beginning with position (0, 1), then (1, 1), and so on.

These assumptions are not rigid. You can use the usual coordinate transformation matrices to map the actual scanning order and representation into this coordinate system. This default coordinate system is called *image space*. At this point, you should notice that we are dealing with three separate coordinate structures: image space, user space, and device space.

The samples that make up this image follow the default coordinate system and so are numbered (0,0) from the bottom left corner, proceed along the bottom row, then move up a row, and so on. In our example, that would make the bottom left corner square (0,0), the bottom right square (8,0), the first square in the next row (0,1), the top left corner (0,14), and the top right corner (8,14). This is also the order that PostScript normally uses to assign values when it reads the data. That is, the first bits are applied to the bottom left corner of the image, the next are applied to the sample value on the left, and so on up the image until all the data are used. The easiest way to encode bit-streams like this is to represent them as hexadecimal digits. Recall from Chapter 2 that PostScript provides a convenient notation for writing hexadecimal strings by enclosing them in the delimiters < >, instead of the usual parentheses. In that case, using hexadecimal notation, the rows of Figure 6-7 are equivalent to the hexadecimal values shown in Figure 6-8.

Figure 6-8. Bit representation with hexadecimal equivalents.

1	1	1	1	0	0	1	1	= <f3>
1	1	1	0	0	0	1	1	= <e3>
1	1	0	0	0	0	1	1	= <c3>
1	0	0	1	0	0	1	1	= <93>
1	1	1	1	0	0	1	1	= <f3>
1	1	1	1	0	0	1	1	= <f3>
1	1	1	1	0	0	1	1	= <f3>
1	1	1	1	0	0	1	1	= <f3>
1	1	1	1	0	0	1	1	= <f3>
1	1	1	1	0	0	1	1	= <f3>
1	1	1	1	0	0	1	1	= <f3>
1	1	1	1	0	0	1	1	= <f3>
1	1	1	1	0	0	1	1	= <f3>
1	1	0	0	0	0	0	0	= <c0>

Then this set of numbers, or characters, would be sent to PostScript as the following hexadecimal string:

<c0f3f3f3f3f3f3f3f3f3f393c3e3f3>

As you see, it begins with the bottommost row and proceeds up the image to the top. The only point to watch out for here is that each row of the sample must start with a new character. In other words, if the example were 9 columns wide, say, you would have to put the ninth bit into a character all alone; the last 7 bits would be thrown out. To illustrate this, let's take the preceding example and add one column of white space on the right edge—another row of all 1s. In this case, each row would have to add another character that would be the same for all the rows: an <80> to set the last bit in the row. A single additional bit does not work. Then the string to represent the image would be changed as follows:

<c080f380f380f380f380f380f380f380f380f3809380c380e380f380>

Once the image is defined to the graphics machinery, it can be mapped into user space. This is necessary in order to place and size the final output image correctly. (The assumption here is that the conversion from user space to device space will be the same for the image as for the rest of the page; if that were not correct, it would be easy enough to encapsulate the image on a "page" by itself and then map that "page" into the final output.) It would, of course, be possible to write a single transformation matrix that took the image from the image space and adjusted it to the final position and size in user coordinates. However, that is somewhat difficult to visualize and to program. An easier technique is to map the image space into a unit square at the page origin, and then position and scale that unit square as desired.

In this process, the first step is to map a square, with corners of $(0, 0)$, $(0, 1)$, $(1, 1)$, and $(1, 0)$, called the *unit square* into the desired output region on the page, using ordinary PostScript translation and scaling techniques. Then, as a second step, the image coordinates are mapped into the unit square. Thus the entire image is correctly transformed into the region set aside for it on the output page.

Image Processing Operators

Now that you have been introduced to the concepts behind image processing, we can discuss the actual PostScript operators that implement it. This is done by two similar operators, **image** and **imagemask.** These two are sufficiently alike that we will discuss one of them, **image,** first, and then explain the differences that distinguish **imagemask.**

The **image** operator takes five operands: sample width, sample height, number of bits per sample, the transformation matrix, and a procedure. You already understand the function of the first four items; only the procedure is new. This is the procedure that **image** executes, repeatedly if necessary, to get the data to generate the sample image. Typically the procedure reads the image data from a file, often the current input file—that is to say, the same file that is supplying the PostScript commands. However, the procedure may use PostScript file operations and any system-provided file structure to read the data from some external source. In the case where the data come over the standard input file, the data are embedded into the command stream immediately after the **image** operator. In any case, the **image** operator obtains the data by executing the procedure. If the image area defined by the first three operands has not been filled by the time the procedure has finished executing, **image** executes the procedure repeatedly until sufficient data have been obtained.

There are several advantages to this method of producing images on the device. First, there is no need for the entire image to reside in PostScript memory in order for the image to be generated onto the output device. The sample data may also be processed as it is read, allowing various transformations to be done on the file. For example, the data on the file might be compressed by some algorithm to conserve space and then decompressed by the input procedure to generate the final sample image. It is even possible to generate an image entirely internally by using a procedure that calculates the necessary binary pattern instead of reading the data from some source.

The **image** operator produces images on the page by marking with an opaque paint, as always. The usual PostScript rules apply and the paint covers every portion of the sampled image, overlaying anything that was on the page previously. This is the effective difference between the two operators, **image** and **imagemask.** Here, then, is the definition of the **image** operator in our standard format:

> width height samp matrix proc   **image**   —
>
> renders a sampled image onto the current page. The image is produced by translating streams of data that are presented to the **image** operator as a binary representation of a sampled image. The sampled image consists of a rectangular array of sample points that exist in their own coordinate system. This rectangle is defined to be *width* columns of samples wide and *height* rows of samples high. Each sample point consists of *samp* bits of data, where *samp* may be 1, 2, 4, or 8. The data is presented to the **image** operator as a string of character data that is interpreted as a series of binary integers, grouped according to *samp* to form the sample values. The string of character data is produced by *proc,* which may get the data from any source but must leave them on the operand stack as a string. **image** uses this data to fill out the image rectangle, beginning at point (0, 0) in the image coordinate system and continuing to the point (*width*-1, *height*-1). If the number of values presented on the operand stack is not sufficient to fill the image rectangle, **image** calls *proc* repeatedly until enough values have been presented and processed. However, if *proc* returns an empty string to the operand stack, processing terminates at that point. If any values are left on the operand stack after the image rectangle is filled, they are ignored.

The **image** operator imposes a coordinate system on the source image data, to provide some structure for reconstructing the image. The coordinate system and the scanning order used in the source image are not a consideration, since, whatever they may be, they can be mapped into the image coordinate system used by the **image** operator.

Although this can be done within a single matrix (as can all linear coordinate transformations), it is best to do it in two steps. The first step transforms the user coordinates to map a unit square—that is, a square with corners at the points (0, 0), (1, 0), (1,1), and (0, 1)—into a space of the correct size and shape that is formed by the transformation operators. Thus, for example, suppose we have a rectangular source image with an aspect ratio (ratio of width to height) of 8:14, as in Figure 6-6, and we wish to place this image on the output page in the region bounded by the points (100, 100), (300, 100), (400, 450), and (100, 450). This region preserves the same 8:14 aspect ratio since it is 200 units wide by 350 units high. You can map the unit square into this region by using the following PostScript commands:

    100 100 translate 200 350 scale

which provides the necessary transformation. Obviously any transformation could be used, rotating or otherwise changing the coordinate system. The only concern is that the aspect ratio must be preserved if you don't want to distort the image.

The second step is the process of mapping the image coordinates into the unit square. This is done by providing an appropriate transformation matrix as an operand to the **image** operator. Here is where the versions of the coordinate transformation operators that can be applied to a general matrix can be useful. The **image** operator default coordinates run from the bottom left corner of the sample to the top right corner, filling in the rows as you go up. If the source image was provided in this same sequence of samples and was 8 samples wide by 14 samples high, the required matrix would be

    [8 0 0 14 0 0]

and this matrix could be generated by the PostScript commands

    8 14 **matrix scale**

Notice how the **matrix** operator is used to provide the necessary matrix operand so the **scale** operator produces a matrix as a result on the operand stack and does not interact with or change the coordinate transformation matrix (CTM). If you had the same image data, but it had been scanned from the top left corner to the bottom right, left to right and top to bottom (a usual format, in fact), the required matrix would be

    [8 0 0 -14 0 14]

which maps the coordinates from the image into the unit square quite nicely. Notice that it maps the y-axis in the necessary negative direction since the image coordinates increase down the image, whereas the default coordinates, like the PostScript defaults, increase up the image. Then the translation component is used to move the *y*-axis origin to the top of the image. The transformation is thus complete. A similar process can be used to map rotated images into the unit square, and so on. Although this matrix is probably most easily created by simply writing it in as a matrix, it too can be generated by using standard PostScript operations.

If only a portion of the image is desired, a clipping path can be defined and placed into use by executing the **clip** operator in the region prepared to receive the image data. In this way, the portion of the image that falls outside the clipping region does not leave any marks on the output page.

Therefore, with the addition of a clipping path, we have now established a three-step process to bring any image data into the PostScript application and then render it onto the output page with any desired revision to its shape:

1. Transform the user coordinates to map a unit square into the correct region for placement of the image.

2. Crop the image, if desired, by establishing a clipping path over the unit square.

3. Map the image coordinates into the unit square by using the required transformation matrix as an operand to **image.**

We can use the information that you have been reading so far to put together a short example using the **image** operator. This is not a full exercise, so we will just keep it quite simple, avoiding the complexities of a real application to show just the basic functions of the operator.

Let's redo the runPSInline to call two new wraps: one to set up the image processing and the other to display the image. The image data, in this case, is the hexadecimal string that you saw earlier.

```
void runPSInline (void)
{
PSWsetupImage();
PSWpaintImage();
}
```

That's really short and sweet; just calls to the two wraps involved, which have the following definitions:

```
defineps PSWsetupImage ()
    %define bit mapped data string
    /One
        < c0 f3 f3 f3 f3 f3 f3
          f3 f3 f3 93 c3 e3 f3 >
    def
endps

defineps PSWpaintImage ()
    gsave
        100 100 translate
        40 40 scale
        0 setgray
        8 14 1
            [ 8 0 0 14 0 0 ]
            {One}
        image
    grestore
endps
```

These, too, are very short and to the point. The first, PSWsetupImage, merely defines the required hexadecimal string for the **image** operator. The second does a little more, but not much. PSWpaintImage first moves to the desired location for the display; in this case, the lower left corner of the display will be at the point (100, 100). Next, it scales the image to the desired size, in this case, 40 points. Remember that you are mapping the image into a 1-unit square, so the scale factor here is size that you want the final display to have. Then you set the paint value to black. Now you are ready for the image itself. The width of the image is 8 units, the height is 14 units, and there is 1 bit per sample; all just as we have discussed. Next is the transformation matrix that maps the image into the unit square. Finally the procedure that places the data onto the stack; here, simply a call to the hexadecimal string that you defined in the setup. Once all this is done, you execute the **image** operator to render the image onto the display. You should then see something like Figure 6-9.

Figure 6-9. Image output.

Using Images as Masks

As we discussed earlier, there is also a masking process that functions much like the imaging process. The main difference is that the current color is applied through the mask, and any image data that is on the output page remains in place wherever the mask shields it. This function is provided by the **imagemask** operator, which, for the most part, takes similar operands to the **image** operator. In particular, it uses the same mechanisms to map its data into the output page. The sole differences between the two operators is how they use the data that they are provided and what form that data may take.

The **imagemask** takes the data stream as a series of binary digits, 0 and 1, and uses these as a *mask* to control where the paint is applied. Let's look at Figure 6-8 again. We said earlier that this is a bitmapped image of the number 1. When we were looking at this is relation to the **image** operator, the 0s represented black paint and the 1s were white paint. Now consider this same data as a mask. In that case, the 0s represent where the **imagemask** operator will apply paint—the current color, as set by **setgray**—and the 1s represent where no color is to be applied. Alternatively, the 0s could be used to represent where no color was applied and the 1s where the color was applied—the reverse of the preceding condition. This is the difference between the two operators: **image** paints the sampled data onto the page; **imagemask** applies paint in the current color through the sampled data, using it as a mask.

The **imagemask** operator requires five operands, much the same as **image.** The first pair and the last pair of operands are identical: the width and height, and the transformation matrix and the procedure. The difference is in the third operand. Here, **image** had the number of bits per sample; but, since **imagemask** is a binary mask, there is always only 1 bit per position. Instead of bits/sample, **imagemask** has a boolean operand in this position: if the value is *true*, the 1s are painted and the 0s are blank; if it is *false*, the reverse occurs. Assuming that you wanted to paint the sample in Figure 6-9 in the current color, you would call the **imagemask** with the operands

    8 14 false [8 0 0 14 0 0] { procedure }

which would paint where the 0s are in the mask and leave everything else on the current page alone. This point is important, particularly if you are developing bitmapped characters. Any marks that are already on the page that lie under the nonpainted characters are not affected by the operation. This ensures that if you had built your own font, for example, any graphic image or background that you paint on an output will not be erased by the character that prints on top of it. If you incorrectly used **image,** instead of **imagemask,** with a bitmapped character, it would paint white over anything underneath it.

It is the matter of a moment to demonstrate this; it also allows you a quick look at the **imagemask** operator. Using the same runPSInline that you had earlier, change the two previously defined wraps as follows:

```
defineps PSWsetupImage ()
    %define bit mapped data string
    /One
        < c0 f3 f3 f3 f3 f3
          f3 f3 f3 93 c3 e3 f3 >
    def

    %add a background procedure
    /background
    {
        100 10 translate
        36 36 scale
        .9 setgray
        0 0 1.5 1.5 rectfill
    }
```

```
        def
endps

defineps PSWpaintImage ()
    gsave
        background
        %offset from the edge of the background
        .1 .1 translate
        0 setgray
        8 14 false
            [ 8 0 0 14 0 0 ]
            {One}
        imagemask
    grestore
endps
```

These wraps are virtually identical to those you used earlier, with **image,** with two differences. The major difference here is that you have added a new procedure, **background**, that does two things. First, it makes the required coordinate changes. Second, it paints a gray rectangle as a background for the image. The minor difference is that you **translate** the image a small distance to place it inside the background rectangle. Using these wraps instead of the previous ones gives the output in Figure 6-10.

Figure 6-10. Image mask output.

This quick overview should give you some feeling for how you can manipulate scanned image data in PostScript. This whole area is quite complex, and you can spend a lot of time developing methods of handling and using scanned data. With what you now know, you should be able to begin using scanned data without too many errors and problems. This can be very important, since errors within **image** or **imagemask** processing, particularly errors in the procedures that get the data for the operators, may easily cause the context to lose control and cause abnormal terminations. The application may even lose control of the interpreter and have to be aborted. These are very sensitive areas, and you should test your procedures thoroughly before you turn them loose.

PLACING EPS GRAPHICS

Similar techniques can be used to place Encapsulated PostScript (EPS) files into your display. In these cases, of course, the graphic that you are placing is not a bitmap but instead a complete PostScript graphic image. However, some of the same problems remain. Presumably you have not created the image that you want to include; it comes to you fully formed by some other program and is now ready to be placed into your output. How can you do this without going through the tedious work of decoding the procedures and names that have been used in the generating application?

If the application output is in EPS format, it is quite easy to place these graphics since any EPS file conforms to a strict set of structural conventions. There is not room here to discuss the structural requirements of EPS files in detail; that is well covered in other sources. Here we concentrate on using the graphics generated by someone else.

This special Encapsulated PostScript structure was designed to allow programs to share a PostScript graphic and manipulate it in certain limited ways. In the following discussion, let's call the application that creates the Encapsulated PostScript file the *source* and the application that uses the file the *destination*.

As the name implies, EPS files are intended to be used as separate "capsules" of graphics, and they do not interact in most ways with the rest of the destination application's output. The significant deviations from this are the destination application's ability to position the graphic on a page at any point, and to crop, scale, or rotate the graphic as required for correct placement and viewing on the output page. The destination application is responsible for creating the necessary changes in the output environment to ensure that this occurs correctly and to restore the original environment when it's done.

Note that any change made by the destination program has not redefined any details of the image. It simply transforms the image like a distorting mirror in a fun house, expanding or contracting each dimension as requested; or it may crop the image as you might crop a photograph with scissors. Destination applications can perform this type of change on the EPS file because they can interpret certain information that the file format provides about size and shape. You don't have to understand the PostScript code itself; that is, the destination application does not actually use the internal PostScript code that is being interpreted. As you can imagine, a lot of coordination is required between the two applications so that this process works as smoothly as it does.

There are two essential points for you to take away from this discussion. First, the exchange of graphic information between cooperating applications, using the EPS file format, is quite simple from the users' point of view. They really should have no problem inserting EPS graphics into another application; the process is smooth, easy, and natural. Second, the placement and transformation of such imported graphics within the destination application is always limited to a fairly basic set of options. You see, therefore, that the role and work of each application is quite well defined, and that you do need to understand which application performs which functions to get the maximum productivity out of these graphic arts tools.

Every EPS file must start with a version header and contain a "%%Bounding-Box" comment. As is true for all conforming PostScript files, an EPS file must have a correctly formed version comment as the first comment in the header. This takes the following form:

```
%!PS-Adobe-2.0 EPSF-1.2
```

where the 1.2 may be replaced by any later version number of the EPSF format that is being used.

This comment indicates to the destination application that the file conforms to both the structuring conventions generally and to the EPSF format conventions in particular. The structure version number is given following the word "Adobe", and the EPSF version number follows "EPSF". This comment also indicates to a destination application that the file is intended for EPSF use; without it, the destination application may reject the file or may not display the graphic information correctly.

The following comment specifies the area on the page that is included in the image produced by the PostScript program and represented by the graphic information:

%%BoundingBox: llx lly urx ury

where the coordinates *llx, lly* are the position of the lower left corner of the image in the default PostScript coordinates, and the coordinates *urx, ury* are the position of the upper right corner. This pair of coordinates defines a standard bounding box for the image that is produced by the PostScript code that follows.

This comment is required for an EPS file. As you will see later in this section, this bounding box information is the essential ingredient for placing and adjusting the EPS graphic. If this comment is not present, the destination application may issue an error message and refuse to import the file.

The basic requirements to print an EPS file are quite straightforward, given the information that you now have. To display an EPS file, you must provide two things: positioning information for the graphic image and a proper coordinate system for its execution. In addition, you may wish to modify the image by transformation, rotation, or cropping. We will discuss the basic requirements first.

An EPS file is designed to be included in a page generated by another PostScript program. In other words, the source of the EPS file expects you to take the entire PostScript output from the EPS file and include it with some other PostScript code. To do that successfully or to display the file by itself, you need to define several things: where on the page you want to place the EPS graphic, what coordinates it uses, and what size you want it to be. The first two issues must always be addressed; the second need only be taken care of if you don't want to use the graphic at the same size as it was created.

Setting Up the EPS Display

The issues of placement, coordinates, and size can be taken care of by two PostScript operators: **translate** and **scale. translate** positions the graphic on the new output page and adjusts the coordinates, if required. **scale** sets the size of the graphic on the new page. In all cases, some housekeeping should be done to ensure that the EPS file does not interfere with the other graphics on the page in the process. This can be done using the **save, restore** operators with which you are familiar. The **save** and **restore** are preferable to the **gsave, grestore** pair because **save** and **restore** remove all the composite objects, all definitions, and all other side effects of the EPS processing, whereas the **gsave, grestore** pair only restores the graphics state.

To successfully place an EPS file onto your display, three things must generally happen:

1. You must move the display origin to the position where you want the new graphic to appear.

2. You must scale the graphic to fit the space that you want it to show in.

3. You must reset graphic to its internal origin so that you can display it properly.

These calculations can be done either in your C application, when it gets the EPS file, or in the PostScript code that is placed around the EPS code to display it. Here we will do all of the calculations to place and display the EPS file in PostScript. At this point, you should have no trouble translating these into a mixture of C and PostScript if you want to keep the calculations in your application code for maximum efficiency.

This sequence can be done by the following wrap, which is presented here without any associated C code. This can be compressed into one or two lines of PostScript code, but it is expanded to multiple lines here to help you see all the operations and the stack results more clearly.

```
defineps PSWsetEPS ( float BBox[4], PBox[4] )
    %first readjust origin for new display
    \PBox[0] \PBox[1] translate                              %1

    %calculate the width of new window
    \PBox[2] \PBox[0] sub                                    %2
    %calculate width of graphic
    \BBox[2] \BBox[3] sub                                    %3
    %use two results on stack for ratio
    div                                                      %4
    %and leave result on stack

    %calculate the height of the new window
    \PBox[3] \PBox[1] sub                                    %5
    %calculate height of graphic
    \BBox[3] \BBox[1] sub
```

```
        %use two results on stack for ratio
        div

        %now both x and y scale are on stack
        %so issue scale command
        scale                                                    %6

        %finally readjust for original coordinates in EPS
        \BBox[0] neg \BBox[1] neg translate                      %7
endps
```

The wrap is called with two arguments, both arrays. The first array is the bounding box of the EPS graphic; you can get this information by looking at the %%BoundingBox: comment, which contains the four values that you require. The other array contains the equivalent bounding box information for the placement of the graphic; in other words, this is the bounding box information for the output space where you want to place the graphic. In both cases, the contents of the arrays are identical: *llx, lly, urx,* and *ury* coordinates for each of the boxes.

Note that there is one new feature in this wrap: this time the input arguments, which are arrays (as you have seen before), are not used as a set of numbers, but instead the components of the array are used individually. The wrap shows how this is done: the individual element is called by giving the name of the array, preceded by a backslash character \, and followed by an opening square brace, [, the element number (as always, counting from 0), and then the closing square brace,]. No white space is allowed between the backslash, \, and the closing brace,]. This is a very straightforward way to reference individual input array elements.

The first change that you have to make is to move the graphic to its new location. As is always the case in PostScript, you will reposition the lower left corner of the image by repositioning the origin. Since you want to move the output graphic so that its lower left corner is at the new position (Pbox[0], PBox[1]), you issue the **translate** on line %1, which moves the graphic to the point you wanted.

Next you want to make your EPS input fit on a defined space in the new page output. This can be done with the help of the BBox argument information. In this case, you want to adjust the height and width of the existing output to fit into some new space, as defined by the PBox.

Suppose that the new space to be filled has a width of w and a height of h. Then, scaling the EPS graphic to this area means simply that the width of the graphic must be scaled to *w* and the height, in similar fashion, scaled to *h*. For example, if the area that you wanted to fit was 1 unit by 1 unit and the graphic was 2 by 4, you would have to scale the graphic by 1 divided by 2 in width and 1 divided by 4 in height. This gives us the general approach for scaling a graphic: the new dimension divided by the old dimension is the scale factor for that coordinate. Thus you see that the width of the graphic is determined by subtracting the two *x* coordinates from one another, and the height by subtracting the two *y* coordinates. Therefore, the scale factor for width is *w*/(*urx* – *llx*) and for height it is *h*/(*ury* – *lly*). Obviously you can use the same method to compute the width and height of the new window as you used to compute the width and height of the EPS graphic, by subtracting the *x* and *y* coordinates of the lower left and upper right corners.

And that is what you do in the code here. In line %2, you calculate the width of the new area by subtracting PBox[0] from PBox[2]. Then line %3 does the same for the EPS graphic, and the results are divided in line %4 according to the preceding formula. The code beginning with line %5 performs the same calculation for the height. This puts the *x* and *y* ratios on the stack in the correct order for the **scale,** which you issue in line %6.

You also must correct for the default coordinates used in the EPS file. Without any adjustment, there is a good chance that the EPS graphic will be drawn off of the top or bottom of the normal output and you won't be able to see it. Furthermore, you cannot rely on the fact that the EPS file uses the default page origin. As you know, it is quite easy and possible for the origin of any PostScript page to have been moved to any arbitrary location. Since the origin of a PostScript page may have been placed anywhere, you need an adjustment mechanism that allows you to readjust the coordinates independently of the default settings.

The necessary adjustment can be easily made by using the information provided by the BBox array argument. The requirement is to move the lower left corner of the EPS graphic to the new origin. This is done by the **translate** in line %7. This readjusts the coordinates for the output to a position that is –*llx* and –*lly,* since the **neg** operator just reverses the sign of the given number. That means that the EPS graphic begins at point (*llx* – *llx*) (*lly* – *lly*), or (0, 0), since subtracting something from itself always results in zero. Once the origin of the graphic is translated to (0, 0), the coordinates on the EPS page will map correctly into those of the output page.

ERROR HANDLING

When you are creating robust applications, you must be particularly concerned with handling errors that occur during processing. All programmers deal with this subject as a normal part of creating good application code. Generally a good application tries to control or recover from an error condition, whatever its cause. Error recovery usually means that the program can fix an error and continue processing. Controlling the error might include isolating the error condition, reporting it, and waiting for some corrective action. As a last resort, a well-constructed and friendly application notifies the user that an error has occurred in some way that allows the user to understand what the error is and how it affected processing, and then will shut itself down in some regular fashion, closing files, cleaning up, and generally being "well behaved" with regard to its system environment.

Creating applications that behave like this relies on some combination of two strategies. The first is to understand points where errors may be introduced and to avoid them. This is one of the functions of edit routines and similar program features. The second is to set up some notification and control process that is activated, in some way, when an error occurs. This latter strategy, in particular, requires some cooperation from the system to support the processing. This process is called *trapping errors*.

PostScript in general, and the Display PostScript environment in particular, present some unique challenges in this area. PostScript is an interactive language, which means that some errors, such as syntax or module errors, that would be caught at the compile or linkage stages in compiled languages, may occur while the application is executing. The problem here, of course, is that compile or link errors occur while the programmer is watching; interpreter errors occur to a user, who may not understand anything about the language being used or the processing being done. Of course, a complete range of data errors and similar occurrences can still happen outside of these language errors; it is just that language errors are much more difficult to explain to the user in any comprehensible way.

In a batch PostScript environment, there is normally not much, if anything, that an application can do to handle data errors. The application is processing data that has been previously created and transmitted; the most it can do is attempt to diagnose the data error precisely, give some kind of intelligible error message, and proceed to either skip processing anything associated with the bad data or terminate processing altogether. In any case, appropriate processing is very limited.

In Display PostScript, however, you are often working in an interactive environment where the user can be notified of an error and may be able to take corrective action that allows processing to continue successfully. In such an environment, terminating the processing is almost never the best response; think of the user's frustration when the result of a simple data error results in a blank screen or, worse, in a window that no longer responds to commands. An additional complication in Display PostScript is that there are two processing "partners," as it were: the C application and the Display PostScript interpreter. Errors may occur in either area, but somehow the response must be coordinated so that the user has only one reasonable and useful interface for error handling and notification. Display PostScript also raises another problem in this regard since its processes are usually executing asynchronously with the application. This means that any errors that the interpreter discovers may not be recognized and reported until some time later, after the application has continued processing. This makes coordination and even identification of the offending commands difficult.

Between them, PostScript and Display PostScript provide features that allow you to manage all these issues in a reasonable and user-friendly way. The available methods fall into two major areas: handling errors within the PostScript environment itself and communicating errors to the application for external resolution.

PostScript Error Processing

PostScript provides three levels of internal error processing. First, you may avoid potential errors by trapping individual instructions or procedures. Second, you may change handling for individual types of errors. Finally, you may change the global error handling and reporting mechanism. To understand how these methods work, you first need to know something about PostScript error processing.

An error is more correctly and broadly described as an *exception*. An exception is an unexpected condition detected by the interpreter that does not allow the current processing to proceed to normal completion. Obvious examples are not having a current point or a current font for a **show** operator, or executing a mathematical operator without the correct number and types of operands on the operand stack. A more subtle example would be a long **for** loop that did not clear the loop variable from the stack, resulting in an eventual overflow of the operand stack when no more operands could be accommodated. In any case, handling exceptions is the work of a series of PostScript routines.

However, the first level of defense against an error is to ensure that one doesn't happen; or, at least, to ensure that it doesn't get processed by the interpreter at all. This is done by using the **stopped** operator. You have already seen this used once, in Chapter 5, where you were displaying a part of the **Encoding** vector. There you used **stopped** to test whether a current point was set. This prevented an error from occurring, later in the code, when the **show** operator would have failed if there had been no current point. The essential point in that routine, as we discussed, was that you could set a reasonable current point inside the routine (the point XMar, TopMar) if no current point was already set.

Let's discuss exactly how the interpreter handles what is called a *stopped context*. Note that this nomenclature does not relate to the Display PostScript context. The stopped context is simply any process or procedure that is executed by a **stopped** operator. The **stopped** operator has the following definition:

> any   **stopped**   bool
> executes *any,* which is typically a procedure, but may be any executable object. If *any* runs to normal completion, the operator returns the boolean value *false* on the stack. In any other case, the operator returns *true*. In any case, execution continues with the next object in normal sequence.

Therefore, one way to prevent PostScript errors is to catch them before they get reported by providing a **stopped** operator to execute any procedures that might have or cause errors. You should also note that there is a matching **stop** operator that terminates processing and exits a **stopped** context immediately, setting the boolean return value to *true*. This lets you exit a procedure by, in a sense, creating your own error.

Two obvious conditions must be satisfied before you can use the **stopped** operator effectively. First, the condition must be known or predictable. For example, in the exercise in Chapter 5, it was certainly known that any attempt to execute the procedure without a current point would cause an error. Moreover, the current point was being set independently of the procedure execution. Thus it was entirely possible for there to be an occasion when the point was not set, raising this error. Second, there must be some reasonable action that can be taken if the error occurs. Again, in the exercise, if the application had not set the current point, there was an obvious solution: to set it. You could do that because you knew that the left and top margin variables already existed in the private dictionary, and that was a reasonable place to start the display.

Notice that you don't waste time and processing cycles trying to avoid every possible error. For example, you didn't test for the existence of PersDict; there will, indeed, be an error if the application has not correctly initialized the environment by executing the necessary setup code. You have only provided for a foreseeable and correctable error condition. In a very real sense, this is the PostScript equivalent of edit processing.

This represents the most basic level of PostScript error handling: trapping an error at the procedure or instruction level. What about the other two levels of PostScript error handling?

When the PostScript interpreter discovers an exception in its current processing, it determines the type of exception and executes a specific procedure, associated with that particular exception, from the special dictionary *errordict*. The keys in *errordict* are the names of the various possible PostScript exceptions; the values are the procedures to be executed when the named exception occurs. These procedures are, in most cases, simply PostScript programs that perform some sensible function to record the state of the program at the point of the error and then terminate the program. Every possible PostScript error is denominated by one of these names, and *errordict* contains standard procedures associated with these names. In a Display PostScript environment, these standard error procedures all take the following actions:

1. Set the context to private virtual memory allocation mode, thus ensuring that all variables, and so on, are allocated in private virtual memory and that the error does not affect any other contexts that might have been sharing data or procedures with the executing context.

2. Record information about the current state of the interpreter in the special dictionary **$error.** Under usual circumstances, the dictionary always contains the name of the error and the command that raised the error. If the boolean value **recordstacks** is *true,* the process continues to record a picture of the operand, dictionary, and execution stacks at the moment of the error, except in the case of a virtual memory error, when such action is not possible in any case. The default value of **recordstacks** is *false,* so that this information is not recorded.

3. Executes a **stop** operator, thereby exiting the current **stopped** context.

Once the **stop** occurs, the interpreter exits the current program (which, as a matter of fact, is actually run as a large process being executed by a **stopped** operator) and executes a standard error reporting procedure also located in the *errordict*. In basic PostScript, this default procedure is called **handleerror,** and it reports the error back as a text message over the communication channel that sent the program. Then the program is usually flushed. In Display PostScript, the process is somewhat different. To begin with, there are two procedures to report errors: **handleerror** and **resynchandleerror.** We will discuss the differences in these two procedures when we discuss Client Library exception handling. In either case, the error is reported back to the application via the Client Library and a special binary object sequence is used to communicate the error information. This triggers the Client Library exception processing.

Let's follow a concrete example of this. Suppose that you have pushed a number 1 onto the stack, followed that with the string (2), then executed an **add** operator. This clearly does not work since the **add** requires two numbers as operands. The attempt to execute the **add** raises the **typecheck** error condition. This is the name of the PostScript error that has occurred, and it is the name associated with the procedure to handle this condition in *errordict*. Every PostScript error has a name, listed in *errordict* and documented in the PostScript reference materials that you have already read about. The interpreter searches for the procedure associated with the name **/typecheck** in *errordict* and executes that procedure.

This is the first level at which you can modify the error handling process. *errordict* is a writeable dictionary, such that you can redefine the procedure associated with the name **/typecheck** in *errordict* to provide any processing that you want. The trick, of course, is to determine some form of processing that is actually appropriate and correct for the circumstances, taking into account that every conceivable error of this type will execute this code. Here, for example, you might (if you were very ambitious indeed) test the offending command to see if it was a mathematical operator; if so, and any of the operands on the stack were strings, you might change them into integer numbers and reexecute the command if that conversion was successful. More likely, you might automatically set the **recordstacks** boolean to save the stack contents and then execute the standard error processing, thus guaranteeing that you would be able to debug this error in some reasonable fashion. In any case, this is one level of error processing that is provided by the PostScript error handling mechanism.

Generally the processing at the level of the individual error must return, in some fashion, to the standard error processing functions by execution of a **stop** operator. Normally, of course, any changes to the standard error procedures in *errordict* automatically include the standard procedures as a component, to be executed after any specialized processing is completed. In any case, when the **stop** is executed, it returns control to the interpreter, which executes the default standard procedure **handleerror.** Ultimately this processing calls the procedure of that name in *errordict* and executes it. This arrangement allows you to change the **handleerror** procedure in *errordict* to provide alternative processing for all errors uniformly.

At this point in the processing there is not much recovery that you can do. However, you can transmit and retrieve additional information to the application, or you can display the additional information, as you deem appropriate and useful. For example, one of the most common changes at this level in batch PostScript environments is to print the error information instead of transmitting it back over the standard communications channel. In the same way, in the Display PostScript environment, it is possible to send back the operand and dictionary stack information in addition to the standard error information, if that has been recorded in **$error** as described earlier.

Changing the **handleerror** (or **resynchandleerror**) procedure is the last and most global of the changes that you can make in PostScript error processing. So, at this point, we have briefly reviewed the three levels of error processing that we first described: at the level of individual procedures, by using the **stopped** operator; at the level of individual error types, by redefining the error procedure of the given type in *errordict*; and at the global processing level, by redefining the **handleerror** procedure in *errordict*. Each of these methods has a place, and each can be very useful in that place. By now you should have some idea of where and how you might use these methods.

One note of caution needs to be made about all these methods. The recovery procedures, or the alternative handling options, that you implement must be carefully tested and retested before you put them in place. As you can readily imagine, any errors that occur in the course of error handling itself are virtually irrecoverable and are usually fatal to the application and the PostScript context. The more general the process being modified, the greater the potential is for disaster. An error in the procedure to support the **stopped** operator is not likely to be too much more disastrous than an error in your normal code. An error within an error handling procedure may cause total disaster if the error creates an error of the same type. But an error in the error handling procedures is almost certainly fatal since any attempt to recover from it will execute the procedure itself, and so on and on. Keep this in mind if you attempt any changes to the default error processing.

Client Library Exception Handling

All this has shown you what is possible within the PostScript environment itself. What happens if an error is not trapped at that level, but instead is reported back to the application? This is, naturally, the course taken by the default error processing: the default error processing procedures send a coded error message back to the Client Library.

Display PostScript actually defines two error handling procedures: **handleerror** and **resynchandleerror. handleerror,** the default, reports any error back to the Client Library and then terminates execution of the context in which the error occurred. In this case, there isn't much that the application can do, except report the error and either terminate itself gracefully or restart processing from the beginning again, with a new context.

The alternative error processing, **resynchandleerror,** is more interesting. In this case, processing in the context is not terminated, but is suspended. The context waits for the application to send it new commands that will resynchronize the execution of the context with the state of the application; in other words, the application can recover the processing and continue.

The context executes one or the other of these procedures when an exception occurs. The application—that is, you—determines which one to execute. The default is to execute the **handleerror** procedure. However, if you have the context execute the PostScript command **resyncstart,** the context executes the alternative **resynchandleerror.** Obviously there are several methods to do this: you can do it in a setup process; you can do it during a wrap; or you can send it individually to the context from the application.

This latter approach has much to recommend it. It makes the fact that you have executed the **resyncstart** very evident. It means that the application does not have to depend on any particular wraps being present or being run.

Absent a specific DPS or PS Client Library routine to set this up, it seems to me to be the best way to handle this particular issue.

There still must be some procedure for recognizing and dealing with the error after it comes to the Client Library to be passed to the application. The Client Library provides a general-purpose, device-independent way to recognize and respond to exceptions. To use these facilities, you must provide certain special structures in your C application code.

The basic process is to define a part of your application where you are executing the wraps and, as it were, enclose that part of the code in a special structure that allows you to be notified of any errors. You do this by invoking certain Display PostScript macros, which are defined in the library *dpsexcept.h*. The basic format of a C procedure that wishes to handle exceptions looks like this:

```
DURING
    statement;
    statement;
    statement;
    ...
HANDLER
    err_handling statement;
    err_handling statement;
    ...
END_HANDLER
```

This represents a simple schematic of how you can insert exception handling code into your C procedures. Normal execution occurs for the code between DURING and HANDLER, so all of the *statements* are executed as they would be. These are the statements that you have been seeing all along. If, and only if, an exception occurs, ordinary sequential processing is discontinued at the point of the exception and the *err_handling statements* are executed. In either case, processing continues in a normal fashion with the statements after the END_HANDLER macro.

It may, of course, happen that one of the *statements* calls another C procedure, which itself may call other C procedures and so on until one of these calls a wrap, as you have seen several times in the exercises. If an exception occurs in these circumstances, the entire stack of C procedures is interrogated, one by one. At each point, one of three things might happen:

- The procedure may ignore the exception—by not providing any exception processing—in which case the exception is passed on to the calling procedure for handling (if any).

- The procedure may handle the exception entirely by itself, either by restarting the PostScript context or by terminating it, or in any other fashion that seems appropriate. In this case, any calls to procedures below the procedure that handles the exception are terminated, and no procedure above the handling procedure is notified of the exception.
- The procedure may handle the exception and reraise it, thus propagating the exception to the next higher procedure in the calling sequence. This allows procedures above the current procedure to be notified of the exception and take additional action, if desired.

Let's consider each of these in turn. If the exception is not handled at the lower level, the exception is simply passed up the calling stack as you would expect. If one of the procedures has an exception handler, however, the exception becomes the responsibility of that procedure. The options for that procedure are, remember, limited by whether the **handleerror** or **resynchandlerror** procedures have been executed. In the first case, the context is already dead (or dying, since this is an asynchronous process). In the second case, the procedure has the option of restarting the context after some clean-up. In either case, however, the procedure is responsible for handling the situation. If the error handler simply ends, or issues a "return," the exception is not propagated to any calling procedure. If the procedure wishes to pass the error on, either because it cannot handle this specific error or because it has completed its processing, it must explicitly reraise the error.

Let's look at this in a concrete way, by examining how you might use this in the routines with which you have been working. In this situation, the error handling would be placed in the main routine that calls runPSInline. The code for this might look like this:

```
#include <dpsexcept.h>

/* after creating a context, set up exception handling */
DPSContext ctx;

ctx = GetCurrentContext();
DPSPrintf(ctx, "resyncstart\n");

DURING
    runPSInline();
```

```
HANDLER
    /* might have some specific error processing here */
    DPSResetContext(ctx);
END_HANDLER

/* and processing continues here */
```

This gives you an example of how the DURING, HANDLER, and END_HANDLER macros are used. Note first that you must include the library *dpsexcept.h* in your code, either explicitly as here, or implicitly as part of some other library or header, so that the macros expand properly. Next, you send the required **resyncstart** command to the current context. This is all similar to what you have done before, so it shouldn't be unfamiliar. Next you place the DURING macro. This sets up the processing loop for exception handling. Then you call your favorite PostScript routine, runPSInline. Now, if any wrap called by any routine within runPSInline causes an exception, you will return here, to the processing that begins with the HANDLER statement. (This assumes that none of the lower procedures themselves have exception handlers—certainly, none of those presented in the book has had them.)

The exception handler statements, after the HANDLER, might provide specific error recovery if you want. The code here has available to it two local variables: Exception.Code and Exception.Message. These may be interrogated and used to determine specific processing. In any case, as presented here, the exception handler issues a DPSResetContext, which restores the context and makes it ready for further processing. This would allow you, for example, to continue with another PostScript task for the same context, if desired. The exception handling code is terminated by the END_HANDLER statement.

The alternative would be to issue the RERAISE command. This ends the processing at the level of this exception handler and passes the exception on to the calling procedure. Once you execute the RERAISE command, the processing at this level stops, and any further recovery is the reponsibility of any handlers above you in the calling chain. RERAISE is primarily valuable in those circumstances where resources need to be recovered or other clean-up processing done, at the level of the handling procedure before returning to the calling procedure.

You should recognize certain structural restrictions here. You are not allowed to branch out of the code between the DURING and HANDLER; in particular, you cannot issue a direct exit or return command from there.

This could be a problem, but Display PostScript provides two alternatives for these. If you wish to return without any value, you should issue the E_RETURN_VOID macro; if you want to return a value, you issue E_RETURN(x), where *x* is the value that you want returned. Both of these procedures correctly reset the exception handling and perform the indicated return for you.

Obviously, more could be said about errors and exception handling, but this discussion gives you a basic overview of the process and allows you to use these features in your application code.

CONCLUSION

This concludes both this chapter and the book. Although there is certainly more to be said about and practiced in Display PostScript, this chapter has given you an overview of some of the other areas that will arise in your Display PostScript programming.

The first section dealt with several important graphics processes. The first was the concept of view clipping, which is both easy and important. The next section dealt with the related topic of hit detection in complex PostScript graphics. Both of these are important issues for you to understand, so this section of the chapter does have an extensive, if simplified, exercise associated with it.

The second subsection here also dealt with the process of the creation and description of arbitrary curved line segments. These are used in the exercise to show how the view clipping and hit detection might function in a real application environment.

The next section dealt specifically with processing general images in PostScript. These are the operations that deal with bitmapped graphics. An overview was provided for the concepts that are necessary to use these operations, including image sampling techniques and control of such images on the output device. This was followed by a short section that related these same techniques to the placement and display of Encapsulated PostScript files since these are becoming more and more prevalent in graphics work and are likely to be especially prevalent in a Display PostScript platform.

The last section discussed error handling in PostScript and, via the Client Library, in the application environment as well. These are all important and interesting topics, but there are others of equal standing. You still will want to know about file handling within your PostScript program, for example, and the new color PostScript operators. Debugging techniques and the use of multiple contexts are other topics that can be very useful in running your PostScript code and in providing multiple displays. However, you do now have a good grasp of PostScript fundamentals and should be well equipped to discover and explore these, and other, areas for yourself. Having completed this long exploration together, I am sure that you will find both pleasure and challenge in using and mastering Display PostScript.

APPENDIX A

Operator Review

This appendix reviews the operators that are presented in each chapter. You will also see definitions for some new operators when they seem to fit in naturally and when the use of the operator does not require additional explanation over and above what can be presented here. Not every possible operator appears in these reviews; only the operators used in the chapters, or operators closely associated with them, are covered.

CHAPTER 1

Mathematical Operators

These are, without doubt, the most straightforward of all the operators. PostScript supports almost every mathematical operation that you might require for page processing. The following selection of operators is those most useful in regular PostScript page descriptions.

The basic mathematical operators are:

num1 num2   **add**   sum
adds *num1* to *num2* and places the result, *sum*, back on the stack.

num1 num2   **sub**   diff
subtracts *num2* from *num1* and places the result, *diff*, back on the stack.

num1 num2   **mul**   product
multiplies *num1* by *num2* and places the result, *product*, back on the stack.

num1 num2   **div**   quotient
divides *num1* by *num2* and places the result, *quotient*, back on the stack.

The operator that affects the signs of results is:

num   **neg**   -num
reverses the sign of *num*.

The operator that makes integers of fractional results is:

num1   **round**   num2
rounds *num1* to the nearest integer, which is return to the stack as *num2*. If *num1* is equally close to its two nearest integers, the result is the greater of the two.

Graphics Operators

The two following operators were introduced and explained in the examples. They are grouped here for convenience.

string   **show**   —
paints characters of *string* on the page at the current point.

num1 num2   **moveto**   —
sets the current point to *x* coordinate *num1* and *y* coordinate *num2*.

Stack Operators

The operators that directly access or manipulate the stack are:

any1 any2 **exch**   any2 any1
exchanges top two elements on the stack.

any   **pop**   —
discards the top element on the stack.

any   **dup**   any any
duplicates top element and adds copy to top of the stack.

|- anyn   **clear** |-
empties stack.

This last operator introduces a new conventional symbol, |-, which represents the bottom of the stack.

CHAPTER 2

Dictionary Operators

int   **dict**   dict
creates a dictionary *dict* with the capacity for *int* value pairs.

dict   **begin**   —
pushes *dict* onto the dictionary stack and makes it the current dictionary.

—   **end**   —
pops the current dictionary from the dictionary stack.

key value   **def**   —
associates *key* and *value* in the current dictionary.

dict key   **undef**   —
removes *key* and its associated value from the dictionary *dict*.

Control Operators

{proc}   **exec**   —
executes *proc*.

int {proc}   **repeat**   —
executes *proc int* times.

init incr lim {proc}   **for**   —
executes *proc* for values from *init* by steps of *incr* until reaching *lim*.

bool {proc}   **if**   —
executes *proc* if *bool* is true.

bool {proc1} {proc2}   **ifelse**   —
executes *proc1* if *bool* is true; executes *proc2*, otherwise.

{proc}   **loop**   —
executes *proc* an indefinite number of times.

—   **exit**   —
terminates active loop.

Relational Operators

any1 any2   **eq**   bool
tests *any1* equal to *any2*.

any1 any2   **ne**   bool
tests *any1* not equal to *any2*.

num1 num2   **ge**   bool
(str1) (str2)   **ge**   bool
tests *num1* or *str1* greater than or equal to *num2* or *str2*.

num1 num2   **gt**   bool
(str1) (str2)   **gt**   bool
tests *num1* or *str1* greater than *num2* or *str2*.

num1 num2   **le**   bool
(str1) (str2)   **le**   bool
tests *num1* or *str1* less than or equal to *num2* or *str2*.

num1 num2   **lt**   bool
(str1) (str2)   **lt**   bool
tests *num1* or *str1* less than *num2* or *str2*.

Logical Operators

int1 int2   **and**   int
bool1 bool2   **and**   bool
logical or bitwise and.

| int1 int2 | **or** | int |
| bool1 bool2 | **or** | bool |

logical or bitwise inclusive or.

| int1 int2 | **xor** | int |
| bool1 bool2 | **xor** | bool |

logical or bitwise exclusive or.

| int | **not** | int |
| bool | **not** | bool |

logical or bitwise not.

| — | **true** | bool |

pushes boolean value *true* onto stack.

| — | **false** | bool |

pushes boolean value *false* onto stack.

State Operators

| — | **save** | savestate |

saves the current state of the PostScript virtual memory as *savestate*.

| savestate | **restore** | — |

restores PostScript virtual memory to the state indicated by *savestate*.

CHAPTER 3

Path Operators

| num1 num2 | **lineto** | — |

adds a straight line segment to the current path. The new line segments extends from the current point, (*x*, *y*), to the point (*num1*, *num2*). The current point at the end of the operation is the point (*num1*, *num2*).

| — | **newpath** | — |

initializes the current path to be empty and causes the current point to be undefined.

| — | **closepath** | — |

closes the current path by making a straight line segment from the current point to the starting point of this subpath (generally the point specified in the most recent **moveto** or **rmoveto**).

delx dely   **rmoveto**   —

moves the current point from the current point, (x, y), to the point $(x+delx, y+dely)$. Unlike the comparable **moveto** command, the current point must be defined at the beginning of the operation.

delx dely   **rlineto**   —

adds a straight line segment to the current path. The new line segments extends from the current point, (x, y), to the point $(x+delx, y+dely)$. The current point at the end of the operation is the point $(x+delx, y+dely)$.

x y rad ang1 ang2   **arc**   —

adds a curved segment to the current path, possibly preceded by a straight line segment. The curved segment is an arc of a circle drawn counterclockwise in user space, and has radius *rad* and the point (x, y) as a center. *ang1* is the angle of a vector from (x, y) with length *rad* to the beginning of the arc, and *ang2* is the angle of a vector from (x, y) with length *rad* to the end of the arc. If the current point is defined, **arc** constructs a straight line segment from the current point to the beginning of the arc.

x y rad ang1 ang2   **arc**   —

performs the same functions as **arc**, except in a clockwise direction.

x_1 y_1 x_2 y_2 rad   **arct**   —

creates a circular arc in user space of radius *rad*, tangent to the two lines defined from the current point to (x_1, y_1) and from (x_1, y_1) to (x_2, y_2). **arct** also adds a straight line segment to the current line from the current point to the beginning of the arc if the current point and the beginning of the arc are not identical.

x_1 y_1 x_2 y_2 rad   **arcto** xt_1, yt_1, xt_2, yt_2

performs the same functions as **arct**, except that it returns the four coordinates of the tangent points on the stack.

Painting Operators

num   **setgray**   —

sets the current color to a shade of gray corresponding to the value *num*, which must be between 0, corresponding to black, and 1, corresponding to white. Intermediate values correspond to proportional shades of gray.

—   **fill**   —

paints the area enclosed by the current path with the current color and clears the current path.

x y width height   **rectfill**   —

creates a path consisting of the rectangle whose bottom left corner point has coordinates (*x, y*) and whose size is *width* dimension parallel to the *x*-axis and *height* dimension parallel to the *y*-axis and fills it with the current color.

num   **setlinewidth**   —

sets the current line width to *num*. This controls the thickness of the lines painted by subsequent **stroke** operators.

—   **stroke**   —

paints a line following the current path using the current line width.

x y width height   **rectstroke**   —

creates a path consisting of the rectangle whose bottom left corner point has coordinates (*x, y*) and whose size is *width* dimension parallel to the *x*-axis and *height* dimension parallel to the *y*-axis and strokes it.

Font Operators

name   **findfont**   font

obtains the font dictionary, *font*, specified by *name*.

font scale   **scalefont**   newfont

applies *scale* to *font* to create *newfont*, whose characters are enlarged in both the *x* and *y* directions by the given scaling factor when they are output.

font   **setfont**   —

establishes *font* as the current font to be used for all subsequent character operations.

name scale   **selectfont**   —

finds the font dictionary corresponding to *name*, scales it to the size given by *scale*, and makes that scaled font dictionary the current font.

Coordinate Transformation Operators

tx ty   **translate**   —

moves the user-space origin (0, 0) to a new position with respect to the current page, while leaving the orientation of the axes and the unit length along each axis unchanged. The new origin is at the point (*tx, ty*) in the current user coordinates.

angle   **rotate**   —

turns the user-space axes counterclockwise around the current origin by *angle,* leaving the origin and the unit length along each axis unchanged.

sx sy   **scale**   —

modifies the unit lengths independently along each of the current *x-* and *y*-axes, leaving the origin and the orientation of the axes unchanged. The new units of length are *sx* times the current unit in the *x* direction, and *sy* times the current unit in the *y* direction.

Graphics State Operators

—   **gsave**   —

pushes the current graphics state onto the graphics stack, thus saving all the current state variables.

—   **grestore**   —

pops the graphics stack, thus making the state that was on the top of the stack the current graphics state and restoring all the state variables that were in effect at that time.

CHAPTER 4

String Operator

any string   **cvs**   substring

converts *any* arbitrary object into a string representation of that object and stores the result in *string,* overwriting the initial portion. The part of string taken up by the new representation is returned to the operand stack as *substring,* while any remaining part of *string* remains unchanged. If *any* is not a number, a boolean, or another string, then the value returned is the string —nostringval—.

Color Operators

red green blue   **setrgbcolor**   —

sets the values *red, green,* and *blue* as the three components of the current color in the current graphics state, according to the red-green-blue model of color. Each of these operands is a number between 0 and 1 (inclusive) that indicates the respective percentages of red, green, and blue in the current color.

hue sat bright   **sethsbcolor**   —

sets the values *hue, sat,* and *bright* as the three components of the current color in the current graphics state, according to the hue-saturation-brightness model of color. Each of these operands is a number between 0 and 1 (inclusive) that indicates the respective values for hue, saturation, and brightness in the current color

cyan magenta yellow black   **setcmykcolor**   —

sets the values *cyan, magenta, yellow,* and *black* as the four components of the current color in the current graphics state, according to the cyan-magenta-yellow-black model of color. Each of these operands is a number between 0 and 1 (inclusive) that indicates the respective percentages of cyan, magenta, yellow, and black in the current color.

Graphics State Operators

—   **gstate**   gstate

creates a new graphics state object and pushes it onto the operand stack. The value returned is a copy of the current graphics state.

gstate   **setgstate**   —

replaces the current graphics state by the graphics state represented by *gstate*. The new graphics state parameters replace all the previous values, which are discarded. The replacement does not affect the values in *gstate,* and any subsequent changes to the current state parameters are not reflected in *gstate*.

User Path Operators

userpath   **ufill**   —

interprets the user path definition *userpath* and fills the resulting path with the current color. Note that **ufill,** like all the user path operators, uses the standard *systemdict* definitions of all the operations in the user path, unaffected by any redefinitions.

userpath   **ustroke**   —

interprets the user path definition *userpath* and strokes the resulting path using the parameters of the current graphics state. Note that **ustroke,** like all the user path operators, uses the standard *systemdict* definitions of all the operations in the user path, unaffected by any redefinitions.

userpath   **uappend**   —

interprets the user path definition *userpath* and appends the resulting path to the current path. Note that **uappend,** like all the user path operators, uses the standard *systemdict* definitions of all the operations in the user path, unaffected by any redefinitions.

bool   **upath**   userpath

creates a new user path object *userpath* that is equivalent to the current path and returns it to the operand stack. The operand *bool* determines whether the resulting *userpath* is to be included in the cache or not. A value of *true* places the path into the cache, by including the **ucache** operator as the first element; a value of *false* does not include a **ucache.** The current path is unchanged at the end of this operation.

—   **ucache**   —

notifies the PostScript interpreter that the subsequent path operations, which define a user path, are to be included in the cache if not already present. This operator is optional in a user path definition, but, if present, it must be the first element in the user path definition, before the required **setbbox.**

Text Operators

textstring numarray   **xyshow**   —

prints successive characters from *textstring* in the same way as **show** would print them, but instead of moving to the end of the character after the display, it selects a pair of values out of *numarray* and uses those as the *x* and *y* displacements, in user space, of the next character origin.

textstring numarray   **xshow**   —

prints successive characters from *textstring* in the same way as **show** would print them, but instead of moving to the end of the character after the display, it selects a value out of *numarray* and uses that as the *x* displacement and 0 for the *y* displacement, in user space, of the next character origin.

textstring numarray   **yshow**   —

prints successive characters from *textstring* in the same way as **show** would print them, but instead of moving to the end of the character after the display, it selects a value out of *numarray* and uses 0 as the *x* displacement and the selected value as the *y* displacement, in user space, of the next character origin.

CHAPTER 5

Be sure to study each of these operators; in some cases, you will find that they are quite powerful and have additional capabilities that were not discussed in the text. Also, several of the operators are listed in more than one section; most notably **get, put,** and **copy.** Each of these performs somewhat different functions, depending on the nature of the operands that you give it. For that reason, I have chosen to list the operators several times, under each of the types of operand that you might be using. Note that it is the change in operand that determines how the operator's results change; there is no change in the operator itself.

Dictionary Operators

dict   **length**   int

returns *int* as the current number of (key, value) pairs in *dict*. (See **maxlength.**)

dict   **maxlength**   int

returns *int* as the maximum number of (key, value) pairs that *dict* can hold, as defined by the **dict** operator that created *dict*.

dict key   **get**   any

looks up the *key* in *dict* and returns the associated value. If *key* is not defined in *dict*, executes the error procedure **undefined.**

dict key value   **put**   —

uses *key* and *value* and stores them as a (key, value) pair into *dict*. If *key* is already present in *dict*, its associated value is replaced by the new *value*; if it is not present, **put** creates a new entry.

dict1 dict2   **copy**   dict2

copies all elements of *dict1* into *dict2*. The **length** of *dict2* must be 0; that is, *dict2* must be empty when the **copy** takes places; **copy** returns the revised *dict2* onto the stack. *dict2* must have a **maxlength** that is at least as great as the **length** of *dict1*.

Array Operators

int   **array**   array

creates *array* that initially contains *int* null objects as entries. *int* must be a nonnegative integer less than the device-dependent maximum array length.

array index	**get**	any
string index	**get**	any

looks up the *index* in *array* or *string* and returns the element identified by *index* (counting from zero). *index* must be in the range from 0 through *n*-1, where *n* is the number of elements in *array* or *string*.

array index value	**put**	—
string index value	**put**	—

stores *value* into *array* or *string* at the position identified by *index* (counting from zero). *index* must be in the range from 0 through *n*-1, where *n* is the number of elements in *array* or *string*.

array	**length**	int
string	**length**	int

returns *int* as the number of elements that makes up the value of *array* or *string*.

array1 array2	**copy**	subarray2
string1 string2	**copy**	substring2

copies all elements of *array1* or *string1* into *array2* or *string2*. The types of the two operands must be the same, that is, array or string. The length of the second operand must be at least the length of the first; **copy** returns the changed elements of the second operand onto the stack as *subarray2* or *substring2*. If the second operand is longer than the first, the remaining values are unaffected by the **copy.**

array	**aload**	$a_0...a_{n-1}$ array

successively pushes all *n* elements of *array* onto the operand stack, where *n* is the number of elements in *array*, and finally pushes *array* itself.

Font Operators

key font	**definefont**	font

registers *font* as a font dictionary associated with *key,* which is usually a name literal. **definefont** also creates an additional entry in the dictionary, whose key is **FID** and whose value is an object of type fontID; *font* must be large enough to add this entry.

font matrix	**makefont**	newfont

applies *matrix* to *font*, and produces *newfont* whose characters are transformed by the values in *matrix* when they are printed. The operator first creates a copy of *font*, then replaces the **FontMatrix** in the copy with the result of combining the original **FontMatrix** and *matrix*. The resulting *newfont* is returned to the stack.

string bool   **charpath**   —

makes character path outlines for the characters in *string* as if it were shown at the current point using **show.** These outlines are added to the current path, and form shapes suitable for general filling, stroking, or clipping. If *bool* is true, the resulting path is suitable for filling or clipping; if *bool* is false, the result is suitable for stroking. This distinction only affects stroked fonts (**PaintType** 1); when the current font is an outline font (**PaintType** 0 or 2), the results will be identical.

Other Operators

$any_1...any_{int}$ int   **copy** $any_1...any_{int}$ $any_1...any_{int}$

when the top element on the operand stack is a nonnegative integer *int*, **copy** pops *int* and then duplicates the top *int* elements of the operand stack.

$any_{n-1}...any_0$ n int   **roll** $any_{int-1}...any_0$ $any_{n-1}...any_{int}$

performs a circular shift of the contents of the operand stack. The top *n* objects on the stack are shifted by the amount *int*. A positive value of *int* indicates movement up the stack, that is, toward the top of the stack; a negative value indicates movement down the stack. The operand *n* must be a nonnegative integer, and there must be at least *n* elements on the stack below the top two operands.

int1 int2   **idiv**   result

divides *int1* by *int2* and returns the integer portion of the quotient as *result*; any remainder is discarded. Both operands must be integers, and the result is an integer.

CHAPTER 6

View Clip Operators

—   **viewclip**   —

replaces the current view clipping path with the current path in the current graphics state. After setting the view clipping path, the current path is undefined.

x y width height   **rectviewclip**   —

replaces the current view clipping path with the rectangular path described by the operands. The path of the rectangle begins at the point (*x, y*) and extends for *width* distance parallel to the *x*-axis and *height* distance parallel to the *y*-axis, all in the current user coordinate system. The result of using **rectviewclip** is exactly identical to constructing the rectangle described by the operands and then invoking the **viewclip** operator.

Display Operators

x y   **infill**   bool

returns the boolean result *true* if the point (*x, y*) in user space would be painted by a **fill** of the current path in the current graphics state; otherwise, it returns *false*.

x y   **instroke**   bool

returns the boolean result *true* if the point (*x, y*) in user space would be painted by a **stroke** of the current path in the current graphics state; otherwise, it returns *false*.

x y userpath   **inufill**   bool

returns the boolean result *true* if the point (*x, y*) in user space would be painted by a **ufill** of the *userpath*; otherwise, it returns *false*. Except for the manner of determining the path, **inufill** behaves in the same manner as **infill.**

x y userpath   **inustroke**   bool

returns the boolean result *true* if the point (*x, y*) in user space would be painted by a **ustroke** of the *userpath*; otherwise, it returns *false*. Except for the manner of determining the path, **inustroke** behaves in the same manner as **instroke.**

Path Operators

$dx_1, dy_1, dx_2, dy_2, ax_2, ay_2$ **curveto**   —

adds a curved line segment, described by a pair of Bézier cubic equations, to the current path. The curve begins from the current point, which is called the first *anchor point,* with the coordinates (ax_1, ay_1), to the second anchor point, whose coordinates are given by the operand values (ax_2, ay_2). The shape of the curve between the two anchor points is determined by two additional points, called *direction points,* whose coordinates are given by the operands (dx_1, dy_1) and (dx_2, dy_2). The entire curved segment lies within the box connecting these four points.

mvproc lnproc cvproc csproc   **pathforall**   —

enumerates all the elements of the current path, using the procedure operand *mvproc* to process any **moveto** or equivalent operation, the procedure operand *lnproc* to process any **lineto** or equivalent operation, the procedure operand *cvproc* to process any **curveto** or equivalent operation, and the procedure *csproc* to process any **closepath** operations. Each procedure operand is called with the appropriate coordinates for the associated operation, based on the current element of the current path being enumerated.

Graphics State Operator

array offset   **setdash**   —

sets the current dash setting in the current graphics state according to the *array* and *offset* operands. The current dash pattern is defined by the *array*, which consists of nonnegative numbers that represent the alternating length of dashes and spaces along the path to be stroked, and the *offset*, which is the starting point of the dash pattern along the line. An empty array, [], generates a solid line.

Painting Operators

width height samp matrix proc   **image**   —

renders a sampled image onto the current page. The image is produced by translating streams of data that are presented to the **image** operator as a binary representation of a sampled image. The sampled image consists of a rectangular array of sample points that exist in their own coordinate system. This rectangle is defined to be *width* columns of samples wide and *height* rows of samples high. Each sample point consists of *samp* bits of data, where *samp* may be 1, 2, 4, or 8. The data are presented to the **image** operator as a string of character data that is interpreted as a series of binary integers, grouped according to *samp* to form the sample values. The string of character data is produced by *proc,* which may get the data from any source but must leave it on the operand stack as a string. **image** uses these data to fill out the image rectangle, beginning at point (0, 0) in the image coordinate system and continuing to the point (*width*-1, *height*-1). If the number of values presented on the operand stack is not sufficient to fill the image rectangle, **image** calls *proc* repeatedly until enough values have been presented and processed.

However, if *proc* returns an empty string to the operand stack, processing is terminated at that point. If there are any values left on the operand stack after the image rectangle is filled, they are ignored.

width height invert matrix proc   **imagemask**   —

renders an image onto the current page using the source data as a mask of 1-bit samples that govern where to apply paint (in the current color) onto the page. The source data consist of a rectangular array of sample points that exist in their own coordinate system. The coordinates and the mapping of this rectangle onto the user coordinate system follow the same system used by the **image** operator, and the operands *width, height,* and *matrix* all have the same functions. Since **imagemask** always uses 1 bit per sample, there is no need for a *samp* operand; instead, the *invert* operand is inserted. The *invert* is a boolean value that governs the polarity of the mask. If *invert* is true, sample values of 1 allow paint to be applied to the page, while values of 0 mask the page, leaving anything underneath them unchanged. If *invert* is false, the reverse applies, with values of 0 allowing paint to be applied and values of 1 becoming the mask. Finally, the *proc* operand is required to provide the sample data to be processed by **imagemask.** The purpose and operation of *proc* is identical to that under **image.**

Stack Operator

any_n...any_0 n   **index** any_n...any_0 any_n

takes the nonnegative integer *n* as a pointer into the operand stack, and retrieves the *n*th object on the stack, counting the top element as 0. This object is duplicated and placed on the top of the operand stack.

Matrix Transformation Operators

—   **matrix**   matrix

generates an identity six-element tranformation matrix and places it onto the operand stack. The identity transformation matrix is a six-element array with the value [1.0 0.0 0.0 1.0 0.0 0.0]; if this array is applied to any transformation matrix, the resulting transformation is identical to the original matrix.

sx sy matrix   **scale**   matrix

modifies the elements of *matrix* in the same way that the current transformation matrix (CTM) would be modified and returns the modified matrix to the operand stack. The new units of length in the modified matrix are *sx* times the current unit in the *x* direction, and *sy* times the current unit in the *y* direction. This operation does not affect the CTM.

tx ty matrix   **translate**   matrix

modifies the elements of *matrix* in the same way that the current transformation matrix (CTM) would be modified and returns the modified matrix to the operand stack. The origin (0, 0) of the modified matrix is translated to a new position with respect to the original matrix. The new origin is at the point (*tx, ty*) in the previous matrix coordinates. This operation does not affect the CTM.

angle matrix   **rotate**   matrix

modifies the elements of *matrix* in the same way that the current transformation matrix (CTM) would be modified and returns the modified matrix to the operand stack. This effectively turns the coordinate axes represented by *matrix* counterclockwise around the present origin by *angle*. This operation does not affect the CTM.

Control Operators

any   **stopped**   bool

executes *any*, which is typically a procedure, but may be any executable object. If *any* runs to normal completion, the operator returns the boolean value *false* on the stack. In any other case, the operator returns *true*. Execution always continues with the next object in normal sequence.

—   **stop**   —

terminates execution of the currently active instance of a stopped context, which is a procedure or other executable object invoked by a **stopped** operator. **stop** terminates all processing within the invoked procedure. The interpreter then pushes the boolean value *true* onto the operand stack and resumes execution with the next intruction after the **stopped.** This has the effect of making the **stopped** operator appear to report an abnormal termination of the procedure that it was executing.

APPENDIX B

Specific Implementations

This appendix provides a guide to two specific implementations of Display PostScript: on the NeXT computer and as an option in the DECwindows environment. In both cases, the example code shown is intended simply to allow you to run the exercises and examples in the body of this book.

Since this is a book about Display PostScript, and not about the NeXT or DEC systems, we will not discuss the actual code presented in any detail. If you have any questions about how this code works, you should be able to find the information in your system references without too much trouble. I refer you to those manuals for a more complete explanation of how the following code works.

For the same reasons, we will not discuss how to create, compile, or link these modules. In all cases, the code uses standard C conventions, or conventions that are standard in the device environment, for all calls and references.

In both cases, the code shown here was modified and adapted from existing example code that was provided with each system. As I am by no means expert in either system, and since both systems were as yet unreleased when I tested on them, there may well be portions of the code shown here that are not essential to the task at hand, or that are no longer required or even desirable. Nevertheless, the code examples here are sufficiently short that the general requirements in each system should be easy to construct, even with any changes.

DECWINDOWS

We begin with the code required to execute a Display PostScript routine in the DECwindows environment. Because the DEC system uses a relatively standard implementation of display technology, based on UNIX, C, the X Windows standard, and Display PostScript, this is the environment that is most like a "typical" Display PostScript implementations. You should be aware that, unlike the NeXT system, Display PostScript is an additional feature and is not automatically part of every DECwindows system. However, with that caution, I used the following code to test the book procedures on the DECwindows system.

```
#include <stdio.h>
#include <dpsXclient.h>
#include <strings.h>

#include "Xlib.h"
#include "XDPSlib.h"

#define WIDTH  500
#define HEIGHT 500


main (argc, argv)
int argc;
char **argv;
{
```

```
Display *dpy;
DPSContext ctx;
XEvent ev;
long mask;
Window win;
XSetWindowAttributes xswa;

dpy = InitializeDisplay(argc, argv);

win = XCreateSimpleWindow(dpy, DefaultRootWindow(dpy),
                10, 20, WIDTH, HEIGHT, 1,
                BlackPixel(dpy, DefaultScreen(dpy)),
                WhitePixel(dpy, DefaultScreen(dpy)));

xswa.bit.gravity = SouthWestGravity;
xswa.backing.store = WhenMapped;
mask = CWBitGravity | CWBackingStore;
XChangeWindowAttributes(dpy, win, mask, &xswa);
XMapWindow(dpy, win);

ctx = InitializePostScript(dpy, win);

while (1)
{
    mask = (1<<0) | (1<<dpy->fd);
    XFlush(dpy);
    select(dpy->fd+1, &mask, NULL, NULL, NULL);

    if (mask & (1<<0))
    {
        DPSSetContext(ctx);
        runPSInline();
        DPSFlushContext(ctx);
    }
    while (XPending(dpy) > 0)
    {
        /* there are no events we care about */
        XNextEvent(dpy, &ev);
    }
}
```

```
        XFlush(dpy);
}


    Display *InitializeDisplay(argc, argv)
    int argc;
    char **argv;
    {
        Display *dpy;
        char *displayname = " ";
        int i;
        int sync = 0;

        for (i=1 ; i<argc ; i++)
        {
            if (strncmp(argv[i], "-display", strlen(argv[i])) == 0)
            {
                i++;
                displayname = argv[i];
            }
            else if (strncmp(argv[i], "-sync", strlen(argv[i])) == 0)
            {
                sync = 1;
            }
            else
            {
                fprintf(stderr, "usage: %s [-display displayname]\n", argv[0]);
                exit(1);
            }
        }

        dpy = XOpenDisplay(displayname);
        if (dpy == NULL)
        {
            fprintf(stderr, "%s: Can't open display %s.\n", argv[0],
displayname);
            exit(1);
        }

        if (sync)
```

```
        (void) XSynchronize(dpy, True);
}


DPSContext InitializePostScript(dpy, window)
Display *dpy;
Window window;
{
    DPSContext ctx;
    char *rec;

    ctx = XDPSCreateSimpleContext(dpy,window, DefaultGC(dpy, 0),0,
            HEIGHT,  TextOut, DPSDefaultErrorProc, NULL);

    if (ctx == NULL)
    {

        printf("Server does not have PostScript extension.");
        exit(2);
    }

    XDPSRegisterStatusProc(ctx, HandleStatus);

    return ctx;
}


static void TextOut(ctx, buffer, count)
DPSContext ctx;
char *buffer;
unsigned count;
{
    fwrite(buffer, 1, count, stdout);
    fflush(stdout);
}


static void HandleStatus(ctx, status)
DPSContext ctx;
int status;
{
```

```c
    char *ptr, buf[1000];
    switch (status)
    {
        case PSRUNNING:
            ptr = "running"; break;

        case PSNEEDSINPUT:
            ptr = "needs input"; break;

        case PSZOMBIE:
            ptr = "zombie"; break;

        case PSFROZEN:
            ptr = "frozen"; break;

        default:
            ptr = "unknown status"; break;
    }

    frpintf(stderr, "[Status event - %s]\n", ptr);

    if (status == PSFROZEN)
    {
        fprintf(stderr, "Hit CR to continue: ");
        fflush(stderr);
        fgets(buf, 1000, stdin);
        XDPSUnfreezeContext(ctx);
    }
}
```

This code consists of three simple layers of procedures. The first layer is the main procedure, which actually runs the Display PostScript module runPSInline. It uses two auxiliary procedures that form the second layer: InitializeDisplay and InitializePostScript. Each performs the function suggested by its name. The InitializePostScript procedure uses two further auxiliary procedures that form the third level in this program. These are TextOut and HandleStatus. The TextOut procedure provides a default method for the context to process text messages that are returned to the application. Most Display PostScript context creation procedures (which are always environment-specific) include some such requirement. The HandleStatus procedure provides a way of handling abnormal status situations in the context. Procedures that begin with "XDPS" are specific to the DECwindows environment and are defined and discussed in the system reference materials that are provided with your system.

NeXT

The NeXT system environment is quite different from the DEC, or any other system with which I am familiar for that matter. These differences stem from three major factors in the NeXT system design. First, the NeXT system uses an Interface Builder to generate windows and the resulting methods and objects that handle them. Second, the NeXT system is object-oriented and uses Objective-C as its programming language. Third, the NeXT system has a number of extensions to its Display PostScript language that are both useful and desirable in the NeXT environment but which are not usable in any other environment.

The following code was primarily generated by the Interface Builder as a result of creating a simple Custom View graphics window, called PSOutput. The menu was modified to contain the two entries Draw and Clear. drawWindow and clearWindow methods were added to the PSOutput subclass. The code was then added to and modified as is described in the NeXT IB tutorial materials. The result is a simple application that just displays the example code in the desired window. Here are the code modules.

```
/* Generated by the Interface Builder */

#import <appkit/View.h>

@interface PSOutput:View
{
    BOOL DrawSwitch;
}

-drawWindow:sender;
-clearWindow:sender;

-drawSelf:(NXRect *)r:(int)count;
-runPSInline:sender;

@end
```

```
/* Generated by the Interface Builder */

#import "PSOutput.h"

@implementation PSOutput

-drawWindow:sender
{
    DrawSwitch = YES;
    [self display];
    return self;
}

-clearWindow:sender
{
    DrawSwitch = NO;
    [self display];
    return self;
}

-drawSelf:(NXRect *)r:(int)count
{
    PSsetgray(NX_LTGRAY);
    PSrectfill(bounds.origin.x, bounds.origin.y, bounds.size.width,
            bounds.size.height);
    if (DrawSwitch)
        runPSInline;

    return self;
}

-runPSInline:sender
{
    /* insert runPSInline example code here */

    return self;
}

@end
```

This approach uses the menu buttons to send messages to the application either to display the graphics generated by runPSInline or to erase the window. The code shown uses the single-operator Display PostScript calls to erase the window every time, and then executes runPSInline if Draw was pressed.

In the NeXT environment, it is not necessary to create or define a context to be associated with the display. Since Display PostScript is the exclusive output method in the NeXT, the system automatically associates a context with every application. In this case, the application was generated from the Interface Builder, using the standard display and project tools. Notice in the preceding code that runPSInline has become an Objective-C method, and so has a slightly different structure than that shown in the text.

One thing not shown here, but which you must remember, is to include the wrap names in your project file in the Interface Builder. If you don't, the wraps will not be compiled with your project and the application will not run.

INDEX

%%[, as error message delimiters, 103
%, as comment indicator, 49, 83
:, as current point marker, 40
;, separating argument names, 106
< >, as hexadecimal string delimiters, 86, 341
{ }, as procedure delimiters, 83, 93
[ ], as array delimiters, 83, 87, 293
, (comma), separating argument names, 106
( )
    as procedure declaration delimiters, 105
    as string delimiters, 35, 49, 83
", as string constant identifier, 35
\, in strings, 85–86, 256–257
– (minus), 142
+, 142–143
/, as name literal indicator, 51, 65, 67, 83
– (dash), as no-operand/result indicator, 47–48

A

add, 43–48, 68, 370
Adobe Type library fonts, 257, 262, 307
aload, 298, 380
alpha value, 155
anchor point, 316
and, 98, 372
angle brackets (<>), as hexadecimal string delimiters, 86, 341

ANSI standard formats, 12
arc, 170–173, 184, 374
arcn, 173–174, 177
arct, 178–184, 374
arcto, 374
arguments, 106
array, 88, 379
array objects, 91, 93
array operators
    aload, 298, 380
    array, 88, 379
    copy, 298, 380
    get, 300, 380
    length, 298, 380
    put, 380
arrays
    bracket delimiters for, 83, 87, 93
    comparing in PostScript, 97
    described, 87–88
    executable (procedures), 83
    in PostScript wrap arguments, 107, 355
ascender, 166
ASCII
    in PostScript notation, 16, 82
    and transmission of special characters, 256
aspect ratio, 215

axes. *See* coordinates

B

backslash (\), in strings, 85–86, 256–257
baseline (of fonts), 165
begin, 66, 238, 260, 268–269, 371
binary devices, 338
binary object sequence encoding, 17
binary token encoding, 16–17
bitmapped fonts, 274–275, 308
bitmapping, 340
bits per sample, 340–341
black fill-ins, 149–151
bold font style, 165
bool, 95, 96, 98–99
boolean objects, 89–90
boolean wrap arguments, 106
bounding box, 217, 252, 261, 272, 320
braces ({ }), as procedure delimiters, 83, 93
brackets ([]), as array delimiters, 83, 87, 293
branching in PostScript, 94
BuildChar (font dictionary key), 263–264, 308
bullets or open circles, 308
business check design exercise, 208–245
business report exercise, 107–123

C

C language programs
    calling Display PostScript procedures from, 50–51, 57–58
    and error handling, 357–358, 364
    integrating with Display PostScript, 104–107, 245–252, 320, 321
    in PostScript environment, 14, 15, 16, 17, 19, 44, 46
    and required familiarity with, 7
    and this book's coding examples in, 10
The C Programming Language, 12
caching
    of fonts, 274, 275, 306–307
    of user paths, 252
capitalization of names, 80
case sensitivity of names, 64, 79
centering strings, 114
character coordinate system, 271
character metrics, 111, 270–272
character origin, 271
characters. *See also* fonts; strings; text
    modifying, 285
charpath, 381
CharStrings (font dictionary key), 262, 286
check design exercise, 208–245
circles, drawing, 169–173
clear, 371
Client Library
    accessing, 104

and contexts, 125
described, 17, 26
exception handling, 107, 361, 363–367
header files for, 38
clip, 157–159, 346
clipping, 156–162
clipping path, current, 135, 194, 195, 312
clipping paths, 156–162, 312
clipping region, 156
closed paths, 144–149
closepath, 145–149, 373
colon (:), as current point marker, 40
color operators, 376–377
colors
    applying through masks, 348
    for sampled images, 337–338
commas (,), separating argument names, 106
comments. *See also* Display PostScript program exercises
    in C-embedded PostScript wraps, 106
    percent sign indicator for, 83–84
    in PostScript programs, 49
    sending through to interpreter, 106
comparisons, 97
composite characters, 301
composite objects, 91–93, 297
conclusions sections of this book, 10
condensed fonts, 305–306
constants, string, 35
context, current, 125, 195
contexts
    current, 125
    defined, 34
    execution, 124
    handling, 128
    identifiers for, 130
    and standard error procedures, 360, 363
    stopped, 359
control operators
    exec, 94, 96, 371
    exit, 95, 372
    for, 94, 96, 281, 332, 358–359, 372
    if, 95–96, 372
    ifelse, 95–96, 296–297, 372
    loop, 95, 372
    repeat, 94, 96, 299, 371
    stop, 362, 385
    stopped, 282, 359–361, 385
coordinate transformation operators
    rotate, 187, 376
    scale, 187, 192, 197, 237, 376
    translate, 187–190, 375
coordinates
    described, 30–32, 135
    in image sampling, 341
    of mouse position, 313–315

rotating, 190–194
selecting, 52–53, 122–123
transforming, 185–190
of windows, 33, 40
copy (as array operator), 298, 380
copy (as dictionary operator), 379
copy (as stack operator), 381
Courier font, 36, 162, 165
CTM (current transformation matrix), 186, 345
curly brackets. *See* braces ({ })
current clipping path, 135, 194, 195, 312
current context, 125, 195
current dictionary, 65
current fonts, 168, 194, 195, 266
current page, 27–28, 135, 194, 195
current path, 28–29, 135, 194, 195
current point, 28, 36, 194, 195
current transformation matrix (CTM), 186, 345
currentdict, 65
currentfont, 266
currentpoint, 282
cursor, locating, 313–315
curves, 169–184, 315–336. *See also* lines
curveto, 29, 316, 382–383
cvrs, 284
cvs, 232, 376

D

data requirements analysis (in business check design exercise), 221–223
ddd character code, 85–86, 256–257, 283
debugging, 107. *See also* errors
DECwindows environments, Display PostScript on, 387–393
def, 68, 100–101, 260, 371
default dictionaries, 65–66
default system, 185, 194
default user space, 30–31, 185
definefont, 261, 380
defineps, as wrap indicator, 51, 105
descender, 166
device classification, 22–23
device resolution, 21–22, 185
device space, 185
device-independence, of PostScript, 17–18, 25, 26
dict, 66, 294, 371
dictionaries
    current, 65
    default, 65–66
    described, 64–66
    font, 166–167, 258–270
    and the interpreter, 67–69
    and names/objects, 25
    private, 251–252, 323
    removing keys/values from, 127
    search sequence of, 67–68

using, 66–69
dictionary objects, 66, 91, 93
dictionary operators
    begin, 66, 238, 260, 268–269, 371
    copy, 379
    def, 68, 100–101, 260, 371
    dict, 66, 294, 371
    end, 66, 260, 371
    get, 379
    length, 379
    maxlength, 294, 379
    put, 294–296, 379
    undef, 127–128, 371
dictionary stack, 41, 65
dinner menu programming exercise, 287–301
display operators
    infill, 314–315, 382
    instroke, 314–315, 382
    inufill, 315, 382
    inustroke, 315, 333, 382
Display PostScript. *See also* Client Library; coordinates; graphics operations; PostScript; windows; wraps
    in DECwindows environments, 387–393
    described, 1–4
    efficient coding in, 245–253
    error handling, 67, 102–103, 107, 357–367
    imaging model, 134–135
    on NeXT systems, 8, 14, 23–24, 32, 155, 387, 393–395
    and purpose of this book, 4–12
    resource management, 123–130
    speed of, 15
    structure and style recommendations, 15, 76–81, 95–96, 108, 245–252, 329, 332
    and your system, 7, 11–12
Display PostScript program exercises. *See also* errors; wraps
    arcs and circles, 171–184
    business check design, 208–245
        application integration, 245–251
        blank form creation, 221–240, 250–251
        objectives, 208, structure, 209–221
        text entry, 241–245
        use of form sets, 251–252
    business report, 107–123
    clipping paths, 157–162
    coordinate transformation and rotation, 187–194
    curves, 315–336
    extended/condensed fonts, 303–306
    font information access, 267–270
    food and wine menu, 287–301
    independent graphics objects, 196–199
    line drawing, 136–144
    logo creation, 199–204
    StandardEncoding array display, 276–285

Index   399

text, strings, and comments, 37–40, 51–61, 69–76
Display PostScript System Reference Manual, 8
div, 43, 299, 370
dot-matrix printers, 22
dots, drawing, 325
dots per inch (dpi), 22
DPS prefix, 81, 130
dpsclient.h, 104, 129
dpsexcept.h, 104, 129, 364, 366
dpsfriends.h, 104, 129
dpsops.h, 104, 129
drawing
    curves, 169–184, 315–336
    dots, 325
    lines, 136–144
    squares and rectangles, 146–149
    triangles, 149
dup, 296, 321, 371

E

efficiency, programming techniques for, 245–253
Encapsulated PostScript (EPS), 252, 351–356
encoding, of PostScript, 16–17
Encoding (font dictionary key), 261, 265, 286, 309
end, 66, 260, 371
endps, as wrap terminator, 51, 105
Enter key (return), 82
EPS (Encapsulated PostScript), 252, 351–356
eq, 96–98, 372
equality, testing for, 96–98
$error dictionary, 102, 360
errordict, 102, 360
errors
    Client Library exception handling, 107, 363–367
    in dictionary lookups, 67
    operators for, 358–363
    processing of, 102–103, 107
    recommendations for handling, 357–358, 362
event sequencing, 249
examples and exercises. *See* Display PostScript program exercises
exceptions. *See also* errors
    Client Library handling of, 363–367
    defined, 107, 358
exch, 73, 296, 371
exec, 94, 96, 371
execution contexts, 124–125
execution stack, 41
exit, 95, 372
Extensions for the Display PostScript System, 125, 186

F

false, 99, 239, 373
false/true values, 89–90, 98, 296
families of fonts, 165
FamilyName (font dictionary key), 264
feedback, PostScript's ability to provide, 15
FID (font dictionary key), 261, 296
file extensions
    as used in wraps names, 59
    .psw, 50, 105
file objects, 90
files, described, 90
fill, 27, 150–151, 155, 247, 374
findfont, 36, 167–168, 258, 265, 268, 375
floating-point numbers, 89
font bounding box, 261
font cache, 274, 275, 306–307
font dictionaries, 166–167, 258–270
font encoding, 272–285
font families, 165
font metrics, 111–114, 165, 250, 257, 301–306
font operators
    charpath, 381
    definefont, 261, 380
    findfont, 36, 167–168, 258, 265, 268, 375
    makefont, 302–303, 380–381
    scalefont, 36, 167–168, 258, 266, 301–302, 375
    selectfont, 36, 48, 167–168, 247, 258–259, 305, 375
    setfont, 36, 167–168, 239, 258, 266, 375
font tuning, 164
FontBBox (font dictionary key), 261
FontDirectory, 260–261, 265
fontID objects, 91
FontInfo (font dictionary key), 262, 264
FontMatrix (font dictionary key), 261–262, 265, 302, 306
FontName (font dictionary key), 262, 266, 269
fonts
    bitmapped, 274–275, 308
    caching of, 274, 275, 306–307
    character metrics for, 270–272
    condensed and narrow, 305–306
    creating and modifying, 256–258, 285–306, 307–309
    current, 168, 194, 195, 266
    described, 162–165
    dictionary entries for, 260–270
    and font encoding, 272–285
    and font metrics, 111–114, 165, 250, 257, 301–306
    leading of, 52–53, 248–249, 285, 293
    measuring, 111–114
    monospaced and proportional, 165
    multiple, 306–307
    outline, 167, 274
    in PostScript, 36, 166–167, 256–260, 305–306
    screen, 275
    specifying, 36, 167–168, 248–249, 306–307

stroked, 274
styles and sizes of, 165–166, 305–306
FontType (font dictionary key), 262, 308
food and wine menu programming exercise, 287–301
for, 94, 96, 281, 332, 358–359, 372
forall, 294–295
form sets, 251–252
full gray-scale devices, 338
FullName (font dictionary key), 264
function calls, 26, 39

G

garbage collection, 126
ge, 98, 372
geometric shapes, drawing. *See* graphics operations
get, 300, 379, 380
graphic objects
    in business check design exercise, 234–235, 252
    described, 19–23, 196–199
graphic orientation (of PostScript), 18–19
graphics operations. *See also* text
    clipping, 156–162
    drawing curves, 169–184, 315–336
    drawing dots, 325
    drawing lines, 136–144
    drawing squares and rectangles, 146–149
    drawing triangles, 149
    placing EPS graphics, 351–356
    sampled image display, 337–351
    shading, 149–156
graphics operators
    moveto, 370
    show, 27, 35, 36, 40, 48, 52, 135, 272–274, 370
graphics state, 194–199
graphics state operators
    grestore, 195–198, 354, 376
    gsave, 195–198, 235, 354, 376
    gstate, 195, 235, 377
    setdash, 324, 383
    setgstate, 239, 377
graphics state stack, 41
gray fill-ins, 152–155
gray-scale devices, 338
greater/less than symbols. *See* angle brackets (<>)
grestore, 195–198, 354, 376
gsave, 195–198, 235, 354, 376
gstate, 195, 235, 377
gstate objects, 91, 195
gt, 98, 372

H

handleerror, 103, 361–363
header files
    in business check design exercise, 230
    dpsclient.h, 104, 129

dpsexcept.h, 104, 129, 364, 366
dpsfriends.h, 104, 129
dpsops.h, 104, 129
psops.h, 26, 37, 104, 129
Helvetica font, 36
hexadecimal strings, 86, 341
high-level page description, 2

I

idiv, 299, 381
if, 95–96, 372
ifelse, 95–96, 296–297, 372
image, 28, 343–348, 351, 383–384
image space, 341
imageable area, 156
imagemask, 343, 348–351, 384
images
    displaying, 337–343
    and EPS graphics, 351–356
    as masks, 348–351
    processing operators for, 343–348
imaging model, of Display PostScript, 134–135
index, 384
inequality, testing for, 96–98
infill, 314–315, 382
input arguments, for wraps, 106
instroke, 314–315, 382
integer objects, 89
integers, in PostScript wrap arguments, 106
interpreter
    and control of current state variables, 194
    described, 2, 14–15, 26–27
    and dictionaries, 67–69
    and error processing, 358–361
    importance of minimizing use of, 246–248
    sending comments through to, 106
inufill, 315, 382
inustroke, 315, 333, 382
IsFixedPitch (font dictionary key), 264
italic font style, 165
ItalicAngle (font dictionary key), 264

J

justifying, strings, 114

K

keys
    defined, 64, 66, 259–260
    placing in dictionaries, 66
    in PostScript font dictionaries, 261–264

L

landscape/portrait modes, 186–187
Language Reference Manual, 8, 309
layouts, for business check design exercise, 214–221

le, 98, 372
leading, 52–53, 248–249, 285, 293
leftside bearing, 272
length, 298, 379, 380
less/greater than symbols. *See* angle brackets (<>)
line operators, 136–144
lines. *See also* graphics operations
    drawing, 136–144
lineto, 29, 137, 143, 146, 373
literals, as objects, 25
load, 69
logical operators
    and, 98, 372
    false, 99, 239, 373
    not, 98–99, 373
    or, 99, 373
    true, 99, 373
    xor, 99, 373
logos, 199–204, 216–217
loop, 95, 372
lt, 98, 372

M

macros, for exception handling, 364
make (function), 59, 105
makefont, 302–303, 380–381
mapping
    of color values, 338
    of images, 342–343
margins, calculating, 123
mark objects, 87, 91
masks, images as, 348–351
mathematical characters, font for, 36
mathematical operations
    necessity for, 134
    sequencing of, 43–46
mathematical operators
    add, 43–48, 68, 370
    div, 43, 299, 370
    idiv, 299, 381
    mul, 43–48, 101, 370
    neg, 143, 370
    round, 370
    sub, 43–48, 370
matrix, 345, 384
matrix transformation operators
    matrix, 345, 384
    rotate, 385
    scale, 353, 356, 384–385
    translate, 353, 356, 385
maxlength, 294, 379
memory. *See also* stacks
    and composite objects, 91–92
    in execution contexts, 124
    private and shared virtual, 124, 126–128
    recovery of, 126–128

metrics (font), 111–114, 165, 250, 257, 270–272, 301–306
Metrics (font dictionary key), 262
minus sign (–), 142
monospaced fonts, 165
mouse, 312, 314, 330
moveto, 29, 39, 40, 48, 52, 370, 374
mul, 43–48, 101, 370

N

name literals, 51, 64–65, 83–84
name objects, 90
names
    defined, 64
    as objects, 25, 64
    selecting, 77–81
narrow fonts, 305–306
ne, 96–97, 296, 372
neg, 143, 370
negative movement, 142–143
negative numbers, 44, 45, 142–143
nesting (of procedures), 77
newline (return or linefeed indicator), 82
newpath, 29, 137, 144, 373
next character origin, 271
NeXT systems
    color management on, 155
    Display PostScript on, 8, 14, 387, 393–395
    screen management example on, 23–24, 32
nominal objects, 90–91
not, 98–99, 373
/.notdef, 273, 282
Notice (font dictionary key), 264, 270
null objects, 88, 91
numeric objects, 89

O

objects
    described, 25, 82
    in dictionaries, 66
    types of, 88–89
    undefining, 126
oblique font style, 165
octal values of characters, 256–257, 283–284
offset, 324
operand stack, 41, 42, 65–66
operands, 26
operator objects, 90
operators
    array, 88, 298, 379, 380
    color, 376–377
    control. *See* control operators
    coordinate transformation, 186–194, 197, 237, 375–376
    described, 18–19, 26
    dictionary. *See* dictionary operators

display, 314–315, 333, 382
font. *See* font operators
graphics. *See* graphics operators
graphics state. *See* graphics state operators
and the interpreter, 67
line, 136–144
logical, 98–99, 239, 372–373
mathematical, 43–48, 68, 101, 143, 299, 370, 381
matrix transformation, 345, 353, 356, 384–385
miscellaneous, 381
painting. *See* painting operators
path. *See* path operators
as presented in this book, 47–48
relational, 96–98, 296, 372
stack. *See* stack operators
state, 126–128, 354, 373
string, 232, 234, 284, 376, 377
text, 28, 250, 251, 378
user path. *See* user path operators
view clip, 313, 327, 381–382
for windows, 33
or, 99, 373
origin (in coordinate system), 30, 135, 187–188, 271
outline fonts, 167, 274
outline rectangle, 215
output, programming example, 37–40
output arguments, for wraps, 106
output devices, raster, 20–22
output structure, 26–30, 134–135

P

page
    current, 27–28, 135, 194, 195
    described, 27
page-description language, Postscript as, 2
painting operators
    fill, 27, 150–151, 155, 247, 374
    image, 28, 343–348, 351, 383–384
    imagemask, 343, 348–351, 384
    rectfill, 151, 153, 156, 177, 194, 247, 375
    rectstroke, 148–149, 151, 169–170, 177, 375
    setgray, 153–155, 167, 374
    setlinewidth, 137–138, 143, 375
    stroke, 27, 137, 143, 247, 375
PaintType (font dictionary key), 262–263, 265
parameters, 169
parentheses (())
    as procedure declaration delimiters, 105
    as string delimiters, 35, 49, 83
path operators
    arc, 170–173, 184, 374
    arct, 178–184, 374
    arcto, 374
    clip, 157–159, 346
    closepath, 145–149, 373

curveto, 29, 316, 382–383
lineto, 29, 137, 143, 146, 373
moveto, 29, 39, 40, 48, 52, 374
newpath, 29, 137, 144, 373
pathforall, 334, 383
rectclip, 160–161, 177
rlineto, 29, 142, 144, 374
rmoveto, 142, 144, 148
pathbox, 321
pathforall, 334, 383
paths
    clipping, 156–162
    closed, 144–149
    current, 28–29, 135, 194, 195
    current clipping, 135, 194, 195, 312
    and subpaths, 28, 146
    user, 30, 235–236, 252
    view clipping, 312, 329
pause, of display, 37
percent sign (%), as comment indicator, 49, 83
percent sign/bracket (%%[ ]%%), as error message delimiters, 103
pie charts, drawing, 174–177
pitch, 165
pixel, 21
plus sign (+), 142–143
point, current, 28, 36, 194, 195
point (measurement in printing), 31
point size (of type), 52, 166, 293
pop, 297, 371
portrait/landscape modes, 186–187
post-fix notation, 45–46
PostScript. *See also* C language; comments; Display PostScript; errors; graphics operations
    basic concepts of, 25–33
    described, 1–2, 4, 14–20, 25–27
    device-independence of, 17–18, 25, 26
    dynamicism of, 15–16
    efficient use of in Display PostScript, 246–248
    as encoded language, 16–17
    and graphic objects, 19–23
    graphic orientation of, 18–19, 134–135
    as interpreted language, 14–15
    language operations in, 41–51
    measurements and coordinates in, 30–32
    memory management in, 126–128
    and output structure, 26–30
    screen and printer management in, 16, 23–25, 129–130, 312–315
    structure and style recommendations for, 76–81, 95–96, 108, 245–252, 329, 332
    window operations in, 32–33
PostScript Language Reference Manual, 8, 309
prefixes, in names, 81
printers
    dot-matrix, 22

managing in PostScript, 23–25
printing. *See* fonts
private dictionaries, 251–252, 323
Private (font dictionary key), 263
private virtual memory, 124
procedure bodies, 105
procedure declaration, 105
procedures
    calling from C applications, 50–51
    constructing and defining, 50–51, 99–102, 105107
    handling errors from, 102–103, 364–365
    and the interpreter, 67
    naming, 77–78
    as objects, 25
    timing of, 99–100
    transfer of control of, 93–99
program examples and exercises. *See* Display PostScript program exercises
proportional fonts, 165
PS prefix, 81, 129
psops.h, 26, 37, 104, 129
.psw file extension, 50
PSW prefix, 81
pswrap, 17, 50, 104–106, 130
"push-pop" mode of stack access, 42–43
put, 294–296, 379, 380

Q

quotation marks, as string constant identifier, 35

R

raising the error, 107
raster output devices, 20–23, 163–164
real numbers, 106
real objects, 89
recordstacks, 360
rectangles and squares, drawing, 146–149
rectangular coordinates, 169
rectclip, 160–161, 177
rectfill, 151, 153, 156, 177, 194, 247, 375
rectstroke, 148–149, 151, 169–170, 177, 375
rectviewclip, 313, 327, 382
reference point (as character origin), 271
relational operators
    eq, 96–98, 372
    ge, 98, 372
    gt, 98, 372
    le, 98, 372
    lt, 98, 372
    ne, 96–97, 296, 372
relative movement, 141
repeat, 94, 96, 299, 371
report exercise, 107–123
resolution (in pixels/dpi), 21–22, 185–186
resource management, in Display PostScript, 123–130
restore, 126–128, 354, 373
resynchandleerror, 103, 361, 363
resyncstart, 366
return (linefeed indicator), 82
right justification of strings, 114
riser, 166
rlineto, 29, 142, 144, 374
rmoveto, 142, 144, 148
roll, 295–296, 381
rotate, 187, 376, 385
rotating coordinates, 190–194
round, 370

S

sampled images, 337
save, 126–127, 354, 373
save objects, 91
scale (as coordinate transformation operator), 187, 192, 197, 237, 376
scale (as matrix transformation operator), 353, 356, 384–385
scalefont, 36, 167–168, 258, 266, 301–302, 375
scan converison, 164, 185
scanning, of images, 337
screen
    and output modifiability, 16
    PostScript's management of, 23–25, 129–130, 312–315
screen fonts, 275
screening, defined, 20
searching, of dictionaries, 67–68
selectfont, 36, 48, 167–168, 247, 258–259, 305, 375
semicolons (;), separating argument names, 106
setcmycolor, 377
setdash, 324, 383
setfont, 36, 167–168, 239, 258, 266, 375
setFontWidth (C function), 112–113
setgray, 153–155, 167, 374
setgstate, 239, 377
sethsbcolor, 377
setlinewidth, 137–138, 143, 375
setrgbcolor, 234, 376
setvmthreshold, 126
shading, 149–156
shareddict, 65
show, 27, 35, 36, 40, 48, 52, 135, 272–274, 370
simple objects, 89–92
single operator procedures, 104
slash (/), as name literal indicator, 51, 65, 67, 83
space (private virtual memory), 125
spaces (blanks), 64, 82
special characters. *See also* Special Characters Index
    allowed in PostScript notation, 82
    in comments, 84
    incorporating with \ddd notation, 86

in names, 64
in strings, 85–86
special objects, 91
speed, as consideration in Display PostScript, 15
speed, coding for. *See* efficiency, programming techniques for
square brackets. *See* brackets ([])
squares and rectangles, drawing, 146–149
stack operators
   clear, 371
   copy, 381
   dup, 296, 321, 371
   exch, 73, 296, 371
   index, 384
   pop, 297, 371
   roll, 295–296, 381
stacks
   dictionary, 41, 65
   execution, 41
   in execution contexts, 124
   graphic state, 41
   operand, 41, 42, 65–66
   as presented in this book, 46–47
   as used in PostScript, 26, 41–48
StandardEncoding vector
   displaying, 276–285
   modifying, 286–301
state operators
   restore, 126–128, 354, 373
   save, 126–127, 354, 373
state variables, 124
static procedure declarations, 105
stop, 362, 385
stopped, 282, 359–361, 385
stopped context, 359
store, 69
string, 87
string constants, 35
string objects, 91, 92–93
string operators
   cvrs, 284
   cvs, 232, 376
   setcmycolor, 377
   sethsbcolor, 377
   setrgbcolor, 234, 376
strings. *See also* text
   in C vs PostScript, 49
   calculating width of, 110–114
   centering, 114
   comparing in PostScript, 97–98
   described, 35
   parentheses delimiters for, 83, 85
   in PostScript wrap arguments, 107
   right justifying, 114
stringwidth, 110–111
stroke, 27, 137, 143, 247, 375

stroke adjustment, 186
stroked fonts, 274
StrokeWidth (font dictionary key), 263
structure
   concentric nature of, 108–109
   recommendations for PostScript programs, 76–81, 95–96, 108, 245–252, 329, 332
strWidth (C function), 113–114
sub, 43–48, 370
subpaths, 28, 146
suffixes, in names, 81
Symbol font, 36
syntactic objects, 2
systemdict, 65, 67, 90, 259

T

tabs, 82
text. *See also* Display PostScript program exercises; fonts; strings
   adjusting display of, 249–250
   output creation examples, 33, 35–37, 69–76, 110–115
text operators
   xshow, 250, 378
   xyshow, 28, 250, 251, 378
   yshow, 250, 378
tiles, described, 23
Times Roman font, 36, 163
tokens, 25, 82
transformation matrix, 186, 338
   current, 186, 345
transforming coordinates, 185–190
translate, 187–190, 353, 356, 375, 385
trapping errors, 357
triangles, drawing, 149
true, 99, 373
true/false values, 89–90, 98, 296
tuning (of fonts and image boundaries), 22, 164, 186
typecheck, 361
typefaces, 164–165. *See also* fonts
typestyles. *See* fonts

U

uappend, 321, 378
ucache, 378
ufill, 28, 377
undef, 127–128, 371
undefining objects, 126
UnderlinePosition (font dictionary key), 264
UnderlineThickness (font dictionary key), 264
UniqueID (font dictionary key), 263
unit square, 343
unsigned numbers (in PostScript wrap arguments), 106
upath, 236, 321, 322, 378
user path operators

uappend, 321, 378
ucache, 378
ufill, 28, 377
upath, 236, 321, 322, 378
ustroke, 28, 235, 377
user paths, 30, 235–236, 252
user space, 30, 185
userdict, 65–66, 125, 259
ustroke, 28, 235, 377

V

values
   default, 74
   defined, 64, 259–260
   placing in dictionaries, 66
variable names, as name literals, 51, 64–65, 83–84.
       See also names
variables
   naming, 78
   in PostScript, 74
   state, 124
Version (font dictionary key), 264
view clip operators
   rectviewclip, 313, 327, 382
   viewclip, 313, 381
view clipping path, 312, 329
view clips, 157, 312–313
viewclip, 313, 381
virtual memory, private and shared, 124, 126–128
vmreclaim, 126

W

Weight (font dictionary key), 264
where, 69
white space characters, 82, 86
width (of characters), 271
window handles, 34
windows
   coordinates of, 33, 40
   described, 32–33
   and screen management, 312
   setup example, 34–37
wrap body, 51
wraps. See also Display PostScript program
       exercises
   accessing specific contexts with, 130
   arguments for, 106
   in business check design exercise, 231–234,
       236–240, 243–244
   for clipping regions, 157–161
   creating, 58–61, 70–74, 104–107, 117–119
   for curves, 318–335
   described, 50–51
   for display of encoding vectors, 277–285
   for EPS files, 354–356
   for extended/condensed fonts, 303–306

   for food and wine menu, 289–293
   for image processing, 346–348
   for images as masks, 349–350
   for logo, 201–204
   for pie charts, 176–178
   for screen boxes, 179–183, 188–189, 196–197
   for shading, 150–155
   for squares, 146–149
   using specific context identifier, 130
   for Xs, 142–143

X

xor, 99, 373
xshow, 250, 378
xyshow, 28, 250, 251, 378

Y

yshow, 250, 378